Farm Management Pocketbook

by

JOHN NIX

THIRTY-EIGHTH EDITION
(2008)

SEPTEMBER 2007

Copies of this book may be obtained from:
The Pocketbook, 2 Nottingham Street,
Melton Mowbray, Leicestershire LE13 1NW.
(Tel: 01664 564508 Fax: 01664 410505)

PRICE £18.00 +**£1.50 p&p**
5 to 19 copies: £17.00
20 to 99 copies: £15.50
100 to 999 copies: £14.00
Postage & Packaging free for 5 or more copies

ISBN 978-0-9541201-6-0

FOREWORD TO THE FIRST EDITION

This booklet is intended for farmers, advisers, students and everyone else who, frequently or infrequently, find themselves hunting for data relating to farm management - whether it is for blunt pencil calculations on the back of an envelope or for feeding into a computer. The material contained is based upon the sort of information which the author finds himself frequently having to look up in his twin roles as adviser and teacher in farm management. There are several excellent handbooks already in existence, but this pocketbook endeavours to cover a wider field and thus to be substantially more comprehensive. It is intended that most of the data herein contained will have a national application, although there is inevitably some bias towards conditions in the south-eastern half of the country.

The development of farm planning techniques in recent years has outstripped the quality and quantity of data available. It is hoped that this booklet will go a little further in supplying the type of information required. It cannot, however, claim to be the ultimate in this respect. For example, there are many variations in labour requirements according to farm conditions and sizes and types of machine used and there are many more variations in sheep and beef systems than are dealt with here. More detailed data on these lines are gradually becoming available from various sources. It is hoped further to refine the material in this booklet and to keep it up to date in subsequent editions, as the information becomes available. As a help towards this end, any comments or criticisms will be gratefully received.

The author wishes to thank his many friends and colleagues who have given him so much time and help in compiling this information.

John Nix
October, 1966

First published October 1966

Thirty-eighth Edition   September 2007

FOREWORD TO THE THIRTY-EIGHTH EDITION

We are in a very exciting period for the agricultural industry for a variety of reasons. As the 38th edition of the Farm Management Pocketbook is going to press, wheat futures worldwide have exceeded all-time highs, oilseed values are rising, and a global shortage of milk products is lifting milk prices. At the same time, the UK has experienced some of the heaviest summer rain since records began. Other factors that influence farming are moving onto new territories too; for example the dollar is touching a 26-year low against the pound and crude oil has been pushing towards $80 per barrel.

The demands on our industry continue to increase, with markets developing rapidly for agricultural produce in the non-food sector, particularly fuel. Globally, with probably little or no additional land available that can be farmed successfully in the future, world agriculture will find it increasingly difficult to meet all these extra demands on its production.

Most of the figures are predicted forward one year, i.e. to 2008. *Thus the crops data relate to the 2008 harvest, i.e. the 2008/2009 marketing year. The livestock data relate either to the 2008 calendar year (e.g. for milk production) or to 2008/2009 (e.g. for winter finished beef), as appropriate.* In a few cases current (i.e. mid-2007) figures are given, where it seemed particularly difficult to try to forecast ahead. The year to which the figures relate is normally stated.

The figures for yields and prices assume a 'normal', or average, season, based on trends; e.g. for potatoes, looking 18-24 months ahead to 2008/2009, no one can predict what the actual average yield and price for that particular year will be.

The data in this book should always be used with caution. *The figures should be adjusted as appropriate according to circumstances and price and cost differences.* As far as possible the assumptions in the tables are set out so as to enable this to be done fairly readily.

As ever, all the enterprises have been reviewed and revised for this edition. The author would like to thank the Andersons' Business Research team who have assisted greatly in the production of this edition.

John Nix

August, 2007

CONTENTS

I GENERAL

1. THE USE OF GROSS MARGINS

DEFINITION

The Gross Margin of an enterprise is its enterprise output less its variable costs. Enterprise output includes the market value of production retained on the farm. The variable costs must (a) be specific to the enterprise and (b) vary in proportion to the size of the enterprise, i.e. number of hectares or head of stock. The main items of variable costs are: Crops: fertilizer, seed, sprays, casual labour and contract work attributable to the crop. Non-Grazing Livestock: concentrate feed, vet. and med., marketing expenses. Grazing Livestock: as for non-grazing livestock, plus forage crop variable costs.

POINTS TO NOTE

1. The gross margin is in no sense a profit figure. The so-called 'fixed costs' (rent, labour, machinery, general overheads - see pages 169-173) have to be covered by the total farm gross margin before arriving at a profit.

2. The gross margin of an enterprise will differ from season to season, partly because of yield and price differences affecting output and partly because variable costs may vary, e.g. the number and type of sprays required. Different soils and other natural factors, as well as level of management, will also cause differences between farms.

3. Items of variable cost may vary from farm to farm, e.g. some farmers use casual labour (a variable cost) to plant and pick their potatoes, others use only regular labour (a fixed cost); some farmers employ a contractor to combine their cereals (a variable cost), others employ their own equipment (a fixed cost); some employ a contractor to cart their sugar beet to the factory (a variable cost), others have their own lorry (a fixed cost). These differences must be borne in mind in making inter-farm comparisons.

4. Provided points 2 and 3 are borne in mind, comparison of gross margins (particularly averages over several seasons) with standards can be a useful check on technical efficiency.

5. The other main usefulness of gross margins lies in farm planning. This is not simply a matter of substituting high gross margin enterprises for low gross margin enterprises. The gross margin is only one relevant feature of an enterprise, although an important one. It says nothing about the call the enterprise makes on the basic farm resources - labour at different times of the year, machinery,

buildings, working capital requirements, etc. All these factors and more have to be taken into account in the planning process.

6. This is not to argue that these other costs should be allocated. Complete allocation of many farm expenses is only possible on an arbitrary basis, since they are shared by two or more, possibly all, farm enterprises. Allocation can therefore be completely misleading when making planning decisions. The same is true even when regular labour and machinery are employed specifically on certain enterprises, if such costs are calculated on a per hectare or per head basis. This is because when enterprises are substituted, expanded, contracted or deleted the variable costs for each enterprise will vary roughly in proportion to the size of that enterprise, but other costs will not, except possibly for fuel and some repair costs. Most 'fixed' costs may stay the same, others will change - but not smoothly in small amounts at a time. Either the same regular labour force will cope with a revised plan or a smaller or larger number of men will be needed. The same is true of tractors, other machines and buildings. Such cost changes must of course be taken into account, but allocating these costs on a per hectare or per head basis will not aid, and may positively confuse, planning decisions. The only point of making such calculations is for efficiency comparisons, e.g. labour costs per cow.

7. Allocating fixed costs at a flat rate (e.g. per hectare) for all enterprises, deducting this from the gross margin and hence calculating a 'net profit' from each enterprise can also be misleading. It ignores the whole problem of enterprise inter-relationships, differences between enterprises in total and seasonal requirements for labour, machinery and capital, and other factors such as different quality land on the same farm.

8. Changes in the scale of an enterprise may well affect its gross margin per unit, e.g. increasing the area of winter wheat from 30% to 50% on a farm will mean more second and third crop wheats being grown and a smaller proportion of the crop being drilled under the best conditions; hence yields will in all probability fall. Even if yields remain the same, variable costs (e.g. fertilizer use) will probably increase.

9. Gross margins used for planning future changes should also take account of possible changes in price, and the effect of changes in production techniques.

LOW, AVERAGE AND HIGH LEVELS

The three performance and production levels given for most crop and livestock enterprises are meant for the most part to indicate differences in natural factors, soil productivity, and/or managerial skill, *given the level of variable cost inputs.* They refer, at each level, to *an average over several years* taking *trends* into account. The evidence on the effect of significantly higher or lower levels of variable inputs on gross margins is conflicting and highly uncertain, depending on many factors, including soil type, and will vary from season to season.

2. COMPLETE ENTERPRISE COSTINGS

Requests are occasionally made for this book to include 'complete' enterprise costings, by which is meant the allocation of all costs to each individual enterprise, not only the variable costs as in the calculation of gross margins.

In the early days of farm business management teaching and research this was the preoccupation of most of those specialising in the subject. The system was, however, abandoned by nearly all practising farm economists in the 1950s. The main reasons are given in item 6 of the previous section explaining gross margins. Much meaningless and arbitrary allocation of 'joint costs' is required, (attempting 'to allocate the unallocatable'), and the results are often misleading in making farm decisions. Furthermore, it requires a considerable amount of record-keeping - in allocating labour on a mixed farm, tractor and machinery costs, telephone bills and so on. Few farmers are prepared to spend the required time and money to do this, nor do they need to.

Another problem in 'complete enterprise costing' is where to stop. Should interest on capital be included, whether borrowed or not? Further problems of asset valuation and allocation are involved if so. What if management and marketing is supplied by the farmer? Should these be for free, as is usually assumed in such cases?

Variations between farms in their financial situations are considerable as, for instance, between the farmer who owns all his land without any mortgage and has no other borrowings and the one with both a rent to pay for all his land and heavy borrowings in addition.

In some situations, e.g. in some company-owned farms, farm managers are obliged to supply such data to their employers, whether they want to or not. Also, if enterprise costs are used for price fixing purposes, governments, or price negotiators, usually require some such attempt to be made, whatever the difficulties and shortcomings of the methodology employed.

The above problems arise when 'costs per tonne' or 'costs per litre' are calculated. Wheat can be calculated to cost anything between £50 and £150 a tonne according to just what costs are included, how they are calculated (allocated) and the yield level assumed.

This is not to decry the efforts that are sometimes made in this direction. Particularly when product prices are falling it seems a natural thing to want to do - to calculate 'unit costs' to compare with prices received. Sometimes they do make clearer particular costs that need investigating, and highlight opportunities for economies that might be made, thus attracting interest. For these reasons costs per litre of milk are included, although the calculation of some of the 'fixed cost' items is difficult. If a farm has only one enterprise such calculations on that farm are obviously straightforward. However, even on solely dairy farms followers are usually reared, which is a second enterprise to milk production.

If required a cost per tonne of wheat (and other combinable crops) can be readily calculated by adding the fixed costs per hectare of mainly cereals farms (according to size range, given on page 171) to the variable costs per hectare given in the enterprise gross margin data, and dividing by the selected yield.

The allocation of specific labour (e.g. a full-time cowman), machinery (e.g. a potato harvester) and buildings (e.g. a grain store) is relatively simple and can provide useful information both for purposes of efficiency comparisons and partial budgeting. For some enterprises on many mixed farms, however, there are few, if any, such specific items and the question of the other so-called fixed cost items remains, if a full costing is attempted.

3. TOTAL FARM GROSS MARGIN

No attempt is made in this book to compile total gross margins for the whole farm, based on the forecasts made for individual enterprises for 2008, since the possible permutations in terms of enterprise combinations and performance levels are endless. Nor has it ever been the intention in the Pocketbook to include 'historical data', except for some of the material in the Agristats section. Hence total farm survey results, which are inevitably a year or two old by the time they are collated, analysed and published, are not included. Their usefulness for any particular farm is bound to be limited, particularly if the farm systems are broadly defined and cover much of the United Kingdom.

Furthermore, such data is readily available from surveys of farm businesses. These are undertaken on a regional basis by UK agricultural departments;

ENGLAND

The Farm Business Survey (FBS) is the main source of business-level data in England. It is carried out on behalf of DEFRA by a consortium of Universities and Colleges. There has recently been a reorganisation of the FBS which has meant that each individual University/College no longer publishes a booklet for its own region covering all farm types. Instead, the data is collected regionally, and then fed into a national database. This can be found at - www.farmbusinesssurvey.co.uk. The data can be broken down into regional analyses by Government Office regions.

As part of the restructuring every University/College will specialise in a particular enterprise (or enterprises). Each of the centres will produce reports giving more detail on their individual enterprises. Some of these Reports are already available - see www.apd.rdg.ac.uk/AgEcon/research/afit/index.htm

The following institutions are invloved in the FBS;

- Askham Bryan College, York – www.askham-bryan.ac.uk/for_business/rural_business_research_unit
- University of Cambridge – www.landecon.cam.ac.uk/research/eeprg/rbu/index.htm
- University of Exeter – www.ex.ac.uk/crr
- Imperial College, London – www.imperial.ac.uk/wyecampus/research/aebm/themes/fbm/survey.htm
- University of Newcastle – www.ncl.ac.uk/afrd/research/rural/economics/index.htm
- University of Nottingham – www.nottingham.ac.uk/rbru/
- University of Reading – www.apd.rdg.ac.uk/AgEcon/

WALES

The Farm Business Survey in Wales is undertaken on behalf of the Welsh Assembly Government by the University of Wales, Aberystwyth. The results are publsihed at - www.irs.aber.ac.uk/fbs/

SCOTLAND

In Scotland the data for the Farm Accounts Survey is collected by the Scottish Agricultural College. It is available in the publciation 'Farm Incomes in Scotland'. See www.scotland.gov.uk/Topics/Statistics/15631/8884

NORTHERN IRELAND

The Department of Agriculture and Rural Development for Northern Ireland undertakes the Farm Business Survey in the province. Results can be found at www.dardni.gov.uk/index/dard-statistics/statistical-reports/agricultural-statistics-farm-business-survey.htm

II. SINGLE PAYMENT SCHEME

Major reforms of the Common Agricultural Policy were agreed in 2003. They came into effect, for the most part, on the 1st January 2005. Then in November 2005 a major reform of the Sugar Regime was agreed including price cuts and compensation to farmers starting with the 2006 sugar beet crop. At the time of writing further sugar reforms are planned to take effect from 2008, but details have not yet been agreed.

The following account of the new regime(s) is deliberately restricted to the main features. Points of detail, including exceptions that are likely to arise in few cases, are omitted so as not to confound the main aspects; they are available in full in other publications, if required.

1. THE BASICS

The major, essential change is *decoupling*. This means that farm support is no longer linked to what is being produced on the farm during the year, i.e. to the crops being grown or the livestock kept. The 'Single Payment' (still often referred to as the 'Single Farm Payment') will be made according to what was being produced, by each individual farmer who made the claims, during the three years 2000-2002, expressed on a £ per hectare basis. While it was originally conceived (by most people at least) that these would be paid directly to the individuals who originally made the claims ('historic entitlements') an alternative method of distributing the total entitlements gained increasing support during the later months of 2003: paying it as a flat-rate regional average payment per hectare. Various 'hybrids' – combinations of the two methods – were also advocated.

The governments in the various EU member states finally made widely different decisions regarding the distribution of the payment: often varying in different regions within their countries. Differences even occurred within the UK. Essentially (with some relatively small variations), Scotland and Wales decided to adopt an individual historic entitlements basis, and Northern Ireland a static hybrid.

For England the government opted for what may be regarded as a complex 'sophisticated' method: generally referred to as a 'dynamic hybrid' or 'delayed flat-rate'. It consists of some of each, historic and regional average, with the proportions changing over an eight-year period: starting mainly historic and changing in annual steps to become entirely regional average, as follows:

Year	2005	2006	2007	2008	2009	2010	2011	2012
% historic	90	85	70	55	40	25	10	0
% regional	10	15	30	45	60	75	90	100

The regional payments in England will differ according to topography, with three types: lowland (or non SDA), non-moorland severely disadvantaged areas (SDAs) and moorland SDA. Payments for the second of these will be approximately 83% of those in the lowland and those for moorland about 14% (i.e. about a sixth of those in non-moorland SDAs).

In order to receive payment, recipients will have to be farming 'eligible' land (see below). They must also satisfy 'cross-compliance' rules, which are in two parts: 'Statutory Management Requirements' (directives, largely already in force, on public and plant health, animal welfare and the environment) and keeping the land in 'Good Agricultural and Environmental Condition'. They apply to the entire holding. The rules in England include no cultivating, fertilising or spraying within two metres of the centre line of any hedge or ditch, and 1m from the top of a ditch bank. Also, no hedge cutting between 1st March and 31st July, and providing a soil management plan. The area of permanent pasture in each region must be maintained (this is a government responsibility to monitor not an individual farmer responsibility).

A claimant's total reference amount will be calculated by multiplying the area and headage claims by the 2005 aid rates in euros per hectare, per head or per litre. These are as follows:

Arable Area: €/ha		*Livestock: €/head*	
England	371.07	Suckler Cow Premium	237.5
Scotland non-LFA	357.21	Beef Special Premium (steers) .	150
Scotland LFA	328.23	Beef Special Premium (bulls) . .	210
Wales non-LFA	325.71	Slaughter Premium	80
Wales LFA.	318.15	Extensification (lower rate). . . .	40
N.Ireland non-LFA.	328.86	Extensification (higher rate). . .	80
N.Ireland LFA	316.89	Sheep Annual Premium (SAP).	21.79
Other Crops:		SAP LFA Supplement	7
Hops.	480.00	*Dairy: (€/litre)*	
Dried Fodder Aid (€/tonne). . .	68.83	2005	0.02435
		2006	0.03654

Sugar: Compensation for sugar reform price cuts will increase farmers' reference amounts on the basis of their contract tonnage for the 2005 crop. For 2006 the whole amount of £6.58 per tonne was paid separately after receipt of the Single Payment, but subject to modulation deductions. For 2007 onwards compensation will be incorporated into the recipient's reference amount and be subject to the increasing deductions (43% in 2008) under the English regional average scheme. Allowing for these deductions, but not modulation or financial discipline, reference amounts will be increased by £6-7 per tonne for 2007-2009, but will then reduce to approx. £2.40 in 2010 and to zero in 2012.

2. OTHER POINTS

The other important points are as follows:

- As the payments are calculated in euros the £:euro exchange rate remains important, as pre-2005. The rate will be that prevailing on 30th September each year.

- The entitlements were awarded to the IACS claimant of agricultural land in 2005. They will be transferable/tradable: sold with or without land, or if leased only with an equivalent area of land.

- Most farmland is 'eligible'; comprising arable land and permanent pasture, but excluding woodland and land in non-agricultural use. 'Permanent crops' (essentially orchards and nurseries), have been excluded in the past, but are likely to be included after the 2008 scheme year. The land has to be 'at the farmer's disposal' for at least ten months of the year; farmers can choose which ten months, within certain limits. There will be changes to the 10 month rule; no decisions have yet been made, but they may be implemented for 2008.

- Soft fruit, vegetables and potatoes are labelled 'negative list' or FVP crops. Land in such crops cannot be used to validate SFP entitlements in that year under historic systems, but such land can validate payments under the regional average system, though only up to a maximum reference area per farmer – through 'FVP Authorised Entitlements'. This is to discourage producers from starting to grow, or increasing their area of these crops. It is widely expected that the need for FVP Authorised Entitlements in England will be abandoned in time for the 2008 application, and Ministers have just made this decision as we go to print.

- *Set-aside:* In Scotland and Wales 10% of the Arable area Payment claims in the years 2000-02 will give 'set-aside entitlements', which must be validated annually by eligible land in set-aside; these entitlements must be claimed before any others. They can be validated also by the land being part of an agri-environmental scheme or in the Farm Woodland Premium Scheme. They will be transferable. In England, a big difference to pre-2005 set-aside is that under the regional system all land except permanent pasture will generate set-aside entitlements including temporary grass and root crops; consequently set-aside entitlements were based on 8% in English lowland (1.3% in non-moorland SDA) of arable land in 2005. In England the payment will be only at the regional average rate and so will be very low in the early years. The set-aside land can be rotated and non-food cropping is allowed, as are 6 metre strips. Fully organic holdings are exempt from set-aside rules. See further pages 73-74. *For 2008 the EU Commission plans a 0% set-aside rate although the legal steps had not been completed at the time of going to print. It is expected that set-aside entitlements will remain and that farmers will be able to validate them with any eligible land.*

- In 2005 only, farmers could opt for the historic payments to which they were entitled to be paid in full on a smaller area of land than that previously farmed. This provision applied in England, and to a much lesser extent elsewhere.

- A *Dairy Premium* is being paid to milk producers as compensation for price cuts (15% in skim milk powder over three years and 25% in butter over four) which started in July 2004 and restrictions in butter intervention. Details of the payments in 2005 and 2006 are given on page 77. They were decoupled in 2005, based on quota held at 31st March 2005, and converted into per hectare Single Payment entitlements: the value before any deductions is approximately 1.65ppl in 2005, rising to around 2.48ppl in 2006 and thereafter. In England, as with all other payments, the annual historic element will be calculated by multiplying by the relevant annual percentage.

- There are supplements (euros/ha) for protein crops (55.57) and energy crops (45).

- *Sugar Reform*: the main consequence of the reforms for sugar beet growers is savage cuts in minimum beet price over four years. British Sugar has agreed with the NFU to pay farmers close to the minimum beet price plus delivery allowance. If one euro = 68p, beet price would be £19.99 in 2007/08, and £18.94 in 2008/09. Average additions for haulage, late delivery bonus and animal feed supplement might be approx. £3.75 in 2007 and 2008. For 2009/10 the agreed price should not drop below £18.50 and will be linked to wheat price, and should reach £20 per tonne with wheat at £95. The compensation to growers for these cuts is explained on page 7. The ongoing payments are fully decoupled. Other elements of the reform include merging of A & B quota, with the quota system retained until 2014/15. There was an EU voluntary restructuring scheme for sugar factories with compensation if quota was given up. British Sugar did not give up quota although it did close the York and Allscott factories after processing the 2006 crop, and operated its own compensation scheme for growers surrendering contract tonnage or transferring it to growers in the remaining factory areas.

The EU restructuring scheme has been a failure so that 3.8m tonnes of excess sugar quota still needs to be removed. Current proposals would compensate farmers direct for giving up contract tonnage, but in the UK this would still be controlled to a large extent by British Sugar. At the time of going to print all we can say is that for 2008 English growers' contract tonnage entitlement will be cut by 10%.

- A number of *deductions* will be made to the payments, most of them increasing over time. A 'National Ceiling', based on past subsidy receipts led to a 0.17% reduction in England only. Across the UK 4.2% was deducted for the *'National Reserve'*, to provide payments for special cases, e.g. new entrants since the end of 2002 and purchasers of extra land. Up to 10% of direct aids from each sector can be deducted to set up a 'National Envelope' to support specific types of farming or improve product quality/marketing; in the UK this is only being used in Scotland (for beef). There will be compulsory *'Modulation'* (for all EU member states) to fund EU-wide Rural Development projects; this is 3% in 2005, 4% in 2006 and 5% in 2007 and thereafter; member states will keep 1% themselves and each will get back at least 80% of its own total; the first 5,000 euros of aid on every farm will be exempt. Member states may add 'voluntary' modulation to the above. For the UK the voluntary modulation rates are shown below:

%	2006	2007	2008	2009	2010	2011	2012
Scotland	4.5	5	8	8.5	9	9	9
Wales	0.5	0	2.5	4.2	5.8	6.5	6.5
N.Ireland	4.5	4.5	6	7	8	9	9
England	6	12	13	14	14	14	14

Finally, after 2007 there is EU 'Financial Discipline': EU Farm Ministers will decide annually what percentage reductions are needed to keep spending within stipulated budget thresholds; as with EU modulation the first 5,000 euros of aid per farm will be exempt. No Financial Discipline is expected for 2007 or 2008.

3. WINNERS AND LOSERS

The gradual change to a flat-rate area payment in England will clearly create winners and losers. By 2012 a farm in 100% combinable crops will lose around £19/ha (from approximately £234/ha to £215/ha), probably increasing to around £61/ha after deductions. Growers of unsupported crops, such as potatoes and soft fruit, will gain the whole of the payment, though at the cost of having to incur set-aside and cross-compliance rules. Sugar beet growers will see their single payments increase in 2006, but there will be a steep decline after

2009 to the regional average rate in 2012. In the case of dairy farmers the higher their milk yields and the higher their stocking rate the more they will lose, especially if they have a flying herd, i.e. no followers; a low-yielding, extensively stocked dairy farm with many followers may lose little or even gain. Intensive beef producers could lose considerably; a low stocking rate suckler herd could be no worse off. Lowland sheep would have to be stocked at a very high rate to lose from the new system; most should gain, some significantly.

4. TOTAL PAYMENTS PER FARM

It is obvious from the above that every farm will have a different total payment per hectare each year as far as the historic payments are concerned. In Wales and Scotland these differences will persist until they have to change from the wholly historic system, as is likely after 2012. In England the differences will gradually iron out as a higher and higher proportion becomes a flat-rate per hectare across all 'lowland' areas (or all non-moorland SDA or all moorland SDA in the case of the other two areas).

The following are estimates of the flat-rate area payments in 2012 in the three areas (or sub-regions) of England, with one euro = 68p. 'Lowland' covers all non-SDA (Severely Disadvantaged Area) land, which is more than 84% of farmed land. The estimates are made by Andersons and include allowance for the inclusion of Dairy Premium and Sugar Beet compensation in the flat-rate area payments.

The deductions (25% from modulation and financial discipline by 2012, i.e. 5 years ahead) can obviously only be assumed; they may well be higher, for several reasons: the future entry into the EU of more, poorer member states, increasing demands for a faster transference of funds to rural/environmental expenditure, and increasing demands by certain member states for budgetary cuts. The figures are per hectare (with per acre in brackets).

	Lowland £	Non-Moorland SDA £	Moorland SDA £
Payments before deductions	215 (87)	172 (70)	29 (12)
Payments after deductions	161 (65)	129 (52)	22 (9)

As a first example, let us take a 100% combinable cropping farm in England. Assuming one euro = 68p the change in average payments per hectare over time is as follows. The annual % deductions assumed for modulation and financial discipline are: 2005, 5; 2006, 10; 2007, 17; 2008, 19; 2009, 21; 2010, 22; 2011, 23; 2012, 25.

	A. Before Deductions			B. After Deductions
	Historic Part	Flat-rate Part	Total	Total
Year	£	£	£	£
2005	215	19	234	222
2006	200	31	231	208
2007	165	63	228	189
2008	130	94	224	182
2009	95	126	221	174
2010	59	160	219	171
2011	23	193	216	166
2012	0	215	215	161

As a second example, let us assume a lowland farm with a considerable amount of intensive or semi-intensive beef, giving a gross historic payment of approximately £400/ha. The example could also apply to a very intensive dairy farm (i.e. high yield and high stocking rate), except that the figures would be higher in year 2006 than 2005 (because the dairy premium rises, before levelling off). Clearly the rate of the loss compared with pre 2005 increases over time – more quickly than the first example.

	A. Before Deductions			B. After Deductions
	Historic Part	Flat-rate Part	Total	Total
Year	£	£	£	£
2005	348	19	367	349
2006	324	31	355	319
2007	267	63	330	274
2008	211	94	305	247
2009	153	126	279	221
2010	95	160	255	199
2011	38	193	231	178
2012	0	215	215	161

Finally, as a third example, let us assume a lowland sheep farm extensively stocked, giving an historic payment of only £100/ha.

	A. Before Deductions			B. After Deductions
	Historic Part	Flat-rate Part	Total	Total
Year	£	£	£	£
2005	89	19	108	103
2006	83	31	114	103
2007	68	63	131	109
2008	54	94	148	120
2009	40	126	166	131
2010	24	160	184	144
2011	9	193	202	156
2012	0	215	215	161

In this example the farmer gains from the new system increasingly over time.

5. IMPLICATIONS FOR PRODUCTION

1. Despite the enormity of the change made in the gross margins – and even more so in net margins, or profits – of the major enterprises affected, the impact on production (areas planted and number of livestock reared) would appear to have been small so far. They may be greater in subsequent years, although with the current high prices for many arable crops the immediate outlook for these enterprises is for an increase in area grown, quite possibly at the expense of grazing livestock production.

There are a number of reasons for the likely small impact in the short term:

i)   The changes, though considerable, will take time to 'register' for many producers. The instinct to 'wait and see' will be strong. Simple inertia will also play a part. Also in England the continued delay in completing the 2005 and 2006 application process has contributed to the inertia.

ii) Many will continue to sow and to rear as in the past because 'it is what they do': it is what their farm life (which is often the major part of their life) is about. The single farm payment, in many (perhaps most) cases at least will enable this to be done – even if it could be regarded as subsidising unprofitable production.

iii) There will be continuing uncertainty about some of the details of the new policy. How strictly will cross-compliance be enforced, for example? There must be no risk of losing the single farm payments.

iv) There are penalties/restrictions on making some changes that might otherwise be contemplated, e.g. growing more potatoes. In any case, new enterprises often mean more capital, more know-how, risk of overproduction and hence reduced prices. This goes for many diversification, as well as farm, enterprises.

v)   If ones own labour, whether manual or managerial, capital and land is charged at 'the going rate', or opportunity cost, most enterprises that might previously have shown a profit, with an area and headage payment, will no longer do so. However, if one stays farming (or even if one does not) many of these costs will still have to be borne, i.e. they are unavoidable, or inescapable by reducing, or even stopping, production. On many farms, especially small and medium sized ones, little would be saved in the way of 'fixed' costs: they really *are* largely, 'fixed'. Hence even a low gross margin may still be leaving an addition to the net income that one would otherwise not have.

vi) The same point as above needs also to be remembered when considering leaving poorer fields fallow while still cropping the rest. The only actual costs saved on those fields may be the variable costs (primarily seed, fertilizer and sprays) and some fuel and repairs, a total for cereals of around £350/ha (£142/acre), which would be covered by a wheat yield of only 3.5 tonnes/ha (1.4/acre) at £100/tonne. However, there would be benefits of greater timeliness on the rest in difficult seasons and casual labour and 'catch up' contract work may be saved on some farms.

vii) Many arable farmers made heavy investments in expensive new machinery following the high prices for the 2003 harvest crops, many of them with a view to farming more land, particularly in contract farming arrangements; they are unlikely to want to see such investments wasted.

viii) If the equipment is allowed to run down it will be expensive to re-equip if prices suddenly improve markedly in the future, which could well happen. Similarly, well established farmers will not want to lose their skilled workers.

2) However, an increasing number of farmers, particularly those who are older, with no obvious successors, or others simply tired of the work involved, the uncertainties and the paperwork, will no doubt opt for a simpler system of farming, with very low inputs, taking care to abide by cross-compliance rules.

3) Those with a rent to pay on most or all of their land, or who have most of their farm operations done by contractors, will be in different positions than those described above (under1v). Clearly the contractor's cost is saved if one ceases production, which could be crucial, especially where yields are only average or below.

4) The higher the crop yields, or present levels of enterprise profitability, the more clearly it will pay to continue to farm similarly as in the past. Those in the opposite situation who are still farming either have very low (escapable) fixed costs or another source of income. These will be among those likely to turn to more extensive farming, as described above.

5) Also relevant is the level of ex-farm prices. At the time of going to print (August 2007) the price prospects for the 2007 and 2008

harvests at £100 per tonne plus for wheat are likely to keep most growers farming. Beef and sheep prices on the other hand are in the doldrums, but milk prices look like rising strongly from very low levels.

6) More farmers are expected to introduce, or expand existing, diversification enterprises, partly, even entirely in some cases, replacing farm enterprises. For many, however, this is easier said than done.

7) With regard to the so called 'variable' costs, primarily seed, fertilizer and sprays, the initial thought might be to reduce them. However, if the right (economic) level of these was being applied before (where, as an economist would put it, marginal cost roughly equates to marginal revenue) then it remains the right amount. Reducing these costs will reduce the net margin (or remaining gross margin) from the crop, with or without an aid payment. The exception might be some economies, cutting out waste, but these should already have been attended to, regardless of policy changes.

8) However, there is no doubting two possibly major exceptions to the general tenor of the above, suggesting comparatively little change on many farms. That regards milk and beef production. Many dairy farmers have given up milk production: this has been a long-term trend, but now total production is falling well below national quota. It remains to be seen to what extent the higher prices now expected will halt this decline. The beef situation is commented on separately below, at the start of the beef section (page 86). Here was quite the strongest case for leaving an enterprise 'coupled': no doubt partly the reason for Scotland using the 'national envelope' option for beef – a 'per head' payment is made on 'beef' calves. Lower calf or store prices would help some beef enterprises, but obviously not others. Higher end prices, i.e. for the finished animal, would/will obviously help, but this will be limited by the ready availability of imports. Cuts in production could still be severe, once the full impact of decoupling has become clear.

9) Another exception to the general 'little change' tenor above is sugar beet production. Most of the growers delivering to the Allscott and York factories in 2006 have now abandoned beet growing, but most of their contract tonnage has been taken up by growers in East Anglia and the East Midlands, largely through existing growers increasing the scale of their beet growing operations. This trend is likely to continue as the high cereal and oilseed prices attract some to give up beet growing, but their tonnage is likely to be taken up by increasingly specialist large scale growers on land capable of growing very high yields. Total production may still be curtailed by EU policy change.

III ENTERPRISE DATA

1. CASH CROPS

WINTER WHEAT

Feed Wheat

Production level................	Low	Average	High
Yield: tonnes per ha (tons per acre)	6.75 (2.7)	8.25 (3.3)	9.75 (3.9)
	£	£	£
Output:...................................	675 (273)	825 (334)	975 (395)
Variable Costs:			
Seed.....................................		47 (19)	
Fertilizer...............................		130 (53)	
Sprays..................................		126 (51)	
Total Variable Costs....................		303 (123)	
Gross Margin per ha (acre).............	**372** (151)	**522** (211)	**672** (272)

Milling Wheat

Production level........................	Low	Average	High
Yield: tonnes per ha (tons per acre)	6.15 (2.5)	7.55 (3.1)	9.00 (3.6)
	£	£	£
Output:...................................	689 (279)	846 (342)	1008 (408)
Variable Costs:			
Seed.....................................		53 (22)	
Fertilizer...............................		146 (59)	
Sprays..................................		130 (53)	
Total Variable Costs....................		329 (133)	
Gross Margin per ha (acre).............	**360** (146)	**517** (209)	**679** (275)

1. *Prices.* The average feed wheat price for the 2008 harvest crop (i.e. 2008/09 marketing year) is taken to be £100 tonne. The average milling price is taken to be £112/tonne. This is based on a 'full specification' premium of £20 over feed wheat, a medium grade milling specification of £12 and a 25% failure rate of achieving the specification. The average premium achieved varies widely according to quality and season: see further comments below (note 3). Full Specification is defined as NABIM Group 1 wheat with Hagberg of 250 or more, 13% Protein or more and a bushel weight of at least 76Kg/hl.

    Intervention. For the 2008 harvest the intervention price is €101.77/tonne delivered to centre (£69.20 at 68p/euro) in November, rising by €0.46 (31.3p) each month to €104.53 (£71.08) in May, but this excludes most feed wheat on specification issues. Transport and merchant charges are likely to total at least £6/tonne.

2. *Yields.* The overall average yield, for all winter wheat, i.e. all varieties, is taken as 8.0 tonnes per hectare, the trend yield (3.2 tons (64 cwt.)/acre).

3. *Milling v. Feed.* The yield of bread and biscuit wheat (generically known as milling) averages 8.5% below that of feed wheat (the difference could be greater on high-yielding land and less on moderate quality land and also tends to be greater on second than on first wheats). Slightly higher costs for seed, fertilizer and sprays might be expected for milling wheats. The actual price premium in any one season varies according to quality and scarcity. The average premium for full specification breadmaking quality exceeds the £12/tonne (12%) used. However, that for other

16

(biscuit) milling wheat is generally below. Furthermore, not all deliveries achieve full specification. Grade 2 varieties normally achieve a premium of only a few pounds a tonne but their average yields are higher than grade 1 varieties. Overall, the breadmaking premium averaged approximately £13.80/tonne for the five harvest years 2002-2006 with a range of 50p to £35.50/t. This had been exceeded for the 2007 harvest by August 2007. The proportion of the UK wheat area sown with milling varieties fell from 42% in 2006 to 34% for 2007 harvest

4. *First v. Second (Feed) Wheats.* The evidence concerning the effect of different types and lengths of rotational breaks on subsequent cereal yields is inevitably variable given the differences between seasons (weather effects), soils, varieties etc. The table below (for feed wheat) assumes a yield reduction of approximately 10% for second wheats compared with first and higher fertilizer and seed costs as shown; (the later the sowing date the less the yield gap tends to be). The same price is assumed as in the initial table. Only average and high levels are shown. Third wheats could yield 10-15% below second wheats; variable costs are likely to be similar. Large scale NIAB trials from 1996 to 2000 showed second wheats yielding an average of just under 1 tonne/ha less than first wheats; the yield difference varied between varieties. Heavy, well-structured, well-drained clay soils appear to be best suited to second wheats; lighter, silty soils usually have a greater risk of Take-all; a firm seedbed is needed. A seven year Arable Research Centre project gave the average yield of first wheats as being approximately 20% above continuous wheats.

Production level	Average		High	
Year (after break)	First	Second	First	Second
Yield: tonnes per ha (tons per acre)	8.75 (3.5)	7.90 (3.15)	10.00 (4.0)	9.00 (3.6)
	£	£	£	£
Output...	831 (337)	750 (304)	950 (385)	855 (346)
Variable Costs...............................	303 (123)	316 (128)	303 (123)	316 (128)
Gross Margin per ha (acre)...........	528 (214)	434 (176)	647 (262)	539 (218)

5. *Straw* is costed as being incorporated. Average yield is approx. 3·5 tonnes per hectare (range 2·5 to 5); value £10 to £50 per tonne according to region and season but mainly £25 to £30 baled ex-field (£5 less in big bales); (average sale value approx. £85/ha); variable costs (string) approx. £2.30 per tonne. Standing straw (sold for baling): anything from no value to £150/ha (£60/acre), according to type of crop, season and area of the country/local demand: national average around £30/ha (£12/acre), double this in the west, at least treble in a season when straw is in short supply.

6. *Seed.* Seed rates vary according to soil, season, variety, farm policy, etc. Seed: main range £275-375/tonne (C2) with a single purpose dressing; 175kg/ha in good conditions, but more is often applied; 30% farm-saved including grain value, cleaning, dressing, testing and BSPB levy of £32.79/tonne (£5.31 per hectare) for autumn 2007 and spring 2008.

7. *Fertilizer* costs are based on P and K replacement cost for an average yield crop, with straw incorporated. Nitrogen is 170kg/ha for feed wheat and 210kg/ha for milling.

8. *Sprays.* Amounts variable according to season, variety, policy, etc. Typical breakdown: herbicides 43%, fungicides 45%, insecticides 5%, growth regulators 5%, slug pellets 2%.

17

9. If a *Contractor* is employed, extra variable costs will be approximately as follows (see pages 158-160):

Spraying:	£10-£17/ha (LV-HV; material included above)
Drilling:	£25-£26/ha
Combining:	£75/ha (excluding carting)
	£105/ha (including carting)
Drying:	£13.50 for 6% moisture per tonne
Baling Straw:	£40-50 (including string) depending on bale type.

10. *Fuel and Repairs* (per hectare). grain £103, straw £37.

11. *Specialized Equipment Prices*. see pages 141-146.

12. *Labour*. see pages 125-136.

Use Excluding exports, just over half (54%) the UK 2006 harvest wheat crop was used for animal feed, 43% for milling and the remainder for seed, starch and distilling. Additionally, some 14% of the total crop was exported and imports amounted to 6% of the UK crop.

SPRING WHEAT

Production level..........................	Low	Average	High
Yield: tonnes per ha (tons per acre)	4.75 (1.9)	5.75 (2.3)	6.75 (2.7)
	£	**£**	**£**
Output:....................................	518 (210)	627 (254)	736 (298)
Variable Costs:			
Seed.......................................		61 (25)	
Fertilizer.................................		106 (43)	
Sprays.....................................		79 (32)	
Total Variable Costs...................		246 (100)	
Gross Margin per ha (acre).............	**271** (110)	**381** (154)	**490** (198)

1. *Price*: In general, see Winter Wheat (page 16). A higher proportion of spring wheat is sold for milling compared with winter wheat. Here we assume 75% making the average price £109/tonne for the 2008 harvest.

2. *Straw:* See Winter Wheat but yields are considerably lower. Page 17.

3. If a *contractor* is employed, extra variable costs (£/ha) will be shown as for Winter Wheat above.

4. *Fuel and repairs* (per hectare): grain £98, straw £37.

5. *Specialised Equipment Prices*: see pages 147-152.

6. *Labour:* see pages 131-142.

N.B. Normally, only about 1% of the UK wheat area is spring sown although survey data is hard to come by. It is popular after root crops. The percentage is naturally higher after a particularly wet autumn. The percentage is even lower in Scotland (1% or less) than in England or Wales.

WINTER BARLEY

Feed Barley

Production level............................	Low	Average	High
Yield: tonnes per ha (tons per acre)	5.4 (2.2)	6.6 (2.7)	7.8 (3.2)
	£	£	£
Output:....................................	529 (214)	647 (262)	764 (310)
Variable Costs:			
Seed......................................		48 (19)	
Fertilizer................................		116 (47)	
Sprays....................................		91 (37)	
Total Variable Costs...................		255 (103)	
Gross Margin per ha (acre).............	**274** (111)	**392** (159)	**509** (206)

Malting Barley

Production level............................	Low	Average	High
Yield: tonnes per ha (tons per acre)	4.7 (1.9)	5.75 (2.3)	6.8 (2.8)
	£	£	£
Output:....................................	508 (206)	621 (252)	734 (297)
Variable Costs:			
Seed......................................		50 (20)	
Fertilizer................................		82 (33)	
Sprays....................................		99 (40)	
Total Variable Costs...................		230 (93)	
Gross Margin per ha (acre).............	**277** (112)	**391** (158)	**504** (204)

1. *Prices*. The average feed barley price for the 2008 harvest crop (i.e. 2008/09 marketing year) is taken to be £98/tonne, a £2 discount to feed wheat. The winter malting price (£108/tonne) assumes an average premium over feed of £10/tonne. This accounts for malting varieties cropped that do not reach malting standards. The actual premium obtained over feed barley varies according to season and quality: For the best malting barleys the premium in the past has often been £25 and in some years higher. However, in the five harvest years 2002 to 2006 the overall premium has averaged approximately £12.15/tonne. By August 2007, the average malting premium for 2007 harvest was double the average premium for any year over the previous decade. See page 16 for intervention prices.

2. *Straw* is not included. Average yield is approx. 2·75 tonnes per hectare, value £12·50 to £55 per tonne according to region and season but mainly £25 to £40 baled ex-field (£5 less in big bales); (average sale value approx. £100/ha), variable cost (string) approximately £2.30 per tonne. Standing straw (sold for baling): anything to £150/ha (£60/acre) according to crop, season and area of the country (local demand): average around £35/ha (£14/acre), double this or more in the west.

3. *Seed*. Seed includes 25% farm-saved; amounts average 175-180kg/ha, varying according to soil, conditions etc. and BSPB levy of £31.34/tonne (£5.17 per hectare) for autumn 2007 and £34.32 (£6.11 per hectare) for spring 2008.

4. Fertilizer costs are based on P and K replacement cost for a 6.6t/ha crop, with straw incorporated. Nitrogen is 160kg/ha for feed varieties and 100kg/ha for winter malting crops. Fertilizer costs on continuous barley will be approximately £18 higher.

5. *Sprays*. Amounts variable according to season, variety, policy, etc. Typical breakdown: herbicides 47%, fungicides 44%, growth regulators 6%, other 3%.

6. If *Contractor* employed, extra variable costs as shown for Winter Wheat (page 18, note 9).

7. *Fuel and Repairs* (per hectare): grain £104, straw £37.

8. *Specialized Equipment Prices*: see pages 147-152.

9. Labour: see pages 131-142.

SPRING (MALTING) BARLEY

Production level..........................	Low	Average	High
Yield: tonnes per ha (tons per acre)	4.4 (1.8)	5.25 (2.1)	6.1 (2.5)
	£	£	£
Output:.....................................	497.2 (201)	593.25 (240)	689.3 (279)
Variable Costs:			
Seed..		52 (21)	
Fertilizer.................................		69 (28)	
Sprays.....................................		72 (29)	
Total Variable Costs...................		193 (78)	
Gross Margin per ha (acre).............	**304** (123)	**400** (162)	**497** (201)

1. *Prices* .Virtually all spring barley grown is a malting variety, most of it is grown with a premium in mind. Malting premiums for spring barleys are normally significantly higher than for winter varieties. In this schedule, the premium over feed barely is £15/tonne. Again, this allows for failed samples.

2. The notes for *variable costs, straw etc.* are as for Winter Barley above except sprays, which consist typically of: herbicides 54%, fungicides 41%, other 5%.

3. *Areas and Use of Winter and Spring Barley.* Since 2001, spring barley has commanded the majority of the UK barley area (56% in 2006, 59% in 2005). In the 1970's, spring barely accounted for over 90% of the combined crop. This fell to around 40% in the 1990's. Overall barley hectarage has slipped to less than 900 thousand hectares, a halving since the late 1980's.

4. Approximately 58% of the UK 2006 barley crop was used for animal feed in the UK and a third for domestic malting. Some 10% of the total barley crop was exported. However, net trade at around 440 thousand tonnes represents the smallest over the last decade by a considerable margin. Net exports for that period averaged over 1.1 million tonnes per year peaking in 1996/7 at just over two million tonnes.

WINTER OATS

Production level	Low	Average	High
Yield: tonnes per ha (tons per acre)	5.3 (2.1)	6.5 (2.6)	7.8 (3.1)
	£	£	£
Output	473 (191)	585 (237)	698 (282)
Variable Costs:			
Seed		47 (19)	
Fertilizer		86 (35)	
Sprays		64 (26)	
Total Variable Costs		197 (80)	
Gross Margin per ha (acre)	**275** (111)	**388** (157)	**500** (203)

1. Prices are the assumed average for the 2008 harvest crop, i.e. the whole 2008/09 marketing year, at £90 per tonne for milling oats. Milling specification required a minimum bushel weight of 50Kg/Hl. Conservation grade milling oats may obtain a premium of £10/tonne.

2. BSPB levy of £29.03/tonne (£4.36 per hectare) for autumn 2007 and spring 2008.

3. Straw is not included above. Average yield is 3.5 tonnes per hectare; value £20 to £50 per tonne according to region and season; variable costs (string) approximately £2.30 per tonne.

4. If a contractor is employed, extra variable costs will be as shown for Winter Wheat (page 18, note 9).

5. For Naked Oats refer to page 35

6. Fuel and Repairs (per hectare): grain £98, straw £37.

7. Labour: see pages 131-142.

SPRING OATS

Production level	Low	Average	High
Yield: tonnes per ha (tons per acre)	4.5 (1.8)	5.5 (2.2)	6.5 (2.6)
	£	£	£
Output Feed	405 (164)	495 (200)	585 (237)
Variable Costs:			
Seed		51 (21)	
Fertilizer		70 (29)	
Sprays		54 (22)	
Total Variable Costs		175 (71)	
Gross Margin per ha (acre)	**230** (93)	**320** (129)	**410** (166)

1. The notes re. *prices, straw etc.* are as for winter oats above.

2. Around 75% of the oats in Great Britain are winter crops; the proportion increases from north to south; it is normally 90% or more in England and Wales but only 25% to 35% in Scotland. Oats now account for only about 3.5% of the total UK cereals area; however, the area has increased in recent years: 121,000ha in 2006 was 33% more than the 1999 area. The risk of lodging and thus difficult harvesting remains a drawback despite the lower costs of production.

OILSEED RAPE

Winter Rape

Production level.......................	Low	Average	High
Yield: tonnes per ha (tons per acre)	2.25 (0.9)	3.25 (1.3)	4.25 (1.7)
	£	£	£
Output:.....................................	438.75 (178)	633.75 (257)	828.75 (336)
Variable Costs:			
Seed.....................................		40 (16)	
Fertilizer...............................		127 (51)	
Sprays...................................		102 (41)	
Total Variable Costs...................		269 (109)	
Gross Margin per ha (acre).............	**170** (69)	**365** (148)	**560** (227)

Spring Rape

Production level.......................	Low	Average	High
Yield: tonnes per ha (tons per acre)	1.5 (0.6)	2.00 (0.8)	2.75 (1.1)
	£	£	£
Output:.....................................	292.5 (118)	390 (158)	536.25 (217)
Variable Costs:			
Seed.....................................		43 (17)	
Fertilizer...............................		60 (24)	
Sprays...................................		65 (26)	
Total Variable Costs...................		168 (68)	
Gross Margin per ha (acre).............	**124** (50)	**222** (90)	**368** (149)

1. *Prices.* The price assumed for the 2008 crop is £195/tonne, including oil bonuses.

2. *Varieties.:* Winter crops are mainly sown between 10th August and 10th September (before the end of August if possible). Spring-sown crops are best sown between late March and mid-April. Winter crops normally are harvested between late-July and mid-August, spring-sown crops in the first half of September. Inputs are lower with spring-sown crops, pigeons are less trouble and the late summer/autumn workload is eased. However, the later harvesting tends to clash with the winter wheat harvest, there is less time for ground preparation and drilling the following winter cereal crop, and spring droughts are a potential hazard to establishment. Above all, yields average only 60% of those of winter rape; hence normally less than 10% of the total oilseed rape crop is spring-sown (less than 5% for the last 2 years). The proportion of the total area sown with hybrid winter rape is increasing rapidly; an average increase in yield of 0·5 tonnes/ha is claimed by its plant breeders.

3. *Seed.* The price quoted is for standard merchants OSR. However, Hybrid Rapeseed is used on approximately 20% of the UK land area. This seed is dearer, costing in the region of £58 per hectare. Also, £20/ha or so can be saved from the gross margin by home saving although other costs appear elsewhere. BSPB levy of £1640.69/tonne (£8.37 per hectare) for autumn 2007 and spring 2008.

4. *Sprays.* Variable with season, etc. Typically: herbicides 65%, fungicides 25%, insecticides 10%.

5. *Labour.* see page 131-142.

LINSEED

Production level..........................	Low	Average	High
Yield: tonnes per ha (tons per acre)	1.0 (0.4)	1.75 (0.7)	2.75 (1.1)
	£	£	£
Output:....................................	200 (81)	350 (142)	550 (223)
Variable Costs:			
Seed.....................................		57 (23)	
Fertilizer................................		37 (15)	
Sprays...................................		44 (18)	
Total Variable Costs...................		138 (56)	
Gross Margin per ha (acre).............	**62** (25)	**212** (86)	**412** (167)

The price assumed for the 2008 crop is £200/tonne. Contract prices are normally tied to a standard 38% oil content and 9% moisture content. Open market prices are usually lower. Some specialist contracts for specific varieties such as Yellow Linseed can be worth more.

Mainly spring-sown, drilling mid-March to mid-April (best mid-March to end March). Susceptible to frost. Should not be grown more than 1 year in 5. Care is needed regarding the level of nitrogen used: too much (over 75 kg/ha) can cause severe lodging, delayed maturity and excessive weed growth – and hence difficult harvesting, poor quality and lower yields; it should be applied early.

Harvesting: normally not before September and can even be after mid-October in a late season as it does not shed. Moisture content most likely 12-16%: must be dried to 9% for storage.

Winter Linseed

There was a surge in plantings of winter linseed for the 1997 harvest: around 30,000 ha, but this fell to about 20,000 the following year, when crops were again disappointing; there has been little sustained interest since – which has been true of all linseed since 2001. The main attractions are easier establishment and earlier harvesting (about a month before the spring varieties). Higher yields than the spring-sown crop were expected but trials indicated little difference. Yield affected by frost heave, disease and thrips (thunder-bugs), with most varieties susceptible to lodging; pigeons and rabbits can also be troublesome. Early sowing (early to mid-September) appears best, with higher seed rates; otherwise variable costs are similar to spring.

Linola

Edible linseed: the oil contains more linoleic and less linolenic acid than conventional linseed, like sunflower oil. It is difficult to see much future for the crop, because its gross margin is very low. It is grown on contract, with the price based on the oilseed rape price. Spring-sown: agronomy and yield similar to conventional linseed; good weed control is essential.

FIELD BEANS

Winter Beans

Production level..........................	Low	Average	High
Yield: tonnes per ha (tons per acre)	3.0 (1.2)	4.0 (1.6)	5.0 (2.0)
	£	£	£
Output:..................................	365 (148)	475 (192)	585 (237)
Variable Costs:			
Seed.....................................		43 (17)	
Fertilizer................................		30 (12)	
Sprays...................................		93 (38)	
Total Variable Costs...................		166 (67)	
Gross Margin per ha (acre).............	**199** (81)	**309** (125)	**419** (170)

1. *Price*. The 2008 harvest price for feed winter beans is budgeted at £110 per tonne. White hylum varieties can fetch another £15/tonne with no yield penalty. This therefore accounts for the majority of winter beans, most being only one variety. The higher price is achievable subject to meeting minimum quality criteria.

2. *EU Protein Supplement*. Under the Single Payment there is a supplement of €55.57/ha for beans, peas and lupins harvested dry. The output figure above includes the value of this supplement, worth around £35/ha (€1 = 68p) after deducting modulations. This assumes a stipulated maximum EU-wide guaranteed area of 1.648 million hectares is not exceeded. It hasn't yet.

3. *Physical input*s. Seed: 185-220 kg per hectare at £340/tonne. About 60% is farm-saved including BSPB levy of £6.86/ha or £38.97/tonne (winter and spring). Fertilizer: based on 9kg phosphate and 10kg potash per tonne of bean harvested per hectare. No nitrogen is applied. Sprays: Simazine is no longer allowed, so the average cost of pre-emergence herbicides has risen considerably.

4. *Labour*. see page 131-142.

Spring Beans

Production level..........................	Low	Average	High
Yield: tonnes per ha (tons per acre)	2.8 (1.1)	3.7 (1.5)	4.6 (1.9)
	£	£	£
Output:..................................	357 (145)	460.5 (187)	564 (228)
Variable Costs:			
Seed.....................................		56 (23)	
Fertilizer................................		28 (11)	
Sprays...................................		69 (28)	
Total Variable Costs...................		153 (62)	
Gross Margin per ha (acre).............	**204** (83)	**308** (125)	**411** (167)

1. *Price*. Spring beans are all grown for the human consumption market. It is only the poor quality beans (predominantly Bruchid beetle damaged) that are rejected and redirected to feed compounders. Even in some years when supply is particularly tight, these are also exported (North Africa). Hence the spring bean price is budgeted higher than winter at £115/tonne. In a 'normal' year, about 30% of spring beans will not make the export (human consumption) grade. This is accounted for in the price.

2. *Physical inputs*. Seed: 185-220 kg per hectare at £375/tonne. About 40% is farm-saved. Fertilizer and sprays: as for winter beans.

3. *Winter versus Spring Beans*. The key determinant between which to crop is soil type. Winter beans are more suited to heavy soils and springs on lighter land. As the schedules illustrate, there is little real difference between the gross margins.

DRIED PEAS

Production level..........................	Low	Average	High
Yield: tonnes per ha (tons per acre)	3.0 (1.2)	3.75 (1.5)	5.0 (2.0)
	£	£	£
Output:....................................	395 (160)	485 (196)	635 (257)
Variable Costs:			
Seed.......................................		62 (25)	
Fertilizer...............................		28 (11)	
Sprays....................................		110 (45)	
Total Variable Costs...................		200 (81)	
Gross Margin per ha (acre)............	**195** (79)	**285** (115)	**435** (176)

1. *Price*. All peas are now grown for a premium market. Only a small proportion (5%) end up being sent to compounders as second grade peas will go for pet food. Feed value is therefore no longer relevant as a base price. The price forecast here is £120/tonne, taking account of some very high premia and a failure rate. Most peas are Blues, used for micronising and exports. Marofats, the other main group of peas, can achieve premiums over wheat of £60/tonne. They are used for canning, packets and export trade. About a third is grown on a forward contract.

EU Protein Supplement. (See Winter Beans), is included in the above.

3. *Physical Inputs*. Seed: 210 to 250 kg, about 50% farm-saved including BSPB levy of £6.70/ha or £29.50/tonne. Fertilizer: based on 9kg phosphate and 10kg potash per tonne of pea harvested per hectare. No nitrogen is applied. Sometimes the crop is desiccated before direct combining.

4. *Labour*. see page 131-142.

5. In 1998 the area of field beans was 20% above that of dried peas but the difference has widened substantially since then: the area of field beans was more than double that of peas for harvesting dry in 2001 and 2002. By 2006 beans outstripped pea area more than 4 fold.

VINING PEAS

Production level..........................	Low	Average	High
	£	£	£
Output:....................................	800 (324)	1100 (446)	1400 (567)
Variable Costs:			
Seed.......................................		180 (73)	
Fertilizer...............................		28 (11)	
Sprays....................................		105 (43)	
Total Variable Costs...................		313 (127)	
Gross Margin per ha (acre)............	**487** (197)	**787** (319)	**1087** (440)

1. The table above relates to vining peas grown on contract where harvesting (approx. £60/tonne) and haulage (approx. £30/tonne) are paid for separately; the average price in this situation ranges from £170 to £290/tonne depending primarily on quality. The average yield is taken as 4.75 tonnes/ha; the national average (fresh weight) for the last five years has ranged between 4.3 and 5.4 although growers are paid on frozen weight. Top quality ('150 minute') peas have to be grown within 40 miles of the factory. More distant 'long haul' peas will be in the lower price range. A pea viner costs £260,000 - £270,000.

   The average yield of petit pois is lower but the price averages 12 to 15% more.

2. *Fertilizer.* many growers use no fertilizer; but refer to combining peas for details.

3. *Sprays.* both herbicide and aphicide are commonly used with fungicides being used dependant on seasonal requirements.

4. *Labour.* see page 131-142.

5. Around 36,000 ha are grown in the UK annually with a view to vining a 150,000-tonne crop.

LUPINS

The following table refers to spring sown *white lupins*. Differences in yield and price for yellow and blue lupins are given in the accompanying notes:

Production level.........................	**Low**	**Average**	**High**
Yield: tonnes per ha (tons per acre)	2.25 (0.9)	3.00 (1.2)	3.75 (1.5)
	£	**£**	**£**
Output:....................................	305 (124)	395 (160)	485 (196)
Variable Costs:			
Seed.......................................		120 (49)	
Fertilizer.................................		30 (12)	
Sprays.....................................		50 (20)	
Total Variable Costs....................		200 (81)	
Gross Margin per ha (acre).............	**105** (43)	**195** (79)	**285** (115)

**price assumed £120 plus estimated £35/ha protein supplement (net of modulation)

A leguminous crop traditionally associated with light land. Their protein content is about 40 to 50% higher than peas and beans, making lupins a good substitute for soya bean meal in livestock feed compounds.

In 1985 1,300 ha of lupins were grown in the UK but the results were so poor that few were grown for more than a decade. There is now renewed interest in the crop following the development of fully- and semi- determinant varieties that are suitable for cultivation in the UK. In 2001 2,500ha were grown and the area expanded to 4,500ha in 2002, 6,500ha in 2004 and 8,000ha in 2006, virtually all spring lupins. They are a non-GM source of high quality digestible protein. The crop can be cut whole for silage, crimped or milled and fed directly to stock or the grain traded as a cash crop.

Lupins can be grown on all but the heaviest land but are not tolerant of alkaline soils. Lupins need a good cereal seedbed and pre-emergence weed control. Sowing is from mid-March to early April and harvest from mid-August onwards. If the crop is for silage, sowing can be as late as mid-May using an appropriate variety. No nitrogen fertilizer is necessary but P and K at 50-55kg/ha should be replaced later. There are no serious pests of the crop. Anthracnose is a potentially serious threat but plant health measures have so far kept it under control. Other diseases are not yet a problem. Determinant varieties do not generally need pre-harvest desiccants.

Appropriate species and variety choice is important depending on area of the country, soil pH, intended end use and growth habit required. There are three distinct species of spring lupins, white (lupinus albus), blue (lupinus angustifolus) and yellow (lupinus luteus). All are suitable for grain or livestock feed. White lupins have higher protein and potentially greater yield than blue lupins but require a longer growing season. Yellow lupins fall between blue and white on both counts.

About 65% of the national lupin area is white and 30% blue. There is very little yellow lupin remaining. In the South-East and East Anglia 90% of lupins are white. In Scotland 60% are blue 30% white and 10% yellow, with blue and yellow grown for combining or crimping and white for whole crop. In Northern Ireland, where almost all lupins are wholecrop, 90% are white.

Lupins harvested dry are eligible for the EU protein supplement of €55.57/ha, worth about £35/ha in 2008 after deducting modulations; this is included in the output figures given. Over-wintered stubbles are worth 70 points per hectare in the Entry Level Scheme.

Lupin characteristics

	White *Lupinus Albus*	Yellow *lupinus luteus*	Blue *lupinus angustifolius*
Flower Colour	white or blue	yellow	white or blue
Growth habit	semi-determinate	semi-determinate	fully or semi-determinate
pH tolerance	5 to 7.6	<5 to 6.8	5 to 6.8
Protein	36-40%	34-42%	31-35%
Oil content	10%	4%	6%
Main use	Combining in Southern England on acidic land Forage in all areas	Combining in Southern England	Combining in the North (determinate) Forage in the very North (semi-determinate)
Yield	3-3.5 t/ha	2-2.5 t/ha	2-2.5t/ha

MAINCROP POTATOES

Production level...................	Low	Average	High
Yield: tonnes per ha (tons per acre)	36.5 (15)	44.5 (18.0)	53.0 (21.5)
	£	£	£
Output:..................................	3066 (1,242)	3738 (1,514)	4452 (1,803)
Variable Costs:			
Seed.....................................		690 (279)	
Fertilizer................................		223 (90)	
Sprays....................................		456 (185)	
grading..................................	584 (237)	712 (288)	848 (343)
Sundries (levy, sacks, etc.).........	355 (144)	405 (164)	460 (186)
Total Variable Costs...................	2308 (935)	2486 (1007)	2677 (1,084)
Gross Margin per ha (acre).............	**758** (307)	**1252** (507)	**1775** (719)

1. *Prices.* The price assumed above is £90 per tonne for ware and £10 for stockfeed (assumed to be 7½ per cent), which is £84 per tonne for the whole crop. The actual price in any one season will depend mainly on the national average yield. Variations according to quality and market (as well as season) are now considerable. The six-year average GB price for wares between 2001 and 2006 was £107.52/t but the average annual price varied from £69.30 in 2002 to £134 in 2006.

2. *Physical Inputs.* Seed: 60% planted with certified seed: 2.8 tonnes per hectare at £200-270 per tonne (the price varies widely from season to season); 40% with once-grown seed: 2.6 tonnes per hectare at £180 per tonne. Sprays: herbicide, blight control, and haulm destruction.

3. *Casual Labour.* The figure in the table above is for assistance during (machine) harvesting and for grading/riddling (approx. £16.50/tonne); it is assumed that most of the labour for the latter is supplied by casuals.

4. Contract mechanical harvesting: approximately £265/hectare (excl. pickers, carting, etc.). Other contract work see page 159.

5. British Potato Council levy: £39/ha (£15.78/acre) for growers in 2008, £44/ha for late payers; exempt from levy if less than 3ha grown.

6. Potato Land Rentals. Have been falling, from an average of around £750/ha (£300/acre) several years ago to around £500/ha (£200/acre) in recent years.

7. Sacks. Approx. £7.50 per tonne.

8. Fuel and Repairs (per hectare): £257.

9. Specialised Equipment Prices: see page 147-152.

10. Potato Store Costs: see page 186.

11. Labour: see pages 131-142.

EARLY POTATOES

Production level	Low	Average	High
Yield: tonnes per ha (tons per acre)	15.0 (6)	20.0 (8.1)	25.0 (10.1)
	£	£	£
Output:	2250 (911)	3000 (1,215)	3750 (1,519)
Variable Costs:			
Seed		805 (326)	
Fertilizer		221 (89)	
Sprays		229 (93)	
Casual labour		335 (136)	
Sundries (levy, sacks, etc.)		255 (103)	
Total Variable Costs		1845 (747)	
Gross Margin per ha (acre)	**405** (164)	**1155** (468)	**1905** (772)

Notes

1. Prices and Yields. The price assumed above is an average of £150 per tonne for a 20 tonne/ha yield. However, yields increase and prices fall as the season progresses. Thus both depend on the date of lifting, e.g. late May to early June, 7 to 12 tonnes per hectare; July, 20 to 30 tonnes per hectare. Prices in late May to mid June are typically three times those in July; the very earliest crops (early May) can even fetch more than £1,000 per tonne, but the price could be down to £500 by mid May and to £250 or even £200 by the end of May. Thus the average output of £3000 given above could be obtained from 10 tonnes at £300 per tonne, 15 at £200, 20 at £150 or 30 at £100.

2. Casual labour for planting: £122 per hectare, plus help with harvesting/grading.

3. Fuel and Repairs (£ per hectare): £225.

4. Labour: see page 131-142.

Second Early Potatoes

Output (average): 42 tonnes/ha (16.75 tons/acre) @ £75/tonne = £3150 (1275) (lifting

July to early September).

Variable Costs: Seed £555 (225), fertilizer £265 (107), sprays £344 (140), casual labour £647 (262), miscellaneous £400 (162); total £2211 (895).

Gross Margin: £939 (380).

Labour: see page 131-142.

In 2006, the percentages of the total potato area in Great Britain planted in maincrop, early and seed crops respectively were 84, 5 and 11; in England and Wales: 90, 5 and 4; in Scotland: 57.9, 36.7 and 3.6. 19.7% of the total GB potato area was in Scotland.

SUGAR BEET

Production level..............................	Low	Average	High
Yield: tonnes per ha (tons per acre)*	47.0 (19)	59.0 (23.9)	71.4 (28.9)
	£	£	£
Output:..	1039.2 (421)	1304.5 (528)	1578.7 (639)
Variable Costs:			
Seed......................................		147 (60)	
Fertilizer		149 (60)	
Sprays....................................		138 (56)	
Transport (Contract)...............	202 (82)	254 (103)	307 (124)
Total Variable Costs....................	636 (258)	688 (279)	741 (300)
Gross Margin per ha (acre)............	**403** (163)	**617** (250)	**838** (339)

* 'Adjusted tonnes' at standard 16% sugar content (DEFRA)

1. *Prices.* The 'all in' delivered price for the 2008 crop is expected to be £22.11 per adjusted tonne, based on £18.94/tonne contract price (at €1 = 68p) with an average of £3.75 of additional payments and £7.00/tonne surplus beet for bio-ethanol. The additional payments comprise an average haulage bonus of £3.00, late delivery payments averaging 25p/tonne and a pulp payment of 50p although this could end up higher if grain values remain so firm. The 2008 harvest will be the third year of price cuts following the reform of the sugar policy. Refer to page **???** for details.

   At assumed proportions of 95% contract beet and 5% surplus beet, this gives an average delivered price of £22.11/tonne. This is not a reflection of what has happened in the past, but the change in contract and lower prices encourages growers to achieve closer to their contractual tonnage. All the above prices are per adjusted (contract) tonne and are based upon the future Minimum Beet Price as set down in the reformed Sugar Regime which commenced on 1st July 2006.

   The price is altered by approximately 1.1% of the contract price for each 0.1 per cent difference in sugar.

   Late delivery bonus. 26th December — 7th January: 0.8% of UK minimum price; thereafter, the rate rises by 0.2% per day.

2. *Effect of Harvesting Date.* As the season progresses, changes occur in the crop before lifting, approximately as follows, on average:

	early Sept to early Oct.	early Oct. to early Nov.	early Nov. to early Dec.	early Dec to early Jan.
Yield (tons of washed beet /ha)	up 3.75	up 1.9	up 1.25	up 1.25
Sugar Content (%)	up 1%	up ¼%	down ¼%	down ¾%
Yield of Sugar (kg / ha)	up 1000	up 375	up 190	down 60

3. *Sprays.* Herbicides normally comprise between 85% and 92.5% of the total cost of spray materials.

4. *Contract.* Contract mechanical harvesting costs approx. £185 per hectare excluding carting or £220 per hectare including carting.

5. *Transport.* Contract haulage charges vary according to distance to factory. The figure assumed above is approximately £4.50 per (unadjusted) tonne of unwashed beet including loading and cleaning (dirt and top tare assumed at 14% in total).

6. *Fuel and Repairs* (per hectare): £225.

7. *Specialized Equipment Prices*: see page 150-151.

8. *Labour*: see page 131-142.

HERBAGE SEEDS

	Italian Ryegrass		Early Perennial Ryegrass	
	Average	High	Average	High
	£	£	£	£
Yield (tonnes per ha)	1.3	1.7	1.25	1.60
Price per 50 kg (£)	25		27	
Output	650	850	675	864
Variable Costs:				
Seed	60		45	
Fertiliser	131		131	
Sprays	65		65	
Cleaning	208	264	201	250
Total Variable Costs	464	520	442	491
Gross Margin per ha	**186**	**330**	**233**	**373**
Gross Margin per acre	75	133	94	151

	Intermediate Perennial Ryegrass		Late Perennial Ryegrass	
	Average	High	Average	High
	£	£	£	£
Yield (tonnes per ha)	1.3	1.6	1.25	1.60
Price per 50 kg (£)	30		32	
Output	750	960	800	1024
Variable Costs:				
Seed	60		45	
Fertiliser	131		131	
Sprays	65		65	
Cleaning	201	250	201	250
Total Variable Costs	457	506	442	491
Gross Margin per ha	**293**	**454**	**358**	**533**
Gross Margin per acre	118	184	145	216

	Hybrid Ryegrass		Kent Wild White Clover & Kent Indig. Peren. R'grass	
	Average	High	Average	High
	£	£	£	£
Yield (tonnes per ha)	1.2	1.6	0.09 (Clover)	0.11 (C)
			0.6 (R'grass)	0.8 (R)
Price per 50 kg (£)	27		200 (C)	30 (C)
Output	648	837	720	920
Variable Costs:				
Seed	60		45	
Fertiliser	125		59	
Sprays	65		65	
Cleaning	194	243	135	169
Total Variable Costs	444	493	304	338
Gross Margin per ha	**204**	**344**	**416**	**582**
Gross Margin per acre	83	139	168	236

Notes

1. The following were the number of hectares entered for certified seed production for the the main grasses and clovers in the UK for the 2006 harvest;

Italian / Westerwold Ryegrass .	183	Cocksfoot	284
Early Perennial Ryegrass	164	Timothy	64
Inter. Perennial Ryegrass	1,380	Red Fescue	372
Late Perennial Ryegrass	2,038	White Clover	62
Amenity Perennial Ryegrass ..	1,014	Red Clover..............	51
Hybrid Ryegrass	394	Common Vetch	122
Westerwold Ryegrass	45		

   The ryegrasses total 5,173 ha (12,782 acres).

   All herbage seeds total 6,128 ha (15,142 acres).

2. Average *yields* are approximate NIAB recorded averages for cleaned certified seed. The crop is very risky, i.e. yields are highly variable, depending especially on the weather at, and precise timeliness of, harvesting. A considerable amount of skill is necessary to average the 'high' levels over a number of years. Most grasses give their highest yield in their first harvest year, assuming good establishment. Yields can be increased by up to 0.2 tonnes per ha with a combination of higher Nitrogen applications along with a growth regulator.

3. Prices in the table are estimated prices for certified seed for the 2007 year. The figures relate to Diploid varieties. Tetraploid prices are lower (intermediate and late varieties achieving around £25 per 50kg). However, tetraploid yields should be higher. High sugar varieties should command a small premium over the values seen in the tables. *There is no longer any specific Seed Production Aid as this was decoupled and became part of the Single Payment as from 2005.*

4. No allowance has been made above for by-products. Some crops produce 4 to 5 tonnes of threshed hay, which is, however, of low feeding value. This could be worth £150 or more per hectare. Some grasses, especially spring-sown ryegrass, also provide substantial quantities of autumn and winter grazing. Clovers can be either grazed or cut for hay or silage and do not have to be 'shut up' until mid or late May, or, in some cases and seasons, even early June. More grazing (until end of May) and better quality threshed hay is provided with a combination of ryegrass and white clover than with the specialist herbage seed grasses.

5. If the seed crop is to be undersown, specialist growers often reduce the seed rate for the cover crop by up to half and restrict nitrogen dressing: the cereal yield may thus be reduced by up to 0.6 tonnes per hectare. If this is not done the grass seed yield is usually lower in the first year compared with direct drilling, except for ryegrass.

6. Labour: see page 131-142.

RYE

Production level............................	Low	Average	High
Yield: tonnes per ha (tons per acre) ..	4.5 (1.8)	5.80 (2.3)	7.10 (2.9)
	£	£	£
Output:..	472.5 (191)	609 (247)	745.5 (302)
Variable Costs:			
Seed		80 (32)	
Fertilizer................................		116 (47)	
Sprays		82 (33)	
Total Variable Costs	278 (113)	278 (113)	278 (113)
Gross Margin per ha (acre)............	**194** (79)	**331** (134)	**467** (189)

Largely grown on light, infertile, sandy or stony soils, where yields are poor for other cereals. Yields would clearly be higher on better soils, but then rye has difficulty in competing with wheat and barley; it could never do so on good wheat land. The average yield in England and Wales in the six years 2001 to 2006 was 5.83 tonnes/ha.

The area grown in England and Wales increased steadily from 5,700 ha in 1993 to 9,700 ha in 1998, mainly in the south, south-east and East Anglia. It has subsequently fell back to between 5,500 – 6,700 Ha in the last few years (6,700 in 2006). Rye crispbread is a major outlet. It is also milled into flour, used in mixed-grain bread and muesli. About two-thirds of UK requirements are imported, mainly from Canada (which produces the highest quality), Denmark, Germany and Spain. The demand for UK-grown rye has been falling in recent years, owing to increased competition in the crispbread market.

The price assumed above (£105 a tonne) is an estimated 2008 price at harvest. It assumes a milling specification is achieved which produces a price £4-£6 above that for feed wheat. Deductions are made for low quality, particularly if it is only of feed grade (price then between feed wheat and feed barley price). Only a small percentage of the crop is grown for the free market, which is risky.

Rye, which is autumn-sown, is drought tolerant and very hardy, can withstand low temperatures and starts growing early in the spring. It has all-round resistance to wheat and barley diseases, e.g. eyespot, and suffers less from take-all than wheat – hence it is a possible replacement for third or fourth wheat. Its vigour keeps weeds down. Its herbicide, fungicide and fertilizer requirements are lower than for other cereals, except for growth regulators. Harvested earlier than winter wheat (useful for following with oilseed rape).

Drawbacks: it sprouts in a wet harvest: must thus harvest early, at relatively high moisture content. It grows very tall and lodges easily: hence high levels of nitrogen are not possible; but growth regulators help. Its heavy straw crop means very slow combining (takes about twice as long per hectare as wheat and barley), and difficult straw incorporation. New hybrid varieties, with shorter, stiffer straw, are being developed; these would improve the comparative profitability of rye on better soils.

Drilling: 2nd and 3rd weeks September.

Harvesting: by mid-August at relatively high moisture content, then dry to 14-15% (no drying costs include in margin).

TRITICALE

Production level	Low	Average	High
Yield: tonnes per ha (tons per acre) ..	4.4 (1.8)	5.80 (2.3)	7.20 (2.9)
	£	£	£
Output:	422 (171)	563 (228)	698 (283)
Variable Costs:			
Seed		50 (20)	
Fertilizer		105 (43)	
Sprays		58 (23)	
Total Variable Costs	213 (86)	213 (86)	213 (86)
Gross Margin per ha (acre)	**209** (85)	**349** (142)	**485** (197)

A 'man-made' cross between rye and hard wheat. Combines the hardiness of rye and the marketability of feed wheat. It is favoured in livestock feed, particularly pig and poultry rations, due to its high levels of lysine. However, due to the relatively low quantities available it is not widely used by feed compounders. The area grown in England and Wales has risen steadily since the mid-1990's. In 2006, 11,400 hectares were grown. However, the areas grown on the Continent are considerably greater.

The price is usually £3 or £4 a tonne below the price for feed wheat, but this tends to vary from season to season; £97 per tonne is assumed above for the 2008 harvest crop.

The average yield in England and Wales in the six years 2001-06 was only 4.33 tonnes per ha, but in the previous six years it had been 5.93 tonnes per ha. The low yields are a result of it mainly being grown on light land, especially thin, drought-prone, poorish, marginal cereal-growing soils. In these circumstances, it can frequently outyield wheat or barley, especially the former, and it has lower input requirements. Its yields tend to be more consistent on such soil than those of barley. Triticale tends to do well compared with second and subsequent wheats owing to its resistance to drought and fungal diseases.

Lower levels of fungicide are needed because of its good disease resistance, except for ergot, but including take-all (making it a possible replacement for a third or fourth wheat, as indicated above). It is a tall crop, which helps to suppress weeds, but it is susceptible to lodging; growth regulators are beneficial. New semi-dwarf varieties are being developed, to overcome straw strength weakness and susceptibility to rust infections.

The crop is best drilled early (September) on very light, drought-prone soils; otherwise October is satisfactory. Harvesting is at approximately the same time as wheat. There is more straw, which slows combining, and incorporation is difficult; this is less of a problem on poor soils as there is less straw.

Spring Triticale

New spring varieties of this crop have been introduced in the last few years. These have been taken up strongly in livestock areas – the north and west of England, as well as western Scotland, Wales and N. Ireland. Being a spring crop means that winter waterlogging is not an issue, and it can be grown on a wider range of soils. In total over 4,000 ha of spring triticale may well now be grown in the UK.

It has lower yields than winter triticale if it is harvested for grain in the conventional way. However, most is whole-cropped to produce an 'arable forage'. Often it is grown in a mixture with a proteins crop – peas or lupins for example. Inputs for spring triticale will be lower than those for winter varieties.

NAKED OATS

Production level.............................	**Low**	**Average**	**High**
Yield: tonnes per ha (tons per acre) ..	4.5 (1.8)	5.50 (2.2)	6.50 (2.6)
	£	**£**	**£**
Output:..	608 (246)	743 (301)	878 (355)
Variable Costs:			
Seed		60 (24)	
Fertilizer...............................		92 (37)	
Sprays		75 (30)	
Total Variable Costs	227 (92)	227 (92)	227 (92)
Gross Margin per ha (acre)............	**381** (154)	**516** (209)	**651** (264)

Naked oats have a higher protein, energy and oil content than 'traditional' oats, but the fibre content is lower – as the husk is removed during harvesting. Contracts require a maximum moisture content of 14%, wich is also recommended for long-term storage.

The area being grown has increased steadily over the last few years, and naked oats now account for 10% of the traded tonnage of UK oats (i.e. excluding those grown for on-farm use). The traditional markets such as racehorse feed, dog food, and bird feed markets are all increasing. Over recent years the human consumption market has developed so that at least half the crop is now sold for for health foods, fancy breads and breakfast cereals. In future, a further growth area is likely to be from demand for inclusion of the crop in monogastric animal feeds. The poultry industry in particular is setting up supply chains.

The 2008 harvest crop price assumed is £135 per tonne, based on contracts offering premiums 35% above the average feed wheat price. The premium can be reduced according to husk content.

Over 90% of the crop is winter sown, which is assumed above. NIAB survey results have suggested that yields average 20%-25% less than conventional oats. New spring varieties have become available that offer yields much closer to winter crops. The actual difference in yield will depend on the particular season, but are likely to be in the range 20%-5%.

The agronomy of naked oats is similar to that of husked oat varieties. Variable inputs are lower than for wheat or barley. Traditionally, high nitrogen use has not been possible due to the risk of lodging, however, new semi-dwarf varieties with stiff straw have been introduced. As well as increasing the scope for higher fertiliser applications, this means the crop is also suited to more fertile soils, and growth regulators may be avoided. Oats provide a break in the take-all cycle.

Harvest is early (coming just after winter barley). New varieties are less susceptible to shedding than in the past, however care needs to be taken with both the timing of harvest, and the set-up of the combine, to ensure a clean, saleable, sample.

Naked Barley

Naked barley, suitable for roasting, flaking or milling as pearl barley, is now rarely heard of. It is grown like normal barley, but yields are reckoned to be some 15% lower. It could be either autumn or spring sown.

DURUM WHEAT

Production level..............................	Low	Average	High
Yield: tonnes per ha (tons per acre) ..	5.0 (2.0)	6.25 (2.5)	7.75 (3.1)
	£	£	£
Output:..	675 (273)	844 (342)	1046 (424)
Variable Costs:			
Seed		80 (32)	
Fertilizer...............................		114 (46)	
Sprays		90 (36)	
Total Variable Costs	284 (115)	284 (115)	284 (115)
Gross Margin per ha (acre)............	**391** (158)	**560** (227)	**762** (309)

N.B. Extra drying costs estimated at £10 per tonne not shown in the margin.

A Mediterranean crop. As well as pasta, it is used to produce ethnic foods, semolina, biscuits, etc. Must be grown under contract to the one processor in the UK. Domestic demand is relatively small, but expanding; UK consumption per head is approx. 4% that of Italy and 10% that of France but total UK use nevertheless amounts to about 60,000 tonnes a year.

The crop started to be grown in England in the late 1970s and built up to 11,000 ha (27,000 acres) in 1984. A series of years of poor yields reduced this to a few hundred hectares by the mid-1990s. It has now recovered, to around 2,000 ha (5,000 acres) in recent years. Demand from millers is strong and double this area could be accomodated.

Yields well above the average given above are often quoted (typically 75%-80% of conventional feed wheat, which would mean an average of nearly 6.5 tonnes/ha), but average yields obtained from farm surveys have been found to be far lower than this in practice.

Contracts are based on a premium over the feed wheat price. For the 2008 harvest this will be £42 per tonne for 'Grade A' durum. However this is a delivered price to East Anglian mills and will be reduced if the crop does not fully meet quality specifications. In the table above an average premium of £35 per tonne after haulage is assumed, giving an ex-farm price of £135 per tonne. *There is no longer any specific EU area supplement for growing durum in England.*

As with milling wheat, there is a risk of rejection if contaminated with excess foreign seeds, especially self-set cereals from previous crop; thus safer as a first cereal crop. A poor price is obtained if quality is too poor for pasta and thus has to go for feed.

The crop is likely to be grown only in the driest parts of the east/south east, where it can best compete with second and third wheats. It may be either autumn or spring sown; around two-thirds is currently autumn sown and this is assumed in the table. The crop is very sensitive to stress and frost-kill in severe winters; the spring-sown crop is more reliable, and cheaper to grow, but the yield is usually substantially lower. The crop has a higher disease resistance than other wheats, except for eyespot and ergot.

Harvesting is a critital operation; it needs to be done as soon as the crop reaches 20% moisture content, or at most 18%: it is very prone to sprouting and the quality for semolina is reduced if harvest is delayed. Must be dried (slowly) to 15%. It is easier and quicker to dry than normal wheat. The straw is of poorer quality and lesser quantity than conventional wheat straw and is therefore rarely baled.

MINORITY CROPS

Borage

Indigenous to Britain (or at least here since Roman times) it has both grown in the wild, and been cultivated for centuries. Produced principally for use as a dietary supplement, but it may be used in cosmetics and pharmaceuticals. The oil has a high gamma linolenic acid (GLA) content. It was first grown as a field crop in the UK in the early 1980's UK and the area has risen slowly so that currently around 5,000-6,000 hectares are being cropped annually. It is essential for a grower to have a buy-back contract with a reputable company, and the crop should not be grown speculatively.

The crop is spring sown (March-April) into a good seedbed. Its aggressive growth gives good weed control with a high plant density. There are no significant pests and diseases, except for powdery mildew. Low rainfall areas are preferred owing to harvesting difficulties in wet conditions. It is combined in late July/early August, after swathing and drying, which takes a minimum of two weeks. Harvesting can be difficult and seed shedding at maturity is a problem. Seed should be promptly dried to 10% for safe storage. Cleaning may be necessary. Contract prices for 2008 are around £2,100-£2,150/tonne.

Borage should only be considered by those prepared to invest sufficient time in the crop's husbandry, harvest and storage. Borage is a low yield / high risk crop – yields are from virtually nothing to 0.75 tonnes/ha (6 cwt./acre); average 0.4 (3.2).

Yield 0.4t/ha (0.2t/acre), Price £2100/t ex-farm	£/ha	(£/ac)
Output	840	(340)
Variable Costs:		
Seed	110	(45)
Fertiliser	60	(24)
Sprays	20	(8)
Total Variable Costs	190	(77)
Gross Margin per ha (acre).................................	**650**	(263)

Camelina Sativa

Camelina, or Gold of Pleasure, or False Flax is a fast growing spring (or occasionally winter) sown crop. It is easily grown and harvested and is drought tolerant. The oil contains a range of essential fatty acids. It can be used as a food supplement or in industry as a drying oil. A few hundred hectares are being grown at present including 100 ha of organic production. It is thought that current requirements could support around 1,000 ha of the crop. Yields are in the 2.5tonne/ha range. Price is variable depending on the end use but the minimum for 2008 is likely to be £250/tonne.

Crambe - Abyssinian Mustard

Crambe is an industrial oilseed that contains high levels of erucic acid. Converted into erucamide it is used as a slip agent in plastics and is a constituent of heat sensitive dyes. The area of crambe in the UK had grown to around 5,000 ha. However, the future of the crop is in some doubt since the major promoter/buyer of the crop went into receivership.

Crambe is a cruciferous spring crop suited to growing in UK conditions on a wide range of soils. The crop can be managed like spring oilseed rape but needs some care and attention to achieve a good yield and oil content. It requires a fine firm seedbed and can be sown from April till the end of May. Good weed control is essential. The crop has a short growing season, requiring only 100-120 days to reach maturity after emergence. As with oilseed rape timely harvesting is important. Crambe can be combined direct, dessicated and combined or swathed depending on weather, uniformity of maturity and cleanliness of the crop. The crop should be stored and marketed at a moisture content of 9% or less.

Margin below is based on a £20/tonne discount to previous commercial price buy back contracts, which offered prices of £180/tonne. Contract requirements stipulated that the crop must be 98% pure with 35% oil content. There is a bonus/deduction of £2.70/tonne per 1% oil above/below that level.

Yield 2.5t/ha (1.0t/acre), Price £160/t ex-farm	£/ha	(£/ac)
Output	400	(162)
Variable Costs:		
Seed	60	(24)
Fertiliser	93	(38)
Sprays*	55	(22)
Total Variable Costs	208	(84)
Gross Margin per ha (acre)..............................	**192**	(78)

* No desiccant included. Could be less depending on grass weeds and low risk of pollen beetle.

Echium

Echium is a relatively new commercial plant to the UK. It has been cultivated on contract only for the last 6-8 years. Currently there is less than 1,000 ha or so grown in the UK but the area is steadily increasing. It is a member of the Boraginacea family and is rich in stearidonic acid, which is used in cosmetic creams to reduce skin wrinkling and the effects of sunburn. It is essential for a grower to have a buy-back contract with a reputable company, and the crop should not be grown speculatively. In the past prices have collapsed to almost nothing due to over-supply in the market.

The crop can be grown as far north as Yorkshire. It has a husbandry programme similar to that of borage but does not shed its seed as readily as borage. The seed is relatively small in size. Echium is suitable for light to medium land whereas borage performs better on a wider range of soil types.

The crop is sown in April and should come to harvest in July/August. There appear to be no significant pests of the crop. Harvesting is carried out with the use of a swather.

Yield approximately: 250kg/ha (100kg/acre).

Price £3,500/tonne of clean seed contract prices for 2008.

Gross margin: £520/ha (£210/acre).

Evening Primrose

This crop is still an important source of gamma linolenic acid (GLA), but it is no longer grown in the UK and very little is cultivated elsewhere in Western Europe – it has been larely superseded by borage, which is easier to grow. The crop is still widely grown in China where the climate is more suitable, and labour costs are lower. Previous editions have given details of the crop and possible gross margin data.

Hemp

Production is co-ordinated by Hemcore of Essex under licence from the Home Office - growers no longer need individual licences. A new factory in Suffolk will open for the 2008 crop. This has the capacity to process the crop from 4,000 ha. Due to the bulkiness of the crop, the majority of it is still grown in the eastern counties, near to the processing facility.

It is drilled in late April/May and the fibre crop grows 3 to 3.5m (10-12 feet) tall. Hemcore suggests a minimum area of 10 ha. A well-grown crop should have no weed or pest problems. Improved technology in the new factory means fibres do not have to be left to rett in the field for as long. Instead of a retting period of 4-6 weeks, the crop is mowed, and then baled after 2 weeks. This increases saleable yields as the crop is allowed to grow for longer (cutting mid to late August), and there is less field-losses from the rows. Average yields should be around 7 tonnes/ha (2.8t/acre), with target yields at 8.5t/ha (3.4t/acre).

The crop must be stored under cover. It is delivered to the factory throughout the year. The price of the delivered crop is £110/tonne in October. This increases by an increment of £1.50/tonne/month (giving a price of £125 in August). An average delivered price of £115/tonne is assumed in the table below. Transport costs need to taken into consideration. A figure of £12/tonne is used in the table below. This should be applicable up to 50 miles from the factory (less if closer).

The outlook for hemp is good, as new markets have opened up. The main markets are in building insulation, and producing insulating panels for the automotive trade. Some hemp is also goes for the trading use in clothing. In the past, the core or pith of the plant has mainly been used for horse or poultry bedding. There is still a strong demand from this market, but it is also now been used as a binding fibre in plasterboard-type products for the building trade.

Yield 6.0t/ha (2.4t/acre), Price £105/t ex-farm	£/ha	(£/ac)
Output	630	(255)
Variable Costs:		
Seed	125	(51)
Fertiliser	106	(43)
Sprays	0	(0)
Contract cutting, turning and baling*	90	(36)
Haulage to factory (£13/tonne)	78	(32)
Total Variable Costs	399	(162)
Gross Margin per ha (acre)...............................	**231**	(93)

* less if the grower does some or all of these operations; more if the yield is higher.

Dual Hemp

Hemp may also be grown as a dual-purpose crop. Around 20% of the national hemp crop is of this type. The crop is left to mature longer, and then the top can be combined for the seed before the straw is mown and retted. A yield of 0.8-1.0 tonne/ha (0.3-0.4 t/ac) of seed is possible, with a contract price of up to £500/tonne. However, the yield of straw is lower at 4-5 tonnes/ha (1.6-2.0 t/ac), with the price being the same as 'conventional' hemp. The seed is cold-pressed to produce a high-value cooking oil, and is also used for bird feed, fishing bait and in nutritional supplements and cosmetics. Agronomy and costs are likely to be similar to a fibre crop. Because of the time needed to let the seed heads mature, some producers opt for an earlier-maturing variety (e.g. Finola). This has shorter stems so both the straw yield and price per tonne is usually at a discount to conventional hemp. However, being bred for seed, yields of this component can be higher at 1.25 tonnes/ha (0.5 t/ac)

Flax (cut flax for industrial fibre)

Flax was re-introduced into the UK during the 1990s, not as the traditional, pulled, long fibre variety used for linen textiles but as a cut, combinable crop producing shorter fibres for industrial uses – 'short-fibre flax'. As a natural, biodegradable fibre and a renewable resource it was promoted as a 'green' alternative to synthetic fibres and plastics. New markets were developed and several processing plants set up - the area of flax expanded to 20,200 ha in 1996. Following low prices and reform of the subsidy regime, the area fell to less than 2,000 ha by 2003, and the one remaining processing facility in Wales was closed. Little, if any, is currently grown.

The agronomy of flax is similar to that of linseed but it is harvested earlier. It is spring sown, suitable for most soil types although lighter soil is preferred. It is a low input crop but weed control is essential. It grows best in areas of high rainfall such as Wales and the South-west. There are several harvesting options (described in earlier editions). Currently the preferred option is desiccation followed by combining. The straw is left to rett in the field and then baled. Retting takes 10-21 days, depending on weather conditions. The price paid for straw will reflect quality. The fibre content of a reasonable crop is 20-30%.

Grain Maize

Maize is one of the major global grains – with world output being higher than that for wheat. However, the climate of the UK has made it difficult to ripen the crop and most maize is grown for forage rather than grain. A combination of earlier varieties, the development of machinery that copes with wet conditions, and even possibly the effects of warmer summers has improved the prospects of this crop.

There is market potential, as over 1.1 million tonnes of grain maize are imported annually. It is used in animal rations, human foods, and in industrial processes. Marketing the UK crop is a problem at present as consignments are generally not big enough to interest the major buyers. The animal feed market is the likeliest outlet for domestic production - a specialised or local market can be developed, for example feed for pigeons or corn-fed chickens. The basis of pricing in the margin as a £10-£15/tonne premium over feed wheat. A further price premium of £10-25/tonne may be available for GM-free crops.

There is no fundamental difference between forage and grain maize – the same varieties are simply left in the field for 3-6 weeks longer to let the cobs mature. It is difficult to know how much of the total UK maize area is taken for grain but it could be around 3,000 ha. The crop can be grown south of a line from Bristol to East Anglia, excluding the far south-west. Fields should be below 500ft in elevation and south-facing. To maximise heat units, the crop should be drilled as soon as soil temperatures are above 8°c – usually late April/May. Harvest by conventional combine with an adapted header in October/November. In UK conditions grain maize seldom drops below 30% moisture. The crop needs to be dried to 15% for storage which can be expensive and time-consuming. On good land the crop can yield 8-10 t/ha but the average is not likely to be so high.

Yield 7.0t/ha (2.8t/acre), Price £110/t ex-farm	£/ha	(£/ac)
Output	770	(312)
Variable Costs:		
Seed	100	(41)
Fertiliser	115	(47)
Sprays	35	(14)
Total Variable Costs	250	(101)
Gross Margin per ha (acre).............................	**520**	(211)
But note high drying costs:		
£13-17/t on-farm; £15-20/t off-farm	91-140	(37-57)

The majority of grain maize is currently stored as a crimped product. This sees the crop cut at 30-35% moisture from mid October to early November with the 'wet' grain being processed, and an additive added (usually an organic acid). The overall cost of crimping and preservative is around £12/tonne. The grain is clamped or put into large bales or bags. It provides a very digestible dairy feed of high nutrition content. Yields can be 11-13t/ha and it sells of £80-£90/tonne ex-farm.

Contact: Maize Growers Association: Town Barton Farm, Sandford, Crediton, Devon. EX17 4LS. www.maizegrowersassociation.co.uk

Navy Beans

Used for baked beans, for which the UK imports 110,000 tonnes annually from North America. A few years ago there was some interest in the crop, as varieties adapted to the soil types and climate of the UK were introduced. However, disappointing prices, and the lack of area aid discouraged growers. Under the Single Payment navy beans are no longer at a disadvantage and growing contracts are available along the south coast, Kent, and some areas of East Anglia. The crop requires good fertile land and some care in growing. Sowing is in mid-May when there is no further frost risk. Harvesting is late August/early September.

Yields: target yield is 3.0t/ha but the average is likely to be substantially less; average 2.0t/ha (0.8t/acre) assumed.

Price: very little market information is available, but likely to be in the region of £225/tonne. Output at assumed average yield and price, £450/ha (£182/acre).

Variable costs: total £275 (£111).

Gross margin: £175/ha (£71/acre).

Soya Beans

Soya is a sub-tropical crop in origin, grown mainly in North and South America, but also to a small extent in southern Europe. The UK imports 1 million tonnes each year as beans and a further 1 million tonnes as meal, all for animal feed, so there would appear to be a ready market for the home grown product.

Various attempts have been made to commercialise the crop to the UK. In the late 1990's new varieties were introduced and by the early 2000's the area expanded to 1,700 ha. But after several difficult years the planted area has declined. Currently, less than 100 ha are being grown. No significant expansion is expected until more reliable varieties are available to growers. However, the plant breeding process continues and the introduction of types more suited to the UK climate could see the viability of the crop improve. As a legume, soya is a good alternative break crop.

Sown from mid-April, depending on soil temperature, altitude should not exceed 70m above sea level. The crop is combine harvested in September. The crop should be cleaned and dried to 14% moisture and 2% admixture. Fertilizer and spray costs are low. Target yield is 3t/ha but the average achieved is likely to be less, particularly in early years as producers become familiar with the crop.

Yields: target yield is 3.0t/ha but the average is likely to be less; average 2.5t/ha (1.0t/acre) assumed

Price: is largely determined by the price of imported crop. The UK crop is GM free, for which a premium is paid. A further premium may be paid for Identity Preserved UK crop which goes into human consumption or for organically grown soya. The 2008 price is assumed to be £190/tonne. Output at assumed average yield and price, £475/ha (£192/acre).

Variable costs: total £270 (£109).

Gross margin: £205/ha (£83/acre).

Sunflower

The UK imports the equivalent of about 400,000 tonnes of sunflower seed each year, mainly as sunflower oil. Currently none is commercially crushed in the UK. There has been continued interest in sunflower, but late harvests and low yields have restricted the development of the crop. Currently only about 500 to 600 ha are grown, producing some 1,000 tonnes of seed. Almost all UK production goes into the pet-food or bird seed market; with good demand, but only in localised areas. Producers should satisfy themselves of the end-market before planting the crop. The birdseed market takes 20,000 tonnes of sunflower seed annually, so there is scope for import substitution. Some attempts have been made to cold-press sunflowers to produce a UK-sunflower oil, but this market is still in its infancy.

Extra-early maturing semi-dwarf hybrid varieties are the most suitable to conditions in the UK. This should allow harvesting by mid-September without significant yield reduction. Yields of up to 2.5t/ha with oil content of 44% are possible. However, the crop still needs a relatively mild climate and is best grown south-east of a line from the Wash to east Dorset. Although sunflower will grow on a broad range of soil types its capacity to do well in dry and sandy soils and areas of low rainfall is a recommendation. Sowing is from April to early May when the soil temperature is 7-8°C. Pre-emergence weed control may be necessary; at the right plant density weeds should not subsequently be a problem. As it is a broad row crop, chemical or mechanical weed control is possible. Sclerotina and botrytis, in a wet season, may affect the crop; on areas of less than 6 ha bird damage can be serious. The crop is dried to 8 or 9% for safe storage (costs average £60/ha). Sunflower has a low nitrogen requirement, which may offer benefits in areas of restricted nitrogen use and in organic production.

The price is usually based on a premium over the price of oilseed rape, but other pricing mechanisms may be used in specialist markets.

Yield 2.0t/ha (0.8t/acre), Price £205/t ex-farm	£/ha	(£/ac)
Output	410	(166)
Variable Costs:		
Seed	110	(45)
Fertiliser	56	(23)
Sprays*	38	(15)
Total Variable Costs	204	(82)
Gross Margin per ha (acre)...............................	**206**	(84)

*   Note: drying costs can be very high.

Contact: United Kingdom Sunflower Association (UKSA): www.uksunflowers.org.uk

Others

Other crops that have been in the news in recent years as possible new crops for the future (or present crops capable of substantial development) include the following: chickpeas and lentils, fenugreek, meadowfoam, cuphea, peppermint, poppies (for cooking oils and phamaceutical uses), quinoa, buckwheat, honesty and herbs for their essential oils. At present there are no reliable data for these crops on average yield expectations and little on prices or variable costs, when grown on a commercial scale in this country. A number of them are either for the health food market or are sources of oil for industry as replacements for whale oil and light mineral oil. Research continues on many of them. More details may be available from the contact listed below;

Contact: National Non-Food Crops Centre (NNFCC): www.nnfcc.co.uk

HOPS

1. Output data

Average Yield: per ha, 2002-2006: 27.68 zentners (1 zentner = 50 kg); range 26.8 (2003) to 31.6 (2004).

Average Price (£ per zentner)	Contract	Spot	Overall
2000.	204	140	193
2001.	191	131	178
2002.	177	114	142
2003.	160	104	155
2004.	164	67	134
2005.	191	136	186
2006	199	-	198

Main Varieties*	ha 2006	av. yield 2001-2006 (z. per ha)	prices (£ per zentner)					
			2005 contract	spot	overall	2006 contract	spot	overall
Target..........	132	31.6	130	70	116	121	-	121
Challenger . .	77	30.8	228	219	228	214	-	214
Goldings	257	32.7	224	228	224	235	-	235
Fuggles	146	31.8	225	221	224	238	-	238
First Gold....	169	20.3	161	147	161	170	-	170
Phoenix.......	18	32.0	85	77	81	103	-	103
Admiral.......	48	37.9	130	116	127	119	-	119
Others	185(includes Northdown (25), Progress (28) and WGV (24))							200
Organic	10	19.0 (in 2006)				560	-	560

* over 85% of the total area grown.

Total area of hops (ha): 2006: 1,042; 2005: 1,071: 1997: 3,067; 1984: 5,091. Early last century over 28,000 ha (70,000 acres) were grown.

There is no longer any separate Hops Income Aid scheme, as aid has been subsumed into the Single Payment.

2. Variable Costs per mature hectare (acre) (materials only)

	£/ha	(£/ac)
Fertilisers and Manure	135	(55)
Insecticide / Fungicide	394	(160)
Herbicide.......................................	65	(26)
String	147	(60)
Pockets / Bales	52	(21)
Drying Fuel	378	(153)
Total	1171	(474)

3. Average Direct Labour Costs per mature hectare (acre)

	£/ha	(£/ac)
Growing..	963	(390)
Picking...	1123	(455)
Drying..	193	(78)
Total..	2279	(923)

A new hop garden (erecting the poles, wiring and planting) could cost in the order of £16,000 to £20,000 per hectare (£6,475 to £8,095 per acre).

Acknowledgement: Chris Dawes, Sales Director, English Hops and Herbs.

VINEYARDS

As at August 2006 the total area under vines in England and Wales was 923 hectares, although the actual area in production was 747 hectares. There were 362 registered Vineyards; any vineyard over 0.1 hectare must be registered with the Wine Standards Branch of the Food Standards Agency (FSA), though many of the smaller vineyards are run purely as a hobby. The largest vineyard is over 100 hectares but the average just 2.36 hectares. There has been a steady fall in the number of vineyards and the area planted since the mid-1990s (479 vineyards, 1,065 ha in 1993), although numbers have recovered in more recent years. Most of the vineyards that have gone out of production are thought to be smaller non-commercial ones.

In 2006 2.53m litres (3,385 litres per productive hectare) were produced. Around 80% of production is white wine and 20% red. the very warm year of 2003, the plantings of Champagne varieties (Chardonnay, Pinot Noir and Meunier) have increased significantly, and almost all plantings in the last 4 years (2004-2007) has been for the production of sparkling wine. Pinot Noir is probably now the most widely planted variety, followed by Chardonnay. Although these varieties now account for around 50% of the total vine area, the amount of sparkling wine on the market is still small as bottle-fermented sparkling wines take between 2 and 5 years to mature after bottling.

There is no EU ban on planting vines in the UK and there will not be until annual production exceeds 2.5 million litres on a five-year average. A Quality Wine Scheme for England and Wales was introduced in 1991 and a Regional Wine Scheme in 1997. Hybrid varieties may be planted in the UK but may not currently be made into quality wine. They may be used for quality sparkling wine and regional wine. All wines sold in the UK bear the same VAT and duty, irrespective of origin (although the duty on sparkling wines is higher than that for still wines). A significant proportion of home-produced wine is sold at the farm gate but supermarkets and off-licences are increasingly stocking it. It supplies only 0.3% of the home market. UKVA has set up a marketing arm, English Wine Producers, to promote all English wine. From 2003, to conform with EU legislation, English table wine has been called United Kingdom table wine unless it qualifies for a description of regional origin. From the 2003 vintage, regional wines have been allowed to carry details of vintage, vineyard and varieties on their labels. Since then there has been a marked increase in successful applications for Quality and Regional wine labelling.

Vineyards ideally need south facing, well-drained and sheltered land, less than 100 metres (330 ft.) above sea level, in the southern half of England and Wales. A high level of management and marketing is essential, as is expert advice. There is no minimum area for profitable production. A small enterprise selling wine at the farm gate and to local hotels and restaurants may be more profitable than one with 10 hectares selling only grapes. Some vineyards have associated gift shops and restaurants and are involved with corporate entertaining, which provide extra income. It is now possible to grow grapes under contract for several successful vineyards that have run out of suitable land of their own. Contracts vary, but prices can be up to £1,000/tonne for grapes for still wine and £1,500/tonne for sparkling.

There are various growing systems: the intensive Double Guyot, the most common in France and Germany, and now 75% of British vineyards, and the more extensive Geneva Double Curtain. Other systems such as the divided canopy Scott Henry system are being tried. The Double Guyot system will yield little until year 3 and be in full production in year 4. Geneva Double Curtain will not have a full yield until year 5 or 6 but crops more heavily. The Scott-Henry system crops fully in year 4 or 5.

Investment capital (to include materials and labour for planting and the first two years establishment) of £18,000 to £24,000/ha is typically required for the vineyard. Equipment for a winery costs a minimum of £50,000-£60,000 and a suitable building is needed. Contract winemaking is, however, generally considered better for smaller vineyards of less than 4ha as it gives them access to state of the art equipment and techniques.

Yields and quality are very variable, according to the variety of grape, the year and the quality of management, in particular the quality of pest and disease control. In a reasonable year a well-managed vineyard should yield 7.5-10 tonnes/hectare (3-4 tonnes/acre), but higher annual yields are possible. An average yield over ten years could be around 8.65 tonnes/ha (3.5 tonnes/acre). For still wine production, around 950 75cl bottles will be produced from 1 tonne of grapes; for sparkling wine the production will be nearer 750-800 75cl bottles

The following costs refer to a commercial enterprise on a suitable site with a broad variety range. Establishment costs could be double if the site has to be drained and provided with windbreaks and rabbit fencing. Annual growing costs can also be significantly greater, depending on planting density, variety, yield and management.

	Double Guyot		*Geneva Double Curtain*	
	per ha	(per acre)	per ha	(per acre)
Number of Vines........	2,600-3,450*	(1,050-1,400)	1,785**	(725)
	£ per ha	£ per ac	£per ha	£ per ac
Establishment Costs:	over 2 years		over 3 years	
Materials	10,000	(4,045)	7,500	(3,035)
Labour	8,000	(3,240)	7,000	(2,835)
Total Establishment Costs	18,000	(7,285)	14,500	(5,870)
Subsequent Annual Costs:				
Materials	850	(345)	850	(345)
Labour (growing) ...	3,640	(1,475)	3,640	(1,475)
Harvesting	450	(180)	450	(180)
Total Annual Costs	4,940	(2,000)	4,940	(2,000)

*   Lower density is advised to allow some of the more vigorous varieties space to grow without causing excessive shading within the canopy.

** The Scott-Henry System uses a lower planting density, but the extra trellis work means that establishment costs are typically some 5-10% higher.

Prices: Grape prices will vary according to the variety and the vintage. They range from £400 to £1,000 per tonne delivered to a winery. Pinot Noir or Chardonnay for sparkling wine may be £1,200 to £1,500 per tonne. Transport as well as picking costs has therefore to be deducted. Wine prices vary widely but are likely to be in the range £5 to £6.50 a bottle and up to £10 for red wine at retail. English sparkling wine may retail at £15 to £20 a bottle but is more costly to produce. A retail price of at least £4.98 per bottle is necessary to break even for most enterprises.

e.g.   £4.98 less 17.5% vat and £1.33① duty = £2.90②

        Less own winery costs (materials and labour) £1.50 per bottle③ = £1.40.

        At 6.5 tonnes per ha and 800 bottles per tonne = £7,280 per ha (£2,950/acre).

①   Sparkling wine of 8.5% or more has a duty rate of £1.71.

②   An allowance may also have to be made for a retail mark up of 25%.

③   Having wine made under contract costs about £1.90 a bottle.

Acknowledgements:*United Kingdom Vineyards Association*, Mrs Sian Liwicki, General Secretary,PO Box 534, Abingdon, OX14 9BZ. Tel: 01865 390188.

TOP FRUIT

Established crops: per hectare

Note: This section has been completeley updated for this edition to reflect the changes in production systems. The figures indicate a range within which the performance of many, but not all orchards, is likely to fall. The gross margin is calculated as lower yields less lower costs / higher yields less higher costs. In practice, of course, this does not necessarily follow.

	Dessert Apples	Culinary Apples	Pears
Yield: tonnes/ha	15–50	25-45	15-30
Price (£/tonne)	450-750	200-400	450-600
	£	£	£
Output	7500-35000	5000-18000	6750-18000
Variable Costs*			
Orchard Depreciation..........	250-1200	150-300	100-300
Fertilisers/Sprays..............	800-1200	600-1000	600-900
Crop Sundries...................	50-200	50-100	50-100
Picking...........................	525-1750	875-1575	525-1050
Grading/Packing	1800-6000	1500-5400	1800-3600
Packaging.......................	500-2000	300-1800	500-1200
Transport	700-2200	300-1500	500-1300
Commission/Levies...........	500-3000	300-1500	300-1000
Total Variable Costs*..............	5125-17550	4075-13175	4375-7100
Gross Margin.......................	2375-17450	925-4825	2375-10900

* Excludes Storage

1. **Price:** Average of all grades. Varies significantly with gradeout.

2. **Orchard Depreciation:** Establishment costs written off over lifetime of orchard. Establishment includes trees, stakes (at approximately £5-7 per tree) and, in newer plantings, support structures and irrigation. Total establishemnt costs of £4000 - £20,000 per hectare at planting densities of 750 – 3500 trees per hectare.

3. **Orchard Duration:** Traditional apples around 20 years, pears 30 years plus. Denser apple systems likely to be nearer 15 years, with full cropping in years 3-5 (c.f. 6-9 for traditional systems).

4. **Crop Sundries:** Including tree ties, stake replacement, bee hire, picking hods, etc.

5. **Picking:** Based on £35 per tonne average (to include supervision). In practice can vary significantly with yield, apple size and quality, etc.

6. **Grading and Packing:** Based on £120 per tonne. Can vary considerably, particularly with crop quality.

7. **Packaging:** Average of between £30-40 per tonne. Considerable variations arise from both crop quality (i.e. grade-out) and customer.

8. **Transport:** Includes allowance for farm to packer cost, as well as delivery to final customer.

9. **Commission/Levies:** Including both marketeer's and retailer's commission, as well as promotional levies (e.g. English Apples and Pears).

Acknowledgements (Top & Soft Fruit): Andersons Midlands and Farm Advisory Services Team Ltd.

SOFT FRUIT

Established crops:per hectare

Note: This section has been completeley updated for this edition to reflect the changes in production systems. The figures indicate a range within which the performance of many, but not all crops, is likely to fall. The gross margin is calculated as lower yields less lower costs / higher yields less higher costs. In practice, of course, this does not necessarily follow.

	Strawberries Raised Bed June Bearers	Strawberries Everbearers	Raspberries
Yield: tonnes/ha	18-23	20-28	8-15
Price (£/tonne)	2400-2800	2300-2700	4500-5500
	£	£	£
Output...................................	43200-64400	46000-75600	36000-82500
Variable Costs			
Plants/planting/Sterilisation (w/o over 3yrs)	2750-3500	9000-11000	1200-1500
Structures (average annual cost).	5000-8000	5000-8000	5000-8000
Fertilisers/Sprays/Predators......	850-1200	900-1400	700-1000
Fieldwork..........................	1200-2500	1500-3000	2500-4000
Picking..............................	12600-16000	10000-15000	11200-21000
Grading/Packing...................	6000-8000	6000-8000	7200-13500
Packaging..........................	2750-4000	2000-3500	2880-5400
Transport/Commission...........	5000-7500	6000-9000	4680-10730
Total Variable Costs*................	36150-50700	40400-58900	35360-65130
Gross Margin	7050-13700	5600-16700	640-17370

1. **Strawberries – June bearers:** Plants – assumes 35,000 per hectare. Assume 60 day cropping in year 1 followed by 2 further years. Plants/planting/sterilisation written off over crop life of 3 years. Bed making not included as a variable cost.

   Structures – annual cost of polytunnels including both metalwork (w/o 10 years) and plastic (w/o 3 years). Costs also included for erection, dismatnling and venting.

   Fieldwork – weeding, removing runners, leaf thinning etc.

   Picking- including supervision. Variations with crop yield, quality.

2. **Strawberries – Everbearers:** Plants – assumes 25,000 per hectare. Plants/planting written off over crop life of one year. Sterilisation cost w/o over 3 years. Bed making not included as a variable cost.

   Structures – annual cost of polytunnels including both metalwork (w/o 10 years) and plastic (w/o 3 years). Costs also included for erection, dismantling and venting.

   Fieldwork – weeding, removing runners, leaf thinning, etc.

3. **Raspberries:** Plants – 8000 per hectare at 35 pence per plant. Planting at 10 pence per plant.

   Wirework – to include materisl and labour.

   Plants/planting/wirework written off over crop life of 5 years.

   Picking – at £1400 per tonne (£1.40 per kilo). Packing – at £900 per tonne (90 pence per kilo). Packaging – at £360 per tonne (36 pence per kilo).

Blackcurrants

Although a soft fruit, this crop is much more of a field crop grown on arable farms with machine harvesting. The vaste majority of the UK blackcurrant crop is grown for processing into cordial drink. Typical output would be 6 tonnes/ha sold at £650 per tonne = £3900/ha, with annual variable costs at £1150/ha leaving a gross margin of £2750/ha (fert. £150, sprays £425, and casual labour £575). Establishment costs approximately £7,000/ha for bushes with full production in year 2 followed by up to 10 years cropping.

FIELD-SCALE VEGETABLES

Per hectare (per acre in brackets)

Note: The wide range of yields, prices and costs both from farm to farm and season to season, has to be stressed. Thus these figures are only broad guidelines: the output level and costs will be very dependent on the particular supply chain the individual grower is in. The 'other' variable cost figures are intended only as a general indication of their level; survey data on many of these crops is rarely available and, when it is, particularly variable between farms and seasons. *Prices are net of marketing expenses.*

	Carrots (maincrop)	Dry Bulb Onions	Dwarf Beans (for Processing)
Yield: tonnes/ha (tons/acre)...	65 (26.3)	41 (16.6)	7 (2.8)
Net Price (£/tonne)	170	100	350
	£	£	£
Output..................	11050 (4471)	4100 (1659)	2450 (992)
Variable Costs:			
Seed	510 (206)	360 (146)	280 (113)
Fertilizer..............	160 (65)	195 (79)	200 (81)
Sprays	475 (192)	400 (162)	150 (61)
Other*	4295 (1739)	1710 (692)	75 (30)
Total Variable Costs........	5440 (2202)	2665 (1079)	705 (285)
Gross Margin.............	5610 (2269)	1435 (580)	1745 (706)
Regular Labour (hours)......	50-150	40-60	n/a

	Brussels Sprouts	Cabbage	Spring Greens
Yield: tonnes/ha (tons/acre)...	13 (5.3)	32.5 (13)	11 (4.5)
Net Price (£/tonne)	475	230	300
	£	£	£
Output..................	6175 (2500)	7475 (3025)	3300 (1336)
Variable Costs:			
Seed	460 (186)	560 (227)	410 (166)
Fertilizer..............	180 (73)	250 (101)	250 (101)
Sprays	240 (97)	290 (117)	290 (117)
Other*	1150 (466)	3150 (1275)	1200 (486)
Total Variable Costs........	2030 (822)	4250 (1721)	2150 (870)
Gross Margin.............	4145 (1678)	3225 (1304)	1150 (466)
Regular Labour (hours)......	75 (30)	75 (30)	60 (24)

	Cauliflower	Broccoli	Calabrese	Sweetcorn
Yield: tonnes/ha (tons/acre)...	14 (5.7)	14 (5.7)	9.5 (3.8)	12.5 (5)
Net Price (£/tonne)	300	300	550	130
	£	£	£	£
Output..................	4200 (1700)	4200 (1700)	5225 (2115)	1625 (658)
Variable Costs:				
Seed	820 (332)	740 (300)	600 (243)	130 (53)
Fertilizer..............	260 (105)	210 (85)	210 (85)	150 (61)
Sprays	160 (65)	160 (65)	185 (75)	55 (22)
Other*	1370 (555)	1430 (579)	2500 (1012)	290 (117)
Total Variable Costs........	2610 (1057)	2540 (1028)	3495 (1415)	625 (253)
Gross Margin.............	1590 (643)	1660 (672)	1730 (700)	1000 (405)

	Lettuce (Outdoor)	Parsnips	Leeks	Rhubarb
Yield: tonnes/ha (tons/acre)...	23 (9.3)	27 (10.9)	20 (8.1)	47 (19)
Net Price (£/tonne)	500	415	650	600
	£	£	£	£
Output..................	11500 (4656)	11205 (4535)	13000 (5263)	28200 (11417)
Variable Costs:				
Seed	1200 (486)	160 (65)	600 (243)	155 (63)
Fertilizer..............	260 (105)	150 (61)	190 (77)	110 (45)
Sprays	340 (138)	370 (150)	420 (170)	80 (32)
Other*	5400 (2186)	3950 (1599)	8600 (3482)	n/a
Total Variable Costs........	7200 (2915)	4630 (1874)	9810 (3972)	n/a
Gross Margin.............	4300 (1741)	6575 (2661)	3190 (1291)	n/a

* Other = Casual Labour, Packaging, etc.

HORTICULTURE – WHOLE FARM DATA

Comparative whole farm data is less generally available for horticultural holdings than for various types of farm in different regions of the country (see sources of reports listed on page 4). Data from across a wide area of England is presented below. Because the results vary so much from year to year two-year averages are presented: for 2004 and 2005 harvest/cropping years. The data are collected by seven College/University centres: Askham Bryan, Cambridge, Exeter, Newcastle, Nottingham, Reading and Wye.

All financial figures are per hectare. The averages cover a wide range.

Type of Holding	Specialist Glass		Specialist Outdoor	
	Mainly edible crops	Flowers & nursery stock	Fruit	Hortic.
No. of Farms in Sample......	31	56	37	29
Average Size (ha [acres])	0.90 (2.2)	0.66 (1.6)	32 (79)	40 (99)
	£	£	£	£
Gross Output	245,836	488,688	5,627	7,886
Less:				
Bought Seed and Plants......	12,726	135,270	37	976
Market Charges	20,914	13,692	810	265
Packing Materials	13,219	24,945	718	371
Other Variable Costs	0	0	15	29
Net Output................	198,977	314,781	4,047	6,245
Other Costs:				
Labour (inc. Unpaid Manual)	89,484	159,504	2,011	2,580
Glasshouse Fuel............	35,496	16,699	1.5	35
Manures..................	6,775	16,891	49	215
Sprays and Fumigants	2,095	3,005	308	223
Horticultural Sundries	10,591	17,645	311	665
Power and Machinery	19,174	32,520	680	1,022
Land Rent, Glass Deprecn. ...	16,995	22,106	398	526
Other Fixed Costs	17,732	34,099	574	488
Total Other Costs	198,342	302,469	4,333	5,754
Management and Inv. Inc.....	635	12,312	-286	491
Grower and Spouse Labour (+)	21,439	32,223	366	441
Net Income	22,074	44,536	80	932
Tenant's Valuation	184,444	289,409	5,482	4,297

Source: Horticultural Business Data, compiled by R. L. Vaughan and R. T. Crane, Department of Agricultural and Food Economics, The University of Reading, 2007.

Glasshouse Crop Outputs (at 5-year average yields (2001-2005) and 5-year average prices (same period); all figures rounded): Source, Defra.

	Yield t/ha (t/acre)	Price £/tonne	Output £/ha (acre)
Tomatoes, heated...........	423 (171)	835	353,200 (142,900)
Tomatoes, cold	127 (52)	1,020	129,500 (52,400)
Cucumbers................	470 (190)	510	239,700 (97,300)
Lettuce	37 (15)	1,230	45,500 (18,400)

MUSHROOMS

The mushroom industry has changed considerably during the past 5 to 10 years. A significant number of businesses have ceased production, and few if any new growers have entered the business. Probably than 75 firms remain in production. Those that remain are either highly efficient enterprises with strong links to supermarkets or small low cost family-run businesses selling largely to wholesalers. The reasons for this are static consumption levels and competition from cheap imports. There are a few organic mushroom producers who sell at a premium.

Among the firms that remain there have also been changes in the method of production. Traditionally, the majority of UK growers employed Phase 1 compost, which they pasteurised and spawn-ran on the premises, to fill moveable trays or shelves in their growing rooms. Currently, the most prevalent system (perhaps 70% of all growers) uses purchased Phase 2 compost (pasteurised, with spawn added). This is supplied in shrink-wrapped blocks but it is also available in plastic bags as well as in bulk. Phase 3 compost (fully spawn-run) in blocks or bags is used by some growers. Organic Phase 2 and Phase 3 compost is also available.

Type of compost used	Phase 2	Phase 3
	per tonne compost	
Mushroom Yield/tonne compost	250kg	300kg
	£	£
Mushroom Price/kg....................	1.80	1.80
Spent compost	2	2
Output	452.0	542.0
Variable costs:*		
Compost (incl. delivery)	95.0	135.0
Casing...........................	12.5	12.5
Growing labour at 4p/kg.............	10.0	12.0
Picking labour at 35p/kg.............	87.5	105.0
Packing materials at 17.5kg...........	44.0	52.5
Packing labour at 4.5p/kg	11.3	13.5
Energy costs at 5p/kg	12.5	15.0
Other costs at 5p/kg	12.5	15.0
Total Variable Costs	285.3	360.5
Margin/tonne compost.................	166.7	181.5
Variable cost/kg mushrooms	1.14	1.20
Margin/kg mushrooms..................	0.67	0.60

N.B. All labour is included but labour for growing, if not picking and packing, could well be regular.

Output: Growers using Phase 2 compost will fill on an 8-week cycle and produce 6.5 crops per year. Phase 3 compost can be filled on a 6-week cycle and allows 8.5 crops per year. Yields are expressed as kg per square metre of bed or kg per tonne of compost. Commercial yields are 25-35kg/sq m of bed area per crop (250-350kg per tonne of compost) using Phase 2 or 3 compost, but only 18-20kg/sq metre (180-200kg/tonne of compost) using Phase 1. Phase 1 compost costs £25/tonne, Phase 2 £85/tonne and Phase 3 £125/tonne plus delivery which can add £6-15/tonne, depending on distance and size of load.

Labour costs: If Phase 2 or 3 compost is used, labour for growing amounts to 10% of all labour costs while picking is 80% and packing 10%. Using Phase 1 compost labour cost for growing is significantly greater, perhaps 25p/kg or 40% of total labour, but the initial compost is cheaper.

Prices: Mushroom prices are in the range of £2.00/kg supplied to a supermarket to £1.00 or less sold on the wholesale market. Small growers marketing through a producer organisation would get around £1.60/kg delivered. At present 60% of the crop is sold by growers direct to supermarkets. Prices can be volatile and oversupply can lead to mushrooms being sold at a loss. Imports now account for 65% of all mushrooms sold in the UK, and 60% of the value of sales. Almost all imports are from the Netherlands and the Republic of Ireland.

Returns: The data suggest that ex-farm it costs £1.14 to produce 1kg of mushrooms using Phase 2 compost and £1.20 using Phase 3 compost. This does not take into account management or finance costs. The yield of the crop and the number of cycles each year are, of course, crucial.

Establishment Costs: A mushroom farm using Phase 2 compost on an 8-week cycle would require 8 rooms each with a 200sq m capacity. A farm using Phase 3 compost on a 6-week cycle would need 6 rooms of 200sq m capacity. In both cases one growing room would be filled each week using 20 tonnes of compost. To set up such a production system would require a capital investment of £200,000-£300,000 for the rooms, trays or shelves, heating and cooling systems, packing area, hard standings and equipment. If Phase 1 compost is used then buildings and equipment for composting, peak heating and spawning are also required.

Acknowledgement: *Mushroom Growers Association*, c/o Snowcap Mushrooms, Broadway, Yaxley, Peterborough, Cambs. PE7 3EF: www.mushroomgrowers.org.

ORGANIC FARMING

The Organic Sector:

As at January 2006, 3.6% of UK agricultural land (excluding common grazing) was in organic production: almost 4,300 holdings. The breakdown of the UK figures is as follows:

	Fully Organic	In conversion	Total	% of Agric. Area	of UK Organic Area	% of UK Organic Producers
England	238,355	53,223	291,578	3.1	47.0	65
Wales	58,024	12,808	70,832	4.9	11.4	16
Scotland	231,206	16,724	247,930	4.5	40.0	14
N. Ireland	6,317	3,196	9,513	0.9	1.6	5
UK	**533,902**	**85,951**	**619,852**	**3.6**	**100**	**100**

The amount has risen significantly in recent years for a number of reasons: poor prices for conventionally produced crops and livestock, good premium price levels, and increasing demand - owing largely to health concerns. There is also grant aid to help producers during the required conversion period (see following pages). The market potential is shown by the fact that around 34% of primary organic produce sold through UK multiple retailers is currently imported (down from 54% in 2003). Demand has risen considerably in recent years. The Soil Association valued UK retail sales at £1.6 billion in 2005, a 30% increase from 2004. This is approximately 2.3% of total food sales. The Government's aim is to increase the UK share of the total domestic market to at least 70%. However, some organic farmers have reverted to conventional production primarily because of declining premiums (see next page). Imports of organic fruit and vegetables, often of lower standards, are especially high.

Many hill and upland livestock farms have converted to organic production – with inputs already low, management changes need only be small. Similar factors have meant that a sizeable number of lowland beef and sheep producers have also embraced organic production. There is also a strong organic dairy sector. The cropping sector appears to have lagged behind other parts of the industry – causing difficulty in sourcing organic feed in many cases. Approximately 22% of organic land in England is in crops, just under 13% in the UK as a whole.

Organic Systems:

The benefits to the nation claimed for organic farming are as follows:

(i)   lower yields = less surpluses = less national and EU expenditure on storage and disposal; additionally, less need for set-aside

(ii) environmental (including wildlife and water pollution) benefits of non-use of inorganic fertilizers and agrochemical sprays

(iii) reduction in use of fossil energy

(iv) increasing concern over health means a rising demand and thus an expanding market (as noted above)

(v)   a saving in imported produce (again as noted above).

Against these points critics argue that:

(i)   it is unproven that inorganic fertilizers and (tested and approved) agrochemicals harm the environment;

(ii) it is unproven that organically produced foods are more nutritious, healthier or tastier;

(iii) there is insufficient land available to feed the present population adequately if all farming were organic;

(iv) since organic farming requires more land than conventional farming to produce a given amount of food, less land would be available for environmental purposes, recreation and woodland;

(v)   if organic production became widespread in the UK compared with other countries our competitive position in terms of production costs per tonne would become increasingly eroded.

The economics to the farmer (though this is of secondary interest to many organic farmers) depend primarily upon:

(i)   relative yield compared with conventional farming;

(ii) the price premium compared with conventional farming.

In the case of cereals both research and experience suggests that yields of organic crops are typically between 60% and two-thirds of those of conventionally produced crops, but the much higher prices obtained have easily compensated for this to date, with cereals and feed peas and beans £210 to £260 per tonne, in addition to the obvious saving in fertilizer and spray costs. Hence the gross margin is normally much higher. However, there are also the wider whole farm effects to be considered, e.g., unless the farm already has a substantial percentage of its area down to leys this will probably have to be increased in order to maintain yields and this extra grass has to be utilised profitably – which is far from easy, and the extra capital requirements could be heavy.

Furthermore, there is a two year 'conversion period' to undergo before full price premiums can be claimed; (though note the aid scheme, below). Also, in the case of vegetable crops, quality (in the sense of appearance) can be badly affected by pests and diseases.

As regards relative cultivation costs, in one ADAS monitored study these were reported to be 15% higher on the organically grown wheat (approximately £20 more per ha (£8 per acre) at present costs). However no spraying is required. Survey data have indicated overall labour requirements to be 10-30% higher than on conventional farms, with machinery costs generally similar.

In the case of livestock, premiums have been highly attractive. In some sectors, such as milk, this led to many producers converting to organic, creating an excess of supply over demand. This then collapsed the organic premium. A steady increase in demand has since re-balanced the milk market and average prices have returned to around 29.5p/litre. It is a demonstration of the need to consider markets fully in a 'niche' sector like organic. Organic production of grazing livestock is generally speaking of greater value to the larger farm, especially on land that favours grass rather than cash crops, where the reduction in stocking rate caused by the lack of nitrogen fertilizer is less important. Concentrate feed costs per tonne are much higher.

As already stated, the big questions are the relative yields and the price difference. Future price premiums will depend on how much the consumption of organic produce increases compared with increases in supply.

Aid for Organic Farmers:

In England, support for organic farmers is through the Organic Entry Level Stewardship (OELS) (see page 220). In summary, this provides relatively high levels of support per hectare for the two-year conversion period. Rates then drop to a 'stewardship' level thereafter.

Similar schemes, but with different categories and payment rates, are available in Wales and in Scotland.

Under the CAP Reform (Mid-Term Review) holdings that are totally organic will be exempt from the requirement to set land aside in order to activate set-aside entitlements.

Further Information:

No gross margin data for organic enterprises are included in this section because a specialist publication is available on the subject: the '2006 Organic Farm Management Handbook', (7th Ed - Sept 2006) by Nic Lampkin, Mark Measures and Susanne Padel, University of Wales, Aberystwyth. Tel: 01970 622248.

Additional information may be available from the following organisations:

DEFRA (Organic Food and Industrial Crops Division)
Nobel House, 17 Smith Square, London, SW1P 3JR.   020 7238 5605

Organic Farmers and Growers Limited
The Elim Centre, Lancaster Road, Shrewsbury, Shropshire, SY1 3LE.   01743 440512

Soil Association
Bristol House, 40-56 Victoria Street, Bristol, BS1 6BY.   0117 929 0661

Elm Farm Research Centre
Hamstead Marshall, Newbury, Berkshire, RG20 0HR.   01488 658298

Biodynamic Agricultural Association
The Secretary, Painswick Inn, Stroud, Glos. GL5 1QG.   01453 759501

Organic Food Federation
1 Turbine Way, EcoTech Business Park, Swaffham, Norfolk, PE37 7XD. 01760 720444

Organic Centre Wales
University of Wales, Aberystwyth, Ceredigion, SY23 3AL.   01970 622248

Tesco Centre for Organic Agriculture
Nafferton Farm, Stocksfield, Northumberland, NE47 7XD.   01661 830222

Scottish Agricultural College
Organic Farming Unit, Craibstone Estate, Bucksburn, Aberdeen,
AB21 9YA   01224 711293

TURF

The market for turf continues to be good but competition within the sector is strong, particularly among the producers of general contract grade turf. The market is now predominantly supplied with seed sown turf or cultivated lawn turf'. Pasture turf is still available in certain areas, but overall its importance is small and declining. Suitable pasture for turf lifting is hard to find and it can now be cheaper to grow cultivated turf than treat and prepare existing pasture. Special seed mixtures and cultivation techniques produce a range of types of turfgrass that can be matched to particular sites and uses. In some cases special soil mixes are provided for the site as well as the turf. The Turfgrass Growers Association (TGA) has introduced quality standards and buyers are increasingly specifying the precise type of turf they require. It is estimated that there are around 16,000 ha (40,000 acres) of turfgrass grown in the UK. Although several turfgrass companies were originally set up by farmers, the business has moved away from mainstream farming. However, farms may be involved in the following ways:

1. Selling existing pasture turf to a turf company

This is the traditional option but it now represents very little of the turf market and its share will continue to decline. The opportunity will be open to very few farmers indeed. The approach may be by the farmer to the company or vice-versa. Minimum 5-6 year ley/pasture generally needed for spring or autumn lifting, 8-10 year grass is better for summer cutting.

Important features: good root structure, number and type of weeds, level, well-drained, stone-free land; good access; timing (farmer wants lifting completed in time to drill next crop).

Payment varies between £750-£1,500 per hectare (£300-£600 per acre), but mainly £900-£1,200 per ha (£360-£480 per acre). There is usually an initial payment plus further payments as turf is lifted. There may be a penalty clause if lifting delays prevent subsequent timely drilling. Lifting can take from two months to even a year. It can be done at any time of year except when there is snow on the ground. The turf company usually sprays against broadleaved weeds, fertilizes and mows before lifting; the farmer may do these tasks, for payment. He may graze the land, for a rent, if lifting is delayed.

Apparently the effect on the land is not detrimental; some say there are benefits (removal of accumulated pests, etc. in the top half inch of grass, roots and topsoil).

Some local authorities require planning consent for turf stripping. In some instances it has been refused on the grounds that pasture turf is not an agricultural crop. Cultivated turf, however, is deemed to be an agricultural crop. On tenanted land landlord's permission is necessary to cut pasture turf.

2. Farmer cutting, lifting and selling pasture turf himself

Extremely uncommon. The turf must be treated, as in option 1. A small turf cutting machine can be hired for about £60 a day. This slices off the turf which must then be cut into lengths and picked up by hand. Two or three workers are required. It is slow going even in good conditions. The wastage figure is commonly 10-20% of the area, perhaps more. To hire a machine which cuts and picks up the turf may be possible but the charge will be considerably more.

Turf has a short life once cut and stacked - a maximum 1 to 2 days in summer, 3 to 4 days in winter, depending on temperature.

3. Renting land to a turf company for production of cultivated turf

Turf companies rent land for turfgrass production in addition to using their own land. As before, well-drained, stone-free land with good access is required. Typically the land is rented on a per crop basis and one or two crops grown. A turf crop usually takes 12 to 18 months from preparation to harvest but autumn sown crops may be harvested within 12 months. Rent levels depend on the quality of the land, the provision of irrigation and the profitability of competing agricultural enterprises. Currently rents are in the order of £900-£1,500 per hectare per crop (£365-£525 per acre) or £700-£1,000 per ha per year (£285-£405 per acre).

4. Cultivated turf production

On their own land turf producers can grow turf continuously, taking a crop every 18 months to two years on average. On rented land (as in option 3), they take one or two crops and move on. Usually they produce a quick growing type of turf which sells quickly on rented land and cultivate more specialist and slower growing turf on their own land. A high level of agronomic expertise and considerable investment in machinery are needed and labour requirements are heavy. As the business is very competitive a high degree of marketing expertise is essential. While the bulk of the trade goes into general landscaping or garden centres there is an increase in the number of contracts where the quality and type of turf is specified. It is estimated that a turf farm would need to be 150-200 hectares (400-500 acres) or more in size to be viable – in order to justify the machinery and equipment necessary and to produce a succession of turf for the market. There are significant economies of scale. The cost of specialist machinery for turf production can be £350,000. The new one-man harvesting machine costs in the order of £120,000-£200,000 but significantly reduces labour costs.

Costs and Returns

Variable Costs plus Rent:	£/ha	(£/ac)
Seed	495-740	(200-300)
Fertilizer	245-370	(100-150)
Herbicide	70-150	(28-60)
Fungicide	60-185	(25-75)
Rent (for 15 months)	900-1,300	(365-525)
Total Costs	1,770-2,745	(718-1,110)

It may be necessary to irrigate and on occasions use netting to grow the grass through for certain sites.

Labour

Special seed bed preparation (including subsoiling and stone burying), regular mowing (twice a week May/June), picking up clippings, harvesting (2 men on harvester plus one loading lorry) between 0.2-0.4 hectares per day (0.5-1.0 acre). The new one-man harvester can do 2 ha (5 acres) a day.

Total costs of the order of £4,942-£7,413 per ha (£12,000-£3,000 per acre), approximately 56-83p per sq.m. (47-69p per sq.yd.)

Value of Turf (on the field)

	per sq. m	per sq. yd.	per ha*	per acre*
Pasture turf	38-43p	32-36p	£3,420-£3,850	£1,380-£1,570
Hardwearing, domestic general contract	75-95p	65-80p	£6,840-£8,550	£2,755-£3,470
Football, hockey, prestige landscape	115-145p	95-120p	£10,260-£12,825	£4,150-£5,200
High quality/specialist**	190-475p	160-405p	£17,100-£42,750	£6,910-£17,290

* assuming 90% recovery, but some producers work on 85%.

** for some contracts the price may be higher.

Delivery charges 45-55p per sq.m.

Acknowledgements: Turfgrass Growers Association, 133 Eastgate, Louth, Lincolnshire, LN11 9QG. Telephone: 01507 607722. www.turfgrass.co.uk. *Robert Laycock,* Dial Cottage, North End, Seaton Ross, York, YO42 4LX. www.robertlaycock.co.uk.

GOLF

The boom in golf course construction that was seen in the early 1990s, when almost 70 a year were being built, is long over. Golf is still very popular in the UK but the supply of courses comfortably exceeds demand in most areas. According to Sport England, almost a million and a half (1,457,347) people play golf each month, making it the seventh most popular sport and recreational activity in the country behind recreational walking, swimming, going to the gym, recreational cycling, football and running/jogging. This equates to 3.6% of the adult population of England playing golf at least once a month.

Despite having just under 900,000 club members, the dominance in the golf market of private members clubs has waned and a very large proportion of the market is occupied by proprietary golf clubs (built for profit by individuals or companies). Over the past 2 -3 years the market has weakened with over two thirds of the 940 companies monitored by one organisation seeing a fall in sales. This indicates that any market growth is being shared by a small number of proprietary companies, with private members club seeing a further downwards trend in number of members and rounds played.

Currently there are only a few courses under construction, but numerous courses are trying to upgrade old facilities to cope with the new competition. This includes many of private members courses who are having to protect their businesses by investing in courses and facilities to reduce membership attrition. It is virtually impossible to build a new facility for less than the cost of existing trading courses.

Range development has increased with nearly 400 ranges in the UK, but again many are having to diversify to attract business

The opportunity for farmers to be involved in golf course development is so low as to be negligible. There may be isolated opportunities however - there are a few hotels wishing to add golf to their facilities and needing to acquire farmland. But, restrictive planning policies on development in the countryside make gaining planning permission for all but urban fringe locations extremely difficult.

It is important that any new golf facility is near a substantial centre of population that can support the course. A rule of thumb measure is that a population of 25,000 within a 20-minute drive will support an 18-hole course. In some areas this has dropped to one course per 17,000 - resulting in a lack of long term future for many courses.

One ray of hope for farmers is the emerging trend for courses within urban areas to be developed for housing. This generates the need for extremely cash-rich golf clubs to relocate – usually to the urban fringe close to their old location. This is likely to continue as land in urban areas comes under greater pressure caused by Government policies to restrict built development to 'brownfield' sites.

Accidents on course continue and the space needed for facilities increases as longer and longer courses are required.

Type of facility

*   18-hole 7000 yard plus course: 70-80 ha (170-195 acres) with Clubhouse and Pro Shop (600 sq. metres), parking, proper access and maintenance buildings. It takes between 1 and 2 years to construct.
*   9-hole course: 35-40 ha (84-95 acres).
*   9-hole Par 3 course: 7 ha (17 acres).
*   6-hole Par 3 or 4 course: 14 ha (34 acres).

- Driving range: 4 ha (10 acres).
- Pitch and putt course: 1.5 ha (4 acres).

Type of business organisation
- To sell land with planning permission. The cost of development of an average new course can be significantly more than the value of the facility when it is complete. Thus little or no premium over agricultural value can be expected unless the situation or planning consent offers something exceptional.
- To let land to a developer/operator. Assuming the latter pays for constructing the course, a long lease will be required. Rental levels will depend on the expected profitability of the facility.
- To form a joint company with a developer/operator. This obviously means the farmer shares in the success or failure. The land would be all or part of the farmer's equity. A well constructed agreement is essential.
- To develop and operate the course himself. The farmer would need good knowledge of golf and exceptional management ability besides access to substantial capital. In the present circumstances it is not to be recommended.

Construction methods and cost
- Specialist golf course constructor:
  18-hole course (60-75 ha): £2.5m-£3.5m according to drainage, earthmoving and irrigation, but excluding green keepers building and machinery.
  9-hole course (35-40 ha): £800,000-£1.2m.
  9-hole par 3 course (7 ha): £600,000-£900,000.
  6-hole par 3 or 4 course (14 ha): £500,000-£800,000.
  Driving range (4 ha): £250,000-£800,000, to include offices, storage, equipment, fencing and floodlighting.
  Full inventory of new machinery for 18-hole course: £460,000.
  Clubhouse (600 sq. metres): from £700,000 or £1.8m fitted out.
- Direct labour may reduce costs by around a third.
- Using own farm labour it is possible to reduce costs but it is very risky in terms of resultant course quality.

It is crucial to obtain professional advice at the outset for investment appraisal, feasibility study and a business plan. Changes to the national planning system places some obligation on Local Authorities to make allowance for the needs of all sports in their areas but in many emerging plans such information is often missing.

Large scale developments require Environmental Impact Assessments to be submitted with a planning application. These can cost anything from £80,000 to £150,000 on top of the golf designers and architects fees. The design and environmental fees are all at risk if planning approval is not gained.

Returns
Many existing businesses are seeing none or only marginal growth and whereas a successful well-run golf business should achieve more than a 15% return on capital, these returns on new courses are now extremely rare. It would have to be a special circumstance to recommend the construction of a new stand-alone golf development in the UK today. Some situations exist, but it is very wise to proceed cautiously and be certain of the expected financial returns.

Acknowledgement: PGA Design Consulting Ltd., The Old Church, Neath Road, Bristol BS5 9AP. Telephone: 0117 952 7585. www.pgadc.com

BED AND BREAKFAST

It is estimated that around 2,000 farms across the UK offer B&B. Some are seasonal and informally run but many are open for much of the year, inspected under the auspices of the National Tourist Boards and/or the AA, and are members of a Regional Tourist Board and/or an organisation such as Farm Stay UK.

A bed and breakfast enterprise can be rewarding in both financial and social terms. However, the person running the business should enjoy meeting people, have good social skills and be prepared to work long hours. Other members of the family must be willing to share their home with visitors and to lose a certain amount of privacy. In a crowded market, and with rising customer expectations, the standard of the product is increasingly important. The aim must be to provide a standard of accommodation equal to that found in hotels. This is likely to involve some refurbishment of the farmhouse; either before starting the enterprise, to upgrade an existing B&B to modern standards, or just ongoing repair of wear and tear. Very little grant assistance is available to cover capital costs in setting-up a B&B. Any support is likely to be on a regional basis. The relevant Regional Development Agency (RDA) should be contacted as a first step. As with all new ventures, it is good practice, and essential if seeking additional finance, to create a well-thought-out business plan containing realistic projections.

Although they are not necessarily onerous for smaller operations, it is vital to know the planning, legislative and financial requirements involved in B&B provision. '*The Pink Booklet - a practical guide to legislation for accommodation providers*' produced by VisitBritain covers all the points which have to be addressed. In addition a great deal of help and advice is provided by National Tourist Boards (which in England is VisitBritain), the Regional Tourist Boards, and the Regional Development Agencies. A series of information pamphlets is available and one-day tourism training courses are run. In particular, The Daily Telegraph publish a paperback 'Starting and Running a Bed & Breakfast – a Practical Guide to Setting up and Managing a B&B Business' (www.howtobooks.co.uk) whilst VisitBritain have produced two excellent booklets entitled 'How to Run Quality Self-catering Accommodation' and 'How to Run a Quality B&B'.

Marketing is very important. It can be done through a national organisation, in local Tourist Information Centres, in newspapers and magazines, and by word of mouth. Some establishments produce an attractive brochure or card giving details of the B&B, its location, facilities, and quality standards rating. Copies are left at tourist information centres etc and sent to prospective visitors. The internet is an important tool for the promotion of farmhouse B&Bs. Indeed, nowadays it's almost imperative to have a website and e-mail address, whilst many operators are also subscribing to online booking and availability systems.

As there is considerable competition it is useful if the enterprise can offer something special or different such as accommodation for visitors' horses, a welcome for pets or use of a tennis court or pool. Establishments that can accommodate bigger parties are gaining in popularity. The number of B&Bs offering an evening meal has tended to decline in recent years, but providing locally grown produce can also be a draw. If evening meals are not offered it helps to have good local restaurants and pubs that customers can be directed to.

To join a marketing organisation it is important for the B&B to have a Quality Assurance Standard rating. These are awarded either by the official National Tourist Board inspectorate (which in England is Quality in Tourism), or the AA. The rating is at one of five levels, expressed as stars. It is based on guest care and the quality of what is provided following an unannounced overnight inspection visit. The inspection fee depends on the number of bedrooms and the level of charges. The rated establishment gets a listing in the VisitBritain guides and on their internet site. In some areas membership of a Regional Tourist Board is an option; this confers additional benefits including a reduction in inspection fees, access to legal advice, and discounted rates for promotional activities and training courses.

Prices charged will reflect the quality of accommodation and location but cannot be far out of line with other local B&Bs and small hotels. Prices can also vary depending on length of stay and time of year. The price range for one person per night at a farmhouse B&B is usually somewhere between £20-£37.50, with the average being about £30 on the basis of two adults sharing a room. A higher rate usually applies for single occupancy of a double room.

The receipts from the enterprise can be calculated as follows: If the B&B is open for 40 weeks of the year at £30 per person per night, given a 60% occupancy rate the gross return per bed will be just over £5,000. Most farmhouse B&Bs have 4-6 bed spaces, which would generate a gross return of between £20,000 to £30,000 p.a.

As every farmhouse B&B is different and some costs are difficult to apportion between guests and family, it is hard to provide realistic average costings. The following provides some pointers. Variable costs are food, electricity and heating, laundry, cleaning materials and additional help. There will also be regular redecoration costs, repairs, and replacement and renewal of glassware, china, cutlery, towels and bedlinen. Variable costs if no non-family labour is used might average about 20% of the nightly charge. If casual labour has to be included variable costs could amount to 30-35% of the nightly charge. Fixed costs will include insurance, business rates (if they apply), membership of a marketing organisation, regular advertising, repayments on any loans taken out for building and equipment to start the business and regular labour; they are likely to average 30-35% of charges.

Contact: *Farm Stay UK*, NAC, Stoneleigh Park, Warwickshire, CV8 2LG. Tel: 02476 696909. www.farmstayuk.co.uk *VisitBritain* (formerly English Tourism Council), Thames Tower, Black's Road, Hammersmith, London W6 9EL. Tel: 020 8563 3000. www.visitbritain.com. *Quality in Tourism*, Farncombe House, Braodway, Worcs. WR12 7LJ. Tel: 0845 300 6996. www.qualityintourism.com.

CHRISTMAS TREES

About 8 million trees are sold a year in the UK: 7.2 million of them home-grown. Five years ago 80% were Norway Spruce, but this is now down to less than 30%, with Nordman Fir, which retains its needles longer, at 50% (95% in urban areas) and Fraser Fir, a US favourite, 12%. The most popular size has been increasing and is now 5 to 7 feet. Only 5% are sold rooted, although public interest in 'living trees ' is now increasing.

Imported trees in the past have accounted for 20% of total sales, but imports for Christmas 2005 fell to a few hundred thousand, and this trend will continue, putting pressure on supplies and wholesale prices continue to rise. Christmas trees are not eligible for the Single Payment, and as a result, many growers throughout the EU have grubbed-up trees, or not replanting in order to grow crops or pasture that is eligible for support. The supply of trees in mainland Europe has therefore been substantially reduced. UK Christmas tree growers, unlike those in other countries, have never received subsidies and have not cut back production significantly.

There are some 400 British growers, with plantations ranging from less than one hectare to 1,000 ha, all across the country. It is estimated that there are 60 million trees being grown, on some 25,000 ha. The average grower sells 6 to 7,000 a year from about 20 ha. The majority of sales are through the big garden centres, which require a uniform tree, netted and palletised, but there are successful 'choose and cut' operations and the enterprise works well on a farm with a farm shop. Producers need to sell 10 to 15,000 a year to justify buying machinery to assist in cultivation

The enterprise is slow to make a return. Norway Spruce is harvested in years 5 to 7, Nordman and Fraser Firs in years 7 to 9, making the enterprise vulnerable to changing market conditions. About 30% of the crop is harvested in the first harvesting year, 40% in the second, 30% in the third. All species need a well-drained site free from late frosts, with good access. As with any crop, the better the land the better the crop.

Rabbit fencing (£2 per m) and possibly deer fencing (£5.50 per m) are pre-requisites. Spacing is possible from 60cm x 60cm to 1.8m x 1.8m, but 1.2m x 1.2m is recommended. This gives 5,500 plants per ha allowing for 80% land loss for headlands, access, etc. Losses of 5 to 10% in the first year means 300-500 replacements are needed in second year. Norway Spruce transplants 20p-50p each, Nordman Fir 30-60p. Planting, by hand or machine, 10-15p/per plant.

Variable Inputs: Fertiliser in a split top dressing of 350 kg/ha 12: 11:18 + Mg and TE in late March and mid-September. Herbicides for weed control: residual herbicide, as cereals, in first year; subsequently an over-spray in October/November plus spot weeding until the canopy closes over. Weed control costs 26p/per plant over the life of the tree. Pesticides: aphicide three times a year for Norway Spruce, once for Nordman Fir at £16 per ha per application. Acaricide from year 3 to harvest: £126 per ha per year for Norway Spruce, £63 for Nordman Fir.

Pruning and Shaping: This is essential to produce the shape of tree the market demands. Norway Spruce: shaping 15p per tree per year from year 3 or 4. Nordman Fir: basal pruning in year 3 or 4 at 15p-20p per tree plus shaping in the same year at 15p per tree and bud-rubbing every year except harvest at 5-10p per tree per year.

Harvesting: Done over 3 to 6 weeks, for dispatch Nov. 20 - Dec. 12. A full-time person is needed per 3,000 trees sold, or one person per week per 400-500 trees. Cost: Norway Spruce 60-80p per tree, Nordman Fir 70-90p; Norway Spruce may be dipped or sprayed to reduce needle drop. Marketing costs around 10% of output.

Machinery: Inter-row plantation tractors £15,000-£65,000; stump clearing machines £7,000-£25,000; palletiser £13,000-£14,000; mist blowers £8,000-£10,000; hydraulic netting funnel £8,000-£10,000; manual netting funnel £175.

Labour: Planting and pruning can be done in January/February and tagging for height and quality in October/November. Thus it fits in well with combinable cropping.

Whilst the gross margins given are high, these will only be achieved by a high level of expertise and commitment and the long period before any return is obtained must also be stressed, together with the risk this entails.

	Norway Spruce		Nordman Fir	
	£/ha	(£/ac)	£/ha	(£/ac)
4,000 5-7 foot trees per Ha @ price of....	1.20p per ft		£2.00-2.40 per ft	
Output (average)	28,800	(11,655)	52,800	(21,365)
Variable costs:*				
Plants	1,925	(780)	2,475	(1,000)
Planting	675	(275)	675	(275)
Fertiliser	625	(255)	800	(325)
Weed Control	1,450	(585)	1,450	(585)
Pesticides	850	(345)	550	(220)
Pruning and Shaping	2,500	(1,010)	2,500	(1,010)
Harvesting	3,200	(1,295)	3,600	(1,455)
Total Variable Costs	11,225	(4,545)	12,050	(4,880)
Gross Margin (whole period)	17,575	(7,110)	40,750	(16,485)
Gross Margin per Year (over 7 & 9 years)	2,510	(1,015)	4,527	(1,830)

* Labour assumed to be casuals.

Acknowledgements: *British Christmas Tree Growers Association*, 13 Wolrige Road, Edinburgh, EH16 6HX. Tel: 0131 664 1100 www.bctga.co.uk.

FORESTRY

(Estimated for 2008)

A. Establishment Costs (before grant)

1. *Unit Cost of Operations*

Year/s	Operation	Estimated Cost (£)
1.	Trees for planting	
	(i) Bare rooted:	
	Conifers	125-200 per 1,000
	Broadleaves	250-350 per 1,000
	(ii) Rooted in small peat blocks:	
	Conifers	150-200 per 1,000
	Broadleaves	300-360 per 1,000
1.	Tree Protection	
	(i) Fencing (materials and erection)	
	Rabbit	3·00-3·50 per metre
	Stock	3·00-3·75 per metre
	Deer	5·00-7·00 per metre
	Deer and Rabbit	7·00-9·00 per metre
	Split post and rail	6·00-7·00 per metre
	(ii) Tree guards/shelters	
	Spiral and canes (450mm)	30-40 per 100
	Plastic tubes (1,200mm)	60-70 per 100
	Stakes	40-50 per 100
1.	Spot spraying	100 per 1,000 trees
1.	Hand planting at approximately 2m spacing	
	Conifers	150-180 per ha
	Broadleaves*	450-650 per ha
	Machine planting (loams and sand)	130-150 per ha
2-3.	Replacing dead trees**	
	Operation	50-100 per ha
	Plant supply	35-45 per ha
1-4.	Weeding per operation	
	Herbicide***	80-120 per ha weeded
2.	Inter-row mowing	80-120 per ha

Costs specific to location			Upland	Lowland
1.	Ground Preparation:	ploughing	100-150 per ha	50- 80 per ha
		mounding	250-300 per ha	250-300 per ha
1.	Drainage		60- 80 per ha	—
1.	Fertilizing		90-190 per ha	—

* Includes cost of erecting guards/shelters.

** Replacing dead trees (beating up) may be necessary, once in the second year and again in the third year. Costs depend on number of trees.

*** Up to 2 weeding operations may be necessary in each of the first 4 years in extreme situations. Costs are inclusive of materials.

Access roads may need to be constructed and can typically cost between £6,000 and £22,000 per kilometre (£9,600 to £35,000 per mile) depending on availability of roadstone and the number of culverts and bridges required.

2. Total Establishment Costs up to Year 3.

(i) Conifer—Lowland Sites

On a fairly typical lowland site, requiring little or no clearing or draining, the approximate cost before grant of establishing a conifer plantation would be in the range £1,200-£1,800 per hectare. Up to 8 separate weeding operations may be required.

(ii) Conifer—Upland Sites

Establishing a similar conifer plantation on an upland site could cost £1,100 to £1,600 per hectare. Normally some form of site preparation and drainage is required but only one weeding operation may be necessary. Overall costs tend to be £100-£200 per ha less than on lowland sites.

(iii) Hardwoods

Costs of establishing hardwood plantations are highly dependent on the fencing and/or tree protection required. If tubes are needed the overall costs will be influenced by the number of plants per hectare. Costs could be in the range £1,600-£2,500 per ha. Site conditions normally mean that hardwoods being grown for timber production are restricted to lowland sites.

(iv) Farm Woodlands

Establishment costs for farm woodlands may be lower than those indicated for hardwoods in (iii) above if lower planting densities are used. Initial establishment costs in the first year of the order of £1,800 per ha for woods under 3 ha and £1,600 per ha for woods of 3 to 10 ha would be typical.

(v) Size Factor

Savings in fencing and other economies of scale may reduce average costs per ha by 10 to 20% where large plantations are being established; conversely costs for small woods may easily be 25% higher per ha established.

(vi) Method of Establishment

A range of organisations and individuals undertake forestry contracting work and competitive tendering can help to control costs.

3. Re-Stocking Costs

Once trees on a site have been felled the Forestry Commission usually requires the site to be restocked as one of the conditions of awarding a felling licence. Re-stocking can either be done by planting or through natural regeneration by leaving a proportion of the existing trees standing and using seed from these trees to re-stock the site. Only minimum site preparation is usually required if using natural regeneration and grant aid is available (see Grant section).

The costs of establishment given above, and those for maintenance given below in section B, are estimates for England. Costs in Scotland tend to be lower, for a variety of reasons, but some indication of costs there can be obtained from the Forestry Commission Scotland publication "Standard Costs and Specification Booklet", which is accessible on www.forestry.gov.uk and is called 'SFGS Applicant's Booklet online'

B. Maintenance Costs

Once trees have been established they will normally require some maintenance and management work each year. For trees being grown primarily for timber production on a large scale, operations required may include ride maintenance, fence maintenance, pest control, fire protection, management fee and insurance premiums. Costs will normally fall within the range £10-£50 per ha per annum depending upon the size of the plantation and the complexity of management. In upland areas one or more fertilizing operations may be needed in the first 20 years in the life of a tree depending on the quality of the site. Estimated cost £90-£150 per ha, depending on elements applied. For trees being grown for sporting and amenity purposes, annual maintenance costs are likely to be less and may range up to about £10 per ha.

A brashing operation which involves removing branches up to two metres may be required for access reasons as the crop matures. Opening up inspection racks over 5-10% of the crop may cost £30-£60 per ha. Brashing 40-50% of the crop could cost £150-£300 per ha.

C. Production

Production is usually measured in terms of cubic metres (m3) of marketable timber per hectare and will vary according to the quality of the site, species planted and thinning policy. Sites in lowland Britain planted to conifers typically produce an average of 12 to 18 m3 of timber per ha per year over the rotation as a whole and would accordingly be assessed as falling in yield classes 12 to 18. Under traditional management systems thinning begins 18 to 25 years after planting and is repeated at intervals of approximately 5 years until the wood is clearfelled at between 40 and 60 years. Approximately 40-45% of total production will be from thinnings. Broadleaves typically produce an average of between 4 and 8 m3 of timber per hectare per year and fall in yield classes 4 to 8. A felling licence must be obtained from the Forestry Commission before any felling takes place.

Prior to a thinning sale the trees normally have to be marked and measured at an estimated cost of 35p per m3, which is equivalent to £100-£125 per hectare depending on species, crop density and age. For a clearfelling sale the cost can range from £250 to £350 per ha, or about £1 per m3 where a full tariff applies, i.e. where each tree is counted and sample measurements of individual trees are taken.

D. Prices

Prices for standing timber are extremely variable, depending on species, tree size and quality, ease of extraction from site, geographical location (nearness to end user), quantity being sold, world market prices and effectiveness of marketing method used. The use of wood for energy generation is beginning to open up a new market for poorer quality hardwood and conifer logs and forest residues.

Conifers

Average prices paid for standing coniferous timber sold from Forest Enterprise areas in the year to 31st March 2007, were:

Harvesting stage	Average tree size (m3)	Price (£ per m3) England	Wales	Scotland
1st Thinning	Up to 0.074	2.32	1.52	3.87
	0.075-0.124	9.00	3.36	3.33
Subsequent Thinnings	0.125-0.174	9.40	5.57	3.41
	0.175-0.224	10.56	5.23	4.09
	0.225-0.274	9.83	2.92	7.75
	0.275-0.424	10.09	5.60	6.70
	0.425-0.499	12.85	5.67	10.56
Clearfelling	0.500-0.599	9.99	6.59	5.03
	0.600-0.699	11.08	5.20	5.68
	0.700-0.799	15.58	7.35	6.59
	0.800-0.899	17.63	4.08	13.74
	0.900-0.999	13.30	2.42	7.62
	1.000 and over	20.33	15.75	10.89

Source: Forest Enterprise, July 2007.

Hardwoods

The hardwood trade is very complex. Merchants normally assess and value all but the smallest trees on a stem by stem basis. Actual prices fetched can show considerable variation depending on species, size, form, quality and marketing expertise of the seller. Felling usually takes place in the winter months.

Some indicative prices for hardwoods are given below, but it is important to note that actual prices fetched can vary quite widely. Wood quality is particularly important in determining prices.

Harvesting stage	Tree size range (m3)	Price range £ per m3	Possible use
First thinnings	<0.13	0-12	Firewood, board products and pulp wood. Poles for refineries and turnery.
Subsequent Thinnings	0.13-0.3	5- 20	Smaller sizes and lower quality
	0.3 -0.6	8- 22	material may go for fencing or
	0.6 -1.0	10- 40	for use in the mining industry.
Clearfellings	1.0 -2.0	15- 80	Trees over 30 cm in diameter and of better quality may go for planking, furniture or joinery.
	2+	25-150	High quality material may go for veneers and can fetch between £150 and £300 per m3 depending on species and specifications.

Prices for Oak, Ash, Sycamore, Cherry and Elm tend to be significantly higher than for Beech, which seldom exceeds about £45 per m3 standing even for stands containing significant volumes of first quality planking.

E. Timber Marketing

In-house marketing by the owner or agent can be cost effective but only if they have detailed, up-to-date knowledge of timber buyers in the market place. The alternative is marketing through a forestry manager or management company, but this can be expensive and is not guaranteed to test the open market fully.

Nationwide electronic sales of timber by auction and tender are now available for all types and quantities of timber. This cost effective, no-sale-no-fee (1·5 to 2·3% sales commission) method offers full exposure to the trade and should realise the correct market value. (Beacon Forestry: www.beaconforestry.co.uk). For small, unusual or low value timber parcels free advertising is available on the Ecolots website and in a free magazine (www.ecolots.co.uk or tel: 01721 724 788).

F. Market Value of Established Plantations and Woods

The value of woods depends on many factors, such as location, access, species, age and soil type. The table on the following page gives an indication of the range of current (2007) market values of commercial woodlands of different ages, based on recent market sales.

From years 20 to 25 onwards prices of commercial woods will also be increasingly influenced by the quantity of merchantable timber they contain. Depending on the time of clearfelling, the timber may be worth between £900 to £6,000 per hectare (£360 to £2,500 per acre).

Woods with high amenity or Ancient Woodland status can often command a premium over prices fetched for commercial woodlands and also those which are freehold including minerals and sporting rights. Conversely conservation designation can restrict value by preventing economic forest management.

The value of woods containing mature hardwoods will depend on the quality and value of the timber they contain and the quality of access.

Market Value of Commercial Sitka Spruce Woodlands

Age of Commercial Woods and Plantations	Price Range for crop and land	
	£/ha	£/acre
0-5 years	125- 625	(50- 250)
6-10 years	625-1000	(250- 400)
11-15 years	875-1125	(350- 450)
16-20 years	1000-1500	(400- 600)
21-25 years	1250-2375	(500- 950)

G. Grants

With devolution, each part of the United Kingdom has introduced new schemes that replace the previous Woodland Grant Scheme (WGS) and the Farm Woodland Premium Scheme (FWPS). In England, the English Woodland Grant Scheme (EWGS) opened in July 2005 (with some elements becoming later that year). The Scottish Foresty Grant Scheme (SFGS) was introduced in June 2002. In Wales, the Better Woodlands for Wales (BWW) programme began in April 2006. Planting grants will be brought under the BWW umbrella sometime in 2007.

English Woodland Grant Scheme

Initially this scheme will operate in a similar manner across the whole of England. However, it is envisaged that in time variations in levels of support will be introduced on a regional basis to meet the needs of each region. The EWGS will comprise six components and applications can be made for combinations of these components where appropriate.

1. *Woodland Management Planning Grant:* available as a contribution towards the cost of producing plans for existing woodlands, and which meet the UK Woodland Assurance Standard. Rates of grant contribution are £10 per hectare for the first 100 hectares and £5 thereafter. There is a minimum payment of £300 for plans covering more than 3 hectares but less than 30 hectares.

2. *Woodland Assessment Grant:* available as a contribution towards the costs of obtaining additional information about the woodland in relation to ecology, landscape, historic and heritage assessments, and to determine stakeholder interests. A fixed hourly rate of £35 is payable plus a contribution at 80% of a set range of standard assesment costs.

3. *Woodland Management Grant:* aid for providing public benefits and to undertake sustainable woodland management. Potentially eligible activities include public access, maintaining boundaries, protecting archaeological features, management of old wood habitat and open space, soil and ground water protection, controlling non-native species, pest control, woodland health and monitoring sustainability. The rate of grant is in line with ELS payments at £30 per hectare per year.

4. *Woodland Regeneration Grant:* a contribution towards the cost of regenerating woodland after felling. The aim is to promote the replacement of felled woodland whilst changing woodland types for increased public benefit. Grant rates depend on the type of wood being felled and the type of wood which replaces it:

Type of woodland felled	Type of woodland being regenerated	Grant (£/ha)
Conifer plantation	Native species	1,100
	Broadleaved species	950
	Conifer species	360
Broadleaved plantation	Native species	1,100
	Broadleaved species	950
Conifer plantation on Ancient Woodland Site	Native species	1,760
	Broadleaved species	950
	Conifer species...................	0
Broadleaved plantation on Ancient Woodland Site	Native species	1,760
	Broadleaved species	950
Ancient and other semi-natural woodland	Native species	1,100

5. *Woodland Improvement Grant:* a contribution towards the cost of work improve the quality of woodland for social, environmental, and economic benefits. Initially the rate of grant is set at 50% of agreed costs in a five-year plan. The focus is on improving access, biodiversity, and protecting SSSIs. In the course of time regions may choose to vary the rate of contributions or priority areas to reflect regional differences. There will be a maximum grant contribution of £100,000.

6. *Woodland Creation Grants:* aids the establishment of new woodlands. This element of the EWGS is competitive and will be assessed on a points scoring system with the applications that giving the greatest benefits being selected. Woodland creation may be by natural regeneration or by direct seeding. The rates of grant will depend on the type of woodland; Standard (3 ha or more), Small Standard (less than 3 ha), Native Species Only, Community (designed for public access), or Special Broadleaved (species appropriate for growth at wide spacing). Planting density requirements, percentage open space and percentage of shrub element are set for for each woodland type. Rates of grant are as follows:

Woodland category	Broadleaves £/ha	Conifers £/ha
Standard, Native and Community.........	1,800	1,200
Special Broadleaved	700	n/a

In addition to the above grant an extra £500 per ha is paid for woodland established within five miles of 100,000 people or within the National Forest Area, OR where there is an agreement to provide for public access and there is an identified need. Woodland meeting both of these requirements will be eligible to claim £1000 per ha.

Payment is made 80% on the completion of the work, with the final 20% payable after 5 years as long as the plantation is maintained. Applications usually have to be made in the summer prior to the winter/spring when the planting will take place. In 2006 the deadline was 31st August.

Planting on Agricultural Land: Annual payments are available under the EWGS for converting agricultural land to woodland (similar to the old FWPS). Payments will continue for 15 years when new woodlands comprise more than 50 per cent broadleaved species, and 10 years when the percentage broadleaves is less than 50 percent (or fast growing broadleaved species such as poplar). Payment rates will depend on the agricultural land use category being converted to woodland. Current rates are set out below, although they may be subject to revision in future years;

Agricultural Land Category	Annual payment (£/ha)		
	Non-Less Favoured Area (LFA)	LFA: Disadvantaged Areas	LFA: Severely Disadvantaged
Arable Land*	300	230	160
Improved Grassland	260	200	140
Other Cropped Land	260	200	140
Unimproved Land	ineligible	60	60

* defined as land that used to be eligible for AAPS under the old IACS system

More details of the EWGS are available on the Forestry Commission website (www.forestry.gov.uk). There are deadlines for the submission of application forms for the different components of the scheme as funding is limited. Early discussions with one of Forestry Commission England' Conservancy offices is advised. Help and advice can also be obtained from the EWGS helpline Tel: 01223 346004.

H. Woodland and the Single Payment

In general, land being used to grow trees is not eligible to activate Single Payment entitlments. However, farm woodland planted on arable land under the English Woodland Grant Scheme (EWGS) and the previous Woodland Grant Scheme / Farm Woodland Premioum Scheme (FWPS) can be counted towards a farmer's set-aside obligation under the Single Payment Scheme. Farmers receive the annual payments under the FWPS / Woodland Creation Grant payments, not set-aside payments. Short-rotation coppice is not eligible for entry into woodland grant schems but where it is planted on set-aside land, such land will remian eligible for the Single Payment.

I. Taxation

Income from commercial woodlands is no longer subject to income tax, and tax relief cannot be claimed for the cost of establishing new woodlands.

In general EWGS grants are tax free but annual payments under the Farm Woodland Premium Scheme (and now Woodland Creation Grants) are regarded as compensation for agricultural income forgone and are liable to income tax.

The sale of timber does not attract Capital Gains Tax, although the disposal of the underlying land may give rise to an assessment.

Woodlands which are managed commercially or which are ancillary to a farming business may be eligible for either Business Property Relief or Agricultural Relief for Inheritance Tax purposes.

Acknowledgement: The above estimates are based in part on information supplied by John Clegg Consulting Ltd.

A magazine, 'Forestry and British Timber', is published monthly (Miller Freeman, Telephone 01732-377651).

ENERGY CROPS
A. General

The production of "Renewable Energy" has grown considerably over the last three years in response to Britain's (and other countries') attitudes towards tackling global warming. The main factor contributing towards rising global air temperatures appears to be the release of green house gases (GHGs) from human activity. The main GHGs are:

- Carbon Dioxide, which accounts for up to a quarter of the green house gas effect

- Methane accounts for between 4% and 9% of the effect but is about 25 times more potent by volume than carbon dioxide

- Nitrous Oxide, which, whilst very low in concentration in the atmosphere, is about 300 times more potent than carbon dioxide

- Water Vapour. Whilst this is the most voluminous and causes between a third and two thirds of the green house effect, human activity has a negligible effect on it.

Energy crops are a form of renewable energy. They are grown to be used for heat and electricity generation or to produce transport fuels. They are considered 'carbon neutral' which means the carbon released on burning is only what they (recently) took up into the plant when growing, thereby not releasing additional carbon from fossil reserves beyond the requirements for fertiliser and chemicals, mechanical cultivation, harvest and transport to end-use location.

Since 1997, 169 countries have signed a commitment to reduce their emissions of GHGs; the Kyoto Protocol. The UK has a legally binding target under the Protocol to reduce its GHG emissions to 12.5% below 1990 levels between 2008 and 2012. It also has another domestic goal to reduce carbon dioxide emissions (one of the main greenhouse gases) by 20% below 1990 levels by 2010. The March 2007 Draft Climate Change Bill (www.official-documents.gov.uk/document/cm70/7040/7040.pdf) outlines how Government intends to enshrine the commitments in the 2003 Energy White Paper ('Our Energy Future, Creating a Low Carbon Economy' www.dti.gov.uk/files/file10719.pdf) to reduce CO2 emissions by 60% on 1990 levels by 2050; and to achieve "real progress" by 2020 (equating to reductions of 26-32%). This is further reinforced in the May 2007 Energy White Paper, 'Meeting the Energy Challenge' (www.dti.gov.uk/energy/whitepaper/page39534.html).

B. Support and Grants

Under the Single Payment Scheme, an Energy Aid Payment is available to growers of €45 per hectare. This is subject to a Maximum Guaranteed Area throughout the EU of 2.0 million hectares. It is likely this will be exceeded in 2007. If so, the payment will be reduced pro rata. For our gross margins, we have forecast the claimed area to reach 2.6 million hectares, thereby reducing the payment to €34/ha (€45 ÷ 2.6mha x 2.0m) before deductions. The grant is normally split between the grower and processor as the latter has administration to cover and guarantees to finance.

In the UK, the area claimed against the Energy Aid payment has risen since its launch in 2004 as follows:

Energy Aid Payment in UK	2004	2005	2006	2007
Hectares	32,972	99,351	182,394	242,413

The Energy Crops Scheme has been running since 2000 to finance the establishment of Short Rotation Coppice (SRC) and Miscanthus. This will reopen for the 2007-2013 period early in 2008 or possibly earlier. DEFRA has indicated the grant aid available under the scheme will be £800 per hectare for SRC and £1,000 per hectare for miscanthus. Confirmation of these rates is dependent on EU approval of the RDPE. In the previous scheme, the rates were £920 for Miscanthus and £1,000 for SRC. Payment is based on 40% of establishment costs for Miscanthus and 50% for SRC.

The Bio-energy Infrastructure Scheme, whilst not part of the Rural Development fund is also temporarily closed, having completed its first round and is awaiting a second round, probably to open in late 2007. It is designed to help develop the supply chain to harvest, store, process and supply biomass for heat, power and electricity end users.

Further support for energy crops comes via UK legislation that encourages the use of renewable-derived energy. These 'Renewable Obligations' are covered in the following biomass and biofuel sections.

C. Biomass for Power

This area covers crops that are grown to be burnt directly to produce heat and/or electricity. The plant material is chopped, chipped, or baled and is generally either used in boilers in dedicated biomass power stations, or mixed with coal for co-firing in conventional power stations. Biomass includes short rotation coppice, miscanthus, straw, canary reed grass and switch grass as well as forest residues. It could become a significant part of Britain's renewable resources.

The European Union's Renewable's Directive that came into force in 2001 encourages Member States to adopt national targets of deriving energy from renewable sources. The UK government has introduced legislation requiring 10% of UK electricity to be generated from renewable resources by 2010 (subject to the cost to consumers being acceptable) and an aspiration to reach 20% by 2020. The mechanisms for achieving this in the UK are:

- The Non Fossil Fuel Obligation (NFFO) covering England, Wales and N. Ireland

- Renewables Obligation (Scotland)

They are monitored by the Office of Gas and Electricity Markets (OFGEM) through a system of certification. Renewables Obligation Certificates (ROCs) are issued to power generators for providing electricity from renewable sources. Generators failing to meet specified annual targets for renewable generation are 'fined' a 'buy-out' penalty which is paid back to ROC holders. However, it is possible to fulfil the renewables obligation by purchasing surplus ROCs from other generators. Thus ROCs have a market value, their average price at the last auction in April 2007 was £47.50/MWh.

At present the only significant dedicated biomass-only plant is the Ely straw burning facility consuming 225,000 tonnes of feedstock annually and generating 38MW of electricity. Other dedicated plants are still planned. But the greatest current demand for biomass is for co-firing existing coal power stations, most of which now have a co-firing element of energy production. There are also small local markets to supply.

Short Rotation Coppice

Short Rotation Coppice (SRC) is a fast growing species of willow or poplar that when harvested, chipped and dried can be used as a fuel for heat or power generation.

SRC willow needs access to moisture but grows on any cultivable land. It requires a seedbed similar to that of a conventional arable crop, with particular attention to weed control. Planting is carried out in the spring using unrooted cuttings at a rate of 15,000/ha. Rabbit fencing may be necessary. Pest and weed control is essential when the plants are young, until canopy closure is achieved in the second year. In the autumn after planting the willow is cut back to encourage multi-stemmed stools. After 3 years the crop is harvested and then harvested every 3 years throughout its life which can be as long as 30 years but is generally put at 16 years. Fertilizer is applied after each harvest. The harvested crop can be stored on-farm, normally as billets. It is then processed according to the needs of the end processor. Some generators require the wood to be processed into granules which, with transport charges can add substantially to production costs. The first harvest should yield 25-30odt/ha (oven dried tonnes), subsequent ones 32-35odt/ha. Contracts are worth around £45/odt.

The following gives a very broad indication of likely costs and net annual returns. No account has been taken of planting grants that may become available with the new Rural Development Scheme in late 2007/early 2008.

Establishment Costs:	£/ha
Fencing (optional)	200
Pre-planting spraying	80
Fertiliser	25
Cultivations	50
Planting	300
Cuttings	750
Post-planting spraying	90
Cut-back	35
Total Establishment	1,530

Annual Net Returns: Output 27 odt @ £45 every third year; £405/year plus Energy Aid Payment net of deductions of approximately £15/ha. Variable costs per year including fertiliser and sprays are £50/ha, harvesting £100/ha, transport and handling £100/ha and processing £100/ha making a total of £350. Note, this equates to harvesting etc, each costing £350 every 3 years. Remember to amortise the cost of planting (including fencing etc) over the forecast period of the crop. Use the Amortisation Table on page 199.

Miscanthus (Elephant Grass)

Miscanthus is a perennial energy and fibre crop, indigenous to Africa and Asia, now grown commercially in the UK. It differs from short-rotation coppice as it is harvested annually using existing farm machinery. The crop has a useful life of 15-20 years.

There is a range of other uses for miscanthus beyond energy generation. After suitable treatment it makes valuable animal bedding, for which there is a ready market. It can go into paper making and biopolymer manufacture or be used to produce a number of bio-degradable products, such as flowerpots.

Potential cropping zones in the UK are widespread but the crop is vulnerable to late spring frosts and is best grown south of a line from Chester to Lincoln. It can be grown successfully further north but yields may be reduced. Trials have performed well in Scotland and the area in Yorkshire is growing to supply a local power generator. It is suitable for a wide range of soil types and pH values but is not recommended for drought prone soils where again yield can be reduced.

The crop is propagated from rhizomes. New technology has improved planting techniques with a work-rate of 10-20ha per day. Weed control is necessary at establishment and in the following spring. A mature crop should suppress any weed growth. So far in the UK no serious pathogens and pests have been encountered. Fertilizer requirement is low; a small amount (perhaps 40kg/ha N, 40kg/ha P and 40kg/ha K) is applied in the first year, sewage sludge is ideal. Little if any is needed subsequently as the leaf mulch supplies nutrients.

Each spring the crop produces new shoots, usually in April, which grow into strong erect stems up to 4 metres in height by late August. They resemble bamboo canes and contain solid pith. The plants senesce in the autumn, nutrients pass down into the rhizomes and a deep leaf litter forms. All foliage dies after the first frost and the stems desiccate to 50% moisture content during winter. The leafless canes are harvested between January and April, before the crop begins to shoot again. The robust rhizome network provides a platform for harvesting machinery; frosty conditions also help.

71

The harvest method depends on end use. For energy the crop is cut with a mower conditioner and then baled into 5-600kg Heston bales. These are stored outside before being taken to the power station. For other end uses a modified maize harvester can be used. New machinery is being developed to make operations more efficient and cheaper.

In the UK the likely yield of a mature crop should be 12-15 oven dried tonnes (odt)/ha/year. In the year after establishment only as much as 50 to 60% of the full yield is obtained. The price for energy crops ranges mainly between £25 to £45/odt (usually ex-farm). Its energy value is potentially higher than this. Horse bedding can retail for as much as £100/tonne in bulk to £240/tonne, de-dusted in 20kg bags.

There are probably about 10,000ha of miscanthus in the UK although this is difficult to measure. Initially much of the crop was used for propagation material but now it is being planted for both energy and fibre end uses. A number of other biomass projects, supported by the DTI, are in train. Small on-farm boilers, to produce heat and energy, have been developed which also offer potential for miscanthus.

The Energy Crops Scheme bases its £800 per hectare planting grant on 40% of total planting costs of £2,000 per hectare. However, new techniques are making this process cheaper and tend to cost in the region of £1,600 to £2,000 per hectare. Planting miscanthus for long term power contracts can involve an agreement whereby planting costs fall to £1,250, meaning net costs after the grant can be as low as £450. Some agrochemicals will probably be required in the first year.

Crop Longevity (years)	5 years	15 Years	20 years
Yield: 12.5odt/ha (5odt/acre) @ £35/odt		£	
Miscanthus*	304 (123)	393 (159)	404 (164)
Energy Crop Supplement	20 (8)	20 (8)	20 (8)
Output:	324 (131)	413 (167)	424 (172)
Variable Costs:			
Amortised Planting Cost**	213 (86)	96 (39)	83 (33)
Fertilizer/spray		0 (0)	
Harvest, bale and haul/store		200 (81)	
Total Variable Costs	413 (167)	296 (120)	283 (115)
Gross Margin per ha (acre)	-89 (-36)	117 (47)	141 (57)

* calculated as average yield over period including 1st year (no harvest) and 2nd season (½ yield)
** Based on £1,675 less £800 planting grant amortised at 7% for longevity of crop
Acknowledgement: David Croxton, *Bical*.

D. Liquid Biofuels

Liquid biofuels are road transport fuels produced from plants, including several mainstream farm crops. Biodiesel is produced from oilseed crops such as oilseed rape, soybeans and palm and is a replacement for mineral diesel. Bioethanol is a petrol replacement, produced from starch/sugar-based crops including wheat, maize and sugar beet or cane. A 'second generation' of biofuels is being developed which will use cellulosic feedstock. This will enable a higher energy return per hectare of cropped land and the opportunity to process household, manufacturing and agricultural organic wastes.

Policy

In the UK, a fuel excise duty discount of 20ppl is available for biofuels (only for the biofuel component of fuel). These discounts are guaranteed to remain in place until April 2010. Duty rates are 48.35ppl for mineral fuel and 28.35ppl for biofuel, until 1st October 2007 when they increase to 50.35ppl for mineral fuel and 30.35ppl for biofuels.

On 15th April 2008, the Renewable Transport Fuel Obligation (RTFO) will begin. It means that from April 2010 to April 2011, 5% of aggregate road transport fuel sales by volume should be a biofuel. The RTFO starts in 2008/9 at a rate of 2.5% and increases to 3.75% in 2009/10. For every litre of biofuel that excise duty is paid on, a Renewable Transport Fuel Certificate (RTFC) will be issued. Companies that supply at least 450,000 litres of mineral fuel to the UK market annually must participate by either incorporating sufficient biofuel into their sales, buying RTFCs from another biofuel provider or pay a 15ppl buy-out penalty (fine).

This 15ppl "buy-out" figure, coupled with the 20ppl excise duty discount, gives (mineral) fuel companies a financial incentive to incorporate biofuel into their road-fuel sales of 35ppl over mineral based fuel (less the additional costs of biofuel production). After April 2010, the emphasis will move from duty exemption to buy-out-price as the principal support mechanism. As an additional incentive, the 15ppl payment made by non-biofuel-incorporating companies will be rolled back into the industry, redistributed equally to every RTFC issued. These subsidies are essential to make the industry viable, without them, there would be no biofuels.

Biofuel Year[1]	2007-2008	2008-2009	2009-2010	2010-2011
RTFO Obligation [2]	0.0%	2.5%	3.75%	5.0%
Duty Discount [3]	20ppl	20ppl	20ppl	?

[1] The biofuel accounting year is from 15th April to 14th April
[2] The RTFO inclusion obligation is by volume and percentage of fuel sales/use
[3] Fuel Excise Duty reduction from fossil fuel Excise Duty per litre

Supply

By 2010, UK road fuel use will be about 40 million tonnes (diesel exceeding petrol use by about 55:45) meaning 2 m tonnes of biofuel will be required. The RTFO does not differentiate between biofuels so one may dominate the market. But splitting the market proportionately would require roughly 1.1 m tonnes of biodiesel and 0.9m of bioethanol. This would need 2.6 m tonnes OSR (or equivalent feedstock) covering 800 thousand hectares (at 3.25t/ha) and 3 m tonnes of wheat (or equivalent feedstock) covering 380 thousand hectares (at 8.00t/ha). The UK could use its exportable surplus, for wheat, but cannot produce that much additional oilseed rape at today's yields.

Over 30 other countries have biofuel policies. Whilst nationally we can redirect an exportable surplus, this is not possible globally as there is no surplus grain production. More land must be converted into arable cropping or higher yields achieved from existing land to supply this new market.

SET-ASIDE

The Provisions

Set-aside is one of the three conditions of claiming the Single Payment (SP), the other two being land occupation (10-month rule) and cross-compliance. If farmers wishing to claim the SP hold set-aside entitlements (either owned or leased in), they are obliged to claim them before they can claim on any other entitlements. To do this, the farmer must manage 1 hectare of 'arable' land according to set-aside regulations for every set-aside entitlement held. Failure to do this will result in penalties being applied to the SP. One exception to this rule is for farms that are wholly registered as organic or organic conversion. Any set-aside entitlements transferred into an organic holding must be with (organic) land.

However, it is highly likely that, for harvest 2008, the set-aside percentage will be reduced to 0%. This is a one-off derogation reducing set-aside to 0% for the 2008 harvest year – it does not abolish set-aside permanently. That is a topic for discussion within the 'Health Check'. The earliest date for complete and final abolition is the 2009 year, with the expectation it will certainly be ended by 2012.

For 2008, farmers will still have set-aside entitlements, meaning they will still receive the set-aside payment (Regional Average component of the SP only in England), but that they will not be restricted by the set-aside regulations. In other words, any cropping will be allowed on the 'set-aside' land.

Farmers were allocated set-aside entitlements in 2005 by varying methods depending on region: In England, land that was arable status in both 2003 and 2005 was allocated set-aside entitlements at the rate of 8% for lowland areas, and 1.3% for SDA non-Moorland. Note that the definition of arable land has changed since Arable Area Payments (AAP) to include fruit, vegetable, sugar beet, some temporary grass and most horticultural land. This decreased the set-aside percentage from the previous 10% to 8% and 1.3%. In Wales and Scotland, set-aside entitlements were allocated simply as 10% of area claimed under the AAP scheme in the reference period. Those claiming small areas of arable land under the 2005 SPS were not issued with set-aside entitlements (carrying-over the 'small producers' exemption' from the previous AAP scheme). For example, in lowland England, there was an exemption for farmers with less than 19.48 hectares of arable land (122.36 ha in SDA non-moorland areas).

Set-aside entitlements can be freely traded, like all other types of SP entitlement. The requirement to set land aside moves with the entitlement. Therefore, through trading, farmers can end up with a greater or lesser set-aside requirement than their original allocation.

In England, only the regional average component of the SP is paid on set-aside entitlements. In early years of the SP, it is therefore a low value per hectare.

A NOTE ON DIVERSIFICATION

While diversification is to be encouraged, wherever feasible, especially to help maintain incomes when the main farm enterprises are falling in profitability, a number of points need stressing. Many new enterprises require a substantial amount of capital; many need new skills (both in production and management), which take time, or a particular type of personality, to acquire. The market may be limited and there is usually a considerable level of risk attached. Nevertheless, many ventures exist where entrepreneurial skills have achieved notable success. Conversion of surplus farm buildings, for offices, workshops, retail and storage, has been the primary farm diversification activity up to date. A 2006 DEFRA survey found that 46% of farms had diversification activity generating an average income of £10,900 pa. But if letting farm buildings is stripped out, the percentage of diversified farms falls to 19%.

Some 'diversification enterprises' have been included above and there are more in the next section. There are many others, which include;

Alpacas	Sporting Fisheries	Tourism:
Herbs	Game Shooting	Caravans and Camping
Carp and Crayfish	Stalking	Holiday Cottages
Llamas	Clay Pigeon Shooting	Barn Conversions
Quails	Horses:	'Added Value' enterprises:
Snails	Riding School	Yoghurt, ice cream, etc.
	Trekking	Motor Sports
		Adventure Games

2. GRAZING LIVESTOCK

DAIRY COWS

Holstein Friesians (per Cow)

	Low	Average	High	Very High
Performance level (yield (1))	Low	Average	High	
Milk Yield per Cow (litres) (2)	5,500	7,000	8,000	9,000
	£	£	£	£
Milk Value per Cow (3)	1265	1610	1840	2070
Plus Value of Calves (4)	50	45	40	40
Plus Value of Cull Cows (5)	75	75	75	75
Less Cost or Market Value of Replacements (6, 7)	£200	200	200	200
Output	1190	1530	1755	1985
Concentrate Costs (8)	225	300	390	488
Miscellaneous Variable Costs (10)	166	171	179	190
Gross Margin before deducting Forage Variable Costs (inc. Bought Fodder)*	799	1059	1186	1308
Margin of Milk over Concentrates (MOC) [9]	1040	1310	1450	1583

Gross Margins per Cow and per Hectare (acre) at 4 different stocking rates (11)

Performance Level	Low	Average	High	Very High
1. At 1·75 cows per forage hectare (low):				
(0·57 forage hectares (1·4 acres) per cow)				
Forage Var. Costs & Bulk Feeds per Cow (11)	84	84	84	84
Gross Margin per Cow	715	975	1102	1224
Gross Margin per Forage Hectare	1252	1707	1929	2142
Gross Margin per Forage Acre	506	690	780	866
2. At 2 cows per forage hectare (average):				
(0·5 forage hectares (1·25 acres) per cow)				
Forage Var. Costs & Bulk Feeds per Cow (11)	**100**	**100**	**100**	**100**
Gross Margin per Cow	**699**	**959**	**1086**	**1208**
Gross Margin per Forage Hectare	**1398**	**1918**	**2172**	**2415**
Gross Margin per Forage Acre	**565**	**776**	**878**	**977**
3. At 2·25 cows per forage hectare (high):				
(0·45 forage hectares (1·1 acres) per cow)				
Forage Var. Costs & Bulk Feeds per Cow (11)	115	115	115	115
Gross Margin per Cow	684	944	1071	1193
Gross Margin per Forage Hectare	1539	2124	2410	2683
Gross Margin per Forage Acre	622	859	974	1085
4. At 2·5 cows per forage hectare (very high):				
(0·4 forage hectares (1 acre) per cow)				
Forage Var. Costs & Bulk Feeds per Cow (11)	133	133	133	133
Gross Margin per Cow	666	926	1053	1174
Gross Margin per Forage Hectare	1665	2315	2632	2936
Gross Margin per Forage Acre	673	936	1064	1187

1. Performance level refers primarily to milk yield, although increases in this are usually (though not necessarily) associated with higher gross margins. Some increase in concentrate feeding (kg/litre) has been assumed as yield rises: see note 8, page 78.

2. *Yield.* The yield referred to is litres produced during a year divided by the average number of cows and calved heifers in the herd. The average yield given (7,000 litres)

is an estimated national figure for sizeable herds of black and white cows in 2008. Note average yields for *costed* herds are invariably above national averages; they exceeded 7,500 litres in 2007, with the highest yielding 10% exceeding 9,000. The same is true of 'recorded herds', i.e. those in Milk Recording Schemes, where the average yield is well over 1,000 litres above the national average. The average yield for organic milk producers is around 6,000 litres.

3. *Milk Price.* This is assumed (as an average for the 2008 calendar year) to be 23.00p per litre, after deducting transport costs. It incorporates all adjustments: for milk composition, hygiene and seasonality. This is an average for all milk marketing groups, after bonuses etc., assuming an average-sized herd. Variable transport charges according to the amount collected mean that smaller herds will achieve a lower average price.

The average price received by individual producers depends on seasonality of production and compositional quality. Output and Gross Margin per cow are changed approximately as follows by each 0·25p per litre difference in price at each performance level:

Low	Average	High	Very High
±£13.75	±£17.50	±£20.00	±£22.50

Seasonality Price Adjustments. These are diverse between the various dairy companies. An increasing number of companies no longer operate conventional seasonal adjustments but instead have payment systems that encourage a level monthly production, with a range of deductions and bonuses related to the individual producer's spring and autumn deliveries. The average adjustments for a selection of companies operating conventional adjustments were as follows in 2007/08:

April	May	June	July	Aug	Sept	Oct	Nov	Dec	Jan– Mar
–2	–3	–2	0	+1.5	+2	+2	+1.5	+0	0.00

Some companies also offer a premium for a level delivery option if supplies in a calendar month are within 10% of an agreed daily volume; the premium is typically 0·2 ppl. The trend towards new production profile payments is continuing, with more and more co-ops and companies introducing them, along with more individual pricing mechanisms.

Compositional Quality Payments

Constituent values vary widely between buyers and months. As an example, the average values for the major dairies were, in June 2007:

> Butterfat: between 1.45p and 1.80p per litre per 1 per cent; average 1.54p.

> Protein: between 2.00p and 2.80p per litre per 1 per cent; average 2.40p. Some are as high as 3.4p

The *standard litre* price is typically 4·1% butterfat and 3·3% protein.

Average milk composition by breed are as follows (England and Wales, MMB recorded herds, 2-year averages, 1999/00 and 2000/01):

	Cows %*	Butterfat %	Protein %
Holstein Friesian........................	94·1	3·905	3·26
Ayrshire.................................	1·9	4·005	3·33
Dairy Shorthorn.........................	0·6	3·86	3·29
Jersey....................................	1·7	5·365	3·86
Guernsey.................................	1·4	4·68	3·56
All Breeds...............................		3·93	3·27

*1988/9; no later data known. Holstein Friesians probably around 96% in 2007/08.

Within Breed Quality Variation. For Holstein Friesians the range can easily be as follows, without going to extremes: between 3.5 and 4.1 for butterfat and from 3.1 to 3.4 for protein. The difference in value between these two levels combined is around 2p per litre.

Hygiene Price Adjustments. These vary widely between the different dairy companies. A mid-2007 example is as follows:

A. *Bactoscan (bacteria measure)*

Bactoscan Reading	Price Adjustment (ppl)
0- 50,000	+0.5
51-100,000	nil
101-250,000	− 1
Over 250,000*	− 6
Over 250,000**	−10

*1st month. **2nd and any subsequent months.

B. *Somatic Cell Count (Mastitis)*

Count	Price Adjustment (ppl)
0-200,000	+ 0.3
201-250,000	nil
251-300,000	− 0.5
301-400,000	− 2
Over 400,000*	− 6
Over 400,000**	−10

*1st month. **2nd and any subsequent months.

Several milk buyers have no premium for the top hygiene bands – they expect their suppliers to deliver top quality milk in order to receive the standard litre price.

C. *Antibiotics.* The price of all milk in a consignment that fails an antibiotics test ranges from l-5p/litre.

Organic milk. Organic milk price tends to fluctuate over a large range depending on supply and demand. A very rough rule of thumb is that the farmgate organic milk price averages about 10ppl more than conventional farmgate milk price. Organic milk price for 2008 is forecast at 32-33ppl.

4. *Value of Calves.* Average annual value per cow of purebred and beef cross heifer and bull calves, at 10-20 days old, allowing for mortality and an average calving index of 385 days. Calves from lower yield herds will have more beef genetics so be more valuable.

5. *Value of Cull Cows.* £300 allowing for casualties; 25% per annum replacement rate.

6. *Cost of Replacements* (N.B. average in 2008). £800 per down-calving heifer (purchase price or market value (mainly home-reared)); 25% per annum replacement rate.

7. *Herd Depreciation.* thus averages £125 per cow per year, i.e., 25 per cent of £500 (i.e., £800-£300).

Net Replacement Cost = £80 per cow per year, i.e., herd depreciation (£125) less value of calves (£45).

Bull. AI is assumed in the tables; bull depreciation would be approx. £150 a year (£1,500 purchase price less £750 cull value, 5-year herd life); tight calving pattern: 60 cows per bull, well spread calving pattern: 100; 10 to 20 tonnes silage, 0·75 tonnes concentrates a year. Very high yield herds may use more expensive (dairy) bulls reaching £2,500 purchase price).

8. *Concentrate Costs.*

Amounts:	Performance level	Low	Average	High	Very High
	kg/litre (approx.)	0.273	0.286	0.325	0.361
	tonnes/cow	1.50	2.00	2.60	3.25

Price: taken (for 2007) as £125 per tonne, which is an average of home-mixed rations and purchased compounds of varying nutritive value, averaged throughout the year.

A difference of £5 per tonne has approximately the following effect on margin over concentrates and gross margin per cow, on the assumptions made regarding the quantity fed at each performance level:

Low	Average	High	Very High
±£7.50	±£10.00	±£13.00	±£16.25

Seasonality. Typically, specialist spring calving herds (60% or more calvings between January and May), compared with autumn calving herds (60% or more calvings between August and December), use 0.09 kg per litre / 550 kg (£82) per cow per year less concentrates. See further note 12 below.

Typical Monthly Variation in Concentrate Feeding (kg per litre, 7,000 litre herd)

Winter		Summer	
October	0.30	April	0.27
November	0.33	May	0.16
December	0.33	June	0.16
January	0.33	July	0.22
February	0.33	August	0.24
March	0.30	September	0.27
Average winter: 0.32		Average summer: 0.22	
	Average whole year: 0.27		

The actual distribution on any farm will obviously vary according to such factors as seasonality of calving, level of milk yield, grazing productivity during the summer, the quantity and quality of bulk feeds in the winter, and turnout and housing dates. The March figure in particular will be affected by type of soil and seasonal rainfall.

Yield with no concentrates and good quality silage: approximately 4000 litres for spring calvers.

9. Margin over Concentrates and Concentrates per litre

The emphasis in the initial tables should be laid on the differences between the margin of milk value over concentrates per cow; the same large variation can occur with widely differing combinations of milk yield and quantity of concentrates fed.

In the following table, at each yield level figures are given for (a) margin of milk value over concentrates per cow (£) and (b) concentrates per litre (kg) at seven levels of concentrate feeding.

Yield Level	Low		Average		High		Very High	
Milk yiield per cow (litres)	5,500		7,000		8,000		9,000	
	(a)	(b)	(a)	(b)	(a)	(b)	(a)	(b)
	£	kg	£	kg	£	kg	£	kg
1.00 tonne (£150) concs. per cow	1,115	0.18	1,460	0.14	-	-	-	-
1.50 tonne (£225) concs. per cow	1,040	0.27	1,385	0.21	1,615	0.19	-	-
2.00 tonne (£300) concs. per cow	965	0.36	1,310	0.29	1,540	0.25	1,770	0.22
2.50 tonne (£375) concs. per cow	-	-	1,235	0.36	1,465	0.31	1,695	0.28
3.00 tonne (£450) concs. per cow	-	-	-	-	1,390	0.38	1,620	0.33
3.50 tonne (£525) concs. per cow	-	-	-	-	-	-	1,545	0.39
4.00 tonne (£600) concs. per cow	-	-	-	-	-	-	1,470	0.44

10. *Miscellaneous Variable Costs (average)*

	£
Bedding*...	25
Vet. and Med...	42
A.I. and Bull Hire..	30
Recording, Consultancy, Consumables, Dairy Stores..................	53
Total...	150

* Straw can vary from 0.4 to 1.5 tonne per cow and from £10 to £50 per tonne (or even more in some areas in exceptional years).

11. *Stocking Rate and Forage Costs.* The stocking rates given assume that nearly all requirements of bulk foods – both winter and summer – are obtained from the forage area, i.e. little is bought in. On average about 55 per cent of the forage area (or production) is grazed and 45 per cent conserved. Note that as the stocking density increases, gross margin per cow falls, but gross margin per hectare rises.

The levels of nitrogen are assumed to be as follows:

Stocking rate Cows per Ha (acre)	Kg N/Ha	units/acre
1.75 (0.7).......................................	180	143
2.00 (0.8).......................................	220	175
2.25 (0.9).......................................	275	220
2.50 (1.0).......................................	360	287

An increase in potash application is also assumed. Seed costs clearly depend on the percentage of permanent pasture, if any, the length of leys, etc. The following total variable costs per hectare (fertilizer, seed and sprays) have been assumed for grassland:

Stocking rate Cows per Ha (acre)	£/Ha	£/acre
1.75 (0.7).......................................	115	45.6
2.00 (0.8).......................................	152	61.6
2.25 (0.9).......................................	191	77.4
2.50 (1.0).......................................	243	98.4
Forage Maize	250	101

A small amount of purchased bulk fodder is normal, and is included in these costings increasing with the stocking rate as follows (per cow): low £18, average £24, high £30, very high £36.

An increase in stocking density can be obtained not only by intensifying grassland production, as above, but also by buying in winter bulk fodder (assuming the same level of concentrate feeding in both cases). This will cause the gross margin per cow to fall still further, but raise the gross margin per hectare at any given level of grassland management.

Clearly, 'fixed' costs, such as labour and depreciation on buildings are likely to increase per hectare and fall per cow as stocking density rises. Furthermore, husbandry problems such as poaching will multiply, unless zero-grazing is practised - with its further additions to fixed costs and management difficulties. In addition the Nitrate Vulnerable Zone regulations must still be abided by.

12 Seasonality. Price and concentrate feeding differences according to the seasonality of production have already been outlined in notes 3 and 8.

Under similar levels of management mainly autumn calving herds average up to 1,000 litres more milk/cow/year than mainly spring calving herds but feed around a tonne more concentrates per cow/year; spring calving herds should normally only be feeding about 0.15 kg/litre. The average milk price would be expected to be higher for autumn calving herds, but the difference is less than might be supposed and has been steadily reduced with better prices being paid for summer milk.

13. *Quota.* Values are particularly dependent on the levels of farmgate milk prices and national milk production v. quota. For six out of the seven years since 2000, the UK has been under quota, and the trend has been downward for the last decade. Throughout the 2007/08 season, milk quota values have been around 1.9 to 2 pence per litre to buy (clean) and 0.15 to 0.20 pence per litre to lease. These prices are all-time lows. If production rises beyond the present falling trend in 2008/09, the price of quota may rise with it..

14. *Labour*: see page 144.

15. *Building Costs*: see page 184.

16. *Costs per litre* (Holstein Friesians)

	Average (pence)		**Premium** (pence)	
Concentrates	4.29		3.70	
Forage and Bought Bulk Feed...	1.43		1.60	
Vet. & Med.	0.90		0.60	
Other Variable Costs	1.54		1.08	
Total Variable Costs		8.16		6.98
Labour: direct (milking etc.)	4.30		3.10	
: field/farm work	1.05		0.72	
Power and Machinery	2.90		2.28	
Rent/Rental Value	1.50		1.15	
General Overheads	1.10		0.94	
Total Fixed Costs		10.85		8.19
Net Replacement Cost *(Herd Dep'n)*		1.79		1.39
Total (excl. Quota Leasing/Purchase)		**20.79**		**16.56**

Notes on the above

With regard to the average costs the variable costs per litre are derived from the data (and therefore the assumptions made) in the main per cow cost table on page 75. The labour cost is as on page 144. The average fixed costs are as for the medium-sized farm data on page 170, with adjustments made to allow for the greater use of resources by dairy cows compared with followers (and possibly cereals). The 'Premium' figures are as estimated for the average of the most profitable 10% of herds, with lower than average costs per cow (except for concentrates and forage costs) and yields of 8,500 litres or more per cow and an above average stocking rate.

Labour includes farmer and any unpaid family labour.

Power and machinery cover all machinery and equipment costs, including the use of farm vehicles, etc.

General overheads similarly relate to the whole farm, including property repairs.

Where the dairy is part of a farm with other enterprises on a significant scale most of the fixed costs per cow and therefore per litre are difficult to determine.

The net replacement cost is herd depreciation less the value of calves.

As said in the table, the cost of additional quota, whether leasing charges or the annual cost of purchased quota, is not included.

Note too that neither interest on capital nor any management charge have been included.

If leasing or buying extra quota is being considered it is of course not the average but the marginal cost of producing the extra milk that needs to be considered. This will depend largely on whether the extra milk is being obtained through increasing yield per cow or by keeping more cows (or a combination of the two).

Channel Island Breeds

	Low	Average	High	Very High
Performance level (yield (1)).......................				
Milk Yield per Cow (litres) (2).....................	4,150	4,850	5,550	6,250
	£	£	£	£
Milk Value per Cow (3).............................	1162	1358	1554	1750
Concentrate Costs (8)...............................	200	269	341	422
Margin of Milk over Concentrates (MOC).......	963	1089	1213	1329
Herd Depreciation less calf value	65	65	65	65
Miscellaneous Variable Costs....................	166	171	179	190
Gross Margin per cow before deducting Forage Variable Costs	732	853	969	1074
Forage Variable Costs (inc. Bought Fodder)......	78	82	88	92
Gross Margin per Cow.............................	653	770	880	981
Gross Margin per Forage Hectare (2.4cows per ha: 0.42ha/cow)	1568	1849	2113	2355
Gross Margin per Forage Acre (1.05cows per acre: 0.97acre/cow)	635	749	856	954

Notes

1. *Yield.* Average of Jerseys and Guernseys. See Note 2 for Holstein Friesians (page 75). Guernseys average some 300 litres more than Jerseys (i.e. giving an average of approximately 4,700 for Jerseys, 5,000 for Guernseys) but Jerseys achieve a higher average price of above 2.5p per litre. Note that the average for Channel Island costed herds should not be compared with the average national (Pocketbook) figure for Holstein Friesians; costed herd yield averages are invariably well above national averages; (i.e. they will well exceed 5,250 litres for Guernseys and 5,000 for Jerseys in 2007.

2. *Milk Price.* This has been assumed to be 28.00p per litre (average of Jerseys and Guernseys), i.e. 5p above Holstein Friesian milk; (29.25p Jersey milk, 26.75p Guernsey). In addition to the higher price obtained through the higher compositional quality for Channel Island milk some companies pay a premium for Channel Island milk.

3. *Concentrate Costs.*

Amounts:	Performance level	Low	Average	High	Very High
	kg/litre	0.32	0.37	0.41	0.45
	tonnes/cow	1.33	1.795	2.275	2.81

Price: taken (for 2008) as £150 per tonne.

4. Net Annual Replacement Value. (i.e. Value of Calves less Herd Depreciation) were calculated as follows:

	£ per cow in herd
Cost of replacements: 25 per cent of herd per year @ £480	120
LESS Value of culls: 25 per cent of herd per year @ £160	
(allowing for casualties)*	40
Herd Depreciation	80
Annual Value of Calves**	15
Net Annual Replacement Cost	65

* Cull cow prices for Guernseys are about £40 higher than for Jerseys.

** Allowing for calving index of 390 days and calf mortality; mixture of pure bred calves and beef crosses. Guernsey calves, especially crosses, fetch more than Jersey calves, averaging perhaps £10 more per head — but substantially more for some Guernsey beef crosses.

5. *Miscellaneous Variable Costs.* See Note 10 for Holstein Friesians (page 79).

6. *Stocking Rate.* See, in general, Note 11 for Holstein Friesians (page 79). The effect of varying the stocking rate on gross margin per forage hectare is as follows:

Gross Margin per Cow Before deducting Forage V.C.s

Cows per Forage Hectare	Forage Hectares (acres) per cow	Low £732	Average £853	High £969	Very High £1,074	Forage V.C. £ per cow*
			Gross Margin £ per Forage Ha (acre)			
2.1	0.48 (1.18)	1379 (558)	1633 (661)	1877 (760)	2097 (849)	75
2.4	**0.42 (1.03)**	**1568 (635)**	**1859 (753)**	**2137 (865)**	**2388 (967)**	**78**
2.7	0.37 (0.91)	1739 (704)	2067 (837)	2380 (964)	2663 (1078)	87
3.0	0.33 (0.82)	1894 (767)	2257 (914)	2605 (1055)	2920 (1182)	100

* A small amount of purchased bulk fodder is assumed, increasing with the stocking rate as follows (per cow): low £15, average £19, high £25 very high £29.

At the average stocking rate given above for combined Channel Island breeds (2.4 cows per forage hectare) the average figure for Jerseys would be approximately 2.55 and that for Guernseys 2.25.

Ayrshires

Performance level (yield (1))	Low	Average	High	Very High
Milk Yield per Cow (litres) (2)	4,900	5,725	6,550	7,375
	£	£	£	£
Milk Value per Cow (3)	1137	1328	1520	1711
Concentrate Costs (8)	184	236	295	360
Margin of Milk over Concentrates (MOC)	953	1092	1225	1351
Herd Depreciation less calf value	113	113	113	113
Miscellaneous Variable Costs	166	171	179	190
Gross Margin per cow before deducting Forage Variable Costs	675	808	933	1049
Forage Variable Costs (inc. Bought Fodder)	78	82	88	92
Gross Margin per Cow	596	726	845	957
Gross Margin per Forage Hectare (2.4cows per ha: 0.42ha/cow)	1431	1743	2028	2296
Gross Margin per Forage Acre (1.05cows per acre: 0.97acre/cow)	580	706	821	930

Notes

1. *Yield.* See Note 2 for Holstein Friesians (page 75).

2. *Milk Price.* See in general, note 3 for Holstein Friesians (page 76). The price assumed in the above table is 23.2p per litre. The compositional quality of milk from Ayrshires is higher than for the black and white breeds.

3. *Concentrate Costs.* See notes 8 and 9 for Holstein Friesians (pages 78-79). In the above table, the levels of feeding kg/litre (and tonnes per cow) are as follows: low 0.25kg/l (1.225 tonne/cow), average 0.275kg (1.575t), high 0.30kg (1.965t), very high 0.325 (2.397t); price £150 per tonne.

4. Net Annual Replacement Value. (i.e. Value of Calves less Herd Depreciation) were calculated as follows:

	£ per cow in herd
Cost of replacements: 25 per cent of herd per year @ £750..	188
Less Value of culls: 25 per cent of herd per year @ £200 (allowing for casualties and slaughter premium)	50
Herd Depreciation	138
Annual Value of Calves*	25
Net Annual Replacement Cost	113

*Allowing for calving index of 385 days and calf mortality; mixture of pure bred calves and beef crosses.

5. *Miscellaneous Variable Costs.* See Note 10 for Holstein Friesians (page 79).

6. *Stocking Rate.* See, in general, Note 11 for Holstein Friesians (page 79).

Shorthorns. The above data could be used for Shorthorns, although one would expect their average yield to be about 5% lower, their cull and calf prices to be higher and their stocking rate to be slightly lower – similar to Holstein Friesians.

DAIRY FOLLOWERS
(per Heifer reared)

A. Holstein Fresians

Performance Level	Low	Average	High
	£	£	£
Value of heifer (allowing for culls) (1).....	720	720	720
Less Value of calf (allowing for mortality)	100	100	100
Output...	620	620	620
Variable Costs:			
Concentrate Costs (2)	178	162	146
Miscellaneous Variable Costs (3)	108	113	119
Total Variable Costs			
(excluding Forage)...........................	286	275	265
Gross Margin per Heifer, before			
deducting Forage Variable Costs...........	334	345	355
Forage Variable Costs (4)...................	76	93	110
Gross Margin per Heifer...................	257	251	245
Forage Hectares (Acres) per Heifer			
reared (5)......................................	0.95 (2.3)	0.73 (1.8)	0.58 (1.4)
Gross Margin per Forage Hectare (6)...	271	347	426
Gross Margin per Forage Acre...........	110	140	173

B. Channel Island Breeds

Performance Level	Low	Average	High
	£	£	£
Value of heifer (allowing for culls) (1).....	432	432	432
Less Value of calf (allowing for mortality)	15	15	15
Output...	417	417	417
Variable Costs:			
Concentrate Costs	152	138	124
Miscellaneous Variable Costs	97	102	107
Total Variable Costs			
(excluding Forage)...........................	249	240	231
Gross Margin per Heifer, before			
deducting Forage Variable Costs...........	168	177	186
Forage Variable Costs (4)...................	63	86	112
Gross Margin per Heifer...................	105	91	74
Forage Hectares (Acres) per Heifer			
reared (5)......................................	0.68 (1.7)	0.58 (1.4)	0.50 (1.2)
Gross Margin per Forage Hectare (6)...	156	159	148
Gross Margin per Forage Acre...........	63	64	60

N.B. on average Channel Island heifers calve about three months younger than Holstein Fresian Heifers

C. Ayrshires

Performance Level	Low	Average	High
	£	£	£
Value of heifer (allowing for culls) (1).....	600	600	600
Less Value of calf (allowing for mortality)	40	40	40
Output...	560	560	560
Variable Costs:			
Concentrate Costs	161	146	131
Miscellaneous Variable Costs	99	104	109
Total Variable Costs			
(excluding Forage)............................	260	250	241
Gross Margin per Heifer, before			
deducting Forage Variable Costs...........	300	310	319
Forage Variable Costs (4)...................	50	69	90
Gross Margin per Heifer...................	250	241	229
Forage Hectares (Acres) per Heifer			
reared (5)......................................	0.68 (1.7)	0.58 (1.4)	0.50 (1.2)
Gross Margin per Forage Hectare (6)...	370	420	459
Gross Margin per Forage Acre...........	150	170	186

Notes

1. The heifer values are based on the purchase price of down-calving heifers, allowing for culls. Most heifers are home-reared. If heifers are reared for sale, the price of whole batches are likely to be lower than the values given in the tables, by perhaps 10 or 15 per cent. On the other hand the purchaser will often take the batch a few months before the average expected calving date, thus reducing feed and area requirements for the rearer.

2. The lower levels of concentrate costs are the combined result of more economical feeding, lower cost per tonne and a lower average calving age. (Other things being equal, however, including the overall level of management, a lower calving age requires higher levels of feeding.) Average (Holstein Friesians) = £52 to 3 months (see Calf Rearing on page 87) plus 250 kg calf concentrates @ £165/tonne and 500 kg @ £138/tonne.

3. Miscellaneous variable costs include bedding (£25): straw requirements average approx. 1 tonne per heifer reared, but are variable, depending on time of year and age when calved, as well as system of housing and extent of outwintering. Vet. and med. approximately £38 per heifer reared.

4. Forage variable costs. Grass for both grazing and conservation, at £75, £115 and £165/ha respectively (low, average and high) plus a small amount of bought and bulk food (£5, £10, £15 a head).

5. With an average calving age of 2 years 4 months, a "replacement unit" (i.e. calf + yearling + heifer) equals about 1·25 livestock units. The three stocking rates given above are equivalent to approximately 0·64, 0·56 and 0·48 forage hectares (1·6,1·4,1·2 acres) respectively per Holstein Friesian cow.

6. Much higher gross margin figures per hectare can be combined by intensive grazing methods, particularly if combined with winter feeding systems which involve little dependence on home-produced hay or silage (cf. Note 11, last three paragraphs, page 79).

7. Contract Rearing: see page 101-102.

8. Labour: see page 145.

Self-Contained Dairy Herd: Cows and Followers

At average annual replacement rates (25 per cent of the milking herd), nearly one-third of a replacement unit is required for each cow in the herd, i.e. roughly one calf, yearling and heifer for every three cows (including calved heifers), allowing for mortality and culling. At average stocking rates for both, this means more than 1 hectare devoted to followers for every 3 hectares for cows. Since surplus youngstock are often reared and frequently the stocking rate is less intensive the ratio often exceeds 1:2 in practice. 1: 2·75 is about the minimum where all replacement heifers are reared, unless their winter feeding is based largely on straw and purchased supplements, or unless there is a combination of long average herd life and early calving, i.e. at 2 years old or just over.

Gross Margin per Forage Hectare (Acre) (£) for the Whole Herd (i.e., Cows and Followers Combined); (at four levels of performance, including four commensurate levels of stocking rate, for the dairy cows; and three levels of performance, including different stocking rates, for the followers) are as follows, assuming a 2:1 land use ratio (dairy cow area: followers area); (Holstein Friesians only):

			G.M per Forage Hectare (acre) Dairy Cows			
			Low	Average	High	Very High
			£	£	£	£
G.M. per			1252 (507)	1918 (777)	2410 (976)	2936 (1189)
Forage	Low	271 (110)	925 (375)	1369 (554)	1697 (687)	2048 (829)
Hectare	Ave.	347 (140)	950 (385)	**1394** (565)	1722 (697)	2073 (839)
(acre)	High	426 (173)	977 (396)	1421 (575)	1749 (708)	2099 (850)

As an example, the above table indicates that at the average level of performance and stocking rate for both cows and followers, the whole dairy gross margin per hectare (acre) figure falls to £1394 (565) compared with £1918 (777) for the dairy cows alone, a reduction of 27 per cent. If more than the assumed (minimum) number of dairy followers are kept and the ratio is 1·5:1 (i.e. 40% of the dairy herd forage area is devoted to followers rather than a third) the gross margin for the whole forage area figure (on the assumption again of average performance) falls to £1,075 (435), which is a reduction of 44 per cent compared with cows.

BEEF

Outlook for 2008

Events of 2007 have made 2008 a difficult year to predict with any certainty. At the time of writing a second Foot and Mouth outbreak in Surrey had just occurred. The beef industry has made good progress since the lifting of the original export ban in May 2006 in regaining markets for prime beef, cow beef and calf exports. We hope this progress is not undermined by a further long absence of UK beef from international markets.

Producers face a substantial increase of feed prices in winter 2007/08 following upward movements of cereals and straights prices. This is likely to result in feed prices £30 per tonne up in 2008 compared with last year. Many will also have low quality forage following the wet summer of 2007. Producers will be looking for the market to provide better returns to offset these higher costs. Such rises may be difficult to secure with processors facing continued resistance to retail price increases. Imports are also likely to limit producer price rises. Niche markets; for example, organic, breed specific or local branded products are likely to be more sheltered from the impact of price pressures on commodity markets.

Producers have already started assessing their beef enterprises without subsidy support. Together with further price challenges and rising feed costs, it seems inevitable beef cattle numbers will fall more rapidly than previous expectations. This in turn will impact on the slaughtering and processing sector with reduced throughput.

Finished Cattle Prices

Finished cattle prices started 2007 strongly but weakened from April to July, before signs of improving in August only to be interrupted by Foot and Mouth.

Over Thirty Month Beef improved substantially in 2007 with the best continental-cross cows achieving £1.00/kg and dairy types averaging 65p/kg.

The best that can be hoped for in 2008 is to regain the position of early 2007. Budgets for 2008 assume 110p to 115p/kg liveweight for suckler bred types depending on time of marketing, with dairy bred cattle achieving 104p to 108p/kg liveweight, with peak prices in March and April and troughs in September and October. The prices assumed in the following tables relate either to the 2008 calendar year or 2008/2009 for winter finished beef.

Hill Farm Allowances

Hill Farm Allowance Payments (which continue for one more year at least) can be found on page 100-101.

Calf Prices

The calf market is dependant upon many factors, finished beef prices, feed prices, producers' margins and export demand.

After a strengthening of prices in 2007 up to the Foot and Mouth outbreak, values for rearing calves look set to fall due to declining margins for almost all systems. The market for Holstein/Friesian bulls is likely to be almost entirely dependant upon export demand as margins for intensive finishing on cereal based diets appear too low at current cereals prices. Some milk buyers' contracts from 2007 exclude marketing calves for export which will mean less available for this market, potentially leaving an extra numbers on the home market at zero or very low prices. Producers will also want to consider carcase disposal costs for poorer black and white bulls without a market.

Some breeds supplying niche markets may be less affected for example Hereford crosses and Aberdeen Angus crosses.

The value below assumed for 2008 relate to black and white bulls or beef cross calves of all qualities, less than three weeks old.

	Bulls	Heifers
Holstein Friesians.........	25 (export)	-
Holstein Friesians.........	5 (home market)	-
Hereford cross	70	40
Continental cross	120	70

A. Calf Rearing

Early Weaning – Bucket Rearing (per calf)

	3 months	6 months
Value of Calf	200	270
Less Calf (1)	99	99
Output	101	171
Variable Costs:		
Milk Substitute and Concentrates (2)	52	96
Miscellaneous Variable Costs (3)	20	30
Hay (4)	1	8
Total Variable Costs	73	134
Gross Margin per Calf reared	**28**	**37**

1. £99 per calf (Holstein Friesian/Continental beef cross calves, 1-2 weeks old; 4 per cent mortality assumed, mainly in first 3 weeks. Value of pure Holstein Friesian bull calf £100 less; sale value at 3 or 6 months old correspondingly less).

2. Milk substitute: 15 kg @ £1500/tonne = £22.50. Calf concentrates: to 3 months, 160 kg @ £185/tonne = £29.60; to 6 months, additional 290kg @ £150/tonne = £44. Calves fed on machine or lib milk systems will use more milk powder.

3. Misc. Variable Costs include vet. and med.: 8 (3 months), 11 (6 months); bedding: 3 (3 months), 7 (6 months); plus ear tags etc.

4. Hay: 10 kg to 3 months, 200 kg to 6 months. Variable costs assume made on farm; double the cost if purchased.

5. Weights: at start, 45 to 50 kg; at 3 months, 115 kg; at 6 months, 210 kg. Contract rearing charge (both 0 to 3 months and 0 to 6 months): £9 per week. Direct labour cost: approximately £19 per head to 3 months, £32 per head to 6 months.

Labour requirements (all beef systems): see page 145.

Veal Calves

Information on veal calf rearing can be found on page 96

B. Suckler Cows

Single Suckling (per cow): Lowland

System	Spring Calving		Autumn Calving	
Performance Level (1)	Average	High	Average	High
	£	£	£	£
Value of Calf (2)	322	354	385	438
Calf Sales/Valuation. per Cow (3)	290	326	347	403
Less Cow and Bull Depreciation and Calf Purchases (4)	47	47	53	53
Output	243	279	294	350
Variable Costs:				
Concentrate Costs (cow and calf) . . .	25	20	56	50
Miscellaneous Variable Costs (5) . . .	57	52	77	72
Total Variable Costs (excluding forage).	82	72	133	122
Gross Margin per cow, before deducting Forage Variable Costs	161	207	161	228
Forage Variable Costs	70	75	70	75
Purchased Bulk Feed	20	15	20	15
Gross Margin per Cow	**71**	**117**	**71**	**138**
Cows per ha (6)	1.8	2.2	1.65	2.0
Forage Ha (Acres) per Cow	.55	.45	.6	.5
	(1.35)	(1.11)	(1.48)	(1.24)
Gross Margin per Forage Hectare	128	257	117	276
Gross Margin per Forage Acre	52	104	47	112

1. Performance level relates to variations in two factors: weaned calf weight and stocking rate. 'High' refers to the average levels likely to be achieved by the better fifty per cent of producers. It is clearly possible to set still higher 'targets'.

2. Weight of calves (kg) at sale/transfer: spring calving: average 280 (at approximately 7.25 months old), high 295 (slightly older); autumn calving: average 335 (at approximately 10.25 months old), high 365 (11 months old). Price (per live kg): spring calving: average 115p, high 120p; autumn calving: 115p, 120p. These prices are averages for steers and heifers.

3. Calves reared per 100 cows mated: average 90, high 92.

4. *Assumptions.* Herd life: spring calving, 7 years; autumn calving, 6 years. Purchase price £625, average cull value £390. Calves purchased: average per 100 cows mated: spring calving 2, autumn calving 3; at £100. Bull: purchase price £2,100, cull value £525; (one bull per 35 cows on average; 4-year herd life). Dairy cross beef cows have better fertility performance than continental pure bred cows, but lower cull sale prices.

5. *Vet. and med.:* spring calving £20, autumn £25; bedding: spring calving £22, autumn £34; miscellaneous: spring calving £15, autumn £18. *Straw:* where yarded in winter, straw requirements average 0.5-0.75 tonne per cow for spring calvers and around 0.75 tonne for autumn calvers.

6. The forage area includes both grazing and conserved grass (silage and hay) plus any other forage crops, such as kale. The higher stocking density implies better use of grassland. Higher stocking rates can also be achieved by buying in more of the winter bulk fodder requirements, or by winter feeding largely on arable by-products, including straw. Purchased bulk fodder and/or straw balancer concentrates will reduce gross margin per cow but increase gross margin per hectare.

Single Payment: all headage payments have been decoupled under the Single Payment. However, a payment is made in Scotland on three-quarter breed beef calves from Suckler Cows. Headage payments under the Scottish Beef Calf Scheme are around £40/head (or £80/head for the first 10 calves claimed).

In lowland conditions rearing two or more calves per cow is an option, but needs substantially greater labour input. Output is raised by fostering a second purchased calf onto a cow soon after calving, with little impact on costs of keeping the cow. The cow breed needs to be of a quiet temperament and have enough milk to rear two calves.

Single Suckling (per cow): Upland/Hill

System:	Upland/Hill Spring Calving		Upland/HIll Autumn Calving	
Performance Level (1)	Ave.	High	Ave.	High
	£	£	£	£
Value of Calf (2)	305	336	385	438
Calf Sales/Valn. per Cow (3)	278	312	350	407
Less Cow and Bull Depreciation. and Calf Purchases (4).........	48	47	54	53
Output	230	265	296	354
Variable Costs:				
Concentrate Costs (cow & calf)	25	20	56	50
Miscellaneous Variable Costs (5)	57	52	77	72
Total Variable Costs (excl. forage)	82	72	133	122
Gross Margin per cow, before deducting Forage Variable Costs	148	193	163	232
Forage Variable Costs	63	70	63	70
Purchased Bulk Feed	20	15	20	15
Gross Margin per Cow	**65**	**108**	**80**	**147**
Cows per Forage ha (6, 7)........	1.6	1.9	1.25	1.5
Forage Ha (Acres) per Cow	.62	.53	.8	.67
	(1.53)	(1.31)	(2.0)	(1.66)
Gross Margin per Forage Ha	104	205	100	220
Gross Margin per Forage Acre	42	83	41	89

1. Performance level relates to variations in two factors: weaned calf weight and stocking rate. 'High' refers to the average levels likely to be achieved by the better fifty per cent of producers. It is clearly possible to set still higher 'targets'.

2. Weight of calves (kg) at sale/transfer: upland spring calving: average 265 (at approximately 7 months old), high 280 (7.25 months); upland autumn calving: average 335 (at approximately 10.25 months old), high 365 (11 months); Price (per live kg); upland spring calving: average 115p, high 120p; upland autumn calving: average 115p, high 120p. These prices are averages for bull and heifer calves.

3. Calves reared per 100 cows mated: upland average 91, high 93.

4. *Assumptions.* Herd life: spring calving, 7 years; autumn calving and hill, 6 years. Purchase price £600, average cull value £360. Calves purchased: upland average, 3 per 100 cows mated, premium 2, at £95. Bull: purchase price £2,100, cull value £525.

5. *Vet and Med.* Spring calving £20, autumn £25; bedding: spring calving £22, autumn £34; miscellaneous: spring calving £15, autumn £18. *Straw:* when yarded in winter,

requirements average 0.5-0.75 tonne per cow for spring calvers and around 0.75 tonne for autumn calvers.

6. The forage area includes both grazing and conserved grass (silage and hay) plus any other forage crops, such as kale. The higher stocking density implies better use of grassland. Higher stocking rates can also be achieved by buying in more of the winter bulk fodder requirements, or by winter feeding largely on arable by-products, including straw. Purchased bulk fodder and/or straw balancer concentrates reduce gross margin per cow but increase gross margin per hectare.

Support: all headage payments have been decoupled under the Single Payment, apart from the Scottish Beef Calf Scheme (see above margin). Hill payments - Hill Farm Allowance in England, Tir Mynydd in Wales, LFASS in Scotland - are not included in the gross margins. These payments are available in disadvantaged and severely disadvantaged acres and are paid on an area basis (but have a minimum stocking density). See Page 100-101.

C. Rearing / Finishing Stores

Traditional Finishing of Strong Store Cattle (per head) (1)

System	Summer Finishing		Winter Finishing	
	£		£	
Sales	572	(2)	598	(3)
Less Purchased Store	480	(4)	462	(5)
Output	92		136	
Variable Costs:				
Concentrates	5		56	(6)
Miscellaneous Variable Costs	25		45	(7)
Total Variable Costs (excluding Forage)	30		101	
Gross Margin per Head before deducting				
Forage Variable Costs	62		35	
Forage Variable Costs	32		16	
Gross Margin per Head	**30**		**19**	
No. per ha (acre)	4	(1·6)	10	(4)
Forage Hectares (Acres) per Head	0·25	(0·62)	0·1	(0·25)
Gross Margin per Forage Hectare	120		190	
Gross Margin per Forage Acre	48		76	

1. The financial results of this enterprise are highly dependent on the market margin, i.e. the difference between the price per kg paid for the store and the price per kg obtained for the finished animal. Other important factors are the stocking rate and the degree of dependence on cash-crop by-products and the quality of conserved grass (and hence the quantity of concentrates required in relation to the liveweight gain) in the case of winter finishing.

    There is a large price range for store cattle based on quality, which will be reflected in carcase classification results. Heifers tend to finish better off grass with less concentrate requirements and therefore are more appropriate than steers for summer finishing at grass.

2. 520 kg @ 110p.
3. 520 kg @ 115p.
4. 400 kg @ 120p.
5. 420 kg @ 110p.
6. 400 kg @ £140tonne.
7. Including straw: average 0.75 tonne per head

BEEF

Finishing/Rearing on Suckler-Bred Stores (per head):	Winter Finishing		Grass Finishing		Overwintering and Grass Finishing		Grazing and Yard Finishing	
	Average £	High £	Average £	High £	Average £	High £	Average £	High £
Sales	589	610	476	485	524	578	545	599
Less Store (1)	332	329	385	365	321	318	328	308
Output	257	281	91	120	203	260	217	291
Variable Costs:								
Concentrates (2)	94	81	5	3	59	47	68	47
Miscellaneous (3)	48	43	25	23	43	40	42	38
Total Variable Costs (excl. Forage)	142	124	30	26	102	87	110	85
Gross Margin per head before Forage Var. Costs	115	157	61	94	101	173	107	206
Forage Variable Costs	34	28	29	29	40	36	45	45
Purchased Bulk Feed	6	6	-	-	10	8	7	4
Gross Margin per head*	**75**	**123**	**32**	**65**	**51**	**129**	**55**	**157**
No. per ha (acre)	9 (3.6)	10 (4)	4 (1.6)	5 (2)	3.75 (1.5)	4.50 (1.8)	4 (1.6)	5 (2)
Gross Margin per Forage Ha*	675	1230	128	325	191	580	220	785
Gross Margin per Forage Acre*	270	498	51	130	77	232	88	314
Weight at start (kg)	310	310	335	320	300	300	285	270
Weight at end (kg)	540	550	445	445	490	530	500	540
Purchase Price (p per kg LW)	107	106	115	114	107	106	115	114
Sale Price (p per kg LW)	109	111	107	109	107	109	109	111
Concentrates per head (kg)	625	600	40	25	390	350	450	350
Silage per head (tonnes)	3.25	3.25	-	-	3.6	3.6	2.1	2.3

All-System Assumptions:
(1) Allowing for mortality at 1%. (2) Concentrate costs per tonne: winter: average £150, high £135; summer: average £135, high £125. (3) Including vet.& med. and bedding.

Additional Note: The gross margin per ha figures must be treated with considerable caution, especially with regard to winter fattening/rearing systems: small variations in land requirements and margins per head cause wide variations in the per ha figures, and capital requirements are considerable. Differences in buying and selling prices per kg can be critical. Very little recent survey data is available on several of these systems.

BEEF

Finishing/Rearing on Dairy-Bred Stores (per head):	Winter Finishing		Grass Finishing		Overwintering and Grass Finishing		Grazing and Yard Finishing	
	Average £	High £	Average £	High £	Average £	High £	Average £	High £
Sales	594	616	494	525	510	535	530	594
Less Store (1)	400	386	392	389	312	309	258	266
Output	194	230	102	136	198	226	272	328
Variable Costs:								
Concentrates (2)	77	69	7	5	53	44	90	61
Miscellaneous (3)	48	42	24	23	49	45	43	39
Total Variable Costs (excl. Forage)	125	111	31	28	102	89	133	100
Gross Margin per head before Forage Var. Costs	69	119	71	108	96	137	139	228
Forage Variable Costs	29	29	29	29	47	44	46	47
Purchased Bulk Feed	4	2	-	-	7	5	7	4
Gross Margin per head*	**36**	**88**	**42**	**79**	**42**	**88**	**86**	**177**
No. per ha (acre)	7.5 (3)	9 (3.6)	4 (1.6)	5 (2)	3.5 (1.4)	4.25 (1.7)	3.5 (1.4)	4.5 (1.8)
Gross Margin per Forage Ha*	**270**	**792**	**168**	**395**	**147**	**374**	**301**	**797**
Gross Margin per Forage Acre*	**108**	**317**	**67**	**158**	**59**	**150**	**120**	**319**
Weight at start (kg)	385	375	350	350	300	300	230	240
Weight at end (kg)	560	570	475	495	490	505	500	550
Purchase Price (p per kg LW)	104	103	112	111	104	103	112	111
Sale Price (p per kg LW)	106	108	104	106	104	106	106	108
Concentrates per head (kg)	510	510	50	40	390	350	600	450
Silage per head (tonnes)	3.4	3.4	-	-	3.6	3.6	3.5	4.5

All-System Assumptions:
(1) Allowing for mortality at 1%. (2) Concentrate costs per tonne: winter: average £150, high £135; summer: average £135, high £125. (3) Including vet.& med. and bedding.

Additional Note: The gross margin per ha figures must be treated with considerable caution, especially with regard to winter fattening/rearing systems: small variations in land requirements and margins per head cause wide variations in the per ha figures, and capital requirements are considerable. Differences in buying and selling prices per kg can be critical. Very little recent survey data is available on several of these systems.

D. Intensive Beef

Cereal Beef (per head):

System	Continental Cross Holstein/Friesian Bulls		Holstein Friesian Bulls	
Performance Level	Average	High	Average	High
	£	£	£	£
Sales (1)	616	638	515	535
Less Calf (2)	155	155	26	25
Output	461	483	489	510
Variable Costs:				
Concentrates (3)	386	373	386	373
Other Feed	4	4	4	4
Miscellaneous (4)	66	61	66	61
Total Variable Costs	456	438	456	438
Gross Margin per Head	**5**	**45**	**27**	**72**

1. Weight at slaughter (kg): Cont cross bulls, average 560kg, high 580kg; Dairy bulls, average 530kg, high 550 kg. Prices: Cont cross bulls, average 110p/kg, high 110p/kg; Dairy bulls, average 97p/kg, high 97p/kg. All year round production is assumed. Average slaughter age is 14 months, with killing out percentages ranging from 54% to 60%, with the better conformation continental cross bulls achieving higher percentages.

2. £155 for continental cross male calves at 3 weeks of age including mortality; £26 for dairy bulls including mortality. Mortality, average 3%, high 1.5%.

3. £52 calf rearing (to 12 weeks: see page 87) + finishing ration. Finishing ration: 17 parts barley @ £125 per tonne, 3 parts concentrate supplement @ £230 per tonne; plus £10 per tonne milling and mixing. Total, £150 per tonne.

   Feed quantity (kg from 12 weeks (115 kg) liveweight to slaughter; FCR average 5·0, high 4·6): average 2225kg, high 2140kg.

4. Vet. and med. £16, bedding £25, misc. £25.

   Margins are very sensitive to calf price and feed price movements. A £10 per tonne feed price movement equates to a margin change of £22 per head.

Note: Interest on Capital

Beef systems require large capital outlay on livestock and variable costs alone. For cereal beef with an interest rate @ 7% on the calf price, and half the variable costs, interest charges amount to £26 per head.

18 Month Beef and Silage Beef (per head produced*):

System Performance Level	18 month Beef		Silage beef	
	Average	High	Average	High
	£	£	£	£
Sales	589	621	581	616
Less Calf	125	122	125	122
Output	464	499	456	494
Variable Costs:				
Concentrates (and milk substitute)...	183	169	232	194
Other Feed	4	4	5	5
Miscellaneous	73	70	68	62
Total Variable Costs (excl. Forage)	260	243	305	261
Gross Margin per Head before deducting Forage Variable Costs	204	256	151	233
Forage Variable Costs	56	56	40	40
Gross Margin per Head	**148**	**200**	**111**	**193**
No. per ha (acre)	3.4 (1.37)	3.8 (1.54)	8 (3.2)	10 (4)
Forage Hectares (Acres) per Head ...... (.25)	.29 (.72)	.26 (.65)	0.125 (.31)	0.1
Gross Margin per Forage Ha (per year). .	503	760	888	1930
Gross Margin per Forage Acre (per year)	203	308	355	772

*   *N.B. The variable costs, including feed and forage, the forage area and gross margin per head all relate to the full production period - 18 months or less for silage beef. Nevertheless, the gross margins per forage ha or acre* are *per year. During the winter there will be both the 0-6 month old calves and 12-18 month old cattle on the farm.*

Notes: 18 Month Beef

General: Autumn-born dairy-bred calves, beef crosses.

Slaughter weights (kg): average 550kg, high 570. Sale price per live kg: average 107p, high 109p.

Calf price/value: £120 (2 week old beef cross male calves, e.g. Limousin cross); mortality: average 4%, high 2%.

Feed: Concentrates (kg; average with high performance in brackets): milk substitute. £23, rearing concentrates 160kg @ £185; other: first winter 220kg @ £150 (200kg), at grass 90kg @ £150 (80kg), second winter 560kg @ £150 (500kg). Silage: 4.5 tonnes/head total, 0.75 tonne first winter, 3.75 tonnes second. Intensive grazing of fresh leys and good quality silage are needed - especially to achieve the high performance levels.

Other Costs: Miscellaneous (average): vet. and med. £21, bedding £27, other £25.

Notes: Silage Beef

General: Dairy-bred calves (beef crosses) fed indoors on grass silage and concentrates, for slaughter at 14 to 17 months old. Good quality silage is the key to high performance per head (otherwise concentrates per head rise and/or daily liveweight gain falls). High yields of silage per ha raise gross margins per ha.

Slaughter weights (kg): average 540, high 560. Sale price per live kg: average 107.5p, high 110p.

Calf price: £120. Concentrates per head (kg) (from 3 months (£52 to rear including milk powder)): average 1200kg @ £150, high 1050kg @ £135. Silage required: approximately 5.5 tonnes per head.

Other Costs: Miscellaneous (average): vet. and med. £16, bedding £28, other £24.

Note that the gross margin per ha figures must be interpreted with considerable caution: small differences in silage yields can have a large effect and, more important, the working capital and building requirements per ha are extremely high: well above even the high needs of 18 month beef.

VEAL

General points: Veal consumption is very low in the UK: only a small fraction of the per capita consumption in France for example. Continental demand is mainly for white veal, produced in individual veal crates, a system that is illegal in the UK, where the less economic 'welfare system' of groups kept in straw pens is required, producing 'pink veal' at heavier weights. Imported 'white veal' is considerably cheaper.

As very little white veal is now produced in the UK validated economic data is rarely seen. This also applies to 'rose veal' produced at heavier weights, but again mainly on the Continent. Now that calf exports have resumed and, given that some continental countries have retained a headage subsidy payment, it is very unlikely that UK veal systems can make a comeback. *For these reasons the provision of gross margin data has been discontinued.*

SHEEP

A. *Lowland Spring Lambing (per Ewe)*
(Selling lambs off grass)

Performance level......................	Low	Average	High
Lambs reared per ewe (put to ram) (1)	1.3	1.45	1.6
Average price per lamb (£) (2)	38.3	39.8	41.3
	£	£	£
Lamb sales	49.8	57.7	66.0
Wool (3).............................	1.2	1.2	1.2
Cull ewes and rams (4)	6.7	6.7	6.7
Sub-total............................	57.7	65.6	73.9
Less Ewe and ram replacements (4)..........	19.3	19.3	19.3
Output.............................	38.4	46.3	54.6
Variable Costs:			
Concentrates (53 kg ewes, 12 kg lambs) (5)..		10.7	
Vet. and Med........................		4.9	
Miscellaneous and Transport (6)		6.5	
Total Variable Costs (excluding Forage).....		22.1	
Gross Margin per Ewe before deducting Forage Variable Costs	16.3	24.2	32.5
Forage Variable Costs (inc. bought forage and keep)	8.0	8.0	8.0
Gross Margin per Ewe	**8.3**	**16.2**	**24.5**
Stocking Rate (Ewes, with lambs, per forage hectare (acre)) (7)	8 (3.25)	11 (4.45)	14 (5.65)
Gross Margin per Forage Hectare	66	178	343
Gross Margin per Forage Acre.............	27	72	138

Notes

1. *Target Rearing Performance.* Lambs reared per ewe put to ram are based on: -
   Ewes lambing: 92% (2.5% deaths, 5.5% barren)
   Lambs born: per 100 ewes lambing = 168
   Live lambs: born per ewe lambing = 156
   Lamb mortality: 14% (7% at birth, 7% post birth)
   Lambs reared: per 100 ewes put to ram = 145

   These performance figures are assumed for flocks of mature ewes i.e. shearlings and older. Where ewe lambs are lambs and included in flock performance adjustment needs to be made.

   Breed will obviously have a large effect on lambing percentage, liveweight gains and carcase grades.

2. *Lamb Prices.* The UK lamb market has changed significantly over the last few years. Old season lamb prices have not risen significantly from January to April as in the past, with the large retailers contracting New Zealand lamb during this period instead.

   Traditionally prices have been at their highest from April to June, declined with increasing mid-season supplies, and risen again post-Christmas. The large UK retailers have now contracted New Zealand lamb from January to the end of April which has lowered late season prices and meant producers have tried to market increasing numbers mid-season and before Christmas. The 2007 season experienced a difficult start with higher New Zealand imports affecting UK new season lamb prices, plus exports have slowed by strong sterling exchange rate.

The prices assumed for lambs sold for slaughter for the 2008 mid-season lamb crop assumes regaining export markets following 2007 Foot and Mouth outbreak. Most of the lambs are sold from June to the end of October. An average market price of 105p/kg liveweight (equivalent to 223p/kg deadweight) has been assumed giving £41 per finished lamb at an average 39kg liveweight.

The average budget price in the table above allows for 20% sold as stores. Low performance is £1.50 a lamb less, high £1.50 per lamb more for variations caused by differences in weights, time of marketing and proportion sold finished or retained as stores.

3. *Wool.* A substantial fall in world wool prices has resulted in small balance payments in 2007 on the 2006 clip of only around 2p/kg (depending upon quality grade). Advance payments for the 2007 clip have been 12 to 16p/kg. The 2007 wool cheque will not meet producers' cost of shearing. Budget price for 2008 of £1.20/ewe is based on encouraging early auctions for 2007 wool clip to achieve 60p/kg for the 2008 wool cheque at 2kg/ewe.

4. *Flock Depreciation.* (i.e. Market price of replacements less value of culls). It is assumed above that 20 per cent of the ewe flock is culled each year @ £32 each and that, allowing for 4 per cent mortality, 24 per cent are purchased or home-reared at £70 each. Rams: 1 per 40 ewes, 3-year life, purchased @ £300, sold @ £35. The net cost (flock depreciation) is £12.60 per ewe per year. N.B. Cull ewe prices are approximately £4 per head higher for heavy breeds and £4 lower for light breeds. Cull values tend to be highly variable but have been high of late, partly at least through a strong, consistent demand from the ethnic sector of the population. No other changes in flock valuation are assumed.

5. *Concentrate Feeding.* Rising feed costs into 2008 will have a substantial impact on margins for most systems and even question the viability of some systems by individual producers. Concentrate finishing of late season lambs has been common, without an uplift of lamb sale price in late season in the last few years. Producers will as a result start to look at alternative methods of finishing lambs and utilize lower cost forage.

6. *Miscellaneous Costs* include contract shearing @ 75p /ewe, scanning 50p /ewe and lamb tags 25p /ewe, carcase disposal £1 per ewe, straw £1 per ewe, marketing, levy and transport @ £3.00 per ewe.

7. *Stocking Density.* The stocking rates assumed are based on land requirements for the main grazing season (April to October) including land for conservation of winter forage.

Land quality and location will also have an effect on potential stocking density. However higher stocking rates can be achieved by catch crop roots for autumn/winter grazing or away wintering on grass keep which carry higher costs on a per ewe basis. Away grazing costs can range from 40p to 60p/ewe per week depending upon location.

On farms with grazing livestock other than sheep, the ewe flock is able to utilize land in the winter utilized by cattle in the normal grazing season. Alternatively ewes can be winter housed pre lambing to rest the land, but this does carry additional costs e.g. £6/ewe per year for building depreciation and interest over 10 years, plus straw and hay costs.

Ensuring good lamb growth rates and early finishing off grass also eases stocking pressures late in the season. Late lamb finishing into autumn and winter in most cases necessitates additional land available for lamb finishing lambs on catch crops or away grazing for ewes.

Other Costs

1. *Prices of Specialised Equipment*

Troughs (2.75 m).	£50 to £60
Racks (2 to 3 m)	£200 to £225
Foot Baths (3 m)	£100 to £125
Shearing machines.	£650 to £1050
Lamb Creep Feeders	£350 to £650
Footbaths (3 m)	£100 to £125

2. *Fencing:* Approximately £1.70 per metre +85p labour.

3. *Labour:* see page 146.

Home-reared tegs (shearlings)

Output: value £70 (allowing for culling and mortality) less £41 for the lamb, plus wool = £30. Variable costs (including forage) = £15. Gross margin per head = £15, per forage hectare £300 (£120 per acre).

Rearing replacements can be treated as a separte enterprise and margins compared on a per hectare basis. Where ewe lambs replacements are lambed in their first year they can be combined with the breeding flock which will reduce lambing percentage and output (£) per ewe but benefit from a reduction of replacement cost.

B. Other Sheep Systems (average performance level only)

System	Early Lambing per ewe	Winter Finishing of Store Lambs per head	Upland Flocks per ewe	Hill Flocks per ewe
Lambs reared per ewe (put to ram)	1.375	-	1.325	1.10
	£	£	£	£
Average price per lamb sold	52.0	48.0	38.8	36.0
Lamb sales	71.5	47.0	51.4	28.8
Wool	1.2	-	1.1	0.8
Sub-total	72.7	47.0	52.5	29.6
Less Livestock Purchases (net of culls) . .	13.5	35.2	12.7	(+) 3.2
Output	59.2	11.8	39.8	32.8
Variable Costs:				
Concentrates	23.1	2.4	8.2	4.9
	(150 kg)	(12.5 kg)	(50 kg)	(30 kg)
Vet. and Med..	4.5	0.4	4.0	3.2
Miscellaneous and Transport	7.0	2.0	5.8	3.5
Total Variable Costs (excl. Forage)	34.6	4.8	18.0	11.6
Gross Margin per ewe (or head) before deducting Forage Variable Costs	24.6	7.0	21.8	21.2
Forage Variable Costs (inc. bought forage)	7.5	2.3	8.0	6.0
Gross Margin per ewe (or head)	**17.1**	**4.7**	**13.8**	**15.2**
Stocking Rate (No. per Forage Ha [Acre])	14 (5.75)	40 (16)	9.5 (3.85)	-
Gross Margin per Forage Hectare	239	188	131	-
Gross Margin per Forage Acre	98	75	53	-

Support: all sheep headage payments have been decoupled under the Single Payment, Hill payments - Hill Farm Allowance in England, Tir Mynydd in Wales, LFASS in Scotland - are not included in the gross margins above. These payments are available in disadvantaged and severely disadvantaged acres and are paid on an area basis (but have a minimum stocking density). See below.

Notes:

Early Lambing. This system assumes January/early February lambing with all lambs sold by the end of August. Recent years have seen lamb prices peak later in the season, i.e. May rather than the traditional Easter market peaks. This has been due to the large retailers contracting to New Zealand lamb in the first part of the year and switching to UK new season lamb when large enough supplies are available i.e. in May. Hence early marketing of substantial numbers in April has not been beneficial.

This system is also very dependant upon concentrate feed inputs to ewe and lambs which will reduce margins per ewe to a level where there is only a small advantage over the Spring Lambing Flocks. However higher stocking rates for the early lambing system (due to less lambs to graze following early sales) do generate higher margins per forage hectare.

Winter Finishing of Store Lambs. The gross margin per head is particularly variable, being very dependant on the difference between purchase and sale price of the lambs. Some of the forage variable costs consist of bulk feed and agistment. It is risky to assume any great uplift in prices per kg from purchase to sale. Marketing costs and levy are a significant part of total costs so longer keep lambs gaining 8 to 10 kgs liveweight on low cost forage are most likely to be worthwhile.

Hill Sheep. These flocks are self maintained and a high proportion of the ewes bred pure. Only 0.75 to 0.8 lambs are sold per ewe per annum and the wool income includes yearling ewes carried on the farm. Only rams are purchased to maintain the flock. Results vary according to the quality of the hill grazing and stocking density.

Many flocks have historically away wintered ewes for up to six months to maximise ewe premium claims and latterly to be eligible for environmental schemes. Where ewes are away for 6 months £10 per ewe needs to be added to the forage costs set out in the table above.

HILL FARM PAYMENTS

Hill farming support across the UK has been paid on an area rather than headage basis since 2000. The schemes are part of the Rural Development Regulation and therefore are additional to the Single Payment. As part of the new Rural Development Programmes for the period 2007 to 2013 (see page 213) the various UK administrations have been consulting on changes to the current systems.

England

DEFRA has announced that the current Hill Farm Allowance (HFA) system will continue until the 2009 year, after which a new scheme is expected to be in place. This new scheme will be a variant of the Entry Level Scheme (see 'Grants' section for more details of the ELS) tailored to upland conditions. Details of the scheme are not currently available.

The payment rates for 2008 under the present HFA scheme are unknown at the time of writing. They are likely to be similar to those paid under the 2007 scheme; £13.32/ha on moorland and common land, £19.03/ha on disadvantaged land and £35.20/ha on severely disadvantaged land. However, from 2008 onwards there will be no payment under the 'disadvantaged land' category under the HFA.

Only half these rates are paid between 350 and 700 ha and none over 700 ha per holding. A claimant must have at least 10 ha of LFA land and a stocking density of at least 0.15 LU/ha; if it exceeds 1.4 LU/ha there is an inspection to ensure that the land is not being over-grazed. An additional 10% or 20% is available if certain environmental criteria are satisfied including mixed cattle/sheep grazing.

Wales

The Welsh Assembly Government has announced that the current Tir Mynydd scheme will continue for the 2008 scheme year. After that support for upland areas will be through agir-environmental payments. Funding for the scheme is likely to be restored from 2007 levels. Although precise payment levels are not known at the time of writing, the basic per hectare for 2008 are likely to be £25.50 on disadvantaged land and £37.50 on severely disadvantaged land.. The full rates are paid up to 140 ha, 65% between 140 and 640 ha and 30% over 640 ha. The minimum area is 6ha and the stocking density must be between 0.1 and 1.8 LU/ha. T here is a range of enhancements up to 10% or 20% (although the actual uplift paid varies from year to year).

Scotland

An interim Less Favoured Area Support Scheme (LFASS) will continue for the years 2007 to 2009. Changes are expected in 2010 following an EU wide review of the Less Favoured Areas. The precise operation of the interim LFASS was not known at the time of writing, although it is expected to be similar to the present scheme. Under the current LFASS, a minimum of 3 ha is required but there are no size differentials: there is a minimum stocking rate of 0.12 LU/ha and a maximum of 1.4 LU/ha (payments are scaled back if the latter is exceeded). Certain environmental conditions have to be met. Payments vary according to three criteria: location, 'grazing category' and enterprise mix (enhancements). The rates in three different locations were as follows in 2006, the first figure being for grazing categories A and B (see below) and the second for C and D: Islands £47.00 and £41.50, Mainland Peripheral £45 and £39.50, Other LFA £39 and £33.50. Payment rates for 2008 are expected to be similar. These payments are increased if suckler cow livestock units exceed a certain percentage of the total: they are raised by 35% if this percentage is between 10% and 50% and by 70% if over 50%. A fraction of the above rates is paid according to the 'grazing capacity' in LU/ha in year 2001, as follows: A. up to 0.19LU/ha, one-sixth; B. 0.2 to 0.39 LU/ha, one third; C 0.4 to 0.59 LU/ha, two thirds; D. 0.6 LU/ha and over, four-fifths. There is a minimum payment of £350.

GRAZING AND REARING CHARGES:
CATTLE AND SHEEP

Grazing charges vary widely according to the quality of the pasture and local supply and demand. The following figures are typical (estimated for 2007):

Summer Grazing (per head per week)

Store Cattle and in-calf heifers over 21 months, dry cows, and fattening bullocks over 18 months	£3.50-£4.50
Heifers and Steers, 12-21 months	£2.50-£3.50
6-12 months Cattle	£2.00-£2.75
Cattle of mixed ages	£2.50-£3.50
Ewes	40p-50p

Winter Grazing (per head per week)

'Strong' Cattle	£2.25-£3.50
Heifers	£2.00-£3.00
Sheep.	50p-60p

Note: the above figures assume the farmer whose land the livestock are on does all the fencing and 'looking after'. Where the owner of the, say, sheep does the fencing, shepherding, etc., the figures may be halved, or be even less depending on local demand.

Grass Keep (per hectare, per acre in brackets)

Most typically around £150-200 (£60-80), with the best £250-300 (£100-120) and poorish quality £85-£100 (£35-40).

These figures are highly variable, especially between one part of the country and another, and between one season and another. The charge can be very high where the pasture is good, the supply scarce and the demand strong. In an average price year poor quality keep may fetch only £75 (30), top quality (fenced and with mains water) more than £300 (120). For top quality grassland, fertilised, well-fenced and watered, with stock seen daily, prices can be even higher for some lots in the west and north-west in years of grass shortage; a top figure as high as £400 (160) is sometimes reported. The average price can exceed £300 (120) in some years in parts of the west and west midlands but can fall below £100 (40) in some eastern and south-eastern counties.

A lowering of these levels following the introduction of the Single Payment Scheme had been expected but experience of 2005, 2006 and 2007 has seen only minor reductions in averages let at auction in most parts of the country. On the other hand there is increasing evidence in some localities that grassland subject to environmental schemes is fetching very low or negative rents where the landowner is taking the payment.

Winter Keep (Cattle) (per head per week)

Grazing + 9 kg hay and some straw	£8.00
Full winter keep in yards	£7.0-£10.0
Calf rearing for beef (0 to 12 weeks or 0 to 6 months).	£9.00

A typical rental for labour buildings and maintenance diet would be £6 per head per week. These rates apply where feed to achieve maintenance plus some growth is supplied plus labour and buildings and bedding where applicable. A typical rental for labour, buildings and a maintenance diet would be £5 per head per week.

Heifer Rearing Charges

Points to clarify in any arrangement are: who pays for transport, who pays the vet. and med. expenses, who bears the losses or pays for replacements, how often are payments made (monthly payments save the rearer interest compared with lump sum payments when the heifer is returned)?

Two possible arrangements are:

1. Farmer X sells calf to Rearer at agreed price; the calf is then Rearer's responsibility and he pays for all expenses and bears any losses. Farmer X has first option on heifers, which he buys back two months before calving. Approximate price: £775 above cost of calf for Holstein Friesians. Rearer fetches calf; Farmer X supplies transport for heifer.

2. Farmer X retains ownership of calf. Approximate charges: £35 per month from 10 to 14 days old (£38 if two-year old calving), or £33 per month from 6 months old (£37 if two-year old calving), (£40 per month from 10 to 14 days to 6 months). As Rearer has no interest on capital to bear, he supplies transport and pays for vet. and medical expenses. In the case of losses by accident/chance, the rearer either refunds payments or replaces calf (this means Farmer X and Rearer share a loss averaging approximately £35 each per heifer reared, assuming 10 per cent losses at average 6 months old). In the case of losses by negligence, the rearer both refunds payments and replaces calf. (The NFU can supply model agreements).

As livestock and beef margins decline, contract rearing availability may increase as farmers with spare land and buildings look for alternatives with agreed returns and less capital outlay in livestock.

Calf and Heifer Rearing for Shorter Periods

Costs are likely to rise to the levels outlined in line with rising feed and milk powder prices.

Calf, 10 days to 3 months, £125 (for food, labour and housing) to £135 (all costs, and rearer bearing losses). Heifers, average from 3 months old to steaming up: approximately £16 per month in summer, £45 in winter.

RED DEER

A. Breeding and Finishing

	Per 100 hinds
Sales:	£
42 stags (15-18 months) : 55kg dw @ £3·25/kg	7390
33 hinds (15-18 months) : 42·5kg dw @ £3·25/kg	4490
8 cull hinds @ £75	600
Average annual value of cull stags	70
Less average annual cost of replacement stags	500
Output.	12050
Variable Costs:	
Concentrates 10·5 tonnes @ £150/tonne	1500
Vet and Med.	850
Miscellaneous	1250
Total Variable Costs	3600
Gross Margin before deducting forage	8450
Forage Variable Costs (5·5 hinds/ha, £120/ha)	2180
Gross Margin (per 100 hinds)	**6270**
Gross Margin per Forage Hectare (18·2 ha)	345
Gross Margin per Forage Acre (45 acres)	139

B. Selling Calves

	Per 100 hinds
Sales:	£
43 stags @ £80 (45 kg lw)	3440
34 hinds @ £62·50 (40 kg lw)	2125
8 cull hinds @ £75	600
Average annual value of cull stags	70
Less average annual cost of replacement stags	500
Output	5735
Variable Costs:	
Concentrates 7 tonnes @ £170/tonne	1190
Vet and Med.	550
Miscellaneous	700
Total Variable Costs	2440
Gross Margin before deducting forage	3295
Forage Variable Costs (6·5 hinds/ha, £110/ha)	1690
Gross Margin (per 100 hinds)	**1605**
Gross Margin per Forage Hectare (15·4 ha)	104
Gross Margin per Forage Acre (38 acres)	42

C. Finishing Stag Calves

	Per 200 stags
Sales:	£
195 @ 55kg dw @ £3·20/kg	34320
Less : 200 @ £75	15000
Output	19320
Variable Costs:	
Concentrates 15 tonnes @ £125/tonne	1875
Vet and Med.	900

Miscellaneous	2000
Total Variable Costs	4775
Gross Margin before deducting forage	14545
Forage Variable Costs (11 stags/ha, £115/ha)	2090
Gross Margin (per 200 stags)	**12455**
Gross Margin per Forage Hectare (18·2 ha)	684
Gross Margin per Forage Acre (45 acres)	277

Additional Notes

Lowland assumed.

Hind replacements home-reared in systems A and B.

Herd Life: hinds, 12 years; stags, 7 years. 25 hinds per stag.

Calves reared per 100 hinds: 85.

Purchase price of breeding stock (good quality): hinds £275 plus, yearling hinds £225 plus, stags £500 plus.

The venison prices reflect projected sales for 2005/06 to wholesale buyers. Higher prices will be obtained for direct sales to consumers (e.g. farm shops and farmers' markets) and caterers, but extra costs will normally be incurred.

Capital costs: perimeter fencing, £5/metre; internal fencing, £2/metre; handling yard, pens, scales, crush: £10,000—in existing buildings. Total cost of establishing a 100-hind breeding flock is typically in the order of £50,000, including breeding stock and £12,500 for fencing, housing and handling facilities. Labour: with an experienced stockman: 400 plus head with additional help when yarding.

Sources of further information*: 'Introduction to Deer Farming'* (Barony College, Dumfries. Tel: 01387 860251. *British Deer Farmers Association*, The Counting House ,Mill Road, Cromford, Derbyshire, DE4 3RQ. Tel. 01629 827037.

Acknowledgement*: Russell Marchant, Principal and Chief Executive, Barony College.

HORSES: LIVERY

The horse industry is now reported to be the second biggest employer in the rural economy and is also one of the fastest growing. Although there are other equine enterprises that farm business can operate, by far the most common is providing accommodation for horses; i.e. livery. There are many different forms of livery and the charges, therefore, vary widely also. This is apart from the effects of local supply and demand. However, three fairly standard forms are offered on farms:

Grass Livery. Keep at grass, preferably with shelter, water supply and secure area to keep tack and store feed. Some grass livery will provide an exercise arena and off-road riding. Charges average £25 per week; range £20-£40.

DIY Livery. The owner still has full care of the horse but has the facilities of a stable, grazing, and in some cases an all-weather exercise arena. The owner is responsible for mucking out, turning out, grooming, exercising and all vet./med. care and the cost of all feed and bedding. Charges average £30 per week; range £20-£50.

DIY Plus Livery. As the above, except that the yard manager is responsible for certain tasks, such as turning out and feeding. Charges average £40 per week; range £30-£60.

The above are only guidelines. There is a wide variation both within, and between regions. Where more services, such as exercise, are provided by the yard the charges may be fitted to the needs of a particular horse. Full livery charges average £100 per week; with a range between £75-£150. Part livery average £75 per week; range £55-100.

Other Costs:

Grazing. Variable costs will average some £30 per horse per year. Average stocking rates are 0·8 ha (2 acres) for the first horse and 0·4 ha (1 acre) for each horse after.

Hay. Average price £2·75 per conventional bale (approximately 20 kg); has to be of good quality. Average consumption is one to two bales per horse per week: less in the summer depending on the grass quality/quantity and the work of the horse. Some horses now have haylage: more expensive, dust free and higher fibre and energy/protein levels; less required per head.

Concentrate Feed. Can range from almost nil to 3 to 4 kg per day depending, amongst other factors, on breed, size and intensity of work. Compound feed 25 to 30p per kg.

Bedding. Averages around £5 per stabled horse per week for half the year, i.e. £110-£130 per year. Straw might cost only half as much; however, more expensive, but preferable, alternatives (such as wood shavings, shredded paper and hemp fibre) are now increasingly being used.

Vet. and Med. Averages approximately £150 per horse per year. Some yards include worming of the horse in the livery cost.

Further Notes:

The supply of livery yards appears to be increasing, from both farms diversifying and other yards setting up. Filling a yard is, consequently, getting more difficult. The level of service and facilities expected by customers has increased. There is a trend towards greater professionalism in the running and management of livery yards. Livery contracts should be exchanged showing clearly the responsibilities of each party. Comprehensive third party insurance is also important.

To be successful, a livery enterprise needs higher quality facilities than farm livestock. To the owner the horse can be anything from a highly trained athlete to a family pet. Horses are expensive: even modest quality horses cost between £1,500 and £3,000. Good customer relations and an effective security system (including burglar and fire alarms) are crucial to success, as is good market research and effective advertising.

A full livery yard will require stables, a secure room to store tack, a vermin-proof hard feed store, storage for hay and bedding, a muck heap and parking provision with room for horse boxes. Planning permission is required for the conversion of an existing building to stabling or the erection of new, purpose-built stables. Permission is also required for construction of an all weather arena used for training horses and exercising them in bad weather. Hay and straw should be stored away from the stables and down wind of them to minimise the fire risk. A hard standing area with a water supply and good drainage should be provided for grooming and washing down the horses.

Good ventilation in the stables is crucial as horses are prone to respiratory diseases caused by spores and dust. Provision should be made for owners to soak hay in clean water before feeding it, to reduce respiratory problems.

Fences must be sound and must be free of protruding nails, wire etc. Ideally fields should be fenced using post and rail, but this is expensive. Barbed wire should be avoided wherever possible or should be 'protected' with an offset electrified fence. Fields should be divided into smaller paddocks to reduce the possibility of fighting between incompatible horses and to separate mares and geldings. Paddocks may be divided using two or more strands of electrified tape or rope but wire is not advisable as it is not easily visible to the horse.

Off-road riding opportunities on the farm are a real asset. The farmer may provide riding trails, a jumping paddock, or a cross country course. An all-weather ménage for exercising horses, possibly with floodlighting, is highly desirable, and some livery yards have horse walkers too. Good facilities can be rented out to individuals or organisations such as pony clubs. It is sometimes possible to link up with nearby farms to increase the length of riding tracks available.

Construction Costs. The cost of conversion of existing buildings will depend on their quality; prefabricated hardwood and steel internal stable partitions can be purchased from upwards of £750 per stable, depending on size and specification. Free standing timber stables cost between £800 and £2,000 (plus base), depending on size and quality. As horses are fairly destructive animals (they both kick and chew) better quality stables will often prove more economic in the long run. All weather arenas (20 metres by 40 metres) cost between £10,000 and £25,000; construction is a specialist job as good drainage is essential; a badly constructed arena is worthless.

Contact: Further financial information on horse enterprises, including riding schools and equestrian centres, is available in 'Equine Business Guide', 5th Edition, 2005, edited by Richard Bacon, Warwickshire College; Tel. 01926 318338.

OSTRICHES

The sector has contracted from 250 producers in the early 1990s to less than 100 at present. Few are strictly commercial and the British Domesticated Ostrich Association has only 30 members. There is little, if any demand for breeding stock, and producers must make an income from meat and hides. Although it is estimated that 4,000-5,000 birds are slaughtered annually in the UK, the great majority come from one enterprise whose main interest is in hides.

Ostriches have been subject to the Dangerous Wild Animals Act requiring licensing (£45 to £360) and inspection by the Local Authority.

Breeding Stock

Adult breeding stock are normally kept in trios of one male and two females, but pairs and colonies are not unusual. A trio will require about 0.2 ha (0.5 acre) for grazing and room in which to exercise: they must be able to run. (More land will be required if it is not free draining). A stout hedge or smooth wire fence of a minimum of 1.7 metres (5.5 ft) high should surround the enclosure. Adult birds need shelter from wind and rain, and a dry floor on which to sleep. Domesticated ostrich are generally docile and easily handled.

A female from 2-3 years of age lays 30-60 eggs a year (March to October); on average, 75% will be fertile (settable). A female may have a productive life of 20 to 30 years. An experienced producer will aim to hatch and rear at least half the eggs set, but there can be significant losses. A 10% replacement rate is anticipated for breeding stock.

A young fertile trio should cost between £600 and £1,000 for good quality stock. Although there is almost no demand it is unlikely a producer of birds would accept less for breeding stock that the birds would fetch for meat. A good meat bird can be worth £400 or more providing the meat is sold at retail and the hide is of good quality.

Grass and other vegetation can form part of the diet, and specially formulated concentrate, barley, silage and vegetable waste are also fed. Dry matter and silage should be chopped. The birds must be provided with grit when young and small stones (up to 12 to 15mm) for adults, oyster shells, and perhaps vitamin supplement. A breeding ration is fed at 1.5-2.5 kg per day for 180 days a year. A specialist feed can cost up to £200 per tonne but a sheep ration with added minerals is £100-£115 per tonne.

Rearing and Meat Production

In theory, fertile eggs are worth £5-£10 each (infertile eggs can be sold for cooking or crafts for about £3-£5 each.) Incubation lasts 42-45 days. Chicks are reared indoors with access to heat for two to three months and then allowed outside. They are fed starter crumb and then small pellets costing £250 per tonne. A high level of care and expertise is required. Meat birds are grouped according to size rather than age from 12 weeks and kept at 25-35 per hectare (10-14 per acre) up to 6 months and 18 per ha (7.5 per acre) when older.

Birds are slaughtered at 10-16 months at a live weight of 95-110kg, giving 25-35kg of de-boned meat. On-farm slaughtering is permitted under poultry regulations but meat can only be sold locally and the producer will have the added cost of packaging and marketing, which could amount to £1 per kg. The majority of ostriches are processed at one of the very few specialist slaughter facilities, which must have veterinary and meat hygiene inspections. The new EU-wide Slaughter Licence that came into effect on January 2006 means that red meat plants can slaughter ostriches providing they have appropriate de-feathering and chilling facilities. Charges are in the order of £40 per bird if the carcase is returned to the producer or the meat is sold on directly to the wholesaler at £3-£4.5 per kg. For slaughter, butchering and returning the meat vacuum packed to the producer the charge is £80/bird. Transport to the abattoir and return carriage for the meat may add significantly to this sum. The skin is returned, sold on commission or bought directly by the processing company. Birds sold to a slaughterhouse will fetch £100-£150, depending on their condition and skin quality. Meat sold at retail will fetch between £9-£23 per kg.

Ostrich meat sold at wholesale prices does not appear to give producers an adequate return. Individual farmers can exploit local outlets such as farmers' markets or nearby shops but this requires positive marketing initiative.

Ostrich skins can be just as valuable as the meat, but British producers have found it difficult to produce a bird with a highly saleable skin, and quality is all important. A top quality skin can fetch over £100, but in the absence of UK tanning facilities skins are generally exported in a batch at £30-£40 each. Feathers are potentially valuable but no market has been established yet.

Meat Production	per meat bird	per hen
Output:	£	£
Assuming 15 birds produced per hen		
30kg of meat each at £4 per kg.............	120	1,800
Skin at £40	40	600
Output	160	2,400
Variable Costs:		
Feed	90	1,350
Vet and med	1	15
Forage	5	75
Egg + incubation	15	225
Slaughter charge	40	600
Misc. and transport	10	150
Total Variable Costs	161	2,415
Gross Margin	-1	-15
Farmer Retailing (excluding retailing costs):		
30kg meat at £15 per kg	450	6,750
Slaughtering and butchering charge*	90	1,350
Gross Margin	360	5,400

* There may also be a carriage charge for return of butchered meat from slaughterhouse.

Fixed Costs

Housing £6; fencing £4; labour: adult birds require about 25 hours a year and chicks and young birds about 4 hours a year. One stockperson might look after 500 meat birds. Two people are needed at times to handle adult stock.

Contact: British Domesticated Ostrich Association (BDOA), 33 Eden Grange, Little Corby, Carlisle, CA4 8QU. (Tel.: 01228 562946); www.ostrich.org.uk

WILD BOAR

Wild Boar are now being farmed in the UK on more than 60 farms, with a population probably exceeding 2,000 sows. They produce a firm dark meat with a characteristically 'gamey' flavour which is in demand particularly from the hotel and restaurant trade.

Wild Boar come under the Dangerous Wild Animals Act and wild boar farms must be licensed by the Local Authority. There is no uniformity of fee or conditions that have to be met, but typically licences cost £100-£150 and are renewed annually following an inspection of the farm. Enclosures must be secure with strong fencing: a minimum height of at least 1.8m is usually specified and most authorities require 30-80cm below ground plus an additional strand of electric fence inside the main fence. The estimated minimum cost of fencing using approved contractors is from £8 per metre erected plus the hire of a digger. All gates and access areas must be padlocked at all times. However, the Act is under review and there is a recommendation that farmed boar will be exempt, giving them the same legal status as the domestic pig.

Wild Boar are kept in groups of up to 10 sows with a boar. They are nearly always kept outdoors, often on arable land (as outdoor domestic pigs), although rough land with some natural vegetation, such as scrub, or best of all, woodland, is ideal. Good husbandry requires some basic housing, such as arcs. Large arcs are suitable for a group of gestating sows, or sows running with maturing boarlets. Sows should have access to an individual shelter for farrowing and the first few days of lactation. If good vegetation is available sows may make their own farrowing nest away from the main group with satisfactory results.

Stocking rates vary according to the type of land but about a hectare would be needed for a group of 5 sows and a boar. They will forage actively on suitable terrain but this is unlikely to provide a significant part of their diet. They need to be fed a balanced ration (additive free pig concentrate is suitable but specially formulated feeds are available) with supplementary vegetable material. If a good supply of root crops is available this may replace some concentrate. Wild boar mate and farrow naturally and have few health problems, so little if any intervention is needed. Gilts mature at 18 months. In the wild breeding occurs in the autumn and early winter and the sows farrow from February to March after 4 months gestation. One litter per year is the norm. However, most farmed sows maintained at a good nutritional level will give two litters in most years. Young sows produce 2 to 3 boarlets and mature sows 6 to 8. A well-run enterprise should average 7 boarlets per sow per year raised to maturity. Wild boar can live from 12 to 15 years, perhaps more, but in a commercial herd the sows are usually culled at 7 to 8 years old.

The boarlets remain in the family group until they are all weaned together at 8 to 12 weeks (16 at the outside). Although some (usually smaller) producers leave growers to mature in family groups, they are generally separated into grower/finisher groups on rough grass or in open barns. Wild boar will take between 9 and 18 months to reach a slaughter weight of 75-85 kg. This produces a 45-50 kg carcase. They are slaughtered in the same way as pigs. The carcase has more shoulder and less on the hind-quarters than a domestic pig. It can be butchered like a domestic pig or without the skin like venison. The meat from male animals 2 years old or over is too strong, except for sausages, but sows up to 8 years old still have an acceptable carcase and a good cull value. A real problem for some producers is arranging slaughter: abattoirs are currently required to have wild boar specified on their licence and many expect them to be difficult to handle.

Labour requirements are low, owing to the 'hands off' nature of wild boar management. One person might manage a herd of 30-40 sows and fatteners.

In spite of the large and apparently unsatisfied demand for wild boar meat, as with other alternative enterprises, there is no organised marketing system and producers have to develop their own outlets. There are some wholesale butchers and game dealers who will take whole carcase in significant numbers, but many producers organise their own processing into a variety of pre-packed products and arrange their own retailing. Sold at retail the meat commands a considerable margin over the wholesale price, but butchering, packaging and marketing costs have to be considered. Wild boar production can be successful both as a secondary enterprise on a farm or as a stand-alone operation.

Capital Costs

Housing and fencing	£4,000 per ha
Pure bred stock ....boar	£300-600
...........................young sow	£250-500

Output

Finished boarlets per sow per year	7 (6-9)
Finished carcase weight (over 15 months)	45-50kg
Price per kg deadweight	£3.75 (£3-£4.50)
Depreciation per sow per year (1)	£30
Total Output per Sow	£1,095

Variable Costs:	
Concentrates ....sow (2)	200
.......................fatteners (£50 each)	490
Bedding	10
Vet., Med. and Licence	30
Water and electricity	10
Total Variable Costs per Sow	£740
Gross Margin per Sow	£355

1. Cost of sow £400, cull value £200, herd life 7 years, plus share of boar

2. Including share of boar

Contact: *The British Wild Boar Association,* PO Box 100, London W6 0ZJ. Tel: 020 8741 7789; www.bwba.co.uk

SHEEP DAIRYING

		Per Ewe	
Performance Level (yield)	Low	Average	High
Milk Yield (litres)	175	275	350
	£	£	£
Milk Value (1)	140	220	280
Value of Lambs (2)	51	51	51
Cull Ewes (3)	3	3	3
Wool	2	2	2
Output	196	276	336
Variable Costs:			
Concentrates (4)		117	
Miscellaneous (including vet and med)		15	
Forage Variable Costs		15	
Total Variable Costs		147	
Gross Margin per Ewe	**49**	**129**	**189**
Ewes (plus replacements) per ha (acre)		11.25 (4.5)	
Gross Margin per Forage Hectare	551	1451	2126
Gross Margin per Forage Acre	220	581	851

Notes

1. *Price:* 80p per litre at farmgate (range from 75p-90p per litre).

2. *Lambing %:* 175%. Assume a 300 Friesland ewe flock. Retain 50 ewe lambs for flock replacements. Sell 400 finished lambs reared from 2 days old (inc. 14.5% mortality) at £38. If meat-type terminal sires used then cross-bred lamb values increase to £55.

3. *Cull ewes:* 17/20% culled at £15 per head (including mortality).

4. *Concentrates:* Milking ewes: 200 days at 1.5 kg/head/day, 100 days at 0.5 kg/head/day; cost £160/tonne. Ewe lamb replacements and artificially reared finished lambs at £40/head.

5. *Forage costs:* Quality silage: 1 tonne per milking ewe (or hay equivalent). Grazing: early grass in March/April; good grazing on leys or pasture; similar for dry stock and lambs.

Additional Points

Fixed Costs per Ewe: Labour (paid) £65; Power and Machinery £15; Property Costs £10; Other £10; Total excluding Finance and Rent, £100.

Capital Costs of Equipment: Complete milking unit for 300 ewes (including yokes, bulk tank, dairy equipment, installation): £8,000-£15,000. A small 50 ewe unit can be put together for under £5,000. Any building works would be additional to the above costs.

Acknowledgement: Anthony Hyde, FRICS, FBIAC.

GOAT DAIRYING

	Per Goat		
Performance Level (yield)	Low	Average	High
Milk Yield (litres) (1)	500	800	1200
	£	£	£
Milk Value (2)	137	215	273
Value of Kids (3)	48	48	48
Livestock Depreciation (4)	3	3	3
Output	190	268	326
Variable Costs:			
Concentrates (4)		105	
Forage		15	
Miscellaneous (including vet and med)		15	
Total Variable Costs		135	
Gross Margin per Goat	55	133	191
Stocking Rate: Goats per ha (acre) (zero-grazed system)			
(Equivalent) **Gross Margin** per Forage Hectare. . .	620	1495	2150
(Equivalent) **Gross Margin** per Forage Acre	250	605	870

Notes

1. *Yield:* Per 300 day lactation, kidding each year. Autumn kidders tend to yield less.

2. *Price:* 40p per litre; seasonal variation from 33p in June to 53p in November. 12.5% solids delivered.

3. *Kid(s):* Prolificacy relates to age, breed, seasonality and feed level. Assumptions: low 140%; average and high 180%. There is very little trade in kids for meat.

4. *Culls and Replacements:* Replacements at £180/head; culls £17.50, average life 6 years. Bucks: 1 per 40-50 does. Does normally mate in autumn; gestation 150 days; young goats can be mated from 6 months.

5. *Concentrates:* Average 0.55 kg concentrate per litre, at £125 per tonne.

6. *Forage:* Average 0.9 kg DM forage per litre at £80 per tonne DM (part purchased, part home-grown). Goats can be grazed but are normally storage fed to avoid problems with worms, fencing, milk taints and pneumonia. Farmers able to produce maize silage will have a better forage conversion ratio.

7. *Miscellaneous:* Bedding £12, vet and med. £24 (includes treatment for out-of-season breeding, vaccination against Johnes and humane disposal of unsaleable kids), sundries £19.

8. *Stocking rate:* Based on home-grown forage.

9. *Labour:* 1 full-time person per 100 goats is a guide, but very dependent on technology employed.

10. *Markets:* There is no government support for goat produce and a strong pound makes imported produce cheap. Some successful businesses have been built on producer processing and retailing. Bulk purchasers of goats milk are few and far between. Herd sizes in the UK range from 50 to 3,000 milking does. Average herd size is growing rapidly as established producers expand with the market at about 15% average annual growth. Prolificacy and technical improvements allow higher annual growth than the market and there is a cycle in milk and stock prices.

Contact: *The British Goat Society* (Bovey Tracey, Devon (tel. 01626 833168)) registers pedigree animals and publishes a monthly newsletter.

Acknowledgements: The above information originally supplied by *Dr. T. Mottram*, Silsoe Research Institute, Bedford MK45 4HS, amended since by the author.

ANGORA GOATS

	Breeding Does (2)	Subsequent Shearing (2)
Yield of Fibre (kg per year)	14.8	5.45
Price of Fibre (less handling charge) (£ per kg) (3)	3.64	3.48
	£ per Doe	£ per Head
Value of Fibre	53.9	19.0
Value of Kids (1.42 per doe mated) (4)	33.3	-
Value of Cull (5).	3.5	9.4
Less Replacements (5)	9.0	10.0
Output	81.7	18.4
Variable Costs:		
Concentrates (6)	25.0	5.5
Vet and Med	8.0	0.8
Miscellaneous (7)	10.0	3.2
Total Variable Costs (excl. forage)	43.0	9.5
Gross Margin per Doe/Head before Forage Costs	38.7	8.9
Forage Variable Costs	8.5	5.5
Gross Margin per Doe/Head	30.2	3.4
Stocking Rate (Does (incl. followers) per ha (acre))	10 (4)	15 (6)
Gross Margin per ha (acre)	302 (122)	51 (21)

111

Notes

The above figures are for a commercial enterprise. Many UK angora flocks are kept on a semi-commercial or hobby basis, in which case different criteria may apply – does retained longer, mortality rates lower, doe/buck ratio different.

1. Angora goats produce mohair; angora rabbits produce angora; cashgora is produced by angora cross dairy goats; cashmere is produced by improved feral goats (valuable 'down' has to be separated from guard hairs; thus, with cashmere production, 'yield of down' must not be confused with 'weight of clip' as percentage down is low and can vary widely). Goat meat is called 'chevon'. UK mohair output is currently around 10 tonnes per year, which indicates a population of between 2,000 and 3,000 animals.

2. The data for Breeding Does include output and inputs for a proportion (4%) of a buck and the doe's progeny. Progeny are sold after 2 clips for breeding or after 3 clips for meat. Stock may be retained for further shearing. This has become more common, as the demand for breeding stock is small, fibre quality has improved and there is little market for meat.

3. Angora goats are usually clipped twice a year. Yield increases over first four clips, but quality decreases with age. Prices can be volatile, being dependent on fashion and on the world market dominated by South Africa and Texas. Demand and prices are highest for the high quality kid fibre <25 microns in diameter. The following yields and prices have been used:-

   Clip 1: 1.1 kg, £6.5 per kg; clip 2: 2.0 kg, £6.5 per kg; clip 3: 3.0 kg, £4.50 per kg; adult doe: 3.5 kg, adult buck 4.0 kg, £2.78 per kg.

   British Mohair Marketing arranges a collection once a year, usually in April. The fibre is professionally graded and then offered for sale by tender.. There is a handling charge of 50p per kg of fibre. Membership of BMM costs £30. (Some producers improve their return by processing and using the fibre themselves or selling to local spinners. Commercial processing costs are significant: combing about £1.8 per kg and spinning about £6 per kg).

4. 1.5 kids born alive per doe mated; 2% mortality to each clip. Number of doe kids sold for breeding equal to number of replacements (unless the flock size is changing). Value comprises: 0.17 breeders at £50 each, 1.25 kids for meat at £20 each.

5. Culls. Breeding stock in commercial flocks are culled after six years on average. Doe:buck ratio averages 25:1. Subsequent shearing stock culled after a further 4 clips. Value of all cull stock: £20 each. Depending on quality, the skin can be worth £10 before curing or up to £100 after curing. Replacement costs: does, £80; bucks, £150. Shearing stock, £20 (as transfer from breeding enterprise). Show quality stock command a premium.

6. Concentrates. Price: £155 per tonne on average. Quantities: Kids - 50 kg to clip 2, 15 kg to clip 3; Adults - breeding adults 90 kg per year, shearlings 40 kg per year.

7. Veterinary costs can be high. Miscellaneous costs include £1.50 to £2.00 per shearing per head (it may be more) and bedding materials.

8. Angora goats require more management than sheep. Fencing requirements are similar but housing costs rather higher. Margins are particularly sensitive to the value and number of breeding stock sold, yield and value of fibre, kidding percentage and meat values. There is a market for meat from older animals but no market has yet been developed specifically for younger animals. Angoras are probably most successfully run as a subsidiary enterprise on a farm rather than a stand alone operation.

Contact: British Angora Goat Society: www.britishangoragoats.org.uk

Acknowledgements: Stephen Whitley, Corrymoor Angoras, Stockland, Honiton, Devon EX14 9DY socks@corrymoor.com www.corrymoor.com

GRAZING LIVESTOCK UNITS

Dairy cows	1.00	Lowland ewes	0.11
Beef cows (excl. calf)	0.75	Upland ewes	0.08
Heifers in calf (rearing)	0.80	Hill ewes	0.06
Bulls	0.65	Breeding ewe hoggs:	
		½ to 1 year	0.06
Other cattle (excl. intensive beef):		Other sheep, over 1 year	0.08
0-1 year old	0.34	Store lambs, under 1 year	0.04
1-2 years old	0.65	Rams	0.08
2 years old and over	0.80		

Source: as advised by DEFRA for the Farm Business Survey.

Notes

1. Total livestock units on a farm should be calculated by multiplying the above ratios by the *monthly livestock numbers averaged over the whole year.*

2. The ratios are based on feed requirements. Strictly speaking, when calculating stocking density, allowances should also be made for differences in output (e.g. milk yield per cow or liveweight gain per head), breed (e.g. Friesians v. Jerseys), and quantities of non-forage feed consumed.

OTHER LIVESTOCK UNITS

Breeding sows	0.44	Broilers	0.0017
Gilts in pig	0.20	Other table chicken	0.004
Maiden gilts	0.18	Turkeys	0.005
Boars	0.35	Ducks, geese, other poultry	0.003
Other pigs	0.17	Horses	0.80
Cocks, hens, pullets in lay	0.017	Milch goats	0.16
Pullets, 1 week to point of lay	0.003	Other goats	0.11

Source: as advised by DEFRA for the Farm Business Survey.

FORAGE VARIABLE COSTS

£ per hectare (acre) per annum	Grass: Dairying (1)	Grass: Other (1)	Forage Maize (2)	Kale	Fodder Beet
Yield tonnes/ha (tons/acre)	-	-	40 (16)(silage)	45 (18)	80 (32)
Seed	10 (4)	7 (3)	121 (49)	60 (24)	130 (53)
Fertilizer	137 (55)	91 (37)	92 (37)	97 (39)	131 (53)
Sprays	5 (2)	3 (1)	37 (15)	42 (17)	135 (55)
Total	152(62)	101 (41)	250 (101)	199 (81)	396 (160)

	Forage Peas	Forage Rape	Turnips	Stubble Turnips	Swedes
Yield tonnes/ha (tons/acre)	35 (14)	35 (14)	65 (26)	35 (14)	75 (30)
Seed	68 (28)	16 (6)	19 (8)	26 (11)	30 (12)
Fertilizer	46 (18)	74 (30)	91 (37)	80 (32)	91 (37)
Sprays	10 (4)	20 (8)	43 (17)	22 (9)	45 (18)
Total	124 (50)	110 (45)	153 (62)	128 (52)	166 (67)

1. These are average figures. Intensively silaged and grazed grass may have much higher fertilizer costs in particular - even as much as £245 (100) for dairying. The seed costs will vary according to the proportion of permanent pasture and the length of leys. Fertilizer inputs are often less on permanent pasture too, but this depends on the attitude of the farmer/manager, which will also be reflected in the stocking rates and productive levels per animal achieved.

2. Contract work on maize: drilling £38 (15); harvesting £83 (33), or £139 (56) to include carting and clamping. The area grown in the United Kingdom was 137,000 ha in 2006.

   Standing maize crops are typically sold for between £500 and £600/ha (£200-240/acre) but can be as high as £800/ha (£325/acre), depending on the potential yield of the crop and local supply and demand.

   Whole Crop Cereals (winter wheat; fermented). Variable costs as for combined crop (see page 17) plus contract harvesting at £150 per ha (£60 per acre). Fresh yield averages 27.5 tonnes per ha (11 tons per acre) harvested around late June with a 35% dry matter. Urea treatment (for higher dry matter): add £100 per ha (£40 per acre) for urea prills.

   Labour: grass, pages 139-141; kale, page 141; conservation labour, page 140. Conservation machinery, page 149.

Grass Silage and Hay Costs and Value

Estimated average costs (for 2008) of producing and harvesting, on a full costs basis (i.e. including rental value of the land, all labour, share of general overheads, etc.) are: Hay: £90 per tonne; Silage: £25 per tonne.

Approximately half the silage cost is for growing the grass and half for harvesting and storage. The % breakdown of total costs is typically as follows:

Variable Costs:		Fertilizer	Seeds and Sprays	Contract	Sundries
Silage		23	1	10	5
Hay		18	1	2	2

Fixed Costs:	Rent	Labour	Tractors	Deprec. & Reps.	FYM/Lime
Silage	21	10	16	9	5
Hay	25	16	19	12	5

Sale Value of hay and (far less common because of its bulk) silage vary widely according to the region and type of season (supply/demand situation), quality and time of year.

Hay (pick-up baled) has an average ex-farm sale value of £65 to £70 per tonne for seed hay (main range November to May £60 to £75) and £52.50-£57.50 for meadow hay (main range November to May £50 to £65); prices are higher in the west than the east and more after a dry summer (giving low yields of grass) than a wet one. Prices tend to be nearer £80-£90 per tonne for horses. Big bale hay is cheaper, averaging £40 to £45 per tonne, ranging mainly between £30 and £50 per tonne.

Grass silage is typically valued at about £30 a tonne delivered (up to £40 when forage is very short in an area, down as low as £22.50 if it is plentiful), maize silage approx. £25 a tonne.

Relative Costs of Grazing, Conserved Grass, etc.

	Yield DM tonnes/ha (acre)	Cost per tonne DM (£)	MJ per kg DM	Pence per MJ of ME in DM
Grazed Grass	11.1 (4.5)	42	11.8	0.36
Kale (direct drilled)	6.9 (2.8)	42	11.0	0.38
Forage Turnips (direct drilled)	6.9 (2.8)	38	10.2	0.37
Grass Silage	11.1 (4.5)	76	10.9	0.70
Big Bale Silage	11.1 (4.5)	79	10.9	0.73
Purchased Hay (1)		76	8.8	0.87
Brewers' Grains (2)	-	104	11.7	0.89
Concentrates (3)	-	174	12.8	1.36

(1) at £65 per tonne (2) at £25 per tonne (3) 14% CP 14% Moisture, delivered in bulk, £150 per tonne

Note

In interpreting the above figures for use in planning feed use on farm, it is important to remember that own land, labour and capital for equipment are required for home-produced fodder but not for purchased feed, and much more storage is required

The consumption of fodder is limited by its bulk although this very much depends upon its quality/digestibility.

Clearly, the cost of forage will vary enormously depending on growing conditions, soil fertility and type, intensity of farming practice and management ability.

FODDER CROPS, GRASSES AND CLOVERS
SEED PRICES (2008) AND SEED RATES

Crop	Price	Seed Rate per hectare
Fodder Kale	£8 to £11 per kg	5 to 7 kg
Swedes	£25 per kg	3.0 to 4.0 kg broadcast
	£46 per kg graded	0.6 kg precision drilled
Stubble Turnips	£4.00 to £10 per kg	3.7 kg drilled,
		5.0 kg broadcast
Rape	£1.90 per kg	3.8 kg drilled (7.5 kg broadcast)
Mustard	£1.30 per kg	20 to 25 kg
Rape and Turnips	£17 per hectare	1.25 kg rape
		3.70 kg turnips
Kale, Swede and Turnips	£51 per hectare	1.85 kg kale, 0.5 kg swede,
		1.85 kg turnips
Forage Maize: Silage	£100 to £125 per hectare	110,000 to 115,000 seeds
Forage Maize: zero grazed	£143 to £165 per hectare	130,000 to 150,000 seeds
Arable Silage	£85 per hectare	125 kg oats, 60 kg tares
Tares/Vetch	£0.90 per kg	100 to 125 kg
Westerwold Ryegrass	£1.50 per kg	35 kg
Italian Ryegrass	£1.20 to £1.60 per kg	33 to 50 kg
Perennial Ryegrass	£2.18 per kg	35 to 40 kg
Hybrid Ryegrass	£2.20 per kg	30 to 40 kg
Cocksfoot	£3.00 per kg	20 to 25 kg
Timothy	£2.40 per kg	7 to 9 kg
Meadow Fescue	£2.60 per kg	11 to 13 kg
Broad Red Clover	£2.30 – 2.80 per kg	29 kg
Alsike Clover	£4.80 per kg	18 to 22 kg
White Clover	£4.50 to £7.50 per kg	5 kg
Kent Wild White Clover	£7.50 to £9.50 per kg	—
Lucerne	£3.90 per kg	20 kg
Sainfoin	£2.00 per kg	60 to 90 kg
Forage Rye	£0.60 per kg	180 kg
Rye and Ryegrass	£80 per hectare	125 kg rye
		22 kg Italian Ryegrass
1 year leys	£53 to £89 per hectare	—
2 year leys	£50 per hectare	—
4-6 year leys	£88 per hectare	—
Long-term Ley	£74 per hectare	—
White Clover Ley	£80 to £82 per hectare	—
Red Clover Ley	£69 to £82 per hectare	—
Wye College mixture	£60 per hectare	—
Horse grazing	£60 to £86 per hectare	—
Game Cover mixture	£60 per hectare	—
Set-aside mixture	£69 to £184 per hectare	
Field Margin mixture	£78 per hectare	
Gallop mixture	£2.68 per kg	100-250 kg

3. PIGS, POULTRY, TROUT, RABBIT

PIGS

1. Breeding and Rearing (to 32 kg liveweight):
per sow per year and per 32 kg pig reared

Performance Level	Average		High	
	per sow	per pig	per sow	per pig
	£	£	£	£
Weaners: (ave) 21.6 (1) @ £35.00 (3)	756	35.00		
(high) 24.7 (2) @ £35.00 (3)			865	35.00
Less Livestock Depreciation (4)	45	2.08	46	1.85
Output	711	32.92	819	33.15
Variable Costs:				
Food (5)	393	18.20	373	15.10
Miscellaneous (6)	77	3.56	77	3.12
Total Variable Costs	470	21.76	450	18.22
Gross Margin (per year)	241	11.17	369	14.93

Notes

1. Weaners per sow - average: 9.80 reared per litter, 2.2 litters per year = 21.6 weaners per sow per year. (The average has now recovered somewhat following falls in the early 2000's due to the wasting diseases PMWS and PDNS).

2. Weaners per sow - high: 10.50 reared per litter, 2.35 litters per year = 24.7 weaners per sow per year.

3. Price – assumed pig cycle average. (See note 4 on p. 120). Prices for 32kg weaners have varied from £15 to £45 during the past decade but have been between £30 and £40 in the last three years.

4. Average livestock depreciation assumes an in-pig gilt purchase price of £145, a cull value per sow of £70 and a 45% replacement rate (i.e. approximately 6 litters per sow life). Sow mortality 5%. Boars (1 per 24 sows) purchased at £650 (40% a year replacement), sold at £80. 'High' compared with 'Average': higher gilt purchase prices and slightly fewer sows per boar assumed.

5. Food – 2.39 tonnes per sow: sow 1.32, boar (per sow) 0.05, other feed (per sow) 1.02. Price of feed consumed: £164 per tonne; (average of 57% sow (and boar) feed (at £130) and 43% piglet and rearing feed (at £210), and of home-mixed and purchased compounds). High performance: lower sow feed but extra piglet rearing feed for additional weaners. Piglets weaned at average 3.75 weeks, 7.25kg weight.

6. Average: vet. and med. £45, transport £11, straw and bedding £11, miscellaneous £11. (Electricity and gas [£18] and water [£7] included in fixed costs below).

7. Direct Labour Cost per sow: average £173, good £135; per weaner: average £8.00, good £5.47. See further page 150. Other Fixed Costs: approx. £160.

8. Building Costs: see pages 185.

N.B. Outdoor Breeding: see page 119.

Acknowledgement: The main data source for the margins within the Pigs section is the Pig Yearbook (Meat and Livestock Commission), 2007 and previous years, but the pig and feed price assumptions are entirely the author's responsibility. Small differences in the relationship between these can of course cause large differences in margins. Big variations can occur between farms. The weaner price is crucial as regards the relative margins between breeding and rearing, and finishing.

2. Feeding (from 32 kg liveweight): per pig

A. Average Performance

	Pork £	Cutter £	Bacon £
Sale Value	62.70	71.50	78.50
Less Weaner Cost (1)	35.00	35.00	35.00
Mortality Charge	1.60	1.80	1.90
Output	26.10	34.70	41.60
Variable Costs:			
Food	17.10	22.30	27.20
Miscellaneous	4.00	4.50	5.00
Total Variable Costs	21.10	26.80	32.20
Gross Margin	**5.00**	**7.90**	**9.40**
Liveweight (kg)	76	87	96
Deadweight (kg)	56	65	72
Killing Out %	74%	75%	75%
Price per Deadweight (p)	112	110	109
Price per Liveweight (p)	82.5	82.2	81.8
Food Conversion Rate	2.65	2.70	2.75
Food per Pig (kg)	122	154	182
Average Cost of Food per tonne (£) (2)	£140	£145	£150
Food Cost per Kg l/w Gain (p)	37.10	39.15	41.25
Liveweight Gain per Day (kg)	0.62	0.65	0.67
Feeding Period (weeks)	10.6	12.5	14.1
Mortality (%)	4.5	5.0	5.5
Direct Labour Costs per Pig (£)	4.00	5.00	6.00

B. High Performance (same pig price)

Food Conversion Rate	2.55	2.62	2.7
Food per Pig (kg)	117	149	178
Food Cost per Pig (£5/t less than ave.)	15.84	20.91	25.84
Food Cost per Kg l/w Gain (p)	34.43	36.68	39.15
Gross Margin per Pig	**4.20**	**7.40**	**8.50**
Direct Labour Costs per Pig	3.30	3.70	4.20

(1) Weaner cost assumes on farm transfer. If purchased (i.e., feeding only) transport and purchasing costs have to be added: these are very variable but average about £1.75 per weaner.

(2) Average of home-mixed and purchased compounds. There can be big variations in feed costs per tonne between farms, according to whether the food is purchased as compounds or home-mixed, bought in bulk or in bags, size of unit, etc.

Labour: see page 146. Building Costs: see pages 185.

Sensitivity Analysis. The effect of changes in important variables (other things being equal) are as follows;

Change in Gross Margin (£)	Porker	Cutter	Baconer
Price: 5p per kg dw difference	2.80	3.25	3.60
Food Cost per tonne: £10 difference	1.22	1.54	1.82.
Food Conversion Rate: 0.1 difference ...	0.64	0.83	0.99

The effect of differences in the cost per weaner is obvious.

3. Combined Breeding, Rearing, and Feeding: per pig

	Pork £		Cutter £		Bacon £	
Performance Level*	Ave.	High	Ave.	High	Ave.	High
Sale Value	62.70	59.90	71.50	71.50	78.50	78.50
Sow and Boar Deprcn	2.08	1.85	2.08	1.85	2.08	1.85
Mortality Charge	1.60	1.40	1.80	1.60	1.90	1.80
Output	**59.02**	**56.65**	**67.62**	**68.05**	**74.52**	**74.85**
Food	35.30	30.90	40.50	36.00	45.40	40.90
Miscellaneous	7.56	6.62	8.06	7.12	8.56	7.62
Total Variable Costs	**42.86**	**37.52**	**48.56**	**43.12**	**53.96**	**48.52**
Gross Margin per Pig	**16.17**	**19.13**	**19.07**	**24.93**	**20.57**	**26.33**
Gross Margin per Sow	**349**	**472**	**412**	**616**	**444**	**650**
Labour Costs per Pig	12.00	8.77	13.00	9.17	14.00	9.67
Labour Costs per Sow	259	217	281	226	302	239

*   Performance levels refer to breeding and rearing differences as on pages 117-118 and, for feeding, differences in food conversion rate, food costs and labour cost only.

4. Prices - General

Pig prices are notoriously difficult to predict. In 1996 average GB prices per kg deadweight were 138p. By 1999 they had fallen to 79p on average. Over the last three years the range has been 99p to 110p, with the average for the first 6 months of 2007 being 107p. The majority of UK pigs are now taken to baconer weight. The level shown in the finisher margins for baconers above, of 109p, is an estimated average for late 2007 through 2008.

5. Further Performance Data

Source: The Meat and Livestock Commission's 'Pig Yearbook 2007' (data for the year ended Sept. 2006).

	Performance Level		
A. Breeding	Average	Top Third*	Top 10%*
Sow replacements (%)	55.3	47.0	44.1
Sow sales and deaths (%)	44.1	38.8	33.2
Sow mortality (%)	5.3	2.4	3.3
Litters per sow per year	2.27	2.34	2.36
Pigs reared per litter	9.4	10.1	10.6
Pigs reared per sow per year	21.3	23.6	25.0
Weight of pigs produced (kg)	7.7	7.3	7.3
Average weaning age (days)	26.1	26.2	25.1
Sow feed per sow per year (tonnes) .	1.38	1.36	1.36
Feed per pig reared (kg)	70	56	57
Sow feed cost per tonne (£)	104	105	106
Sow feed cost per sow per year (£) .	139	141	138
Feed cost per pig reared (£)	7.32	5.84	5.91

*   selected on basis of pigs reared per sow per year.

B. Rearing	Average	Top Third*	Top 10%*
Weight of pigs at start (kg)	7.2	7.4	7.6
Weight of pigs produced (kg)	35.1	33.3	38.7
Mortality (%)	2.5	2.7	3.7
Feed conversion ratio	1.7	1.7	1.7
Daily Gain (g)	493	487	537
Feed cost per tonne (£)	192	182	158
Feed cost per kg gain (£)	32.8	30.2	27.2
Feed cost per pig reared (£)	9.16	7.82	8.47

C. Feeding	Average	Top Third*	Top 10%*
Weight of pigs at start (kg)	27.2	33.5	40.6
Weight of pigs produced (kg)	98.2	102.0	103.5
Mortality (%)	5.6	4.9	5.1
Feed conversion ratio	2.8	2.8	2.8
Daily Gain (g)	655	706	727
Feed cost per tonne (£)	120	101	89
Feed cost per kg gain (£)	33.0	28.8	24.4
Feed cost per pig reared (£)	23.40	19.73	15.82

** selected on basis of feed cost per kg liveweight gain.

Feed conversion ratio for rearing and feeding combined, from 7.5kg to 98kg liveweight is approximately 2.46.

6.   Outdoor v Indoor Performance

Breeding	Outdoor	Indoor
Sow replacements (%)	57.6	49.5
Sow sales and deaths (%)	42.6	49.2
Sow mortality (%)	5.4	6.1
Litters per sow per year	2.27	2.26
Pigs reared per litter	9.3	9.7
Pigs reared per sow per year	21.1	22.0
Weight of pigs produced (kg)	8.1	7.2
Average weaning age (days)	26.1	26.1
Sow feed per sow per year (tonnes) .	1.30	1.37
Feed per pig reared (kg)	68	63
Sow feed cost per tonne (£)	103	102
Sow feed cost per sow per year (£) .	124	139
Feed cost per pig reared (£)	7.07	6.53

Stocking Rate for outdoor pigs is mainly between 12 and 25 per hectare (5 and 10 per acre), 20 (8) being the most common. Good drainage is essential. A low rainfall and mild climate are also highly desirable. In 2003, MLC's Agrosoft puts the cost of establishing a sow herd on a greenfield site at £1,800 per sow place for an indoor unit and about £600 per sow place for an outdoor unit.

Over 35% of the UK breeding sow herd is now kept outdoors. The percentage of outdoor rearing/finishing pigs is in the order of 5%.

Further details can be found in 'Pig Production in England 2005-06' published by Askham Bryan College, York (address on page 248).

EGG PRODUCTION

(brown egg layers, 52 week laying period)

Level of Perforamnce ..	Cages				Free Range	
	Average		High		Average	
	per bird	per doz eggs	per bird	per doz eggs	per bird	per doz eggs
	£	p	£	p	£	p
Egg Returns	11.96	46.0	12.42	46.0	18.75	75.0
Less Livestock Deprcn ..	2.90	11.2	2.90	10.7	3.10	12.4
Output	**9.06**	**34.8**	**9.52**	**35.3**	**15.65**	**62.6**
Variable Costs:						
Food	6.80	26.2	6.80	25.2	8.06	32.2
Miscellaneous	1.54	5.9	1.54	5.7	1.49	6.0
Total Variable Costs	**8.34**	**32.1**	**8.34**	**30.9**	**9.55**	**38.2**
Gross Margin	**0.72**	**2.7**	**1.18**	**4.4**	**6.10**	**24.4**

Notes:

Hen-housed data are used throughout, i.e. the total costs and returns are divided by the number of birds housed at the commencement of the laying period. IPPC permit and 1st year charges have not been included, but when finalised they are likely to represent a significant cost to egg and poultry meat producers with 40,000 birds or more.

A. Cage Production

1. The yields assumed are:
   - Average .... 312 (26.00 dozen)
   - High .... 324 (27.00 dozen)

2. The average price assumed (for 2008), 46p per dozen, includes all quantity and quality bonuses. Farmer to shop and consumer prices are well above packer to producer levels and normally 35p and 65p per dozen premiums respectively are required.

3. Livestock depreciation—the average point of lay pullet is priced at £2.80 (16/17 weeks old); old hen processors are currently charging between 6.5 and 21.5 pence/bird to take them away.

4. The food price assumed (for 2008) is £160 per tonne. The feed cost is dependent on breed, housing and environmental conditions, quantity purchased and type of ration. Quantity of feed used = 42.5 kg.

5. Direct Labour Costs: average £1.26 per bird, premium £1.00. See page 146.

   Housing Costs: see page 186. Deadstock depreciation averages about £1 per caged bird.

B. Free Range Production

1. Egg yields: 300 (25 dozen).

2. Average price: 75p per dozen.

3. Quantity of feed used = 47.4 kg. Price £170 per tonne.

4. Direct Labour Costs: average £4.00 per bird, dependent on automation.

Acknowledgement: The figures in the whole of the poultry section are provided by Tony Warner, *AAW Poultry Consultancy*, Lilleshall, Newport, Shropshire.

REARING PULLETS

(Average per bird reared)

	£
Value of 16/17 weeks old bird	2.80
Less Chicks 1.01 (1) @ 54p (including levy)	0.55
Output	**2.25**
Variable Costs:	
Food: 6.25 kg @ £160 per tonne	1.00
Miscellaneous (2)	0.73
Total Variable Costs	**1.73**
Gross Margin	**0.52**

1. Assumes 3 per cent mortality, but 2 per cent allowed in price.

2. Excluding transport (16p), but including full vaccination costs.

    Labour (35p); deadstock depreciation (44p).

TABLE POULTRY

A *Broilers* (per bird sold at 41 days)	p
Returns 2.37 kg per bird @ 55.0p per kg lw	130.4
Less Cost of Chick	26.4
Output	**104.0**
Variable Costs:	
Food: 4.12 kg @ £198 per tonne	81.6
Miscellaneous	15.0
Total Variable Costs	**96.6**
Gross Margin	**7.4**

    Capital cost of housing and equipment: £6.65 per broiler space (depreciation cost approximately 5.7p per bird sold). Housing Costs: see page 186.

    Labour: 4.7p, excluding catching and cleaning out (4.6p) but includes management; see page 146.

B *All Year Round Turkey* (per bird sold at 20 weeks, sexed stags)	£
Returns 14.3 kg per bird @ £2.35 per kg O.R	33.6
Less Cost of Poult	2.0
Output	**31.6**
Variable Costs:	
Food: 50 kg @ £210 per tonne	10.5
Miscellaneous	4.1
Total Variable Costs	**14.6**
Gross Margin	**17.0**

    10% mortality allowed in cost of poult figures.

* Rearing turkeys all the year round now tends to be just in the hands of a few large companies. Returns for all year round production have improved recently because of higher European prices, but this is a volatile market. Also with both turkey enterprises there will be considerable variation depending on strain, production system and feeding regime. These figures should therefore be used only as a rough guide.

C   Christmas Turkey (Traditional Farm Fresh - indoor reared)

	Light	Medium	Heavy
	£	£	£
Returns per bird sold	23.49	26.57	25.48
Less Cost of Poult	4.00	4.00	3.35
Output	**19.49**	**22.57**	**22.13**
Variable Costs:			
Food	5.00	6.51	6.99
Miscellaneous	2.53	2.88	3.35
Total Variable Costs	**7.53**	**9.39**	**10.34**
Gross Margin	**11.96**	**13.18**	**11.79**
Killing Age (weeks)	18	22	22
Live Weight (kg)	7.2	8.3	12.0
Oven Ready Weight (kg)	6.1	6.9	9.8
Food Conversion	3.2	3.7	2.8
Food per Bird (kg)	22.7	30.3	33.3
Food Cost per tonne	£220	£215	£210

1.   7, 8 and 10% mortality allowed for in cost of poult figures for light, medium and heavy weights respectively.

2.   Light and medium = slow growing sexed hens.
     Heavy = stags (as hatched).

3.   Price per kilogram:
     Christmas (fresh, eviscerated): hens 350-420p range; stags 230-290p range.

Note: With both turkey enterprises considerable variations will occur between individual strains and because of different production systems and feeding regimes. Free range systems for example will show higher costs and returns. The figures should therefore be used only as rough guidelines.

D   Roaster (Capons) (per bird sold at 12 weeks; Christmas - males only)

	£
Returns 4.8 kg per bird @ £2.75 per kg O.R.	13.20
Less Cost of Chick	0.70
Output	**12.50**
Variable Costs:	
Food: 14.3 kg @ £210 per tonne	3.00
Miscellaneous	1.31
Total Variable Costs	**4.31**
Gross Margin	**8.19**

10% mortality allowed for in cost of chick figures.

E **Ducks** *(Aylesbury type)* (per bird sold at 7 weeks)	£
Returns 2.8 kg per bird @ £4.75 per kg O.R.	13.30
Less Cost of Duckling	2.10
Output	**11.20**
Variable Costs:	
Food: 9.5 kg @ £230 per tonne	2.19
Miscellaneous	1.77
Total Variable Costs	**3.96**
Gross Margin	**7.25**

Heavier ducks of the Pekin type can be grown to 15-16 weeks, when oven-ready weights of 3.5-4.0 kg can be realised.

Day-old costs allow for 10% mortality.

F **Geese** (Traditional Farm Fresh - free range and dry plucked)	£
Returns 5.0 kg per bird @ £7.70 per kg O.R.	38.50
Less Cost of Gosling	6.00
Output	**32.50**
Variable Costs:	
Food: 20 kg @ £220 per tonne	4.40
Miscellaneous	2.10
Total Variable Costs	**6.50**
Gross Margin	**26.00**

Day-old costs allow for 6% mortality.

RAINBOW TROUT

	£ per tonne of fish
Returns 1 tonne of fish @ £1.60 per kg	1,600
Less 4000 fingerlings @ 5.5p each	220
Output	**1,380**
Variable Costs:	
Food: 1 tonne @ £750 per tonne	750
Vet and med; Miscellaneous	125
Miscellaneous	20
Total Variable Costs	**895**
Gross Margin	**485**

Notes

1. Fish growing to 350g from fingerlings at 4.5g.

2. Prices are estimated ex-farm to processor or wholesaler. Higher prices of up to £4.20 per kg can be achieved by selling direct to retailers, caterers and consumers at, say farmers markets, but significant additional costs are associated with such sales.

3. Fingerlings price: varies according to quantity ordered and time of year.

4. Average feeding period, 10 months. Mortality, from fingerling to market size, 15%. Food conversion ratio, 1.0:1. The price for fish food is for a pigmented high oil expanded pellet.

5. Current capital costs for construction of earth pond unit approximately £60 per cubic metre, to include buildings, holding systems and installation of water supply and services, but excluding land.

6. Labour requirement: the basic norm has in the past been 1 man per 50 tonnes of fish produced per annum on a table fish farm, but to remain competitive farmers now need to produce at least 150 tonnes per annum of table fish per man.

The figures given above must only be considered illustrative. Trout farming varies across the UK – from Cage Farming in Scottish lochs (freshwater and marine) through to 'traditional' river farming. It also encompasses both the table and restocking sectors. As such feed costs, conversion rates etc do vary which obviously has an effect on the costings for the enterprise.

Acknowledgement: British Trout Association, The Rural Centre, West Mains, Ingliston, Edinburgh, EH28 8NZ. Tel: 0131472 4080 www.britishtrout.co.uk

MEAT RABBITS

Although the consumption of rabbit meat in the UK is low, at less than 2oz per person per year, most of it is imported. Commercial rabbit production is an intensive livestock enterprise and will probably require planning permission and building regulation approval from the Local Authority.

A meat rabbit unit needs a weather- and vermin-proof building, which is insulated, well-drained and has good ventilation, lighting and a water supply. Housing can be fully environment controlled to give good feed conversion rates and better winter conditions for both stock and personnel, or be natural environment, which has lower capital and running costs and possibly keeps animals healthier. Rabbits are kept in wire cages, usually in one tier, ideally suspended; a single tier system needs 10-12 square feet per cage. Feed hoppers, drinkers and nest boxes are required. Some experimental work to provide less intensive conditions for the animals, possibly with outside access, is in progress, but is at an early stage.

New Zealand White or Californian stock is used. Young does are bought in at 12 weeks and mated at 16-20 weeks. Bucks are bought at 16 weeks and first mated at 20 weeks. A ratio of one buck to 10-20 does is recommended. Gestation is 31 days. Average litter size is 8-9, of which 6-7 should be successfully fattened. Re-mating can be immediately post-partum or up to 6 weeks afterwards; the average is about 21 days. A doe can have a useful life of 10-12 litters over 18 months; less productive animals may be culled sooner. An overall mortality rate of up to 12.5% can be expected.

Young rabbits are weaned at 35-42 days at about 2.5-3 lb and then fed ad-lib until they are ready for marketing at 5.5-6.5lb liveweight at 11-13 weeks. Food conversion rate, including the doe's feed and a share of the buck's is around 4:1. A balanced ration can be obtained for £165 per tonne in bulk but may cost up to £185 per tonne. A doe should produce around 50 meat rabbits each year but experienced producers would aim for 60-70. Health, hygiene and good stockmanship are crucial to the enterprise. One full-time person can look after 250-300 does and their progeny.

There are only a few buyers and processors of meat rabbits in the UK and they do not cover all parts of the country. Hence transport costs may have to be allowed for. The demand for rabbit meat is seasonal - more is eaten in the winter than the summer, which can pose marketing problems. Producers are advised to adjust their production by 15 to 20% in summer to allow for this. An individual producer may develop local markets but this will require initiative. There may be a market for the manure but again this would have to be developed.

Capital Costs	£	No. per 50 does	£ per 50 does
Doe at 12 weeks	10	50	500
Buck at 16 weeks	12	3	36
Cage	10	87	870
Drinker	5	87	435
Nest Box	4	50	200
Building (new):			
(10 sq.ft/cage at £3/sq.ft x 1.75) ..	52.50/doe		2,625

Gross Margin	£/doe/year	£/50 does/year
48 young @ 2.60 kg @ £1.30/kg (1)	162.2	8,112
Less Depreciation (2)	4.6	228
Output	**157.7**	**7,884**
Variable Costs:		
Feed	97.3	4,867
Vet and med	1.7	85
Bedding	1.8	90
Miscellaneous (including electricity) ..	4.0	200
Total Variable Costs	**104.8**	**5,242**
Gross Margin	**52.8**	**2,642**

1. £1.20 to £1.40 depending on delivery and collection

2. Cull value: Does £1.5 over 2 years. Bucks £1.5 over 3 years. Both 10% mortality.

3. Food conversion 4:1 at £195 per tonne including allowance for doe and share of buck.

Acknowledgement: David Blythe, *Woldsway Foods Ltd.* Tel: 01754 890641. www.woldsway.co.uk

IV. LABOUR

1. LABOUR COST

1. Statutory Minimum Wage Rates

The following rates are applicable from 1st October 2007. The minimum weekly rates relate to a 39-hour standard week of normal hours worked on any five days between Monday and Saturday.

A. *Normal Hours (Standard Rates)*

Grade			Weekly Rate	Hourly Rate	Overtime per Hour
			£	£	£
1.	Initial Grade	Over 16 years	215.28	5.52	8.28
		Under 16 years	-	2.76	4.14
2.	**Standard Worker**		**234.00**	**6.00**	**9.00**
3.	Lead Worker		257.40	6.60	9.90
4.	Craft Grade		276.12	7.08	10.62
5.	Supervisory Grade....................................		292.50	7.50	11.25
6.	Farm Management Grade..........................		315.90	8.10	12.15
	Apprentice:	Year 1	134.94	3.46	5.19
		Year 2 ~ 16-18 years	134.94	3.46	5.19
		Year 2 ~ 19-21 years	179.4	4.60	6.90
		Year 2 ~ 22 years and over	215.28	5.52	8.28

Night work rates are £1.18 per hour; standby rates £23.78 per day; dog rates £6.58 per week.

B. *Flexible Working*

Grade		Number of days basic hours worked	Weekly Rate	Hourly Rate	Overtime per Hour
			£	£	£
1.	Initial Grade (16+ only)	4 to 5	226.20	5.80	8.28
		6	230.49	5.91	8.28
2.	Standard Worker	4 to 5	245.70	6.30	9.00
		6	250.38	6.42	9.00
3.	Lead Worker........................	4 to 5	270.27	6.93	9.90
		6	275.34	7.06	9.90
4.	Craft Grade..........................	4 to 5	289.77	7.43	10.62
		6	295.62	7.58	10.62
5.	Supervisory Grade...............	4 to 5	307.32	7.88	11.25
		6	313.17	8.03	11.25
6.	Farm Management Grade....	4 to 5	331.89	8.51	12.15
		6	338.13	8.67	12.15

Notes

1. The new grading structure, comprising six grades instead of the previous five, was introduced in 2005. The manual Harvest Worker category, introduced in 2003, was abolished. Flexible working rates were set for each of the six new grades. In 2006 the Basic Trainee Grade was renamed the Initial Grade. All age differentials were abolished apart from the under 16 category in the Initial Grade.

2. Part standby duty days are paid at half the rates given above.

3. A deduction up to £30.10 a week or £4.30 a day for non-house accommodation can be made. There are specified provisions for sick pay, paid bereavement leave and paid paternity leave (3 days).

Full details are available from the Agricultural Wages Board for England and Wales (Telephone: 0207 238 6523).

Holiday Pay

Holidays with pay. The number of days holiday that workers are entitled to in a year depends on the number of days worked each week. Those working full-time, 5 days a week, have 23 days per year. There are rules as to timing.

For part-time workers the number of days worked per week is based on the total hours worked over the 12 months ending on the last 5th April.

2. Estimated Average Earnings, Year 2008

Government statistics are no longer available for different categories of worker as listed above; the last year such data was available was 1997. The figure below for all hired men is approximately 43% more than the 1997 average, which is by how much the statutory minimum wage has risen between 1997 and 2007; the retail price index has risen by approximately 30.2% over that period. The differentials for the listed categories of worker are based on the average differentials for the three years 1995 to 1997 (they differed very little indeed during those years). The same applies to the hours of work.

| Type of Worker | Average Total Earnings | | Total Hours |
	Annual	Per Week	Per Week
	£	£	
All Hired Men	20,534	395	47.4
Foremen	24,557	472	47.4
Dairy Herdsmen	24,871	479	52.7
Other Stockmen	20,638	397	46.5
Tractor Drivers	21,840	420	49.4
General Farm Workers	19,070	367	46.7
Horticultural Workers	17,294	332	42.4

3. Typical Annual Labour Cost

Estimated for the 2008 calendar year, based on a Standard Worker.

	Average Annual Cost(1)	Average Weekly Cost	Average Hourly Cost(2)
	£	£	£
Minimum Wage (basic standard worker rate)	12,168	234.00	6.93
National Insurance Contribution and Employers Liability Insurance	1,679	32.30	
Minimum Cost	13,847	266.30	7.89
Overtime, average 10 hrs per working week (45) @ £9.0 (+ NIC, ELI)	4608	88.63	
	18,455	354.93	10.52
'Premium' over basic rate average £45.00 per week (+ NIC, ELI)	2,663	51.20	
Total Cost (3,4)	21,118	406.10	12.03

NIC = National Insurance Contribution = 12.8%;

ELI = Employer's Liability Insurance = 1%

1. Estimated average annual cost higher than 2007 AWB rate as figures based on calendar year rather than Oct-Oct AWB year.

2. Hours, excluding overtime, based on 45 weeks (of 39 hours) per year, i.e. statutory holidays (23 days), public holidays (8 days) and illness (4 days), have been deducted.

3. Annual cost (or net value) of cottages, value of perquisites, contribution towards payment of the council tax, etc., would have to be added where appropriate.

4. Total average worker's gross earnings on the above assumptions = £18,557 a year, £356.90 a week, £7.99 an hour.

4. Assessing Annual Labour Requirements

The regular labour staff required for a farm is sometimes assessed by calculating the total number of Standard Man-Days (Man-Work Units), as given on page 227-228. The number of days supplied by casual labour is first deducted, then 15% is added for general maintenance work; no allowance is made for management, for which 7.5% may be added if required. It is assumed that 275 Standard Man-Days are provided annually per man, including national average hours of overtime and allowing for holidays and illness; allowance needs to be made for any manual labour supplied by the farmer himself. A full-time dairyperson will average 300 SMD a year, again including overtime. (1 SMD = 8 labour hours a year.)

This is a crude calculation in that it makes no allowance for seasonality and the special circumstances of an individual farm, such as soil type, level of mechanization, and condition and layout of the buildings.

The following sections supply the type of data that should be used in assessing labour requirements.

2. LABOUR HOURS AVAILABLE FOR FIELD WORK

(per man per month)

	Total Ordinary Hours (1)	Adjusted Ordinary Hours (2)	% Workable	Available Ordinary Hours (3)	Available Overtime Hours (4)	**Total Available Hours**	Total Available '8-hour Days' (5)
January	177	148	50	74	28 (61)	**102** (135)	13 (17)
February	160	134	50	67	33 (55)	**100** (122)	12½ (15)
March	172	149	60	89	69 (82)	**158** (171)	20 (21½)
April	161	139	65	90	86	**176**	22
May	171	151	70	106	110	**216**	27
June	170	150	75	112	112	**224**	28
July	177	157	75	118	113	**231**	29
August	169	150	75	112	104	**216**	27
September	172	152	70	106	82 (69)	188 (195)	23½ (24½)
October	177	153	65	99	63 (83)	162 (182)	20 (23)
November	172	144	50	72	26 (59)	98 (131)	12 (16½)
December (16½)	161	135	50	67	25 (65)	**92** (132)	11½

(1) 40 hour week, less public holidays. No deductions have been made for other holidays because they may be taken at various times of the year.

(2) After deducting (a) for illness (10 per cent Nov. to Feb., 7½% March, April and Oct., 5% May to Sept.), and (b) for contingencies and non-delayable maintenance (½ hour per day).

(3) Adjusted Ordinary Hours x percentage Workable.

(4) Maximum 4 overtime hours per day summer, 3 hours winter, and 12 to 14 hours' work at weekends, according to season. Same adjustments for illness and percentage workable as for ordinary hours. Figures in brackets indicate hours available if headlights used up to limit of overtime stated. The percentage overtime (without headlights) available from weekend work as opposed to evenings = (January to December respectively): 100, 78, 58, 50, 40, 40, 41, 42, 53, 67, 100, 100.

(5) Total available hours ÷ 8.

Notes

(1) These figures relate to medium land. The percentage workability will be higher with light soils and less with particularly heavy soils. On heavy soils, of course, the land may be virtually 100 per cent unworkable between late November and early March (or still later, according to the season), particularly if undrained. A rough estimate of variations in workability according to soil type (compared with the figures in the above table) are as follows. Heavy land — March, October, November: one-third less; April: one-fifth less; September: 10% less; May to August: no difference. Light land — October to April: one-sixth more; May and September: 10% more; June to August: no difference.

(2) When these figures are used for planning, it must be remembered that indoor work, e.g. livestock tending or potato riddling, can be continued over the full working-week, i.e. the hours available are the Adjusted Ordinary Hours, plus overtime. Also, some handwork in the field has to continue even in rain, e.g. sprout picking.

(3) To be precise, percentage workability varies according to the particular operation, e.g. compare ploughing and drilling.

(4) Furthermore, some operations are limited by factors other than soil workability, e.g. combine-harvesting by grain moisture content.

(5) Factors touched upon briefly above are discussed fully in Duckham's 'The Farming Year'.

3. SEASONAL LABOUR REQUIREMENTS FOR

CROPS AND GRASS

On the following pages, data on labour requirements for various crops and types of livestock are given. Two levels are shown: average and premium. The average figures relate to the whole range of conditions and farm size, i.e. small and medium-sized farms as well as large; the figures give all farms equal weight. The premium rates do not denote the maximum rates possible, for instance by the use of especially high-powered tractors under ideal conditions, but relate to rates of work estimated to be obtainable over the whole season, averaging good and bad conditions, with the use of wide implements, relatively large tractors (75 to 90 kW) (100-120 hp) and high capacity equipment in 8 hectare fields and over, where no time is wasted. Most farmers with more than 200 hectares (500 acres) of arable land are likely to achieve at least the premium levels shown. Those with over 400 hectares (1,000 acres) will have still bigger machines and therefore faster work rates, and thus require 15 to 25% less labour than even the premium levels given.

The rates of work include preparation, travelling to fields, allow for minor breakdowns and other stoppages. They relate broadly to medium and medium-heavy land; some jobs, such as ploughing, may be done more quickly on light soils. Operations such as combine harvesting can obviously vary according to many factors to do with the topography and other natural features of the farm.

The usual times of year when each operation takes place are shown; these relate to lowland conditions in the south-eastern half of Britain. They will obviously vary between seasons, soil types, latitude and altitude. In particular, on light land, land can be ploughed over a longer winter period and a high proportion of cultivations for spring crops may be completed in February in many seasons. All such factors must be allowed for in individual farm planning. Conditions in different seasons will also affect, for instance, the number and type of cultivations required in seedbed preparation. Typical monthly breakdowns of requirements are given for various crops.

To illustrate the type of questions that need to be asked for full details of seasonal labour requirements on the individual farm, 'Critical Questions affecting Timing' are listed for cereals. Similar questions would, of course, need to be asked for other crops.

WINTER CEREALS

Operations	Labour-hours per hectare		Time of Year
	Average	Premium	
Plough (1)	1.4	1.0	July to October (according to previous crop)
Cultivate (often power harrow)	1.0	0.7	September to October (according to previous crop) (½ Aug if ploughed in July)
Drill (often with power harrows) followed by roll	1.1	0.7	Mid-September to 3rd week October (according to previous crop and soil)
Apply Fertilizer	0.3	0.2	
Spray	0.3	0.2	October-November
Top Dress (three times [2])	0.9	0.6	March and April
Spray (three or four [2])		1.0	0.5 Spring/early summer
Combine, Cart Grain, Barn Work Sept	2.5	1.9	Mid-Aug to approx. 10th
Later Barn Work (3)	0.7	0.4	September to June
Total	**9.2**	**6.2**	
Straw: Bale	1.3	0.8	Mid-August to end
Cart	3.5	2.6	September

Typical Monthly Breakdown

Month	Average	Premium	Notes
October	2.4	1.7	Approx. 60% of Ploughing,
November	—	—	Cults., Drill, Harrow
December	—	—	
January	—	—	
February	—	—	
March	0.4	0.2	Part Top Dress
April	0.8	0.5	Part Top Dress, Spraying
May	0.3	0.2	Spraying
June	0.3	0.2	Spraying
July	—	—	
August	1.7	1.3	⅔ of harvesting (4)
	(+2.4 Straw)	(+1.7 Straw)	
September (harvest)	0.9	0.6	⅓ of harvesting (4)
	(+2.4 Straw)	(+1.7 Straw)	
September (prepn. drill)	1.7	1.1	40% of Ploughing, Cults., Drill, Harrow

Notes

1. Some cereal crops are direct drilled or drilled after reduced, or minimal, cultivations, i.e. without traditional ploughing. Direct drilling reduces man-hours per hectare by about 2.5 (average) or 1.8 (premium), and minimal cultivations by about 1.2 (average) and 0.9 (premium).

2. Winter wheat; winter barley will often have one less top dressing and spraying and oats two less.

3. Later barn work excluded from monthly breakdown.

4. Winter wheat (see page 133 for harvest times for winter barley and oats).

SPRING CEREALS

Operations	Labour-Hours per hectare		Time of Year
	Average	Premium	
Plough (1)	1.4	1.0	July to October (according to previous crop and soil type)
Cultivate (often power harrow)	1.0	0.7	March (½ in second half February on light land)
Apply Fertilizer	0.3	0.2	
Drill (often with power harrow), plus roll	1.2	0.8	March (½ at end February on light land)
Top Dress (once, some possibly twice)	0.4	0.2	
Spray (two or three)	0.7	0.3	May
Combine, Cart Grain, Barn Work	2.4	1.8	Last ¾ of August (affected by variety and season)
Later Barn Work (2)	0.6	0.4	September to June
Total	**8.0**	**5.4**	
Straw: Bale (unmanned sledge)	1.3	0.8	Mid-August to end
Cart	3.5	2.6	September

Typical Monthly Breakdown

Month	Average	Premium	Notes
October	0.4	0.3	Ploughing. How much in
November	0.8	0.5	October depends on area
December	0.2	0.2	W. Wheat, Potatoes, etc.
January	—	—	
February	—	—	
March	2.4	1.6	All Cults. Drilling, Rolling, (nearly half in February on light land)
April	—	—	
May	1.1	0.6	Spray and Top dress
June	—	—	
July	—	—	
August(3)	2.4 (+2.6 Straw)	1.8 (+1.8 Straw)	Harvesting
September	— (+2.2 Straw)	— (+1.6 Straw)	

Notes

1. See note 1 on page 136.

2. Later barn work excluded.

3. Spring barley; spring wheat and oats partly September (see page 138).

In a *normal* (i.e. neither early or late) *season*:

WINTER WHEAT
Drilling mid-September to 3rd week October.
Harvesting mid-August to approx. 10th September.

WINTER BARLEY
As for winter wheat, except that:
Ploughing unlikely to start before cereal harvest, as usually follows a cereal crop.
Harvesting some weeks earlier: mid July to approx. 10th August.

WINTER OATS
As for winter wheat, except that:
Drilling usually first full half of October.
Harvesting earlier (late July or first half of August).

SPRING BARLEY
Drilling end of February to end of March or early April.
Harvesting last half/¾ of August.

SPRING WHEAT
As for spring barley, except that:
Drilling is on average one or two weeks earlier (should be finished in March) — lose more if later than barley.

Harvesting, on average, is two weeks later: last week of August/first half of September (two-thirds in September).

SPRING OATS

As for spring barley, except that:

Drilling is usually a little earlier.

Harvesting is later than spring barley, earlier than spring wheat: end of August/beginning of September.

Critical Questions affecting Timing (Autumn-sown Cereals)

1. Previous crops (affects time available and need for ploughing and cultivations).
2. Will the crop be ploughed traditionally, chisel ploughed, minimally cultivated, or direct drilled?
3. Earliest and latest drilling date, by choice.
4. Effect on yield if drilling is delayed.
5. Autumn weed control?
6. In the spring: (a) whether crop is rolled, and when,
                         (b) whether crop is harrowed, and when,
                         (c) time of top dressings,
                         (d) number of spray applications.
7. (a) Average period for harvesting.
   (b) Earliest dates for starting and finishing harvest, and latest dates for starting and finishing harvest, ignoring extreme seasons (one year in ten).

Critical Questions affecting Timing (Spring-sown Cereals)

1. Previous crops.
2. Will the crop be ploughed traditionally, chisel ploughed, minimally cultivated, or direct drilled?
3. Months when winter ploughing is possible, on average. (Where relevant).
4. Is spring ploughing satisfactory? (Where relevant).
5. Average period of cultivations and drilling.
6. Earliest dates for starting and finishing spring cultivations/drilling and latest dates for starting and finishing cultivations/drilling, ignoring extreme seasons (1 year in 10).
7. Effect on yield if drilling is delayed.
8. Is the crop rolled (a) within a few days of drilling or (b) later?
9. (a) Average period of harvesting.
   (b) Earliest dates for starting and finishing harvest, and latest dates for starting and finishing harvest, ignoring extreme seasons (one year in ten).

MAINCROP POTATOES

Operations	Labour-Hours per hectare		Time of Year
	Average	Premium	
Plough...............................	1.4	1.0	September to December
Cultivating, Ridging, Destoning/			
Clod sep. (as required)	6.5	5.0	March, early April
Plant and Apply Fertilizer (1).....	4.5	3.5	Last quarter of March, first
Apply Herbicide	0.3	0.2	three-quarters of April
Spray for Blight (av. 6 times).....	1.2	0.9	July, first half August
Burn off Haulm	0.3	0.2	End September, early
			October
Harvest, Cart, Clamp (2)	15.0	10.0	End September, October
Work on Indoor Clamp	4.8	3.2	November
Riddle, Bag, Load......................	40.0	30.0	October to May
Total	**74.0**	**54.0**	

(1) Automatic planter. Hand-fed planters: approx. 12 hours plus 8 that could be casual labour.

(2) Mechanical harvester, excluding up to 25 hours for picking off on harvester—usually casual labour. None may be needed on clod and stone-free soils. Hand harvesting: additional approx. 80 hours of casual labour.

Typical Monthly Breakdown

Month	Average	Premium	Notes
October	12.2	8.2	80% of harvest, ½ burn off
November	5.9	4.0	Clamp work and ¾ plough
December....................................	0.3	0.2	¼ plough
January.......................................	—	—	
February.....................................	—	—	
March..	7.8	6.0	All fert', ½ cults', ¼ plant
April..	3.5	2.7	½ cult's, ¾ plant
May...	—	—	
June...	—	—	
July..	0.9	0.7	3 blight sprays
August...	0.3	0.2	1 blight spray
September...................................	3.1	2.0	20% harvest, ½ burn off

Note: These figures exclude casual labour and riddling.

EARLY POTATOES

Operations	Labour-Hours per hectare		Time of Year
	Average	Premium	
Plough	1.4 (1)	1.0 (1)	September to December
Cultivating, etc	6.5 (1)	5.0 (1)	Late February, early March
Plant and Apply Fertilizer	4.5 (1)	3.5 (1)	Late February, early March
Apply Herbicide	0.3 (1)	0.2 (1)	1st half March (some in
			February on light land or
			in early season)
Further Spraying.........................	0.3 (1)	0.2 (1)	
After-Cultivation/Spray..............	0.3 (1)	0.2 (1)	April, early May
Harvest, bag, load.......................	30.0 (1)	25.0 (2)	2nd week June onwards.
			All June or till mid-July

(1) Excluding 80 hours picking—usually casuals.

(2) Excluding 60 hours picking—usually casuals.

SECOND EARLY POTATOES

| Operations | Labour-Hours per hectare | | Time of Year |
	Average	Premium	
Plough	1.4 (1)	1.0 (1)	September to December
Cultivating, etc	6.5 (1)	5.0 (1)	March
Plant and Apply Fertilizer	4.5 (1)	3.5 (1)	March
Apply Herbicide	0.3 (1)	0.2 (1)	Half 2nd half March, half 1st half April
Further Spraying	0.9 (1)	0.7 (1)	End April, May, early June
Harvest	15.0 (1)	10.0 (2)	Mid-July to end August

(1) Spinner or elevator-digger, excluding picking and riddling—usually casual labour.

(2) Mechanical harvester, excluding picking off on harvester and riddling—usually casual labour.

SUGAR BEET

| Operations | Labour-Hours per hectare | | Time of Year |
	Average	Premium	
Plough	1.4	1.0	September to December
Seedbed Cults	3.2	2.2	Mainly March (some early April. Some late February in good seasons)
Load, Cart, Apply Fertilizer	0.7	0.4	
Drill (and Flat Roll)	1.8	1.1	Between mid-March and mid-April
Spray (herbicide: pre- and post-emergence)	0.6	0.3	Late March/April
Spray (x 2)	0.6	0.3	May/June
Spray (aphis)	0.3	0.2	July
Harvest (machine)	14.0	9.0	End September, October, November
Load	3.4	2.5	End September to early January
Total	**26.0**	**17.0**	

Typical Monthly Breakdown

Month	Average	Premium	Notes
October	7.2	4.6	45% harvest; + loading
November	8.2	5.3	45% harvest; ¾ ploughing; + loading
December	1.0	0.8	¼ ploughing; + loading
January	0.5	0.4	Loading
February	——	——	
March	3.8	2.3	Fert., most cults., some drilling
April	2.5	1.7	Some cults., most of drilling
May	0.3	0.2	Spray
June	0.3	0.15	Spray
July	0.2	0.15	Spray
August	——	——	
September	2.0	1.4	10% harvesting; + loading

VINING PEAS

Operations	Labour-Hours per hectare		Time of Year
	Average	Premium	
Plough................................	1.4	1.0	September to December
Cults, Fert. and Drill..................	2.3	1.6	Mid-Feb. to April
Post Drilling and Spraying.........	1.5	0.8	
Harvesting................................	19.0	14.0	July and early August
Total.........................	**24.2**	**17.4**	

Note

Drilling is staggered in small areas through the season, ranging from early varieties to late varieties.

DRIED PEAS

Month	Labour-Hours per hectare		Notes
	Average	Premium	
October................................	1.2	0.8	
November................................	0.8	0.5	Stubble cult., Plough
December................................	—	—	
January................................	—	—	
February................................	0.2	0.1	Cult. x 2, harrow; drill & fert.
March................................	2.8	1.9	(80% March); light harrow
April................................	0.6	0.4	roll; and spray
May................................	2.5	1.2	
June................................	0.2	0.2	Scare pigeons; spray
July................................	1.8	1.1	Possible spray desiccant;
August................................	2.2	1.3	combine and cart, dry
September................................	0.5	0.3	Stubble cult.

Assumes direct combining.

FIELD BEANS

A. Winter Beans

Operations	Labour-Hours per hectare		Time of Year
	Average	Premium	
Broadcast Seed............................	0.6	0.4	
Apply Fertilizer............................	0.3	0.2	
Plough................................	1.4	1.0	September/October
Power Harrow............................	1.0	0.8	
Spray (pre-emergence)...............	0.3	0.15	
Spraying (two or three times).....	0.8	0.35	Spring
Combine and cart and			
Barnwork..................................	3.0	2.4	August

B. Spring Beans

Operations	Labour-Hours per hectare		Time of Year
	Average	Premium	
Plough..	1.4	1.0	September to December
Cultivate (often power harrow)..	1.0	0.7	
Apply Fertilizer	0.3	0.2	
Drill, Roll....................................	1.2	0.8	End Feb, early March
Spray (two or three times)..........	0.8	0.4	
Combine and cart and			
Barnwork	3.0	2.4	September

OILSEED RAPE

(Autumn Sown - Desiccated)

Month	Labour-Hours per hectare		Notes
	Average	Premium	
October			
November	0.6	0.3	Spray herbicide and
December..........................			insecticide if necessary
January..............................	—	—	
February............................	—	—	
March.................................			
April..................................	0.8	0.4	Top dress twice
May	—	—	
June...................................	—	—	Desiccate (1st half July);
July....................................	2.4	1.7	combine (½ 2nd half July
August...............................	2.0	1.4	½ 1st half Aug.); dry
August...............................	1.6	0.9	Cults. (x 2), spray, drill, fert.;
September	1.6	0.9	harrow, roll, barn work (0.5)

HERBAGE SEED *(first production year)*

A. Undersown

Operations	Labour-Hours per hectare		Time of Year
	Average	Premium	
Undersow...................................	0.6	0.4	March, April
	⎧ (0.6	(0.4)	Straight after drilling
Roll	⎨ 0.4	0.3	September
	⎩ 0.4	0.3	Late February, March
Harvest (by Combine): Mow......	1.4	0.9	3 to 4 days before combining
Combine and Cart......................	4.5	3.5	Ital. Ryegrasses and Early
			Perennials: late July.
			Intermed. Perennials: late
			July/early August.
			Late Perennials/White
			Clover: mid-August
	6.0	4.5	Meadow Fescue: early July
	7.0	5.0	Cocksfoot: early July
	10.0	7.0	Timothy: mid-August
			Red Clover: late September

B. Direct Drilled in Autumn

Operations	Labour-Hours per hectare		Time of Year
	Average	Premium	
Plough..	1.4	1.0	
Seedbed Cults.............................	2.2	1.6	Depends on previous crop—
Load, Cart, Apply Fertilizer........	0.3	0.2	Usually July or August
Drill (with harrows behind)........	0.8	0.6	As early as previous crop allows. This may be up to mid-Sept for ryegrass without detriment to the yield.
Roll (soon after drilling)............. cocksfoot	0.6	0.4	Meadow fescue and are best sown no later than July and it is risky to sow Timothy much later than this.

GRASS

A. Production

Operations	Labour-Hours per hectare		Time of Year
	Average	Premium	
Plough..	1.4	1.0	Autumn drilling: may not
Seedbed Cults.............................	2.2	1.6	
Load, Cart, Apply Fertilizer........	0.3	0.2	
Drill*..	0.7	0.5	Mid-March to mid-April (1) or end July to mid-Sept.
Roll	0.6	0.4	Soon after drilling
Load, Cart, Apply Fertiliser*:			
(three lots)...................................	0.9	0.6	March to mid-August (2)
Top*..	1.3	0.8	Mid-June to mid-July; if grazed only.

Notes

1. Spring drilling may continue to mid-May to enable extra cleaning cultivations or the application of farmyard manure.

2. P. and K. may be applied in September—especially on undersown ley in year sown.

* Only these operations apply where the seeds are undersown in a spring cereal crop soon after drilling. One extra harrowing and rolling is needed if undersown in an autumn-sown cereal crop.

B. Conservation

Operations	Labour-Hours per hectare Average	Premium	Time of Year
Plough..	1.4	1.0	Autumn drilling: may not
Hay (5.5 tonnes per hectare)			
Mow....................................	1.2	0.9	
Turn, etc...............................	2.6	1.9	Two-thirds June, one-third
Bale......................................	1.3	0.9	July
Cart	6.0	4.5	
Total per hectare..........................	11.1	8.2	
Total per tonne.............................	2.0	1.5	
Silage (17 tonnes per hectare)			
Mow....................................	1.2	0.9	
Turn, etc...............................	0.7	0.5	Two-thirds May, one-third
Load.....................................	2.3	1.7	June
Cart	3.0	2.3	
Clamp	2.3	1.7	
Total per hectare..........................	9.5	7.1	
Total per tonne.............................	0.56	0.42	

Specialized Equipment Prices for Grass Conservation: see page 143.

Typical Monthly Breakdown

A. *Production* (figures averaged over the life of the ley)

	1-year ley undersown in spring		3-year ley undersown in autumn (1)		1-year ley drilled		3-year ley drilled	
	Ave.	Prem.	Ave.	Prem.	Ave.	Prem.	Ave.	Prem.
March..........	0.9	0.5	0.7	0.5	0.6	0.3	0.6	0.3
April............	0.9	0.5	0.7	0.5	0.6	0.3	0.6	0.3
May.............	0.6	0.3	0.6	0.3	0.6	0.3	0.6	0.3
June.............	0.6	0.3	0.6	0.3	0.6	0.3	0.6	0.3
July.............	0.6	0.3	0.6	0.3	0.6	0.3	0.6	0.3
August.........	0.3	0.2	0.3	0.2	5.0	3.4	1.9	1.4
September...	0.6	0.3	0.3	0.2	3.2	2.2	1.4	1.0

Note

1. On land ploughed after a cereal crop, drilled early August to mid-September.

	1-year ley drilled in autumn (1)		3-year ley drilled in spring		Permanent Pasture	
	Ave.	Prem.	Ave.	Prem.	Ave.	Prem.
March.................	3.0	2.1	1.4	1.0	0.6	0.3
April..................	1.8	1.2	0.9	0.7	0.6	0.3
May....................	0.3	0.3	0.6	0.3	0.6	0.3
June...................	0.6	0.3	0.6	0.3	0.6	0.3
July....................	0.6	0.3	0.6	0.3	0.6	0.3
August...............	0.3	0.2	0.2	0.2	0.3	0.2
September..........	—	—	—	0.2	0.2	0.2
October	0.9	0.5	0.6	0.3	—	—
November	1.4	1.0	1.0	0.3	—	—
December...........	0.7	0.5	0.6	0.2	—	—

B. Conservation

	Hay				Silage			
	per hectare		per tonne		per hectare		per tonne	
	Av.	Prem.	Av.	Prem.	Av.	Prem.	Av.	Prem.
May	—	—	—	—	6.3	4.7	0.37	0.28
June	7.4	5.6	1.3	1.0	3.2	2.4	0.19	0.14
July	3.7	2.6	0.7	0.5	—	—	—	—

KALE

(Growing only)

A. Production

	Labour-Hours per hectare		
Operations	Average	Premium	Time of Year
Plough	1.4	1.0	September onwards
Seedbed Cults	2.2	1.6	March, April, early May
Fertilizer	0.3	0.2	April, early May
Drill	1.3	1.0	May
Roll	0.6	0.4	Straight after drilling
Spray (weedkiller)	0.3	0.2	6 weeks after drilling

B. Catch Crop

Kale may be drilled up to the first week of July; the crop will be smaller but either an early bite or silage crop may have been taken from a ley earlier in the year, or the ground may have been fallowed and thoroughly cleaned during the spring and early summer. The smaller crop is also easier to graze using an electric fence.

The above operations will still apply although the times of the year will obviously be different, but there may be an additional three or so rotavations and two or three heavy cultivations if fallowed for the first half of the year or ploughed after an early bite. This means approximately an extra 10 (average) or 8 (premium) man-hours per hectare in April, May, June.

FIELD SCALE VEGETABLES

(Labour hours per hectare unless otherwise stated)

Cabbage Transplanting	Hand 150-160. Spring cabbage, Sept.-Oct.; summer, April; autumn, May-June Machine (3.5 gang). Spring cabbage 75, summer 85, autumn 100. Pulling and dipping plants. 20 per hectare transplanted.
Cabbage Harvesting	Early spring cabbage, 210, Feb.-April; hearted spring, 250, April-June; summer, 220, June-July; autumn, 220, Oct.-Dec.
Brussels Sprouts Transplanting	45 (machine) to 55 (hand), May-June.
Brussels Sprouts Picking	320-400: picked over 3-5 times, maximum approx. 3 hectares per picker per season. Early sprouts, Aug.-Dec.; late, Nov.-Mar.
Peas Hand Pulling	475-525 (150 per tonne). Early, June; maincrop, July-Aug.
Runner Beans (Picked)	Harvesting. 625 (175 per tonne), July-Sept.
Runner Beans (Stick)	Harvesting. 675, July-Sept.
Runner Beans (Stick)	Erecting Canes and String. 100-150, May-June.

Carrot Harvesting.	Elevator-digger: 260 (1 man + 12 casuals, 20 hours per hectare). Earlies, July-Aug.; maincrop, Sept.-Feb. Harvester: 30 (3 men, 10 hours per hectare). Riddle and Grade: (1° per tonne), Dec.-Feb.
Beetroot Harvest and Clamp.	25, Oct.-Dec. 12-15 man-hours per tonne to wash and pack.

Source: The Farm as a Business, Aids to Management, Section 6: Labour and Machinery (M.A.F.F.). (N.B. This data is now very dated, but it is still the latest known to the author.)

4. LABOUR FOR FIELDWORK

Gang Sizes and Rates of Work

Basic information on Rates of Work is given on pages 153-156, where both 'average' and 'premium' rates for many operations are listed.

The following data relate to rates of work with gangs of different sizes. The rates of work are averages for good and bad conditions throughout the season, including preparation time and travelling to the field, and assume an 8-hour day, unless otherwise stated. Obviously these rates can be exceeded by overtime work in the evenings.

Combine Harvesting

Gang size can vary from 1 to 4 men per combine (excluding straw baling) according to the number of men available, size and type of combine, distance from grain store, crop yield, type of grain drier, and degree of automation in the grain store. The main possibilities are:

1 man: all jobs (trailer in field)
2 men: 1 combining, 1 carting and attending to grain store
3 men: 1 combining, 2 carting and attending to grain store
3 men: 1 combining, 1 carting, 1 attending to grain store
4 men: 1 combining, 2 carting, 1 attending to grain store

Three men is most typical, although two is quite feasible with a fully automated grain store with in-bin or floor drying, unless transport times are excessive owing to distance or lack of good connecting roads. Four men is most usual with two combines, but an extra man may be needed with a continuous drier.

Except in the case of the small area cereal producer operating on his own, the rate of work will normally depend on the speed of the combine, sufficient tractors and trailers being provided to ensure that combining does not have to stop because of their absence.

Assuming a 9-hour combining day, typical rates of work are:

Size of combine (metres cut)	No. of Men	Ha/day
3 to 4.2	1	4.5 to 7.75
	2 or 3	6 to 10
4.25 to 5.4	2 or 3	8 to 12
5.5 and over	3 or 4	10 to 15

Straw Carting

2 men, 1 or 2 tractors and trailers 'traditional system'	2.5 to 3.25 ha a day
3 men, 1 to 3 tractors and trailers	3.25 ha a day
1 man, 1 tractor with front and rear carriers	2.5 ha a day
2 men, flat 8/10 accumulator mechanised system	10 to 15 ha a day
2 or 3 men, big bale system	8 to 15 ha a day

Potato Planting

Hand planting (chitted seed) 3 men, 16 women	2 ha a day
Hand planting (unchitted seed) 2 men, 12 women	2 ha a day
(women working a 6-hour day only)	
2-row planter (chitted seed) 3 workers	1 ha a day
3-row planter (chitted seed) 4 or 5 workers	1.75 ha a day
2-row planter (unchitted seed) 3 workers	1.5 ha a day
3-row planter (unchitted seed) 4 workers	2.25 ha a day
2-row automatic planter (unchitted seed) 1 worker	2.5 ha a day
(part-time help loading and carting seed additional; this may be	
full time if fertilizer is applied with an attachment to the planter)	

Potato Harvesting

Hand harvesting (piecework) 3 to 5 men, 10 to 15 women	0.65 to 0.85 ha a day
(women working a 6-hour day only)	
Machine harvesting (1-row) 4 men, 3 women	0.65 to 0.9 ha a day
Machine harvesting (2-row) 5 men, 3 women	1 to 1.5 ha a day
(lower end of range for heavy land, upper end for light land	
and good work organization)	

Potato Riddling

3 to 5 workers	10 to 15 tonnes a day

Sugar Beet Harvesting (1-row)

Gang can vary from 1 to 5 (1 or 2 on harvester, 2 or 3 carting, 1 at clamp) but is usually 3 or 4.

3 or 4 men	0.9 ha a day
2 men	0.8 ha a day
1 man	0.7 ha a day
(add 20% for light loams and silts)	

Vining Peas

Drilling (2 men)	7 to 10 ha a day
2.5-3 m. cutter (1 man)	2 ha a day
Pea pod picker, and carting, 5 or 6 men	0.4 ha a day
(large-scale growers: two 12 hour shifts worked per day)	

Carting Hay Bales

2 men, 1 or 2 tractors and trailers	7 to 9 tonnes a day
3 men, 1 to 3 tractors and trailers	9 to 14 tonnes a day

Silage-Making with Forage Harvester (excl. mowing but inc. clamping; 15 tonne/ha crop)

1 man gang (1)	1.25 ha a day
2 man gang (1,3)	2.25 ha a day
3 man gang (1,3)	3.5 ha a day
4 man gang (2,3)	4.5 ha a day
(1) trailers towed behind, in line	
(2) trailers towed alongside	
(3) man with buckrake at clamp full-time	

Farmyard Manure Spreading

1 man: front loader and mechanical spreader	28 tonnes a day
4 men: front loader and 3 mechanical spreaders	90 tonnes a day

5. LABOUR FOR LIVESTOCK

DAIRY COWS

Herd size (no. of cows)	60	80	100 or more
	hours per cow per month		
January	3.3	2.9	2.5
February	3.3	2.9	2.5
March	3.3	2.9	2.5
April	3.0	2.7	2.4
May	2.7	2.4	2.2
June	2.7	2.4	2.1
July	2.7	2.4	2.1
August	2.7	2.4	2.1
September	2.7	2.4	2.2
October	3.0	2.8	2.4
November	3.3	2.9	2.5
December	3.3	2.9	2.5
Total per cow per year	36	32	28
Total hours per year	2160	2560	2800
Total hours per week	42	49	54
Total cost per annum	£22,070	£26,380	£29,630*
Total cost per week	£424	£507	£570*
Total cost per cow per annum	**£368**	**£330**	**£297***
Cost per litre: 6000 litres/cow	6.13p	5.50p	4.95p
Cost per litre: 6500 litres/cow	5.66p	5.08p	4.57p
Cost per litre: 6650 litres/cow	5.53p	4.96p	4.47p
Cost per litre: 7000 litres/cow	5.26p	4.71p	4.24p
Cost per litre: 7500 litres/cow	4.91p	4.40p	3.96p
Cost per litre: 8000 litres/cow	4.60p	4.13p	3.71p
Cost per litre: 8500 litres/cow	4.14p	3.88p	3.49p
Cost per litre: 9000 litres/cow	4.09p	3.67p	3.30p

* For more than 100 cows per man (i.e. without additional help) the cost per week per additional cow is likely to be in the order of £2 per week (approx. £100 per annum), with the cost per cow per annum falling by around £1. Labour hours per cow will fall very little.

Note

These *costs* (note, not *earnings*) are *estimates for 2008* and are based on the average number of *direct* hours of work per cow for different herd sizes obtained from University costings; they do not include fieldwork, such as hay and silage making. The costs include craftsman addition and any other premiums paid, overtime, national insurance payments, and holidays with pay. They also include the cost of relief milking, including during annual holidays.

Earnings. The average earnings of all 'dairy herdsmen' in 2008 are estimated to be approximately £24,871 a year (£479 for an average 53-hour week).

DAIRY FOLLOWERS AND BEEF

Note

No recent survey work has been published on labour requirements for beef animals and dairy followers. The following data can therefore only be taken as 'best estimates'. They are for average performance under average conditions, excluding fieldwork (see page 228, note 5). Substantial variations can occur from farm to farm, e.g. through economies of scale with widely differing herd sizes.

A. *Calves* (per head, early weaning)

Age Group	Labour hours per month	
	Average	Premium
0-3 months..	2.3	1.6
3-6 months..	0.9	0.6
(av. 0-6 months...	1.6	1.1)
6-12 months, yarded.....................................	1.1	0.8
6-12 months, summer grazed..........................	0.3	0.2
(av. 0-12 months, during winter (1).................	1.3	0.9)
(av. 0-12 months, during summer (1).................	0.9	0.6)

Note

1. Assuming 6 to 12-month olds housed in winter and grazed in summer, and calvings or calf purchases fairly evenly spaced throughout the year.

B. *Stores* (per head)

Yearling, housed.....................................	1.0	0.7
2 year olds and over, housed......................	1.4	0.8
Outwintered store..................................	0.7	0.5
12 months and over, summer grazed.............	0.2	0.1

C. *Dairy Followers*

(Per 'replacement unit', i.e. calf + yearling + in-calf heifer.) (1)

During winter.......................................	2.9	2.0
During summer......................................	1.2	0.8

Note

1. Assuming calvings fairly evenly spaced throughout the year and heifers calving at 2 to 2.5 years old.

D. *Beef Finishing* (per head)

Housed...	1.8	1.2
Summer Grazed.....................................	0.2	0.1
Intensive Beef (0-12 months).....................	1.3	1.0

E. *Suckler Herds (per cow)*

Lowland Single suckling (av. whole year)......	0.9	0.6
Lowland Multiple suckling (av. whole year)...	2.9	2.1
Upland/Hill Single suckling (av. whole year)...	1.1	0.7

SHEEP
(per ewe)

	Labour hours per month	
	Average	Premium (4)
January	0.3	0.2
February	0.3	0.2
March	1.0 (1)	0.7
April	0.4	0.25
May	0.3	0.2
June	0.4 (2)	0.3
July	0.2	0.15
August	0.2	0.15
September	0.25	0.15
October	0.25	0.15
November	0.2	0.15
December	0.2	0.15
Total	4.0 (3)	2.75

1. Assuming mainly March lambing.
2. 0.3 if shearing is by contract.
3. A full-time shepherd, i.e. one who did no other work on the farm, would have to have a flock of at least 600 ewes for the average 4 hours per ewe per year to be achieved, assuming full-time assistance during lambing time.
4. In a national survey conducted in 1999 the average annual requirement for flocks exceeding 500 ewes was 2.9 hours.

PIGS

	Labour hours per month	
Age Group	Average	Premium
Breeding and Rearing, per sow	1.5	1.20
(Average 130 sows per worker, Premium 160)		
Feeding only, per 10 pigs	1.6	1.25
No. at a time, per worker:		
Average 1,200 per man, Premium 1,600		
No. per year, per worker:		
Average: 6,000 porkers, 4,800 cutters, 4,450 baconers		
Premium: 8,000 porkers, 6,400 cutters, 5,750 baconers		
Breeding, Rearing and Feeding, per sow (with progeny)		
Porkers, average 90 sows per worker, premium 110	2.4	2.0
Cutters, average 80-85 sows per worker, premium 100-105	2.6	2.1
Baconers, average 75-80 sows per worker, premium 95-100	2.8	2.2

POULTRY
(large scale, automated)

	Labour hours per month
Laying hens: battery cages (18,000 per full-time worker)	1.1 per 100
free range	4 per 100
Broilers: 32,500 at a time per full-time worker*	
(225,000 a year)	1.0 per 100

* N.B. additional help needed for catching and cleaning out (included in labour hours per month)

V. MACHINERY

1. AGRICULTURAL MACHINERY PRICES

(Estimated Spring 2008 prices for new machinery, net of discounts and ex. V.A.T.)

1. *Tractors*

(a) *Two-Wheel Drive*

£

43-49 kW (57-66 hp)	17,000-20,000
50-56 kW (67-75 hp)	18,000-22,700
57-66 kW (76-89 hp)	20,500-25,000
67-75 kW (90-100 hp)	22,700-27,000

(b) *Four- Wheel Drive*

43-50 kW (57-67 hp)	16,400-24,000
56-65 kW (75-87 hp)	22,700-28,000
66-75 kW (88-100 hp)	28,000-32,500
76-90 kW (101-120 hp)	31,000-39,000
94-105 kW (125-140 hp)	37,500-46,700
115-134 kW (154-180 hp)	46,700-56,700
140-165 kW (187-220 hp)	54,600-60,000
170-200 kW (228-268 hp)	69,700-80,000

(c) *High Road Speed*

15-130 kW (155-175 hp)	51,000-62,500
140-165 kW (188-221 hp)	62,500-72,800

(d) *Crawlers*

175-225 kW (230-300 hp) rubber track	112,000-123,000
225-300 kW (340-400 hp) rubber track	129,000-150,000
336-410 kW (450-550 hp) rubber track	156,000-172,000

2. *Cultivating Equipment*

£

(a) *Ploughs*

	Fixed width	Variable width	
		Mechanical Adjustment	Hydraulic Adjustment
Reversible:			
3-furrow	6,100-6,700	6,700-8,500	—
4-furrow	7,100-8,000	7,800-10,600	10,600-13,800
5-furrow	8,000-9,000	9,100-12,000	12,400-16,000
6-furrow		11,700-15,000	14,000-17,500
6-furrow (semi-mounted)		13,800-15,900	15,700-15,500
7-furrow (semi-mounted)		14,800-17,000	16,400-20,800
8-furrow (semi-mounted)		19,000-21,200	19,600-23,800
9-furrow (semi-mounted)			22,800-27,600

(b) *Furrow Presses*

1.6-1.8 m double row	2,400-2,900
2.0-2.4 m double row	2,800-3,800
2.6-3.0 m double row	3,600-5,300
3.2-3.6 m double row	5,300-6,600
3.8-4.0 m double row	6,400-7,400
Front Press Arm – hydraulic	1,200-1,300

(c) *Front Presses (excluding linkage)*

1.5 m single row	1,900-2,100
3.0 m single row	2,900-4,000
4.0 m single row — hydraulic folding	4,300-5,300

(d) *Front Press Linkage*

1.5 to 2.0 tonne..	1,600-1,900
3.5 to 5.5 tonne..	2,200-2,800

(e) *Other Cultivating Equipment*

Sub Soiler 2-3 leg		2,100-2,700
Soil Looseners	(3 m)......................................	4,900-5,900
	(4 m)......................................	7,600-8,700
Vibrating Compaction Breaker	(2-2.5m)	5,600-6,600
	(3 m)...................	7,600-8,700
Straw Incorporating Disc Cultivator	(2.5-3 m)	6,200-7,200
Stubble Cultivator	(3 m):.....................................	4,300-4,900
(heavy duty)	(4 m): hydraulic folding..........	7,600-8,700
	(6 m): hydraulic folding..........	11,000-13,300
Spring-tine Cultivator	(3-4 m):	1,800-2,600
	(5-6 m): hydraulic folding.......	4,900-5,900
Combination Harrows	(2.5-4 m)...............................	3,700-5,800
	(5-6 m): hydraulic folding.......	9,900-10,600
Levelling Harrows	(2.5-4.2 m).............................	1,300-2,100
	(3.7-6.1 m): hydraulic folding	3,300-4,900
Disc Harrows	(2.7-3.6 m): trailed	9,900-10,900
	(4.25-6.25 m): trailed, , folding	17,500-25,500
Harrows (5-6 m): light-medium, hydraulic folding		2,100-2,500
Rotovator	(up to 100 kW tractor)	5,800-6,900
	(150 kW tractor)....................	9,500-10,600
Power Harrow (with crumbler roller)		
	(2.5-3 m).................................	5,300-6,000
	(3.5-4m).................................	7,500-8,800
	(5-6m): folding........................	16,500-18,500
Roller Packer for power harrow	(2.5-4 m)	1,100-1,500
	(5-6 m)	1,800-2,500
Rolls: triple gang, hydraulic folding	(6 m)......................	5,800-6,900
five gang, " "	(12m)	14,000-15,300

3. *Fertilizer Distributors, Seed Drills, Sprayers* £

(a) *Fertilizer Distributors*

Mounted Spinners

(500-750 litre)...	1,300-1,800
(700-1,200 litre): twin disc, hydraulic control1	1,900-2,400
(1,300-1,700 litre): twin disc, hydraulic control	3,200-3,500
(1,650-2,300 litre): twin disc, electronic control........	5,300-5,800
(3,200 litre): twin disc, electronic control	6,900-7,100
Bag lifter (850-1,000kg)..	1,300-1,600

(b) *Seed Drills*

Grain: mounted	3 m, gravity fed, 25 row..........	5,300-6,600
	3-4 m, pneumatic, 24-32 row..	10,900-13,300
	6 m, pneumatic, 48 row	21,700-25,500

(c)   *Combined Cultivator and Pneumatic Drill*

3-4 m, 24-32 row	15,400-18,500
6 m, 48 row	31,000-35,000

(d)   *Combined Power Harrow and Pneumatic Drill*

3-4 m, 24-32 row	16,400-22,000
6 m, 48 row	38,000-43,500

(e)   *Direct Drill*

6m, 32 chisel openers	54,000-60,000

(f)   *Sprayers*

Mounted, 400 litre tank, 6 m boom	1,700-2,100
Mounted, 600-800 litre tank, 12 m boom	3,200-3,600
Mounted, 1,000-1,300 litre tank, 20-24 m hydraulic boom..	13,100-16,500
Mounted, Air Assisted, 1,000 litre tank, 18 m boom	18,500-22,000
Trailed, Air Assisted, 2,500-3,000 litre tank, 24 m boom	33,000-38,000
Trailed, 2,500-3,000 litre tank 18-24 m boom	24,500-27,500
Trailed, 3,000-3,500 litre tank 24-30 m boom	28,500-33,000
Self-propelled, 24-36 m boom, 4-wheel drive	64,000-76,000

4.   *Grass Conservation and Handling Equipment*   £

(a)   *Silage Equipment*

Forage Harvester: trailed, precision chop	21,000-27,500
Self-propelled (3 m pick-up 280-375 hp)	106,000-120,000
Maize attachment, 4-6 row	21,000-27,500
Silage Trailer, 10 tonne, tandem axle	5,800-6,900
Silage Trailer, 12 tonne, tandem axle	6,500-8,200
Buckrake (push off)	1,700-1,900

(b)   *Haymaking Equipment*

Mower (1.6-1.8 m, 2 drum)	2,000-2,700
Mower (2.0-2.4 m, 5-6 disc)	3,600-4,100
Mower (disc) Conditioner, mounted (2.4-3.2 m)	7,400-8,500
Mower (disc) Conditioner, trailed (2.8-3.2 m)	11,700-12,700
Tedder (5-7 m, 4-6 rotors)	3,700-5,800
Windrower, (3.9-4.2 m)	3,500-4,000
Balers and Bale Handling: see 5(c) and (d) below	

(c)   *Silage Handling Equipment*

Silage shear bucket (1-1.2 m)	1,900-2,800
Silage grab	1,400-1,800
Big Bale Silage Feeder, mounted	5,300-6,900
Diet-feeder Wagon (8-14 m)	18,500-22,800
Clamp Silage Mixer (12-18m^3)	17,500-22,800

5.   *Grain and Straw Harvesting and Handling Equipment*   £

(a)   *Combines*

Engine size kW (hp)	Cutterbar width metres (feet)	
150-165 (200-220)	4.5-5.0 (14-16)	89,400-93,800
165-185 (220-249)	4.5-5.5 (14-18)	94,700-130,000
186-223 (250-299)	5.4-6.1 (18-20)	103,500-140,700
223-298 (300-399)	6.0-7.7 (20-25)	125,000-198,000
Over 300 (400 up to 530)	9.0-9.15 (29-30)	188,000-290,000

(b)	*Yield monitoring/mapping*	6,500-8,000

(c) *Pick-up Balers (twine tying)*

Small rectangular bales	8,500-9,500
Small rectangular bales, heavy duty models	10,600-12,700
Big round bales, twine tying	14,800-15,900
Big round bales, twine tying and net wrap	14,800-18,000
High density rectangular bales	58,000-64,000

(d) *Bale Wrappers*

Big Bale Wrapper: mounted/trailed	8,500-9,600
Big Square Bale Wrapper: mounted	12,700-13,800
Combined Baler and Wrapper	35,000-41,000
Bale Trailers, 5-8 tonne	2,600-3,500
Accumulator, flat 8, mechanical	1,800-2,300
Loader, flat 8	750-1,000
Big Bale Spike	185-270
Big Bale Handler	550-800
Big Bale Shredder, silage or straw	5,300-6,400

(e) *Drying, Handling, Food Processing Equipment*

Grain driers and Grain storage: see pages 163 and 181	
Cleaner/grader, 10-20 tonnes/hour	8,000-11,300
Grain augers 100 mm, 3.3-7.3 m	500-650
Grain augers 150 mm, 6-8.5 m, with trolley	1,600-2,000
Grain conveyors, (25-50t/hour)	1,300-1,600 + 120-150 per m
Specific gravity separator, (5-10t/hour)	12,700-15,000
Bucket elevator, (25-50t/hour)	1,750-2,300 + 150-200 per m
Hammer mill, 7.5-15 kW	2,900-3,200
Roller mill, 4-5.5 kW	2,500-2,900
Mixer, 750-1000 kg	3,200-3,700
Mill and mixer, 1,000-1,300kg, 3.7-5.5 kW	5,300-6,400
Grain weigher, 25 tonne/hour	1,600-1,900

6. *Potato, Sugar Beet and Vegetable Machinery* £

(a) *Potato Machinery*

Stone separator, 1.6 m (1 bed)		35,000-40,000
Bedformer, 2 row		3,200-3,500
Bed cultivator, 1.7-1.8 m (1 bed)		6,600-7,100
Planter:	2 row mounted	8,500-10,600
	4 row mounted	26,500-30,000
Haulm pulveriser:	2 row	5,300-6,000
	2 row cross conveyor	8,200-9,200
Elevator-Digger,	2 row	5,300-6,000
Harvesters (trailed):	1 row, 2-3 tonne bunker	32,000-38,000
	2 row, elevator manned/unmanned	58,000-69,000
	2 row, 6 tonne bunker	75,000-88,000
Store loader (heavy duty)		19,800-23,300
Flat belt conveyor, 3-8 m		1,800-3,000
Soil elevator (rubber belt)		5,500-6,000
Self-unloading hopper, 3-5 tonnes		8,000-9,000
Clod separator		8,000-9,000
Sizer, 5-30 tonnes/hour		8,000-12,000

Sponge drier, 0.9-1.2m			11,000-12,000
Barrel washer, 8-10 tonnes/hour			16,000-18,000
Roller inspection table, 1.2 x 2.4 m			3,000-3,500
Weigher, automatic, 8-10 tonnes/hour			5,000-6,000
Box tipper with cross conveyor			14,000-16,000
Box filer, automatic			12,000-13,000
Bag stitcher (hand held)			800-1,000
Complete out of store grading line:	20 tonnes/hour		30,000-37,000
	30 tonnes/hour		70,000-75,000
Box filler (30 tonnes/hour)			11,000-13,500

(b) *Sugar Beet Machinery*

Precision Drill:	6 row (pneumatic)		8,500-10,000
	12 row-18 row (pneumatic)		17,000-26,500
Hoe:	6 row-12 row (heavy duty)		5,600-10,600
Harvesters:	Trailed, 2 row, tanker		53,000-58,000
	Trailed, 3 row, tanker		64,000-70,000
	Trailed, 4 row, tanker		74,000-80,000
Self-propelled, 6 row (including power unit), 18 tonne tank			254,000-286,000
Cleaner-loader, with engine, 1-3 tonnes per minute			21,000-24,000
Fodder beet harvester			5,800-6,400

(c) *Vegetable Machinery*

Onion windrower			7,800-9,000
Root crop digger:	1 webb		5,500-6,000
	2 webbs		6,400-7,500
Top lifting vegetable harvester:	single row, bunker		42,000-48,000
	twin row, bunker/elevator		74,000-90,000
	four row, elevator		95,000-112,000
	four row, self-propelled		254,000-275,000
Leek harvester (mounted)			15,900-26,500

7. *General* £

Trailer, 4 tonne tipping	2,000-2,300
Trailer, 5-6 tonne tipping; grain/silage	2,700-3,200/3,200-3,700
Trailer, 10 tonne tipping, tandem axle; grain/silage	4,800-5,300/5,800-6,300
F.Y.M. Spreaders, (4-6 tonne)	3,200-3,700
F.Y.M. Spreaders, (6-8 tonne)	4,200-5,300
Loaders, front mounted	3,700-4,200
Pallet loader, self levelling (1,000-1,600 kg)	4,200-5,300
Materials Handler, telescopic boom (2.5-3.0 tonne)	34,000-40,000
Skid steer loader (500-600 kg)	14,000-16,000
Slurry Stores (metal), including base for 120 day storage period for:	
100 cows	£230 per cow
200 cows	£210 per cow
400 cows	£185 per cow
Vacuum Tankers (5,000-6,000 litre)	4,200-4,700
Low Ground Pressure Tankers (9,000-11,000 litre)	9,000-10,600
Slurry pump	3,200-3,700
Cattle crush	900-1,200
Cattle crush with weigher	1,700-1,900
Cattle trailer (twin-axle)	1,900-2,500
Yard scrapers	550-700

Rotary brush (2-2.5 m)	1,500-1,900
Grassland roll, ballastable (2.5-3 m)	900-1,100
Pasture topper (2.0-3.0 m)	1,900-2,700
Hedger: hydraulic angling; flail head	9,700-12,000
Ditcher: fully slewing	7,500-8,500
Carrier box	500-600
Post hole digger/driver	1,000-1,300/1,600-2,500
Saw bench	1,600-1,800
Log splitter	650-800

2. TYPICAL CONTRACTORS' CHARGES, AVERAGE FARMERS' COSTS, AND RATES OF WORK FOR VARIOUS FARM OPERATIONS

Contractors' charges vary widely according to many factors: those given below are estimates for 2008. Farmer-contractors often charge less, since their overheads and machinery fixed costs are largely covered by their own farming operations, but the service may not always be so complete, including specialist advice.

Farmers' own costs (which include the value of the farmers' own manual labour) vary even more widely; those given below (estimated for Spring 2008) are averages in every respect — covering different types of soil, size of farm, and so on; they are based on accounting cost procedures in that labour, tractor and machinery fuel, repairs and depreciation are included — but no allowance has been added for general farm overheads, interest on capital, supervision/management or under-occupied labour during slack times. They assume four-wheel drive 75-90 kW (100-120 hp) tractors for ploughing, heavy cultivation and other work with a high power requirement. Four-wheel drive 55-65 kW (75-87 hp) tractors are assumed to be used for most other operations. The figures should not be used for partial budgeting.

For a typical set of farm operations, excluding harvesting, the breakdown of the farmers' costs averages very approximately one third each for labour, tractors and implements/machines. The larger the farm, the lower the labour element and the higher the machine element, and vice versa. However the input from contractors may affect these costs.

The contract charges and average farmers' costs are put side-by-side for tabular convenience, not to facilitate comparisons. Apart from the fact that contractors' charges must cover expenses omitted from the farmers' cost, the advisability or otherwise of hiring a contractor for a particular job depends on many factors, varying widely according to farm circumstances; furthermore, there are advantages and disadvantages not reflected in a cost comparison alone.

Machinery rings. Prices charged by farmers offering services through machinery rings are extremely variable but are generally between average farmers' costs and contractors' charges. There are exceptions, which mainly relate to relatively expensive items of machinery (e.g. precision drills, destoners and combine harvesters), where the charges for services offered through machinery rings are close to and often less than average farmers' costs.

Four-wheel drive 120-150 kW (150-200 hp) tractors are assumed where appropriate to achieve the 'Premium' rates of work (which will be achieved on most farms with more than 200 hectares (500 acres) of arable land); obviously, still larger wheeled tractors and crawlers could achieve still faster rates of work, particularly on light land. The rates of work include preparation, travelling to and from the fields and allow for minor breakdowns and other stoppages. See further page 131, first paragraph.

All charges and costs below are per hectare unless otherwise stated.

Operation	Contract	Average Farmer's Cost	Rate of Work (Ha per 8 Hr day)	
			Average	Premium
	£	£		
Cultivations				
Ploughing (light/heavy soils)	37.10-43.90	43.75-57.00	5-6½	7½-9
with furrow press	Extra £5.00	50.00-66.75	4½-6¾	7-8½
Deep Ploughing (over 300 mm)	48.00-52.00	69.00-86.00	3-3¾	5-6½

Operation	Contract	Average Farmer's Cost	Rate of Work (Ha per 8 Hr day)	
			Average	Premium
	£	£		
Rotovating	59.90-65.00	74.00	4½	6
			(ploughed land)	
		112.00 (grass)	3	4
Subsoiling	46.90	39.40	6	10
Stubble Cultivating	25.30	21.60	12	16
Heavy Disc Cultivating	28.40	31.10	10	15
Disc Harrowing	22.20	16.20	12	16
Power Harrowing	32.00	30.00	10	15
Spring tine Harrowing	22.20	16.60	12	18
Seedbed Harrowing	17.90	13.60	12	20
Rolling (flat 3-4 tonne)	19.20	23.30	6	10
(ring, set of 3, 6 m)	13.00	12.40	15	25
Fertilizer Distributing (including loading and carting):				
Broadcast (125-375 kg/ha)	9.00-11.50 (fert. in field)	6.40	30	60
Broadcast (500-750 kg/ha)	—	10.10	22.5	45
Broadcast (1,000-1,250 kg/ha).	—	15.20	15	30
Pneumatic (125-375 kg/ha)	—	14.50	25	40
Drilling:				
Cereals : conventional	25.30	21.20	14	18
Cereals : combi-drilling	39.50	37.40	10	14
Direct drilling	37.10	15.90	11	15
Roots/Maize (inc. fertiliser)	33.40-38.00	64.90	3½ (4 row)	5 (6 row)
Sugar Beet—precision drill	39.50	38.00	6 (6 row)	10 (12 row)
Destoning potato land	148-214.00	188.10	3.25	4
Potato Planting automatic	—	126.40	2½ (2 row)	3½
Potato Ridging	36.50-46.50	30.10	5½	7
Spraying (excl. materials):				
(extra £1-£2 for < 20ha)	11.10-15.00			
Low Volume (up to 175 l/ha)	—	8.00	35	75
Medium Vol. (200-300 l/ha)	—	9.30	30	60
High Volume (over 800 l/ha)	—	16.80	25	50
Tractor Hoeing Sugar Beet	—	37.90	5	8
Combine Harvesting:				
Combine Harvesting Cereals:			(hectares per hour)	
100 ha/year		121.00	¾-1	1-1¾
200 ha/year	71.70 - 75.00	78.50	1	1½
300 ha/year		68.30	1½	2
600 ha/year		59.00	2¾	3¼
Carting to barn add	11.10	17.70/hr		
Straw Chopper incorporated	4.90			

Operation	Contract £	Average Farmer's Cost £	Rate of Work (Ha per 8 Hr day)	
			Average	Premium
Straw chopping (sep. operation).	24.10			
Oilseed rape (direct)	71.70	as cereals + 10%	⅔-1	¾-1¼
Beans	71.70	as cereals + 10%	⅔-1	¾-1¼
Peas	72.90	As cereals	¾-1	1-1½
Windrowing Oilseed Rape	34.60	—	1.2	1.4
Pick-up Baling (incl. string)	27p per bale	23.0p Per bale	0.8 per hour	1.25 per hour
Big Baling (round)	1.70-1.90 per 150x100 cm bale	1.84 per bale	—	—
Crop Drying (inc. intake and pre-cleaning) (per tonne)				
Cereals:				
by 6 per cent	13.50	9.90	—	—
by 10 per cent	17.75	12.50	—	—
Oilseed Rape:				
by 5 per cent	18.75	12.00	—	—
by 10 per cent	24.00	15.60	—	—
Cleaning without drying (£/t)	8.50	—	—	—
Mobile Seed Cleaning (cereals)				
(per tonne) (inc. chemicals)	69-100	—	—	—
Grain Storage (per tonne per week)	32p	(see page 168)	—	—
Handling into store (per tonne)	£1.50	£1.30		
Handling out of store (per tonne)	£1. 50	£1.30		
Potato Harvesting	£63/hour (2-row unmanned)	—	0.75	2
Sugar Beet Complete Harvesting	175	191	3.5	4.5
	(excl. carting)			
	195	218		
	(incl. carting)			
Grass Mowing/Topping				
(inc. Set-aside)	21.00	23.50	8	12
Swath Turning/Tedding	11.70	15.80	11	15
Forage Harvesting:				
First cut	51.90	—	—	—
Other cuts	42.00	—	—	—
Forage harvesting, carting and ensiling grass				
First cut	103.80	—	—	—
Other cuts	89.00	—	—	—
carting and ensiling maize				
25-30 tonnes/ha	129.70	—	—	—
F.Y.M.: Tractor and Spreader	27.25/hr per hour	—	—	—

Operation	Contract	Average Farmer's Cost	Rate of Work (Ha per 8 Hr day)	
			Average	Premium
	£	£		
F.Y.M.: Tractor and Loader	21.00 per hour	—	—	—
Lime Spreading	4.00 Per tonne	—	—	—
Hedge Cutting	19.50 per hour			
Tractor Hire (inc. driver and fuel):	Per hour			
2 wheel drive, 56 kW (75 h.p.)	17.50	—	—	—
2 wheel drive, 75 kW (100 h.p.)	18.75	—	—	—
4 wheel drive, 75 kW (100 h.p.)	21.25	—	—	—
4 wheel drive, 112 kW (150 h.p.)	22.25	—	—	—
Trailer (with driver and tractor)	24.00 per hour	17.70 per hour	—	—

Acknowledgement. The above estimates for contractors' charges are based in part on information kindly supplied by the National Association of Agricultural Contractors.

Contract Charge for All Operations (Cereals and Combinable Break Crops, 'stubble to stubble' i.e. up to and including Combine Harvesting and Carting the Grain to Store): £220 to £270/ha (£90-110/acre). Variations depend upon such factors as distance away, area contracted, size of fields, type of terrain, quality of soil and level of inputs (as affecting weight of crop to be harvested and carted). The charge is most typically £235 to £247/ha (£95-£100/acre).

Management Agreements. The contract charge can be as low as £200/ha (£80/acre) where a proportion of the profit is also taken by the contractor or a neighbouring farmer after payment of a prior charge to the landowner. This was usually between £220 and £270/ha (£90-£100/acre) in 1995-8, but is now likely to average £200 to £210/ha (£80-£85/acre) owing to the fall in farm profitability. The percentage share of total gross margin less these two deductions has been typically 70%-80% to the contractor and 20%-30% to the landowner.

One sometimes sees farmers' total power and machinery costs compared with stubble to stubble contractors' charges. It has of course to be remembered that the former include many cost items not included in the latter, e.g. the cost of farm vehicles, fixed plant such as grain stores and general farm maintenance.

Total Cultivations cost typically £75/ha (£30/acre) on light land, £110/ha (£45/acre) on heavy land.

Haulage Costs
Great Britain average costs per tonne in December 2004, 2005 and 2006 are summarised as follows:

	2004	2005	2006
10 miles	£4.05	£4.29	£4.09
20 miles	£4.52	£4.77	£4.57
40 miles	£5.47	£5.74	£5.53
60 miles	£6.42	£6.71	£6.50
100 miles	£8.31	£8.65	£8.43
150 miles	£10.68	£11.08	£10.84

(Home-Grown Cereals Authority).

3. TRACTOR HOURS

(per annum)

A. Crops	per hectare	
	Average	Premium
Cereals	9	7
Straw Harvesting	3.5	2.5
Potatoes	25	15
Sugar Beet	20	12
Vining Peas	20	12
Dried Peas	10	8
Field Beans	9	7
Oilseed Rape	9	7
Herbage Seeds:		
1 year undersown or 3 year direct drilled	7	5
1 year direct drilled	11	8
Hops (machine picked)	125	—
Kale (grazed)	8	6
Turnips/Swedes: folded/lifted	12/35	10/25
Mangolds	50	35
Fallow	12	7
Ley Establishment:		
Undersown	2	1
Direct Seed	7	4
Making Hay	12	8
Making Silage:		
1st Cut	12	8
2nd Cut	9	6
Grazing:		
Temporary Grass	3	2.5
Permanent Grass	2	1.5

B. Livestock	per head Average
Dairy Cows	6
Other Cattle over 2 years	5
Other Cattle 1-2 years	4
Other Cattle ½-1 year	2.25
Calves 0-½ year	2.25
Housed bullocks	3
Sheep, per ewe	1.25
Store sheep	0.8
Sows	1.75
Other pigs over 2 months	1
Laying Birds	0.04

1. For livestock, annual requirements are the per head requirements above multiplied by average numbers during the year (i.e. average numbers at end of each month).

2. As with labour, the number of tractors required by a farm depends more on the seasonal requirements and number required at any one time than on total annual tractor hours. These can be calculated from the seasonal labour data provided earlier in this book. The soil type and size/power of tractors purchased are obviously other relevant factors.

Tractor Power Requirements		hp/acre		hp/ha		kW/ha	
		av.	prem.	av.	prem.	av.	prem.
Combinable crops:	heavy land	.75	.65	1.85	1.5	1.4	1.1
	light land	.5	.45	1.25	1	0.95	0.75
Mixed cropping:	heavy land	1	.75	2.5	1.85	1.85	1.4
	light land	.7	.5	1.75	1.25	1.3	1.95

The average size of tractors purchased in 2006 was 94.5kw (126.5hp), a very small rise on the previous year and the second highest year. The number of units sold at 13,874 was 4.3% higher than in 2005 (Agricultural Engineers Association).

4. TRACTOR COSTS

(Estimates for Spring 2008)

	Two-Wheel Drive 43-49 kW (56-66 h.p.) £18,500		Four-Wheel Drive 56-65kW (75-85 h.p.) £26,000	
Initial Cost..............................				
	per year £	per hour £	per year £	per hour £
Depreciation............................	1,110	2.22	1,625	3.25
Insurance................................	231	0.46	293	0.59
Repairs and Maintenance..............	740	1.48	1,040	2.08
Fuel and Oil.............................	1,576	3.15	2,514	5.03
Total.....................................	3,657	7.31	5,473	10.95

	Four-Wheel Drive			
	76-90 kW (101-120 h.p.) £38,000		115-134 kW (154-180 h.p.) £51,000	
Initial Cost..............................				
	per year £	per hour £	per year £	per hour £
Depreciation............................	2,470	4.94	3,570	7.14
Insurance................................	391	0.78	486	0.97
Repairs and Maintenance..............	1,520	3.04	2,040	4.08
Fuel and Oil.............................	3,481	6.96	4,835	9.67
Total.....................................	7,863	15.73	10,931	21.86

	Crawlers			
	60 kW (80 h.p.) £23,000		200 kW (266 h.p.) £117,000	
Initial Cost..............................				
	per year £	per hour £	per year £	per hour £
Depreciation............................	1,610	3.22	8,190	16.38
Insurance................................	257	0.51	1,026	2.05
Repairs and Maintenance..............	920	1.84	4,680	9.36
Fuel and Oil.............................	2,476	4.95	8,250	16.50
Total.....................................	5,262	10.52	22,149	44.30

Depreciation is based on the assumption that small two-wheel drive tractors are sold for 40% of their original value after ten years and that small, medium and large four-wheel drive tractors (including crawlers) are sold for 37.5, 35 and 30% respectively of their original value after ten years. Annual repair costs have been calculated at 4 per cent of initial cost for all tractors. No interest on capital has been included. Fuel has been charged at 39 pence per litre.

The hourly figures are based on a use of 500 hours per year. A greater annual use than this will mean higher annual costs but possibly lower hourly costs. On large arable farms and contracting businesses, many tractors do over 750 hours per year, or even 1,000 in some cases. Early replacement at a given annual use will increase depreciation costs per hour but should reduce repair costs. The hourly figures are averages for all types of work: heavy operations such as ploughing obviously have a higher cost than light work.

5. ESTIMATING ANNUAL MACHINERY COSTS

Annual machinery costs consist of depreciation, repairs, fuel and oil, contract charges, and vehicle tax and insurance. These can be budgeted in three ways, assuming there is no available information on past machinery costs on the farm:

(a) Per hectare, by looking up an average figure for the district, according to the size and type of farm. Approximate levels are shown in the tables of whole farm fixed costs (pages 170-173). This is obviously a very rough and ready measure.

(b) Per standard tractor hour. The crop area and livestock numbers can be multiplied by the appropriate standard (average) tractor hours per hectare and per head as given on page 157. The total can then be multiplied by the machinery cost per standard tractor hour as calculated from farm surveys. The following average figures (estimated for 2007/08) are based on 2001-2004 levels in South-East England.

Farm Type	Cost per Standard Tractor Hour
Mainly Sheep/Cattle, over 100 ha............................	£10.00
Sheep/Cattle and Arable, over 100 ha	£14.00
Mainly Sheep/Cattle, under 100 ha	£15.00
Mainly Dairying, under 60 ha...............................	£18.00
Mainly Dairying, over 120 ha...............................	£18.00
Mainly Arable, over 200 ha	£18.00
Dairying and Arable..	£18.00
Sheep/Cattle and Arable, under 100 ha.....................	£18.00
Mainly Dairying, 60-120 ha	£18.00
Mainly Arable, 100-200 ha.................................	£21.00
Mainly Arable, under 100 ha...............................	£32.50

Premium levels are about 15 per cent lower.

The capital element of leasing (but not the interest) is included in depreciation.

The percentage composition of the total cost (based on Cambridge, Reading and Wye Farm Business Survey data) varies with size and type of farm but averages approximately:

Depreciation	Repairs	Fuel/Elec.	Contract	VTI*
35.5	22.5	17.5	20	5

*Vehicle tax and insurance.

This method may be used as a check on the per hectare calculation.

(**N.B.** The standard tractor hour is used only as a convenient measure of machinery input. The costs incorporate not only tractor costs but all other power and machinery expenses, including field machinery and implements, fixed equipment, landrovers, vans, use of farm car, etc.)

(c) Fully detailed calculation, costing and depreciating each machine in turn, including tractors, estimating repairs and fuel costs for each, and adding the charges for any contract work. The following tables give, for different types of machine, estimated life, annual depreciation, and estimated repairs according to annual use.

1. Estimated Useful Life (years) of Power Operated Machinery in relation to normal use

Equipment	Annual Use (hours)				
	25	50	100	200	300
Group 1:					
Ploughs, Cultivators, Toothed harrows, Hoes, Rolls, Ridgers, Potato planting attachments, Grain cleaners……………..	12+	12+	12+	12	10
Group 2:					
Disc harrows, Corn drills, Grain drying machines, Food grinders and mixers……	12+	12+	12	10	8
Group 3:					
Combine harvesters, Pick-up balers, Rotary cultivators, Hydraulic loaders…...	12+	12+	12	9	7
Group 4:					
Mowers, Forage harvesters, Swath turners, Side-delivery rakes, Tedders, Hedge cutting machines, Semi-automatic potato planters and transplanters, Unit root drills, Mechanical root thinners……	12+	12	11	8	6
Group 5:					
Fertilizer distributors, Combine drills, Farmyard manure spreaders, Elevator Potato diggers, Spraying machines, Pea cutter windrowers……………..	10	10	9	8	7
Miscellaneous:					
Beet harvesters…………………..	11	10	9	6	5
Potato harvesters……………….	—	8	7	5	—
Milking machinery………………	—	—	—	12	10

	Annual Use (hours)					
	500	750	1,000	1,500	2,000	2,500
Tractors…………	12+	12	10	7	6	5
Electric motors…	12+	12+	12+	12+	12	12

2. Depreciation: Average annual fall in value

(per cent of new price)

Frequency of renewal. Years	Complex. High Depreciation Rate e.g. potato harvesters, mobile pea viners, etc.	Established machines with many moving parts, e.g. tractors, combines, balers, forage harvesters	Simple equipment with few moving parts, e.g. ploughs, trailers
	%	%	%
1	40	30	20
2	27½	20	15
3	20*	16*	12½
4	17½†	14½	11½
5	15‡	13†	10½*
6	13½	12	9½
7	12	11	9
8	11	10‡	8½†
9	(10)	9½	8
10	(9½)	8½	7½‡

* Typical frequency of renewal with heavy use.

† Typical frequency of renewal with average use.

‡Typical frequency of renewal with light use.

Tractors. For the results of a study giving variations in tractor depreciation according to size and annual use as well as age when sold see P. Wilson and S. Davis, 'Estimating Depreciation in Tractors in the UK (etc)', 'Farm Management', Vol. 10, No. 4, Winter 1998/99, pp. 183-193.

3. Net Purchases and Closing Value of Farm Machinery in the Eastern Counties, 2004/05

£ per ha (% of total in brackets)

Type of Farm	Mainly Cereals	Mixed Cropping	Mixed Farms
Tractors	34 (46)	44 (35)	23 (26)
Vehicles	9 (12)	26 (21)	11 (12)
Harvesters	7 (10)	16 (13)	18 (20)
Other Equipment	24 (32)	40 (31)	37 (42)
Total	74 (100)	126 (100)	89 (100)
Total 2003/2004	88	137	87
Total 2002/2003	67	74	101
Closing Value (2004/2005)..........	411	587	360

Source: Report on Farming in the Eastern Counties of England, 2004/2005. University of Cambridge, Rural Business Unit, 2006. This data has not been updated for 2005/06.

4. Depreciation: Percentage rates

A. Straight-Line

Trade-in, Second-hand or Scrap Value as % of New Price

Years Retained	5%	10%	20%	25%	33%	40%	50%	60%
3	—	—	—	—	—	20	16	13
4	—	—	—	—	17	15	12	—
5	—	—	—	15	13	12	—	—
6	—	—	13	12	11	10	—	—
8	—	11	10	9	—	—	—	—
10	9	9	8	—	—	—	—	—
12	8	7	—	—	—	—	—	—
15	6	—	—	—	—	—	—	—

Example: If a machine costing £10,000 is retained for 8 years, at the end of which the trade-in value is 20% of the new price (i.e. £2,000), the average depreciation per annum has been £8,000 over 8 years = £1,000 (i.e. 10% of the new price).

B. Diminishing Balances

Trade-in, Second-hand or Scrap Value as % of New Price

Years Retained	5%	10%	20%	25%	33%	40%	50%	60%
3	—	—	—	—	—	26	21	16
4	—	—	—	—	24	20	16	—
5	—	—	—	24	20	17	—	—
6	—	—	23	20	17	14	—	—
8	—	25	18	16	—	—	—	—
10	25	20	15	—	—	—	—	—
12	22	17	—	—	—	—	—	—
15	18	—	—	—	—	—	—	—

Example: If a machine costing £10,000 is retained for 4 years, at the end of which the trade-in value is 40% of the new replacement price, the annual depreciation on the diminishing balances method is: Year 1, £2,000 (i.e. 20% of £10,000); Year 2, £1,600 (i.e. 20% of £8,000 [the written-down value]); Year 3, £1,280 (i.e. 20% of £6,400); Year 4, £1,024 (20% of £5,120). The total written-down value at the end of Year 4 is therefore £4,096 (i.e. £10,000 less the total depreciation of £5,904). This is approximately 41% of the new price. (Taking the percentages in the above table to decimal places would give the trade-in prices stated more precisely).

Note. The trade-in value taken for purposes of the calculation must exclude any 'disguised' discount on the price of the new machine.

Calculations of data collected as part of the Farm Management Survey in 1982/83 found the following to be the best estimates of the real diminishing balance rates of depreciation for machines sold during that year: (source: S. Cunningham, University of Exeter, Agricultural Economics Unit, 1987):

Tractors	15%	Potato harvesters	21%
Combine harvesters	15%	Forage harvesters	21%
Balers	18%	Beet harvesters	23%

For other machinery and equipment an average rate of 15% is suggested (author).

Tax Allowances on Machinery. See page 207-208.

5. Estimated Annual Cost of spares and repairs as a percentage of purchase price* at various levels of use

	Approximate Annual Use (hours)				Additional use per 100 hours
	500	750	1,000	1,500	ADD
	%	%	%	%	%
Tractors..	5.0	6.7	8.0	10.5	0.5

	Approximate Annual Use (hours)				Additional use per 100 hours
	50	100	150	200	ADD
Harvesting Machinery:	%	%	%	%	%
Combine Harvesters, self-propelled and engine-driven.........................	1.5	2.5	3.5	4.5	2.0
Combine Harvesters, p.t.o. driven, metered-chop forage harvesters, pick-up balers, potato harvesters, sugar beet harvesters.....................	3.0	5.0	6.0	7.0	2.0
Other Implements and Machines:					
Group 1					
Ploughs, Cultivators, Toothed harrows, Hoes, Elevator potato diggers......................................	4.5	8.0	11.0	14.0	6.0
Group 2:					
Rotary cultivators, Mowers, Pea cutter-windrowers..................	4.0	7.0	9.5	12.0	5.0
Group 3:					
Disc harrows, Fertilizer distributors, Farmyard manure spreaders, Combine drills, Potato planters with fertilizer attachment, Sprayers, Hedge-cutting machines..	3.0	5.5	7.5	9.5	4.0
Group 4:					
Swath turners, Tedders, Side-delivery rakes, Unit drills, Flail forage harvesters, Semi-automatic potato planters and transplanters, Down-the-row thinners.............................	2.5	4.5	6.5	8.5	4.0
Group 5:					
Corn drills, Milking machines, Hydraulic loaders, Potato planting Attachments.............................	2.0	4.0	5.5	7.0	3.0
Group 6:					
Grain driers, Grain cleaners, Rolls, Hammer mills, Feed mixers Threshers.................................	1.5	2.0	2.5	3.0	0.5

* When it is known that a high purchase price is due to high quality and durability or a low price corresponds to a high rate of wear and tear, adjustments to the figures should be made.

6. IRRIGATION COSTS

(Estimated for 2008)

A. Capital Costs
(before any grant)

1. Pumps (delivering from 20 to 200 cubic metres per hour from a surface water source, all with portable suction and delivery fittings)

Tractor pto shaft driven c/w monitoring equipment	£2,700-5,200
Diesel engine driven c/w monitoring equipment	£4,800-20,000
Electric motor driven (c/w switch gear)	£2,500-36,000
Optional remote/wireless monitoring controls	£2,000-5,200

2. Pipelines (averages per m)

   Portable: (excl. valve take offs) 50mm, £2.50; 75 mm, £3.00; 100 mm, £4.50; 125 mm, £5.50; 150 mm, £7.75; (incl. valve take offs) 75 mm, £4.75; 100 mm, £6.00; 125 mm, £7.00; 150mm, £10.00.

   Permanent Underground P.V.C. pipe 12.5 bar rating (supply and laying) per metre: 75 mm, £4.50; 100 mm, £5.50; 150/160 mm, £7.75; 200 mm, £11.00; 250mm, £15.00. Hydrants: 100 mm x 100 mm, £200; 150 mm x 125 mm, £240.

3. Application Systems

   (a) Traditional portable hand move sprinkler systems

   75mm (3 inch) diameter. Sprinkler line assemblies:

1 move/day/six day cycle	£785/ha
2 moves/day/six day cycle	£420/ha
3 moves/day/six day cycle	£290/ha

   (b) Solid set sprinkler lines – semi-permanent systems

   63mm dia. pipework assemblies at

   18m x 18m triangulated spacings
   £1,365/ha

   As above but infra-red automated hand-held controls
   £1,575/ha

   (c) Drip irrigation systems

   16.5mm non-recoverable tape (excluding header mains, control valves and filtration equipment)
   £370/ha

   (d) Hose reel systems using rain guns (average cost per machine)

		Manual controls	Electric Controls
Small	6-15m³/hr	£4,000	–
Medium	20-40m³/hr	£10,000	£11,500
Large	40-80m³/hr	£14,000	£15,500

   (e) Hose reel systems using irrigation booms (average cost per unit)

Small including	20m boom	£7,200
Medium including	40/50m boom	£13,500
Large including	70/80m boom	£27,000

   (f) Pivot and linear systems

Small pivot	200m radius (12.5ha)	£1,300/ha full circle
Large pivot	600m radius (113ha)	£775/ha full circle
Linear machine (dependent on length)		£1,500-2,100/ha

4. Total

If no source works are needed, as with water from a river, or pond, total capital costs are likely to vary between £1,000 and £2,000 per hectare requiring irrigation at regular intervals, depending on the levels of sophistication and automation of the system installed.

B. Water Sources

An abstraction licence is required if more than 20m³ of water per day are taken from surface or underground sources. Abstraction charges vary widely, depending on the region, season and whether or not the source is supported by Environment Agency operations. Winter abstraction charges typically range from £2 to £3 per 1000m³ and summer rates from £15 to £30 per 1000m³ for sources that are not supported by the Environment Agency operations. Abstraction charges during the summer can be up to £100 per 1000m³ in areas where supplies are supported by Environment Agency operations. A charge of £3 per 1000m³ equals 75p per 25mm hectare whilst a charge of £25 per 1000m³ would cost £6.25 per hectare per 25mm application. Mains water at 107p per m³ would cost £265 per application of 25mm per hectare.

New time limited abstraction licences are difficult to obtain, especially for summer abstraction. Hence there is an increasing trend towards constructing reservoirs that can be used to store water abstracted during the winter months. The cost of clay-lined reservoirs varies widely but would typically be of the order of £1 per m³ of water stored. The cost of storing 4546m³ (1 million gallons) could easily be £4,000. This price could double if the reservoir is lined and fenced.

A subsistence charge is payable, calculated by a formula combining the following factors together:

- Volume – annual licensed
- Whether the source is Environment Agency unsupported, supported or tidal
- Season – summer, winter or all year round
- Level of losses
- A minimum charge of £25

An application charge of £135 and advertising administration charge of £100 is due, alongside a standard unit charge (SUC), a charge for the region in which the abstraction is authorised to be made. For 2007/08 they are:

Region	2006/7 Standard Unit Charges (£/1000m³)
Anglian	24.37
Midlands	13.74
Northumbria	24.86
North West	12.71
Southern	17.88
South West including Wessex	19.44
Thames	13.05
EA Wales	12.85

C. Overall Operating Costs

Because of variations in individual farm circumstances in terms of source works and the irrigation system used the overall cost of applying 25mm per hectare can range widely, from £60 to £120. Very sophisticated systems distributing mains water over intensive specialist crops could be much more expensive.

The (approximate) imperial equivalents for metric values commonly used in irrigation are as follows:

1 cubic metre = 1,000 litres = 220 gallons.

A pump capacity of 100 cubic metres per hour is equivalent to 22,000 gallons per hour (366 gallons per minute).

In terms of water storage 1,000 cubic metres (1 million litres) is equivalent to 220,000 gallons (1 million gallons = 4,546 cubic metres).

1,000 cubic metres is sufficient to apply 25 millimetres of water over 4 hectares, which is approximately equivalent to applying 1 inch over 10 acres. An acre inch is therefore 101 cubic meters (22,000 gallons), or a hectare centimetre is 100 cubic meters.

---

7. FIELD DRAINAGE

(Estimated for 2008)

1. Installation (costs per metre of excavating a trench, supplying and laying the pipe and backfilling with soil).

Plastic pipes:	60mm diameter	1.60—1.90
	80mm diameter	1.85—2.35
	100mm diameter	2.70—2.90
	125mm diameter	3.60—3.85
	150mm diameter	4.10—4.60
	300mm diameter	9.60—10.60

The above rates apply to schemes of 5 hectares or more; smaller areas and patching up work can cost up to 50% more.

Supplying and laying permeable backfill to within 375mm of ground level will add between £2.40 and £3.00 per metre to costs.

Digging new open ditches (1.8m top width, 0.9m depth) costs £1.75-£2.25 per metre compared with improving existing ditches at £1.25 to £1.75 per metre.

Subsoiling or mole draining will cost in the region of £50-£65 per hectare.

2. *Total*

Costs per hectare for complete schemes will vary depending on the distance between laterals, soil type, size of area to be drained, region of the country and the time of year when the work is to be undertaken. The cost of a scheme with 20m spacing between laterals and using permeable backfill will typically be in the range £2,250 to £2,750 per hectare (£900-£1,100 per acre). Backfilling with soil, rather than with permeable material such as washed gravel, may reduce the cost by almost half but is only possible on certain types of soil. Equally, certain soil types which are particularly suitable for mole drainage may permit spacing between laterals to be increased to 40m or even 80m in some instances. Where this is possible costs will be reduced proportionately.

8. GRAIN DRYING AND STORAGE COSTS

(Estimated for 2008)

A. Drying

Capital Costs: vary widely according to type and capacity of drier. A standard 20 tonne per hour heated air drier would cost in the region of £110,000 including the wet bin and associated handling requirements (to feed drier and empty it). On a 200 hectare arable farm (1125 tonne harvest), over 10 years, this capital cost represents £10 for every tonne of grain regardless of drying requirements. Over 15 years it will fall to £6.50. Amortised (including finance) at a low 5% and assuming only 75% of the grain requires drying, over the 15 year period, this figure rises again to £12.56/tonne.

A 20 tonne per hour operating for 12 hours a day 7 days a week for 6 weeks could theoretically cope with 10,000 tonnes of grain. Under this 'full' capacity, the amortised capital cost per tonne over 15 years falls to £1.04/tonne.

Annual fixed costs: depreciation and interest £3.00 to £6.50 per tonne.

Running costs: Fuel: A useful 'rule of thumb' is 1 litre of fuel per 1% moisture per tonne. Thus 700 tonnes drying an average of 5% would be 3,500 litres. At 38ppl this makes £1.90 per tonne. Maintenance: for new driers, 1% of purchase price, rising as drier ages. Additional repairs might be necessary. Electricity of 17.5Kw/hr for the burner and dischargers, as much again for the handling apparatus, totalling 35Kw/hr. Over a season, (approximately 150 hours use) at 10p/Kw is £525. This represents 47p per tonne grain.

Little labour is required for modern automatic driers unless grain has to be passed over the drier several times.

Central grain stores have grain drying services of about £5.50 to £11.75 per tonne for 5% moisture drying for members and non-members respectively.

Acknowledgement : JW Installations

B. Storage

Capital Costs: from approximately £75 per tonne (on-floor storage in a purpose-built building) to over £215 per tonne for an elaborate plant, including pit, elevator, conveyors, ventilated storage bins etc. in a new building.

Typical costs are given on page 191.

Depreciation and Interest: £175 per tonne depreciated over 20 years, with 6 per cent interest, equals £15.25 per annum; over 15 years, at 8 per cent interest, £20.45. (In highly mechanized bulk plants, part of this may be charged against harvesting and drying rather than entirely against storage).

Fuel and Repairs: £2.20 per tonne.

Extra Drying: Additional drying costs will be borne if storage necessitates further moisture reduction. Average £3.00 per tonne where own drier, £4.50 if dried on contract, for an additional 4% moisture extraction.

Loss of Weight: the value of the weight of grain lost should be considered as an additional cost of storage if storage requires extra drying. 2% = £1.30 to £1.60 per tonne.

Interest on Grain Stored: from 58p (£100 per tonne grain, at 7%) to 80p (£120 per tonne grain, at 8%) per month.

Contract Storage: typically £1.25 per tonne per month with a handling charge of around £1.50 per tonne for loading into store and out of store.

VI. OTHER FIXED COSTS DATA

1. WHOLE FARM FIXED COSTS

The following are a *broad indication* of the levels of fixed costs (£) per hectare (acre) for various types and sizes of farm, estimated for 2008, *including the value of unpaid family manual labour*, including that of the farmer and his wife. Regional survey results, from which these costs are derived, can be obtained from reports published annually by the agricultural economics departments of certain Universities and Colleges. These are listed on page 4, but note the change in availability of this data which makes this year's updates less reliable. In future years we expect completely new data sets to be available, albeit in a different format.

All of these costs can of course vary widely according to many factors, especially the intensity of farming, e.g. the number of cows per 100 hectares on the mainly dairying and dairying and arable farms, or the hectares of intensive crops on the mixed cropping farms.

Furthermore, *the figures provided are only averages. 'Premium' farms of the same level of intensity can have labour, machinery and general overhead costs at least 20% lower.* However, the most profitable farms are often more intensive and therefore have higher fixed costs associated with the great intensity — but with substantially higher total farm gross margins; it is the net amount (TGM-TFC) that matters.

Regarding the under 75 or 100 hectare figures; these relate only to full-time holdings and do not include very intensive holdings occupying very small areas.

The term 'fixed costs' is used here as it is in gross margin analysis and planning: a full explanation of the differences between fixed and variable costs in this context is given on pages 1 and 2. *Note that all casual labour and contract work have been included under fixed costs.* In calculating enterprise gross margins on the individual farm these costs are normally allocated as variable costs if they are specific to a particular enterprise and vary approximately in proportion to its size, i.e. are approximately constant per hectare of a particular crop or per head of livestock. Otherwise they are included as fixed costs. In both cases, however, they could be regarded as substitutes for regular labour and/or the farmer's own machinery — which are both items of fixed cost. It is therefore simpler if both are included, fully, as fixed costs. If one is comparing results from accounts set out on a gross margin basis, and some or all of the casual labour and contract work have been included as variable costs (especially on cropping farms, e.g. for potato harvesting using casual labour or a contractor's machine), the necessary adjustments need to be made in making the comparisons.

Notes

Unpaid Labour. Refers to the value of unpaid family manual labour, including that of the farmer and his wife.

Depreciation. This is based on the 'historic' (i.e. original) cost of machinery, not on the current (i.e. replacement) cost. Although the latter is a truer reflection of the real loss of value of machinery (as is apparent when replacement becomes necessary), virtually all farm accounts use the historic cost method. Hence the use of the latter facilitates efficiency comparisons. It should, however, be noted that depreciation is based on current costs in the University/College reports listed on the previous page; on average this increases the figure by about 10%. Both this item and Repairs include vehicles.

Leasing Charges: The capital element, but not the interest, is included in depreciation; the proportion paid as interest varies according to the rate of interest paid and the length of the leasing period, but is typically 7 to 10 per cent.

Rental Value. Estimated rent for owner-occupied land, based on actual rents of farms of similar type and size (established tenancies; i.e. not new / farm business tenancies). 'Landlord-type' expenses average about 40 per cent of the estimated rent.

General Overheads include general farm maintenance and repairs, office expenses, water, insurance, fees, subscriptions, etc. 'Farm maintenance', i.e. repairs to property (buildings, roads, etc.), averages approximately one-quarter of total general farm overhead expenses.

In making comparisons with fixed costs taken from farm accounts it is important to note that in the figures below unpaid manual labour and a rental value for owner-occupied land are included. Very low 'target' figures given in press articles often omit these items and can therefore be misleading; usually, too, they relate only to large, very well appointed farms. Note too that the figures given below do not include management, whether paid or unpaid, nor interest on capital - again whether paid or unpaid. The margin after deducting the fixed costs below from the total gross margin plus any other farm receipts represents the total return to the management supplied and the capital utilised.

Labour, machinery and buildings are the main items of 'fixed' costs subject to change with major alterations in farm policy. Each has a separate section in this book.

Mainly Dairying

	Under 75 ha (Under 185 acres)		75-125 ha (185-310 acres)		Over 125 ha (Over 310 acres)	
Regular Labour (paid).......	80	(32)	125	(51)	170	(69)
Regular Labour (unpaid).....	540	(219)	345	(140)	185	(75)
Casual Labour.............	20	(8)	20	(8)	20	(8)
Total Labour	**640**	**(259)**	**490**	**(198)**	**375**	**(152)**
Machinery Depreciation	100	(40)	90	(36)	95	(38)
Machinery Repairs..........	70	(28)	65	(26)	70	(28)
Fuel, Elec., Oil.............	65	(26)	60	(24)	60	(24)
Contract..................	90	(36)	90	(36)	95	(38)
Vehicle Tax and Insurance ...	15	(6)	15	(6)	10	(4)
Total Power and Machinery	**340**	**(138)**	**320**	**(130)**	**330**	**(134)**
Rent/Rental Value..........	200	(81)	190	(77)	200	(81)
General Overhead Expenses..	160	(65)	130	(53)	120	(49)
**Total Fixed Costs..........	**1340**	**(542)**	**1130**	**(457)**	**1025**	**(415)**

Dairying and Arable

	Under 100 ha (Under 250 acres)		100-200 ha (250-500 acres)		Over 200 ha (Over 500 acres)	
Regular Labour (paid).......	230	(93)	240	(97)	240	(97)
Regular Labour (unpaid).....	225	(91)	155	(63)	65	(26)
Casual Labour.............	25	(10)	20	(8)	5	(2)
Total Labour	**480**	**(194)**	**415**	**(168)**	**310**	**(125)**
Machinery Depreciation	120	(49)	100	(40)	110	(45)
Machinery Repairs..........	75	(30)	60	(24)	55	(22)
Fuel, Elec., Oil.............	70	(28)	50	(20)	50	(20)
Contract..................	90	(36)	90	(36)	60	(24)
Vehicle Tax and Insurance ...	15	(6)	10	(4)	10	(4)
Total Power and Machinery	**370**	**(150)**	**310**	**(125)**	**285**	**(115)**
Rent/Rental Value..........	185	(75)	165	(67)	160	(65)
General Overhead Expenses..	140	(57)	120	(49)	105	(42)
**Total Fixed Costs..........	**1175**	**(471)**	**1010**	**(409)**	**860**	**(348)**

Mainly Cereals*

	Under 100 ha (Under 250 acres)		100-200 ha (250-500 acres)		Over 200 ha (Over 500 acres)	
Regular Labour (paid).......	100	(40)	70	(28)	85	(34)
Regular Labour (unpaid).....	190	(77)	100	(40)	40	(16)
Casual Labour.............	20	(8)	10	(4)	10	(4)
Total Labour	**310**	**(125)**	**180**	**(73)**	**135**	**(55)**
Machinery Depreciation	110	(45)	75	(30)	70	(28)
Machinery Repairs..........	45	(18)	40	(16)	45	(18)
Fuel, Elec., Oil.............	45	(18)	35	(14)	35	(14)
Contract..................	65	(26)	50	(20)	25	(10)
Vehicle Tax and Insurance ...	15	(6)	10	(4)	10	(4)
Total Power and Machinery	**280**	**(113)**	**210**	**(85)**	**185**	**(75)**
Rent/Rental Value..........	155	(63)	155	(63)	155	(63)
General Overhead Expenses..	120	(49)	90	(36)	65	(26)
Total Fixed Costs..........	**865**	**(350)**	**635**	**(257)**	**540**	**(219)**

* With combinable break crops.

Mixed Cropping*

	Under 100 ha (Under 250 acres)		100-200 ha (250-500 acres)		Over 200 ha (Over 500 acres)	
Regular Labour (paid).......	75	(30)	85	(34)	170	(69)
Regular Labour (unpaid).....	230	(93)	140	(57)	35	(14)
Casual Labour.............	20	(8)	15	(6)	10	(4)
Total Labour	**325**	**(132)**	**240**	**(97)**	**215**	**(87)**
Machinery Depreciation	100	(40)	100	(40)	100	(40)
Machinery Repairs..........	60	(24)	60	(24)	70	(28)
Fuel, Elec., Oil.............	50	(20)	50	(20)	45	(18)
Contract..................	60	(24)	65	(26)	70	(28)
Vehicle Tax and Insurance ...	15	(6)	15	(6)	10	(4)
Total Power and Machinery	**285**	**(115)**	**290**	**(117)**	**295**	**(119)**
Rent/Rental Value..........	160	(65)	165	(67)	160	(65)
General Overhead Expenses..	115	(47)	100	(40)	80	(32)
Total Fixed Costs..........	**885**	**(358)**	**795**	**(322)**	**750**	**(304)**

* With potatoes and/or sugar beet and/or field vegetables; grade 1 or 2 land.

Large-Scale Arable Farms (over 400 ha (1,000 acres))

There is no conclusive evidence from tables for different sizes of farm published in Cambridge University's Farm Business Survey in the Eastern Counties that total labour and machinery costs per hectare are on average significantly lower on arable farmers exceeding 400 ha (1,000 acres) than the average figures given above for such farms over 200ha (500 acres).

However, the lowest cost large-scale cereals and combinable crop farms average around £260/ha (£105/acre) for paid labour and machinery, which is the sort of figure at which farm management companies would be budgeting.

Mainly Sheep/Cattle (lowland)

	Under 100 ha (Under 250 acres)		100-200 ha (250-500 acres)		Over 200 ha (Over 500 acres)	
Regular Labour (paid).......	40	(16)	40	(16)	65	(26)
Regular Labour (unpaid).....	315	(127)	185	(75)	125	(51)
Casual Labour.............	20	(8)	10	(4)	5	(2)
Total Labour	**375**	**(152)**	**235**	**(95)**	**195**	**(79)**
Machinery Depreciation.....	75	(30)	75	(30)	70	(28)
Machinery Repairs..........	50	(20)	40	(16)	40	(16)
Fuel, Elec., Oil.............	45	(18)	40	(16)	35	(14)
Contract..................	45	(18)	40	(16)	35	(14)
Vehicle Tax and Insurance ...	10	(4)	10	(4)	10	(4)
Total Power and Machinery	**225**	**(91)**	**205**	**(83)**	**190**	**(77)**
Rent/Rental Value..........	130	(53)	135	(55)	130	(53)
General Overhead Expenses..	120	(49)	90	(36)	75	(30)
**Total Fixed Costs..........	**850**	**(344)**	**665**	**(269)**	**590**	**(239)**

Sheep/Cattle and Arable

	Under 100 ha (Under 250 acres)		100-200 ha (250-500 acres)		Over 200 ha (Over 500 acres)	
Regular Labour (paid).......	35	(14)	50	(20)	90	(36)
Regular Labour (unpaid).....	270	(109)	140	(57)	70	(28)
Casual Labour.............	20	(8)	15	(6)	10	(4)
Total Labour	**325**	**(132)**	**205**	**(83)**	**170**	**(69)**
Machinery Depreciation.....	65	(26)	70	(28)	60	(24)
Machinery Repairs..........	35	(14)	40	(16)	35	(14)
Fuel, Elec., Oil.............	40	(16)	35	(14)	30	(12)
Contract..................	40	(16)	30	(12)	25	(10)
Vehicle Tax and Insurance ...	15	(6)	10	(4)	10	(4)
Total Power and Machinery	**195**	**(79)**	**185**	**(75)**	**160**	**(65)**
Rent/Rental Value..........	135	(55)	135	(55)	130	(53)
General Overhead Expenses..	100	(40)	80	(32)	75	(30)
**Total Fixed Costs..........	**755**	**(306)**	**605**	**(245)**	**535**	**(217)**

Arable and Pigs/Poultry*

	Under 100 ha (Under 250 acres)		100-200 ha (250-500 acres)		Over 200 ha (Over 500 acres)	
Regular Labour (paid).......	380	(154)	220	(89)	215	(87)
Regular Labour (unpaid).....	220	(89)	105	(42)	35	(14)
Casual Labour.............	15	(6)	10	(4)	10	(4)
Total Labour	**615**	**(249)**	**335**	**(136)**	**260**	**(105)**
Machinery Depreciation	135	(55)	110	(45)	110	(45)
Machinery Repairs..........	95	(38)	85	(34)	70	(28)
Fuel, Elec., Oil.............	100	(40)	80	(32)	70	(28)
Contract..................	75	(30)	75	(30)	75	(30)
Vehicle Tax and Insurance ...	15	(6)	15	(6)	10	(4)
Total Power and Machinery	**420**	**(170)**	**365**	**(148)**	**335**	**(136)**
Rent/Rental Value..........	200	(81)	190	(77)	180	(73)
General Overhead Expenses..	185	(75)	160	(65)	130	(53)
Total Fixed Costs.........	**1420**	**(575)**	**1050**	**(425)**	**905**	**(366)**

* The number of pigs in relation to the total farm area varies widely, and so, therefore, can these per hectare (per acre) figures.

Livestock Rearing

	Upland		Hill	
	(per adjusted hectare (acre))*			
Regular Labour (paid).....................	70	(28)	45	(18)
Regular Labour (unpaid)...................	105	(42)	75	(30)
Casual Labour...........................	10	(4)	5	(2)
Total Labour	**185**	**(75)**	**125**	**(51)**
Machinery Depreciation....................	65	(26)	45	(18)
Machinery Repairs........................	20	(8)	15	(6)
Fuel, Elec., Oil..........................	30	(12)	20	(8)
Contract................................	30	(12)	10	(4)
Vehicle Tax and Insurance..................	5	(2)	5	(2)
Total Power and Machinery	**150**	**(61)**	**95**	**(38)**
Rent/Rental Value........................	100	(40)	50	(20)
General Overhead Expenses.................	75	(30)	45	(18)
Total Fixed Costs........................	**510**	**(206)**	**315**	**(127)**

* Divisors to give the actual area figure = upland 1.33, hill 2.2.

Horticultural Holdings

See page 50.

2. RENTS

Unless otherwise stated the figures in this section relate to farms let with a combination of crops, grass and rough grazing in England; they include housing and buildings, as available.

It has to be borne in mind that rough grazing, including upland, is included in the figures given below. Some farms are likely to be let at below competitive rates, for various reasons. **The average rent for lowland, excluding woodland and rough grazing, for farms under full agricultural tenancies is likely to be approximately £150 per ha, £60 per acre, in 2008.** Rents for land have been tending to fall, but this is being offset by higher rents for housing and buildings so that overall per hectare rents are stable. The surge in some commodity prices in 2007 has not so far affected rental levels. The levels on large mixed arable farms (i.e. including potatoes, sugar beet and/or vegetables) on very good soil, or well-equipped dairy farms, will tend to average £160 to £210 per ha, £65 to £85 per acre. Rents on moderate, below average, quality farms, particularly with full repairing and insuring leases, are likely to average £110 to £120 per ha, £45 to £50 per acre. Some future rents, at least, are likely to be affected by the Single Payment Scheme provisions which started in 2005; it is, however, too early as yet to speculate; the situation will vary from farm to farm and differ between the different regions/countries of the UK. The tenant is the only person who can claim the single farm payment, except in some seasonal agreements where the landlord may be able to claim.

Farm Business Tenancy rents will remain higher than those above for traditional tenancies, although significantly lower on average than those initially offered when such tenancies first became available, in 1996, at a relatively prosperous time. Farmers who already own land, with little or no mortgage, can afford to offer a higher figure than bidders with no other farm. £200/ha (£80/acre) for cereals land of reasonable quality was still common in 2007 in east and south-east England.

The following data all relate to 2006. The figures are rounded to the nearest 50p/ha or 25p/acre.

Average Rent by Type of Agreement:	£/ha (acre)
Full Agricultural Tenancies...........................	114 (46.25)
Farm Business Tenancies for 1 year and over	133 (53.75)
Seasonal Lets of less than one year	102 (41.25)

Average Rent by Farm Type: (£ per ha [acre])	Full Agricultural Tenancies		Farm Business Tenancies*
	Land Only	**Other**	**All Agreements**
Cereal	129.00 (52.25)	127.50 (51.50)	148.50 (60.00)
General Cropping	114.00 (46.25)	142.50 (57.75)	167.00 (67.50)
Dairy	106.50 (43.00)	137.50 (55.75)	168.50 (68.25)
Cattle and Sheep (Lowland)	93.50 (37.75)	111.50 (45.25)	89.00 (36.00)
Cattle and Sheep (LFA)	29.00 (11.75)	40.00 (16.25)	42.00 (17.00)
All	101.00 (40.75)	116.00 (47.00)	133.00 (53.75)

* for a year and over

Source of Data

DEFRA (Farming Statistics): Tenanted Land Survey - England, 2006. The survey's results were based on approximately 7,300 agreements, covering 9% of all tenanted land in England by area. This survey is now undertaken every two years.

3. LAND PRICES

Sale Value of Farmland, England and Wales (£ per hectare (acre)

(1) Auction Sales (with Vacant Possession only) :
Oxford Institute/Savills(1) *series, 1937-2000*

Year	Current Prices		Real Values(2)		Index (3)	Year	Current Prices		Real Values(2)		Index (3)
1937-9	0	(24)	2030	(822)	33	1982	4557	(1844)	8373	(3389)	136
1945	111	(45)	2246	(909)	37	1983	5145	(2082)	9041	(3659)	147
1955	198	(80)	3274	(1325)	53	1984	4888	(1978)	8180	(3310)	133
1960	198	(80)	2643	(1070)	43	1985	4781	(1935)	7542	(3052)	123
1965	304	(123)	3608	(1460)	59	1986	4193	(1697)	6398	(2589)	104
1970	581	(235)	5857	(2370)	95	1987	4944	(2001)	7242	(2931)	118
1971	605	(245)	4872	(1972)	79	1988	6716	(2718)	9376	(3794)	153
1971	647	(262)	4761	(1927)	77	1989	6558	(2654)	8493	(3437)	138
1972	1473	(596)	9603	(3886)	156	1990	6346	(2568)	7505	(3037)	122
1973	1871	(757)	11793	(4773)	192	1991	6007	(2431)	6708	(2715)	109
1974	1572	(636)	8529	(3452)	139	1992	5441	(2202)	5859	(2371)	95
1975	1332	(539)	5817	(2354)	95	1993	5456	(2208)	5783	(2340)	94
1976	1814	(734)	6798	(2751)	111	1994	5028	(2035)	5204	(2106)	85
1977	2449	(991)	7922	(3206)	129	1995	6140	(2484)	6140	(2485)	100
1988	3279	(1327)	9794	(3964)	160	1996	8797	(3560)	8591	(3477)	140
1979	4371	(1769)	11513	(4659)	188	1997	8065	(3263)	7636	(3090)	124
1980	4265	(1726)	9521	(3853)	155	1998	7250	(2934)	6637	(2686)	108
1981	4272	(1729)	8525	(3450)	139	1999	13920	(5634)	12565	(5085)	205
						2000	7895	(3196)	7125	(2885)	116

(1) Savills after 1988. (2) At 1995 general price levels. (3) Real Values, 1995 = 100.

From 1970, figures were based on sales reports in the Estates Gazette and the Farmers Weekly, plus some unpublished sales, with a minimum size of 10 hectares

The series was discontinued after 2000.

(2) Current Agricultural Prices (CALP and CALP/RICS) series *(vacant possession only)*

Covers sales of 5 ha and above but excludes land sold for development or forestry, gifts, inheritances and compulsory purchases. Includes sales of bare land as well as land with dwellings, buildings, etc. Calculated by dividing the total value of sales by total area sold.

CALP series (England only) data collected jointly by ADAS (Agricultural Development and Advisory Service) AMC (Agricultural Mortgage Corporation) and CLA (then Country Landowners Association) and were published by the AMC until 1993. A CALP/RICS Farmland Price Index (England and Wales) began in 1995.

(i) *CALP Annual Figures*

	Average price (A)	Average price (B): in 1995 £	Index (of B) (1995 = 100)
1978	3160 (1280)	9438 (3820)	176
1979	4140 (1675)	10497 (4248)	196
1980	3975 (1610)	8874 (3591)	166
1981	3940 (1595)	7863 (3182)	147
1982	4125 (1670)	7579 (3067)	142
1983	4630 (1875)	8288 (3354)	155
1984	4555 (1845)	7622 (3085)	142
1985	4340 (1755)	6846 (2771)	128
1986	3675 (1485)	5608 (2270)	105
1987	3780 (1530)	5537 (2241)	103
1988	5350 (2165)	7469 (3023)	139
1989	5595 (2265)	7245 (2932)	135
1990	4440 (1795)	5251 (2125)	98
1991	4145 (1675)	4629 (1873)	86
1992	3658 (1480)	3939 (1594)	74
1993	3608 (1460)	3824 (1548)	71
1994	5085 (2060)	5263 (2130)	98
1995	5355 (2170)	5355 (2170)	100
1996	6940 (2810)	6778 (2743)	127
1997	7295 (2955)	6907 (2795)	129
1998	7055 (2855)	6459 (2613)	121

Series discontinued : superseded by (ii) below

(ii) *CALP/RICS Farmland Price Index**

	2002	2003	2004	2005	2006
Jan. – Mar.	7906 (3200)	7817 (3163)	9526 (3855)	9099 (3682)	8,785 (3,555)
Apr. – Jun.	7579 (3067)	7910 (3201)	9255 (3745)	8834 (3575)	10,030 (4,059)
Jul. – Sept.	7694 (3114)	7629 (3087)	10670 (4318)	9781 (3958)	-
Oct. – Dec.	6390 (2586)	8367 (3386)	9828 (3977)	9513 (3850)	10,378 (4,200)

* Average prices weighted to remove the effect of exceptional sales.

Sales of vacant possession land in England and Wales, excluding residential value where more than 50% of total sale price; value of milk quota excluded. Calculated by dividing total value of sales by total area sold. Figures for the most recent quarters are subject to revision as further information becomes available. In 2006 twice as much land was sold as in 2005 and that year saw an increase of 30% compared to 2004. The higher area sold in 2006 has not seen lower prices, reflecting a very strong market at present.

(iii) **FPD Savills Farmland Value Survey** *(vacant possession, lowland, excluding houses)*

	March	June	September	December
1993	2995 (1212)	3145 (1272)	3290 (1332)	3440 (1393)
1994	3500 (1417)	3565 (1442)	3625 (1467)	3685 (1491)
1995	3960 (1603)	4240 (1715)	4520 (1829)	4800 (1942)
1996	5035 (2037)	5265 (2131)	5310 (2149)	5355 (2167)
1997	5405 (2187)	5450 (2206)	5390 (2181)	5325 (2155)
1998	5155 (2086)	5035 (2038)	4860 (1967)	4755 (1925)
1999	4740 (1918)	4775 (1932)	4780 (1934)	4705 (1904)
2000	4575 (1852)	4560 (1846)	4445 (1799)	4405 (1782)
2001	4360 (1765)	4360 (1764)	4365 (1766)	4360 (1765)
2002	N/A	4370 (1769)	N/A	4325 (1751)
2003	N/A	4330 (1752)	N/A	4440 (1797)
2004	N/A	4845 (1961)	N/A	5145 (2083)
2005	N/A	5410 (2190)	N/A	5780 (2339)
2006	N/A	6030 (2440)*	—	—

This series includes farm buildings but not houses or cottages. A static portfolio of nine types of equipped VP land in 25 regions in Britain is valued quarterly by a panel of expert agricultural valuers, taking into account local transactions and any special circumstances.

* Prime arable 7250 (2935); arable 6480 (2622); poor arable 4620 (1870); dairy 6360 (2574); pasture 5150 (2084); poorer pasture 3960 (1602).

(3) Inland Revenue Returns (England only; Oct.-Sept. 30 years)

	Vacant Possession		Tenanted	
Year(1)	Farms(2)	Bare Land	Farms(2)	Bare Land
1980/1	3568 (1444)	3325 (1346)	2334 (945)	2354 (953)
1981/2	3503 (1418)	3281 (1328)	2644 (1070)	1340 (542)
1982/3	3766 (1524)	3525 (1427)	2549 (1032)	2210 (894)
1983/4	3761 (1522)	3835 (1552)	2389 (967)	2511 (1016)
1984/5	4258 (1723)	3466 (1403)	2879 (1165)	2310 (935)
1985/6	4055 (1641)	3477 (1407)	2192 (887)	2217 (897)
1986/7	3703 (1499)	3023 (1223)	2141 (866)	1777 (719)
1987/8	3750 (1518)	3140 (1271)	2252 (911)	2476 (1002)
1988/9	4739 (1918)	3521 (1425)	3178 (1286)(3)	1929 (781)
1989/90	5355 (2167)	4080 (1651)	2143 (867)	2093 (847)
1990/91	5515 (2231)	3750 (1517)	2090 (846)	2505 (1014)
1991/92	5015 (2030)	3370 (1363)	2505 (1015)	1465 (592)
1992/93	4405 (1785)	3120 (1265)	1680 (680)	2045 (830)(3)
1993/94	4319 (1748)	3235 (1309)	2102 (851)	1116 (452)
1994/95	4661 (1886)	3608 (1460)	1860 (753)	1720 (696)
1995/96	5058 (2047)	3936 (1593)	2605 (1054)	1490 (603)
1996/97	6224 (2519)	4548 (1841)	4513 (1826)	2623 (1062)

Series discontinued: see (4) below.

1. There was invariably a delay between the dates when a price was agreed and when it was notified to the Inland Revenue and thus included in the above figures; this time-lag was thought to average about 9 months.

2. Farms = Land and Buildings, including the farmhouse.

3. High figure caused by a few untypically high-priced transactions.

The above figures related to all sales of agricultural properties of 5 ha and over except those for development and other non-agricultural purposes. They included any sales at prices below ruling open market value (as between members of a family), sales where the vendor retains certain (e.g. sporting) rights, sales in which the farmhouse represented a substantial part of the total value, and sales of land which may, in the purchaser's view, have had an element of development value.

Vacant Possession Premium

On the basis of the Inland Revenue Returns above the average price of tenanted land as a percentage of vacant possession land in the five years 1992/93 to 1996/97 was 50% for whole farms and 49% for bare land. In individual years the figure varied from 38% to 73% for whole farms and from 35% to 65% for bare land. A sudden jump (for whole farms) from a previous high of around 50% to 72.5% in 1996/97 could have been attributed to the introduction of farm business tenancies in 1995. For later figures, see (4) B below.

(4) Valuation Office Agency Transactions (England only)

This relatively new series, issued now by DEFRA, uses the same basic data source as the Inland Revenue Returns series above, which it has replaced, but the sales are now analysed on the basis of the time period when the transactions actually take place, not when validated by the Inland Revenue on average nine months later. Hence there is no longer a time-lag. Some restrictions and technical adjustments mean that the new series is not strictly comparable with the old one. The figures are subject to revision for up to three years as late returns are received, but the later revisions are expected to be minor. The 2002 to 2004 figures below are therefore denoted as provisional estimates. (Number of sales: 1999, 3,437; 2000, 3,227; 2001, 2,603; 2002, 3,029; 2003, 2,459; 2004, 1570).

A. By Property Type	Land and Dwellings	Land and Buildings	Land only
1993	4,532 (1,834)	3,315 (1,342)	3,297 (1,334)
1994	5,257 (2,127)	3,918 (1,586)	3,565 (1,443)
1995	5,557 (2,249)	5,125 (2,074)	4,177 (1,690)
1996	7,111 (2,878)	5,596 (2,265)	5,333 (2,158)
1997	7,698 (3,155)	6,565 (2,657)	5,528 (2,237)
1998	7,076 (2,864)	6,294 (2,547)	5,414 (2,191)
1999	9,754 (3,947)	6,217 (2,516)	5,282 (2,138)
2000	10,488 (4,244)	6,922 (2,801)	5,603 (2,268)
2001	11,411 (4,620)	6,466 (2,617)	5,674 (2,296)
2002	10,471 (4,239)	6,565 (2,658)	5,466 (2,213)
2003	11,671 (4,725)	6,756 (2,735)	5,404 (2,188)
2004	11,359 (4,599)	7,460 (3,020)	6,213 (2,515)

B. By Tenure	Vacant Possession	Tenanted
1993	3,829 (1,550)	1,855 (751)
1994	4,323 (1,750)	2,069 (837)
1995	4,946 (2,002)	2,566 (1,038)
1996	6,132 (2,482)	3,227 (1,306)
1997	6,579 (2,662)	3,504 (1,418)
1998	6,191 (2,505)	3,652 (1,478)
1999	6,631 (2,684)	8,391 (3,396)*
2000	7,112 (2,878)	3,996 (1,605)
2001	7,353 (2,976)	13,581 (5,496)*
2002	6,946 (2,812)	3,179 (1,287)
2003	7,284 (2,949)	3,995 (1,617)
2004	7,666 (3,104)	7,495 (3,034)

* Tenanted figures in 1999 and 2001 affected by a small number of high value sales.

C. By Size Group	5-49.9 ha	50-99.9 ha	100 ha and over	All sales
1993	4,487 (1,816)	3,808 (1,541)	2,944 (1,191)	3,791 (1,534)
1994	5,138 (2,079)	4,272 (1,729)	3,145 (1,273)	4,229 (1,711)
1995	5,933 (2,401)	4,902 (1,984)	3,555 (1,439)	4,788 (1,938)
1996	6,962 (2,817)	5,737 (2,322)	5,161 (2,089)	6,058 (2,452)
1997	7,259 (2,938)	6,118 (2,476)	5,578 (2,257)	6,448 (2,609)
1998	7,126 (2,884)	6,326 (2,560)	4,873 (1,972)	6,134 (2,482)
1999	7,349 (2,974)	5,866 (2,374)	5,975 (2,418)	6,673 (2,701)
2000	7,531 (3,048)	6,686 (2,706)	6,298 (2,549)	7,082 (2,866)
2001	8,357 (3,382)	6,878 (2,783)	5,825 (2,357)	7,406 (2,997)
2002	8,069 (3,267)	6,571 (2,660)	5,010 (2,027)	6,915 (2,799)
2003	8,753 (3,544)	6,508 (2,635)	5,037 (2,039)	7,172 (2,904)
2004	8,768 (3,550)	6,858 (2,777)	5,799 (2,348)	7,654 (3,099)

D. By Land Class*	Grade 1 and 2	Grade 3	Grade 4 & 5	Ungraded
1995	5,144 (2,082)	5,473 (2,215)	2,677 (1,083)	3,397 (1,375)
1996	6,798 (2,751)	6,396 (2,588)	3,700 (1,497)	4,474 (1,811)
1997	7,348 (2,974)	7,217 (2,921)	3,135 (1,269)	3,738 (1,513)
1998	6,974 (2,822)	6,569 (2,658)	4,066 (1,645)	3,384 (1,369)
1999	7,354 (2,976)	7,313 (2,960)	4,043 (1,636)	2,576 (1,042)
2000	6,948 (2,812)	7,589 (3,071)	5,266 (2,131)	5,029 (2,035)
2001	7,072 (2,862)	7,904 (3,199)	5,297 (2,144)	5,271 (2,133)
2002	6,696 (2,710)	7,610 (3,081)	4,818 (1,950)	4,158 (1,683)
2003	7,043 (2,851)	7,659 (3,101)	6,143 (2,485)	4,325 (1,750)
2004	7,256 (2,938)	8,289 (3,356)	6,572 (2,661)	4,016 (1,625)

* predominant grade of land.   % total area, England and Wales: Grade 1, 2.3%; 2, 16.9%; 3, 54.7% (a 19.3, b 35.4); 4, 15.0%; 5, 11.1%.

E. By Region (all sales)	2002	2003	2004
North East	4,282 (1,733)	3,563 (1,443)	8,620 (3,490)
North West	6,329 (2,561)	7,705 (3,119)	6,294 (2,548)
Yorkshire and Humber	5,504 (2,228)	6,060 (2,453)	5,614 (2,273)
East Midlands	6,786 (2,746)	7,341 (2,971)	7,852 (3,178)
West Midlands	7,288 (2,949)	6,673 (2,702)	7,930 (3,211)
East of England	7,357 (2,977)	6,729 (2,724)	6,524 (2,641)
South East	9,082 (3,675)	9,285 (3,759)	9,999 (4,046)
South West	7,954 (3,220)	8,944 (3,621)	8,605 (3,484)
England.	6,915 (2,799)	7,172 (2,903)	7,654 (3,098)

Regrettably, due to a lack of data it has not been possible to continue the series and its future is uncertain.

Sale Value of Forests and Woodlands

(1) General

The figures in this section relate to planted land sold (over 25 hectares) so that values include the value of the property (land) and the timber. Timber prices have been improving, but by a much smaller margin than the rise in forest values. Despite transactions increasing by 15% in the year to September 2006, area sold fell by 11% compared to last year, indicating sales of smaller plantations. The average size of plantation sold was 122 ha, some 37ha smaller than that for the previous year.

In the forest sector average prices were up 7% in the year to September 2006 compared to 2005 and have risen by 60% over the last four years. However on further analysis the 7% rise understates the actual increase in like for like sales. Adjusting for crop age and yield class, average values have increased by approximately 20% over the past year.

(2) Forests

For forests the figures are for the UK and are predominantly upland with at least 50% coniferous content. Values vary with many factors and only size of block and age are recorded here, but yield class is also important.

A. By Size Range (approx.)	2005	2006
	£/ha (£/acre)	£/ha (£/acre)
Below 51 hectares	2,700 (1,093)	3,300 (1,337)
51 to 100 hectares	2,550 (1,032)	2,600 (1,053)
101 to 200 hectares	2,050 (830)	2,500 (1,012)
Above 200 hectares	1,950 (789)	2,200 (874)

B. By Age Band	2005	2006
	£/ha (£/acre)	£/ha (£/acre)
Young (1 to 10 years)	900 (364)	1,900 (769)
Mid-rotation (11 to 20 years).	1,500 (607)	1,850 (749)
Semi-mature (21 to 30 years)	2,100 (850)	1,950 (789)
Mature (over 30 years)	2,300 (931)	2,350 (951)
Mature (over 40 years)	3,200 (1,295)	3,450 (1,397)

(3) Woodlands

Whilst timber prices remained relatively stable into 2007, small woodland values continued to increase, attributable to the general rise in land values. Values are at their highest adjacent to centres of population and for properties of high amenity value. Sales in the South of England are often recorded in the £8-10,000/ha range, whereas £2-5,000/ha is more typical for more remote propeties, or where amenity values are lower.

Source: Tilhill and FPD Savills.

4. BUILDINGS

A. Building Costs

Building costs are notoriously variable. Many factors influence a contractor's price, including distance from his yard, size of contract, site access, site conditions, complexity of work, familiarity with the type of work and his current work load. There will also be differences in efficiency and standard of work between contractors and, as is often the case with farm buildings, the absence of detailed specification by the client may mean that different contractors will not have quoted for identical buildings. The number of extras that are found to be required after a contract has been agreed will also vary.

The costs given below can only be taken as an approximate guide. They refer to new buildings, erected by contractor on a clear level site and exclude VAT and any grants that may be available. The costs were provided by SAC Buildings Design Services, Aberdeen, in 2007. More detailed information is available in the following publications. The books and journals giving general building cost information generally assume knowledge of how to take off quantities for building work.

Specialised Information on Farm Building Costs

Farm Building Cost Guide published by SAC Building Design Services, Aberdeen.

Standard Costs Part 1: Specifications; Part 2: Costs. Published by DEFRA and the Agricultural Departments in Scotland, Wales and Northern Ireland. Used when claiming government grants on a standard-cost basis.

General Building Cost Information

Books are produced by a number of publishers with annual or more frequent new editions and updates. Examples are Laxton's Building Price Book, Spon's Architects' and Builders' Price Book, and Wessex Comprehensive Building Price Book. Regularly updated cost information is also given in several professional and trade journals.

1. Constituent Parts

Frame, Roof and Foundations	*per m2 floor area*

1. Open-sided timber framed pole barn with round pole uprights on concrete bases, sawn timber rafters and purlins, high-tensile galvanised steel cladding to roof and gable ends above eaves, hardcore floor, eaves height 4.8 m, 9 m span, no side cladding, rainwater drainage to soakaways. — £55

2. Open-sided steel portal-framed building with fibre-cement or plastic coated steel cladding to roof and gables above eaves, hardcore floor, eaves height 4.8 m, no side cladding, rainwater drainage to soakaways.

9 m span	£105
13.2 m span	£90
18 m span	£85

3. Cost breakdown of 2 above;

Materials:	portal frame and purlins	26%
	foundations	3%
	roofing	16%
	rainwater and drainage	3%
	hardcore and blinding	2%
	Total Materials	50%

	Erection:	portal frame and purlins	19%
		foundations	2%
		roofing	19%
		rainwater and drainage	5%
		hardcore and blinding	5%
		Total Erection	50%

Roof cladding   *per m²*

1. Natural grey fibre-cement, 146 mm corrugations fixed with drive screws

Materials	£7.90	
Fixing	£15.50	
Total		£23.40

2. Extra for coloured sheet   £1.90
3. Deduct for translucent sheets   £0.12
4. Deduct for PVC-coated steel   £4.50
5. Deduct for high-tensile corrugated galvanised steel sheeting   £7.80
6. PVC 150 mm half-round gutter on fascia brackets, including stop-ends and outlets   £20.25
7. PVC 100 mm rainwater pipe with fixings, swanneck and shoe   £39.00

                                                               per m run

8. Fibre-cement close-fitting ridge   £33.25
9. Fibre-cement ventilating ridge   £36.00

Walls and Cladding   *per m²*

1. Concrete blockwork, fair faced and pointed both sides
150 mm thick	£39.40
215 mm thick	£56.20
215 mm thick hollow blocks	£58.50
215 mm thick hollow blocks, filled and reinforced	£71.50

2. Extra for rendering or roughcast to blockwork on one side   £18.75
3. Vertical spaced boarding 21x 145 mm with 19 mm gaps including horizontal rails, all pressure treated   £23.20
4. Fibre-cement vertical cladding, including rails   £36.20
5. Corrugated high-tensile steel side cladding, including rails   £29.20
6. Wall element: 215 mm thick blockwork, including strip foundation (base 750 mm below ground level), 2.5 m height above ground level   £147 per m run

Floors   *per m²*

1. Concrete floor 100 mm thick, Gen 3 mix, on 150 mm hardcore, including excavation: £29.60

   Breakdown:
(a)	excavate, level and compact	£2.70
(b)	hardcore	£4.20
(c)	blinding	£2.00
(d)	damp-proofmembrane	£1.70
(e)	premixed concrete spread and compacted	£15.60

(f)	float finish	£3.40

2. Extra to above for
   (a) 150 mm instead of 100 mm — £5.00
   (b) laying concrete to falls — £1.40
   (c) broom or textured finish — £1.70
   (d) Carborundum dust non-slip finish — £2.90
   (e) insulating concrete — £8.40

3. Reinforced concrete slatted floors for cattle
   (a) cattle loading — £64.00
   (b) tractor loading — £71.50

4. Reinforced concrete slats for pigs — £47.00

5. Insulating floor, including excavation and base
   (a) 27 mm expanded polystyrene, 38 mm screed — £41.50
   (b) insulating concrete with lightweight aggregate — £33.00
   (c) as (b) with 20 mm screed — £42.00

6. Form channel in concrete — £3.90 per m run

7. Excavate for cast 1 m3 in-situ concrete bases for stanchions — £105 each

Services and Fittings	*per m²*

1. Drainage: 100 mm PVC pipe laid in trench, including 750 mm deep excavation and backfill — £21.20 per m run
   Breakdown:
   (a) excavate and backfill — £13.50
   (b) 100 mm PVC pipe laid — £7.70
   Extras:
   (c) add to (a) for 1 m deep — £3.20
   (d) add to (b) for 150 mm pipe — £5.60

2. Excavate soakaway and fill with stones — £92.50 each

3. Trap and grid top, 100 mm PVC — £18.00 each

4. Yard gully with heavy duty road grating 400 x 300 mm — £165 each

5. Inspection chamber 900 mm deep, 450 x 600 mm opening and medium duty cast iron cover — £335 each

6. Above-ground vitreous enamel slurry tank on concrete base, 1000 m³ — £37500 each

7. Reception pit, 20 m³ — £3.500 each

8. Slurry channel beneath (not including) slats, 1.8 m deep, 3m wide — £375 per m run

9. Lighting: 1.5 m 60W single fluorescent unit, including wiring and switch — £115 each
   Extras:
   (a) PVC conduit — £72
   (b) screwed steel conduit — £95

10. Power: 13A switched outlet — £75 each

11. Diagonal feed fence, fixed, including posts (painted) — £72 per m run

12. Tombstone feed fence, fixed, including posts (painted) — £85 per m run

13. Feed bunker — £50 per m run

14. Hay rack, wall fixing — £55 per m run

15. Cubicle division, galvanised, fixed in place — £75 each

16.	Fencing: three-rail timber with posts, all pressure treated	£21.50 per m run
17.	Gate, 3 m wide, galvanised steel, including posts set in concrete	
	(a) medium duty	£172 each
	(b) heavy duty	£235 each
	Deduct for painted instead of galvanised finish	£32

2.   Complete Buildings

Fully Covered and Enclosed Barn

Portal frame, 18 m span, 6 m bays, 6 m to eaves, 3 m high
blockwork walls with sheet cladding above, 6 m sliding   £155 per m² floor
doors at either end, 150mm thick concrete floor   area

Cows and Cattle Housing

1.	Covered strawed yard, enclosed with ventilated cladding, concrete floor, pens only, with 4.0 m² per head floor area	£620 per head
2.	Extra to 1 for 4.0 m wide double-sided feeding passage, barrier and troughs	£260 per head
3.	Kennel building	£390 per head
4.	Portal framed building with cubicles	£1200 per head
5.	Extra to 4 for feed stance, feeding passage, barriers and troughs	£550 per head
6.	Extra to 4 for slatting of cubicle passages	£550 per head
7.	Covered collecting yard, 1.1 m² per cow	£180 per head
8.	Milking parlour building, example: 5.5 x 11.5 m for 8/16 parlour	£14,000
9.	Parlour equipment, herringbone parlours:	
	(a) low level, 1 stall per point	£3,200 per point
	(b) pipeline	£2,950 per point
	(c) extra for meter and auto cluster removal	£1,850 per point
	(d) auto feed dispenser	£770 per point
10.	Dairy building	£250 per m² floor area
11.	Bulk tank and washer	£5.80 per litre
12.	Loose box, 16 m² floor area laid to falls, rendered walls	£290 per m² floor area
13.	Bull pen and open run	£9,750
14.	Cattle crush and 20 m race	£4,200
15.	Slatted floor cattle building for 120 growing cattle (1.7 m² pen space per head) with drive-through feed passage/troughs	£900 per head

Silage

		per tonne stored
1.	Timber panel clamp on concrete base with effluent tank	£55
2.	Precast concrete panel clamp with effluent tank	£80
3.	Glass-lined forage tower and unloader	£190

Waste Storage

		per m³ stored
1.	Lined lagoon with safety fence	£32
2.	Glass-lined steel slurry silo	
	small (400 m³)	£45
	medium (1,200 m³)	£37
	large (3,600 m³)	£35
3.	GRP below-ground effluent tank, encased in concrete	
	small (12 m³)	£400
	large (36 m³)	£350

Sheep Housing

1.	Penning, troughs, feed barriers and drinkers installed in suitable existing building	£27.50 per ewe
2.	Purpose-built sheep shed with 1.35 m² pen space per ewe concentrate troughs, feed passage and barrier for forage feeding	£175 per ewe
	Extras:	
	(a) softwood slatted floor panels, materials only	£7.00 per m²
	(b) slatted panels as (a), made up, plus supports	£23.50 per m²

Pig Housing

		per sow and litter
1.	Farrowing and rearing	
	(a) Prefabricated farrowing pens with crates, side creep areas, part-slatted floors, including foundations, electrical and plumbing work	£2,750
	(b) Steel-framed farrowing house with insulated blockwork walls, part-slatted pens with side creeps in rooms of eight with off main passage	£3,150
	(c) Flat-deck rearing house 3-6 weeks with fully perforated floors to pens, 0.25 m² per pig pen area	£115 per weaner
	(d) Prefabricated verandah house including foundations, electrical and plumbing work, 0.3m² per pig internal lying area	£90 per weaner
2.	Finishing	per baconer
	(a) Prefabricated fattening house with part-slatted floors, trough feeding	£205
	(b) Prefabricated fattening house with part-slatted floors, floor fed	£190
	(c) Steel framed building with insulated blockwork walls, part-slatted floors, trough fed	£260
	(d) Automatic feeding systems for items (a), (b) and (c) above:	
	dry-feed system with ad-lib hoppers	£550
	dry on-floor feeding	£11
	wet feeding	£17
3.	Dry sows and boars	per sow
	(a) Yards with floor feeding	£295
	(b) Sow cubicle system	£490
	(c) Yards with electronic feeders	£810
	(d) Yards with individual feeders	£900

(e)	Two-yard system with flat-rate feeding	£930
(f)	Boar pens as part of sow house	£2,200 each

4. Complete pig unit

Building costs calculated on basis of three-week weaning,
23 pigs per sow per year to bacon, excl. external slurry or
dung storage, feed storage and handling/weighing facilities:

(a)	Breeding and rearing only	£1,600 per sow
(b)	Breeding with progeny to bacon	£2,900 per sow

Poultry Housing and Equipment   *per bird*

1.	Intensive enriched cages with automatic feeding and egg collection; (new traditional cages were banned from 1st January 2003;only enriched cages complete with nest box, perches and scratching area are now allowed)	£18.00-£20.50
2.	Perchery/barn	£17-00-£21.75
3.	Free Range: new sites stocked at 9 birds per m², smaller mobile units will cost	£20.00-£27.50 £24.50 plus
4.	Broiler Breeders, deep litter, 0.167 m² per bird	£23.50
5.	Pullets (cage and floor reared)	£10.60
6.	Broilers, deep litter, 0.05 m² per bird	£6.60-£6.90
7.	Turkeys, 20,000 pole barn fattening unit (cost varies with size of unit and degree of automation)	£16.50-£23.00

(N.B. Source of Poultry Housing costs: as for poultry, see page 121)

Grain Storage and Drying   *per tonne stored*

1.	Intake pit, conveyor, elevator, overhead conveyor and catwalk, storage bins within existing building	£165
	extra for low volume ventilation of bins	£65
2.	As 1 in new building	£240
3.	Portable grain walling for on-floor storage in existing building	£37.50
4.	On floor grain storage in purpose-built building	£95
	Extras:	
	(a) low volume ventilation	£6.70-£7.20
	(b) on-floor drying with above-ground main duct and laterals	£100.00
	(c) add to (b) for below-ground laterals	£12.00
5.	Sealed towers for moist grain, including loading and unloading equipment	£135-£150

Potato Storage   *per tonne stored*

1.	Pallet-box store with recirculation fans	£175
	Pallet boxes, 1 tonne	£57
2.	Bulk store, building only	£160
	Ventilation system: fans, main duct, below-floor lateral ducts	£35

Roads and Fences   *per m length*

3.2 m wide hardcore road with drainage ditches using locally
excavated material   £24

using imported hardcore (£6.15/m³)   £36

extra for bitumen macadam surfacing, two coats   £42

Traditional 7-wire stock fence   £5.10

High tensile 7-wire stock fence   £3.90

Construction Equipment Hire   *hourly rate, with driver*

Excavator   £18-£25

Tipping lorry   £29.00

10-tonne crane   £32

                                                                weekly rate

Concrete mixer, 100 litre (5/3)   £40

Compressor and heavy breaker   £105

B. Standard Costs

Standard costs are published by the Scottish Executive on the basis of the cost of farm or casual labour and new materials. They do not include an allowance for overheads and profit: in most cases building contractors would add 15-30% to cover them. Standard costs are therefore usually lower, sometimes by a larger percentage than this, particularly where the labour content of the item is high. The following examples are based on standard costs issued in 2002. Farm buildings costs generally will have risen by about 21% between that year and 2007. Crown copyright material is reproduced from 'Standard Costs' with permission of the Controller of HMSO and the Queen's Printer for Scotland.

                                                           per m² floor area
Open-sided framed building with cladding to roof and gable peaks only, hardcore
floor, rainwater drainage to soakaways:

9 x 18 m   £35

13.2 x 24m   £32.50

                                                         per m² wall or roof

Corrugated cladding to roof or walls, including supports
(purlins or rails):

fibre cement sheeting   £16.80

extra for coloured sheeting   £0.80

extra for PVC coated steel instead of fibre cement   £0.60

deduct for metallic coated (e.g. galvanised) steel   £4.90

Spaced boarding   £18.80

Wall element, concrete blockwork 190-324 mm thick with
strip foundation (base 750 mm below ground level) and
2.5 mm height above ground level   £92 per m run

Extra for rendering blockwork on one side   £6.50 per m²

Concrete floor, 100 mm thick, including
excavation, hardcore and waterproof membrane   £11.50 per m²

Concrete floor, 150 mm thick as above   £15.50 per m²

Reinforced concrete slats for cattle (supports not included) £47.50 per m²

Yard gully with heavy grating   £251 each

Drainage pipes, 100 mm, jointed in UPVC, clayware or spun concrete including 900 mm trench and backfill	£10.70 per m run	
Drainage pipes 150 mm as above	£19.00 per m run	
Tank for water, effluent etc., 20 m³	£2,966 each	
Gate, 3 m wide, steel, including posts concreted in: light duty	£106.40 each	
cattle yard type	£141.90 each	

	per m² floor area
Fully covered enclosed building with concrete floor, and rainwater drainage to soakaways	
10 x 18 m	£72.50
15 x 24 m	£54.60

C. Storage Requirements

Bulk (cubic metres (feet) per tonne):

Beans		1.2	(43)
Wheat, peas		1.3	(46)
Barley, rye, oilseed rape, linseed, fodder beet		1.4	(50)
Oats		1.9	(68)
Potatoes		1.6	(57)
Dry bulb onions		2.0	(71)
Concentrates:	meal	2.0	(71)
	cubes	1.6	(57)
Grass silage:	18% DM	1.3	(46)
	30% DM	1.6	(57)
Maize silage		1.3	(46)
Silage: large round bales		2.5	(88)
Wheat straw ⎤		13.0	(464)
Barley straw ⎬ small bales		11.5	(411)
Hay ⎰		6.0	(214)
Wheat straw ⎱		20.0	(714)
Barley straw ⎱ large round bales		18.0	(643)
Hay ⎦		8.0	(286)
Brewers' grains		0.9	(32)

(With straw and hay the storage requirement clearly depends on the packing density; the above are simply typical averages).

Boxes (floor area in square metres (feet) per tonne):

Potatoes:	0.5 tonne boxes, 5 boxes high	0.52	(5.6)
	1.0 tonne boxes, 4 boxes high	0.52	(5.6)
	1.0 tonne boxes, 5 boxes high	0.45	(4.8)

Bags (floor area in square metres (feet) per tonne):

Feedingstuffs:	2 bags high	1.6	(17)
Fertilizer:	6 bags high	1.1	(12)
	10 bags high	0.7	(8)

VII. CAPITAL, TAXATION AND GRANTS
1. CAPITAL

(i) *Tenant's Capital consists of:*

   (a) *Machinery.* Costs of new machinery are given on pages 147-152. Written-down values in 2008 are likely to be averaging about £500 per hectare (£200 per acre) taking all farm types together.

   (b) *Breeding Livestock.* Over all types of farm the 2008 average is estimated to be about £450 per hectare (£180 per acre), but the figure varies from zero to over £1,250 (£505) for a small, intensive dairy farm. Approximate average market values (£) of various categories of breeding livestock (of mixed ages in the case of adult stock) are as follows (actual value will vary according to average age and weight, quality and breed):

Holstein Friesian Dairy Cows (inc. dry cows): 700.
Channel Island Dairy Cows (inc. dry cows): 450.
Other Dairy Cows (inc. dry cows): 575.
Beef Cows: 550.

Other Cattle:	Dairy Followers		Beef Cattle
	Holstein Friesians	Ayrshires and C.I. Breeds	
In-calf heifers	725	500	600
Over 2 years.	525	375	500
1-2 years.	435	305	400
6-12 months.	330	220	300
Under 6 months.	180	110	200

Ewes: 60.   Rams 275
Sows and In-pig Gilts: 110.   Boars   500.

   (c) *Working Capital.* This is defined as the current assets of a business less its current liabilities. It is the liquid capital needed to finance the cash flow through the production cycle, the length of which varies considerably between different crop and livestock enterprises and different combinations of these enterprises. It can include the cost of purchased fattening stock, feed, seed, fertilizers, regular labour, machinery running costs, general overhead costs, rent and living expenses. This capital may be only £100 per hectare (£40 per acre) or so on an all-dairying farm but £400 or more per hectare (£160 per acre) on an all-cereals farm where the crop is stored until the spring. The average is likely to be about £325 per hectare (£130 per acre) in 2008.

(ii) *Return on Capital*

   (a) *Tenant's capital.* For all lowland farms (excluding intensive pig and poultry units, fruit and glasshouse production), total tenant's capital will average about £1,300 per hectare (£525 per acre) in 2008 (for range, see table on page 191). If the average UK management and investment income in year 2008 were, say, £75 per hectare (£30 per acre), the average return on tenant's capital would be 5.8 per cent. 'Premium' levels (the average of the top 50 per cent of farms) would be likely to be some 50 per cent higher (i.e. close to 9 per cent), with the levels achieved for mixed cropping on the very best soils and top dairy farms at least double the average. Note that no charge has been included for management (but that a rental value for owner-occupied land and the value of the unpaid labour of the farmer and wife have been deducted).

(b) *Landlord's Capital* (i.e. land, buildings, roads, etc.). With farms in 2008 averaging, say, £7,800 per hectare (£3,160 per acre), with vacant possession (assuming no special amenity or house value), an average lowland rent of, say, £150 per hectare (£60 per acre) (see p. 174), and assuming ownership expenses at £60 per hectare (£24 per acre), the (net) return (£90 per hectare (£36 per acre)) averages 1.3 per cent. If land is taken at its tenanted value, with a vacant possession premium of say one-third, the return increases to 2 per cent. If farm business tenancy rents were paid, at say 33% above the average level for established tenants (i.e. £200/ha [£80/acre]), the return would average 2 per cent with land at the vacant possession price assumed and 3 per cent with land at the tenanted value assumed. Full repairing and insurance leases clearly raise the returns above these levels. Above average quality farms acquire higher rents but also obviously command higher prices than the average levels quoted above.

(c) *Total Owner-Occupier's Capital* (i.e. land plus 'tenant's' capital). The combined (net) return on the above assumptions (£165 per hectare, or £66 per acre) on total capital, (£8,100 per hectare, or £3,280 per acre), with land at its vacant possession value, averages 2.03 per cent. This increases to 2.83 per cent if land is taken at its tenanted value and this is two-thirds the vacant possession value. If higher rent levels are assumed (given the same farming return), the overall return remains the same, the distribution simply being reallocated in favour of the land ownership share at the expense of the farming share. 'Premium' farming returns (as defined above), assuming the same capital requirements, raise the returns to 2.5 per cent with land at the vacant possession price and 3.5 per cent with tenanted land values.

(iii) Average Tenant's Capital per hectare (per acre in brackets) for Different Farm Types, as estimated for 2007, are as follows:

Farm Type Group	Average No. Hectares	Livestock £	Crops, Cultivns., Stores £	Machinery and Equipment* £	Total Tenant's Capital £	£
Mainly Dairying:						
under 75 ha..........	40	1250	150	800	2200	(890)
75 to 125 ha.........	100	1050	175	675	1900	(770)
Over 125 ha.........	150	900	200	525	1625	(660)
Mainly Arable:						
under 100 ha.........	60	100	375	575	1050	(425)
100 to 200 ha.......	150	100	350	475	925	(375)
over 200 ha..........	350	75	375	425	875	(355)
Dairy and Arable:						
under 100 ha.........	70	725	250	575	1550	(625)
100 to 200 ha........	150	650	275	550	1475	(595)
over 200 ha..........	350	475	325	525	1325	(535)
Mainly Sheep/Cattle:						
under 100 ha......	65	550	150	350	1050	(425)
over 100 ha..........	175	525	125	325	975	(395)
Sheep/Cattle and Arable:						
under 100 ha.........	70	600	175	350	1125	(455)
100 to 200 ha........	150	550	200	325	1175	(435)
over 200 ha..........	300	500	250	300	1050	(425)
Dairy, Sheep/Cattle and Arable:	275	450	250	475	1175	(475)
Intensive Arable:						
Fruit...................	90	0	3250	1250	4500	(1820)
Field Vegetables....	60	0	450	2200	2650	(1075)
Mainly Pigs Poultry:						
(per £1000 output).	—	200	75	200	475	

* Based on current (i.e. replacement) costs.

Note: The above (deliberately rounded) data are based on Farm Business Survey results compiled annually by University/Colleges centres (as listed on page 5), where actual figures for previous years can be found. None includes the value of milk quota on farms with dairying, even though a case can be made for this on the grounds of opportunity cost; obviously the cost of additional quota must be included when budgeting for, and calculating the return on capital of, introducing or expanding a dairy herd — whether by increasing yield per cow or the number of cows or both.

(iv) *Return on Capital to Individual Enterprises* on a mixed farm is virtually impossible to ascertain, except perhaps for a full-time pig or poultry enterprise, nor would it be of very much use even if it could be determined. It would require the arbitrary allocation both of costs and capital inputs that are common to several, in some cases all, of the enterprises on the farm.

What is relevant and important is the extra (net) return from an enterprise either to be introduced or expanded, as calculated by a partial budget, related to the extra (net) capital needed. The 'net' in brackets relates, as regards return, to the addition to gross margins less any addition to (or plus any reduction in) 'fixed' costs, bearing in mind that another enterprise may have to be deleted or reduced in size; and, as regards capital, to the fact that deletion or reduction of another enterprise may release capital.

In most cases of 'marginal' substitution, it is differences in the value of breeding livestock and differences in variable costs that are particularly relevant, but the timing of both inputs and sales are also obviously very important.

(v) *'Marginal' Capital Requirements* for small changes in crop areas or livestock numbers can be estimated as follows:

Crops: variable costs till sale.

Dairy Cows and Egg Production: value of the cow* or hens, plus food until payment of product.

Other Breeding Livestock: average value of stock*, plus variable costs to sale (payment) of the progeny (e.g. lambs) – or their transfer to another enterprise (*e.g.* weaners to the pig fattening enterprise). Rearing Breeding Livestock (*e.g.* heifers, tegs, gilts, pullets): cost of the calf, lamb, weaner or chick, plus variable costs till they produce their first progeny/eggs.

Fattening Livestock and Production of Stores: cost of stock, plus variable costs till sale.

* Value of breeding stock, including dairy cows: either the average value over their entire breeding or milk producing life (see table on page 194) or their value when they first produce progeny can be taken. The latter will give the lower return on (marginal) capital and is thus the severer test.

Home-reared stock: where stock to be used for milk or egg production, breeding or fattening are home-reared, there are two possibilities:

(i) either they can be valued at variable costs of production when they are transferred from the rearing to the 'productive' enterprise; in this case the return on (marginal) capital will be estimated over the combined rearing and 'productive' enterprise.

(ii) or they can be valued at market value at point of transfer. This is the procedure if one wishes to work out a return on (marginal) capital for the rearing and the 'productive' enterprises separately.

(vi) Return on 'Marginal' Capital. This is sometimes expressed as the gross margin less fuel and repair costs of the enterprise expanded as a percentage of the 'marginal', or extra, capital. However, two points have to be remembered:

(i) If another enterprise has had to be reduced in size to enable the enterprise under consideration to be expanded, the capital released and the gross margin forfeited by reducing the size of the first enterprise must be brought into the calculation in estimating the net result of the change.

(ii) All the above statements on 'marginal' capital refer to small changes. If the change is large enough to cause changes in labour, machinery or building requirements the capital changes brought about may be considerably greater.

(vii) Return on Investments in Medium-Term and Long-Term Capital. Rate of Return and the Discounted Yield.

Example: If £5,000 investment results in an annual net return of £500 (after deducting depreciation, but ignoring interest payments):

$$\textit{Rate of Return on Initial Capital} = \frac{500}{5,000} \times 100 = 10\%$$

$$\textit{Rate of Return on Average Capital} = \frac{500}{2,500} \times 100 = 20\%$$

It is more accurate to calculate the 'Discounted Yield', which is the discount rate that brings the present value of the net cash flows (which means ignoring depreciation) to the value of the investment.

The tables on pages 194 and 195 may be used.

'Short-Cut' Estimates of the Discounted Yield on depreciating assets. The Discounted Yield falls between the simple Rates of Return on Initial and Average Capital. In fact, for investments lasting 5 to 15 years, when the Rate of Return on Initial Capital is 10 per cent and on Average Capital 20 per cent, the Discounted Yield will be almost exactly halfway between, i.e. about 15 per cent. However, this is only so providing the anticipated annual net cash earnings are fairly constant — or fluctuate unpredictably around a fairly constant level.

There are three circumstances when the Discounted Yield will get closer to the Rate of Return on Initial Capital (i.e. the lower per cent return) and further from the Rate of Return on Average Capital:

(a) The longer the life of the investment.

(b) The higher the Rate of Return.

(c) The higher the net cash flow is in the later years of the investment compared with the earlier years.

When the opposite circumstances obtain, the Discounted Yield will be closer to the Rate of Return on Average Capital (i.e. the higher per cent return).

Granted that there are inevitably varying degrees of estimation and uncertainty in calculating future net annual earnings of investments, the following short-cuts might reasonably be used where the annual net cash earnings are expected to be fairly constant — or fluctuate unpredictably (e.g. through weather effects on yields) around a fairly constant level. (W.O. period = write-off period; R.R.I.C. = rate of return on initial capital).

1. Where (i) the W.O. period is 5 years or less,

   (ii) the W.O. period is 6 - 10 years and the R.R.I.C. is 15 per cent or less,
   (iii) the W.O. period is 11 - 20 years and the R.R.I.C. is 10 per cent or less,

   calculate the Return on Capital as being approximately midway between the Rates of Return on Initial and Average Capital, i.e. by calculating the Rate of Return on 2/3 of the original investment.

For example, following the earlier example:

$$\frac{500}{3,333} \times 100 = 15\%.$$

2. Where (i) the W.O. period is 6 to 10 years and the R.R.I.C. exceeds 15 per cent,

   (ii) the W.O. period is 11 to 20 years and the R.R.I.C. is between 10 per cent and 25 per cent,

(iii) the W.O. period exceeds 20 years and the R.R.I.C. is 10 per cent or less,

calculate the Return on Capital on 80 per cent of the original investment.

For example, again following the earlier example:

$$\frac{500}{4,000} \times 100 = 12\frac{1}{2}\%.$$

3. Where (i) the W.O. period is 11 to 20 years and the R.R.I.C. exceeds 25 per cent,

     (ii) the W.O. period exceeds 20 years and the R.R.I.C. exceeds 10 per cent, take the Return on Capital to be the R.R.I.C.

In borderline cases, use method 1 rather than 2, or 2 rather than 3 if there is a tendency for the cash flow to be higher in the earlier years, e.g. because of tax allowances on machinery. Take 2 rather than 1, and 3 rather than 2, if the likelihood is that the cash flow will be lower in earlier years and increase in later years.

However, where the annual cash flow is expected to vary (apart from unpredictable fluctuations) it is safer to make the full D.C.F. calculation. This is particularly so where the variation is both up and down and where further periodic investments are to be made during the life of the project.

Discounting Table A

Discount Factors for Calculating the Present Value of Future (irregular) Cash Flows

Year	Percentage																
	3%	4%	5%	6%	7%	8%	9%	10%	11%	12%	13%	14%	15%	16%	18%	20%	25%
1	0.971	0.962	0.952	0.943	0.935	0.926	0.917	0.909	0.901	0.893	0.885	0.877	0.870	0.862	0.847	0.833	0.800
2	0.943	0.925	0.907	0.890	0.873	0.857	0.842	0.826	0.812	0.797	0.783	0.769	0.756	0.743	0.718	0.694	0.640
3	0.915	0.889	0.864	0.840	0.816	0.794	0.772	0.751	0.731	0.712	0.693	0.675	0.658	0.641	0.609	0.579	0.512
4	0.888	0.855	0.823	0.792	0.763	0.735	0.708	0.683	0.659	0.636	0.613	0.592	0.572	0.552	0.516	0.482	0.410
5	0.863	0.822	0.784	0.747	0.713	0.681	0.650	0.621	0.593	0.567	0.543	0.519	0.497	0.476	0.437	0.402	0.328
6	0.837	0.790	0.746	0.705	0.666	0.630	0.596	0.564	0.535	0.507	0.480	0.456	0.432	0.410	0.370	0.335	0.262
7	0.813	0.760	0.711	0.665	0.623	0.583	0.547	0.513	0.482	0.452	0.425	0.400	0.376	0.354	0.314	0.279	0.210
8	0.789	0.731	0.677	0.627	0.582	0.540	0.502	0.467	0.434	0.404	0.376	0.351	0.327	0.305	0.266	0.233	0.168
9	0.766	0.703	0.645	0.592	0.544	0.500	0.460	0.424	0.391	0.361	0.333	0.308	0.284	0.263	0.225	0.194	0.134
10	0.744	0.676	0.614	0.558	0.508	0.463	0.422	0.386	0.352	0.322	0.295	0.270	0.247	0.227	0.191	0.162	0.107
11	0.722	0.650	0.585	0.527	0.475	0.429	0.388	0.350	0.317	0.287	0.261	0.237	0.215	0.195	0.162	0.135	0.086
12	0.701	0.625	0.557	0.497	0.444	0.397	0.356	0.319	0.286	0.257	0.231	0.208	0.187	0.168	0.137	0.112	0.069
13	0.681	0.601	0.530	0.469	0.415	0.368	0.326	0.290	0.258	0.229	0.204	0.182	0.163	0.145	0.116	0.093	0.055
14	0.661	0.577	0.505	0.442	0.388	0.340	0.299	0.263	0.232	0.205	0.181	0.160	0.141	0.125	0.098	0.078	0.044
15	0.642	0.555	0.481	0.417	0.362	0.315	0.275	0.239	0.209	0.183	0.160	0.140	0.123	0.108	0.084	0.065	0.035
20	0.554	0.456	0.377	0.312	0.258	0.215	0.178	0.149	0.124	0.104	0.087	0.073	0.061	0.051	0.037	0.026	0.012
25	0.478	0.375	0.295	0.233	0.184	0.146	0.116	0.092	0.074	0.059	0.047	0.038	0.030	0.024	0.016	0.010	0.004
30	0.412	0.308	0.231	0.174	0.131	0.099	0.075	0.057	0.044	0.033	0.026	0.020	0.015	0.012	0.007	0.004	0.001

Example: The Present Value of £500 received 10 years from now, at 12 per cent discount rate of interest = 500 x 0.322 = £161.

Conversely, £161 invested now, at 12 per cent compound interest, will be worth £500 in 10 years' time.

Discounting Table B

Discount Factors for Calculating the Present Value of Future Annuity (i.e. Constant Annual Cash Flow) Receivable in Year 1 to n inclusive.

Year	Percentage																
	3%	4%	5%	6%	7%	8%	9%	10%	11%	12%	13%	14%	15%	16%	18%	20%	25%
1	0.971	0.962	0.952	0.943	0.935	0.926	0.917	0.909	0.901	0.893	0.885	0.877	0.870	0.862	0.847	0.833	0.800
2	1.913	1.886	1.859	1.833	1.808	1.783	1.759	1.736	1.713	1.690	1.668	1.647	1.626	1.605	1.566	1.528	1.440
3	2.829	2.775	2.723	2.673	2.624	2.577	2.531	2.487	2.444	2.402	2.361	2.322	2.283	2.246	2.174	2.106	1.952
4	3.717	3.630	3.546	3.465	3.387	3.312	3.240	3.170	3.102	3.037	2.974	2.914	2.855	2.798	2.690	2.589	2.362
5	4.580	4.452	4.329	4.212	4.100	3.993	3.890	3.791	3.696	3.605	3.517	3.433	3.352	3.274	3.127	2.991	2.689
6	5.417	5.242	5.076	4.917	4.767	4.623	4.486	4.355	4.231	4.111	3.998	3.889	3.784	3.685	3.498	3.326	2.951
7	6.230	6.002	5.786	5.582	5.389	5.206	5.033	4.868	4.712	4.564	4.423	4.288	4.160	4.039	3.812	3.605	3.161
8	7.020	6.733	6.463	6.210	5.971	5.747	5.535	5.335	5.146	4.968	4.799	4.639	4.487	4.344	4.078	3.837	3.329
9	7.786	7.435	7.108	6.802	6.515	6.247	5.995	5.759	5.537	5.328	5.132	4.946	4.772	4.607	4.303	4.031	3.463
10	8.530	8.111	7.722	7.360	7.024	6.710	6.418	6.145	5.889	5.650	5.426	5.216	5.019	4.833	4.494	4.192	3.570
11	9.253	8.760	8.306	7.887	7.499	7.139	6.805	6.495	6.207	5.938	5.687	5.453	5.234	5.029	4.656	4.327	3.656
12	9.954	9.385	8.863	8.384	7.943	7.536	7.161	6.814	6.492	6.194	5.918	5.660	5.421	5.197	4.793	4.439	3.725
13	10.635	9.986	9.394	8.853	8.358	7.904	7.487	7.103	6.750	6.424	6.122	5.842	5.583	5.342	4.910	4.533	3.780
14	11.296	10.563	9.899	9.295	8.745	8.244	7.786	7.367	6.982	6.628	6.302	6.002	5.724	5.468	5.008	4.611	3.824
15	11.938	11.118	10.380	9.712	9.108	8.559	8.061	7.606	7.191	6.811	6.462	6.142	5.847	5.575	5.092	4.675	3.859
20	14.877	13.590	12.462	11.470	10.594	9.818	9.129	8.514	7.963	7.469	7.025	6.623	6.259	5.929	5.353	4.870	3.954
25	17.413	15.662	14.094	12.783	11.654	10.675	9.823	9.077	8.422	7.843	7.330	6.873	6.464	6.097	5.467	4.948	3.985
30	19.600	17.292	15.372	13.765	12.409	11.258	10.274	9.427	8.694	8.055	7.496	7.003	6.566	6.177	5.517	4.979	3.995

Example: The Present Value of £500 a year for the next 10 years, at 12 per cent discount rate of interest = 500 x 5.650 = £2,825. This is the same answer that would be obtained by multiplying 500 by each discount factor (at 12 per cent) in Table A for each year from 1 to 10, and adding together the ten resulting figures.

To obtain the Discounted Yield of a constant annual net cash flow, divide this into the original investment and look up the resulting figure in the table above, against the number of years. Example: an investment of £1,000 is estimated to produce £80 a year additional profit over 10 years (before charging interest). Add £100 depreciation a year = £180 annual net cash flow. 1000 / 180 = 5.56. This equals just over 12 per cent (the 10 years /12 per cent figure being 5.650).

Compounding Table A

The Future Money Value of £1 after n Years with no additional payments made

Year									Rate of Interest								
	3%	4%	5%	6%	7%	8%	9%	10%	11%	12%	13%	14%	15%	16%	18%	20%	25%
1	1.03	1.04	1.05	1.06	1.07	1.08	1.09	1.10	1.11	1.12	1.13	1.14	1.15	1.16	1.18	1.20	1.25
2	1.06	1.08	1.10	1.12	1.14	1.17	1.19	1.21	1.23	1.25	1.28	1.30	1.32	1.35	1.39	1.44	1.56
3	1.09	1.12	1.16	1.19	1.23	1.26	1.30	1.33	1.37	1.40	1.44	1.48	1.52	1.56	1.64	1.73	1.95
4	1.13	1.17	1.22	1.26	1.31	1.36	1.41	1.46	1.52	1.57	1.63	1.69	1.75	1.81	1.94	2.07	2.44
5	1.16	1.22	1.28	1.34	1.40	1.47	1.54	1.61	1.69	1.76	1.84	1.93	2.01	2.10	2.29	2.49	3.05
6	1.19	1.27	1.34	1.42	1.50	1.59	1.68	1.77	1.87	1.97	2.08	2.19	2.31	2.44	2.70	2.99	3.81
7	1.23	1.32	1.41	1.50	1.61	1.71	1.83	1.95	2.08	2.21	2.35	2.50	2.66	2.83	3.19	3.58	4.77
8	1.27	1.37	1.48	1.59	1.72	1.85	1.99	2.14	2.30	2.48	2.66	2.85	3.06	3.28	3.76	4.30	5.96
9	1.30	1.42	1.55	1.69	1.84	2.00	2.17	2.36	2.56	2.77	3.00	3.25	3.52	3.80	4.44	5.16	7.45
10	1.34	1.48	1.63	1.79	1.97	2.16	2.37	2.59	2.84	3.11	3.39	3.71	4.05	4.41	5.23	6.19	9.31
11	1.38	1.54	1.71	1.90	2.10	2.33	2.58	2.85	3.15	3.48	3.84	4.23	4.65	5.12	6.18	7.43	11.64
12	1.43	1.60	1.80	2.01	2.25	2.52	2.81	3.14	3.50	3.90	4.33	4.82	5.35	5.94	7.29	8.92	14.55
13	1.47	1.67	1.89	2.13	2.41	2.72	3.07	3.45	3.88	4.36	4.90	5.49	6.15	6.89	8.60	10.70	18.19
14	1.51	1.73	1.98	2.26	2.58	2.94	3.34	3.80	4.31	4.89	5.53	6.26	7.08	7.99	10.15	12.84	22.74
15	1.56	1.80	2.08	2.40	2.76	3.17	3.64	4.18	4.78	5.47	6.25	7.14	8.14	9.27	11.97	15.41	28.42
20	1.81	2.19	2.65	3.21	3.87	4.66	5.60	6.73	8.06	9.65	11.52	13.74	16.37	19.46	27.39	38.34	86.74
25	2.09	2.67	3.39	4.29	5.43	6.85	8.62	10.83	13.59	17.00	21.23	26.46	32.92	40.87	62.67	95.40	264.7
30	2.43	3.24	4.32	5.74	7.61	10.06	13.27	17.45	22.89	29.96	39.12	50.95	66.21	85.85	143.4	237.4	807.8

Compounding Table B

The Future Money Value of £1 after n Years*

Year									Rate of Interest								
	3%	4%	5%	6%	7%	8%	9%	10%	11%	12%	13%	14%	15%	16%	18%	20%	25%
1	1.03	1.04	1.05	1.06	1.07	1.08	1.09	1.10	1.11	1.12	1.13	1.14	1.15	1.16	1.18	1.20	1.25
2	2.09	2.12	2.15	2.18	2.21	2.25	2.28	2.31	2.34	2.37	2.41	2.44	2.47	2.51	2.57	2.64	2.81
3	3.18	3.25	3.31	3.37	3.44	3.51	3.57	3.64	3.71	3.78	3.85	3.92	3.99	4.07	4.22	4.37	4.77
4	4.31	4.42	4.53	4.64	4.75	4.87	4.98	5.11	5.23	5.35	5.48	5.61	5.74	5.88	6.15	6.44	7.21
5	5.47	5.63	5.80	5.98	6.15	6.34	6.52	6.72	6.91	7.12	7.32	7.54	7.75	7.98	8.44	8.93	10.26
6	6.66	6.90	7.14	7.39	7.65	7.92	8.20	8.49	8.78	9.09	9.40	9.73	10.07	10.41	11.14	11.92	14.07
7	7.89	8.21	8.55	8.90	9.26	9.64	10.03	10.44	10.86	11.30	11.76	12.23	12.73	13.24	14.33	15.50	18.84
8	9.16	9.58	10.03	10.49	10.98	11.49	12.02	12.58	13.16	13.78	14.42	15.09	15.79	16.52	18.09	19.80	24.80
9	10.46	11.01	11.58	12.18	12.82	13.49	14.19	14.94	15.72	16.55	17.42	18.34	19.30	20.32	22.52	24.96	32.25
10	11.81	12.49	13.21	13.97	14.78	15.65	16.56	17.53	18.56	19.65	20.81	22.04	23.35	24.73	27.76	31.15	41.57
11	13.19	14.03	14.92	15.87	16.89	17.98	19.14	20.38	21.71	23.13	24.65	26.27	28.00	29.85	33.93	38.58	53.21
12	14.62	15.63	16.71	17.88	19.14	20.50	21.95	23.52	25.21	27.03	28.98	31.09	33.35	35.79	41.22	47.50	67.76
13	16.09	17.29	18.60	20.02	21.55	23.21	25.02	26.97	29.09	31.39	33.88	36.58	39.50	42.67	49.82	58.20	85.95
14	17.60	19.02	20.58	22.28	24.13	26.15	28.36	30.77	33.41	36.28	39.42	42.84	46.58	50.66	59.97	71.04	108.7
15	19.16	20.82	22.66	24.67	26.89	29.32	32.00	34.95	38.19	41.75	45.67	49.98	54.72	59.93	71.94	86.44	137.1
20	27.68	30.97	34.72	38.99	43.87	49.42	55.76	63.00	71.27	80.70	91.47	103.8	117.8	133.8	173.0	224.0	428.7
25	37.55	43.31	50.11	58.16	67.68	78.95	92.32	108.2	127.0	149.3	175.8	207.3	244.7	289.1	404.3	566.4	1318
30	49.00	58.33	69.76	83.80	101.1	122.3	148.6	180.9	220.9	270.3	331.3	406.7	500.0	615.2	933.3	1418	4034

* Equal payments made at the beginning of each year.

198

Amortisation Table

Annual Charge to write off £1,000

Write-off Period (Years)	3	4	5	6	7	8	9	10	11	12	13	14	15	16	18	20
											Rate of Interest					
5	218	225	231	237	244	250	257	264	271	277	284	291	298	305	320	334
6	185	191	197	203	210	216	223	230	236	243	250	257	264	271	286	301
7	161	167	173	179	186	192	199	205	212	219	226	233	240	248	262	277
8	142	149	155	161	167	174	181	187	194	201	208	216	223	230	245	261
9	128	134	141	147	153	160	167	174	181	188	195	202	210	217	232	248
10	117	123	130	136	142	149	156	163	170	177	184	192	199	207	223	239
11	108	114	120	127	133	140	147	154	161	168	176	183	191	199	215	231
12	100	107	113	119	125	133	140	147	154	161	169	177	184	192	209	225
13	94	100	106	113	120	127	134	141	148	156	163	171	179	187	204	221
14	89	95	101	108	114	121	128	136	143	151	159	167	175	183	200	217
15	84	90	96	103	110	117	124	131	139	147	155	163	171	179	196	214
16	80	86	92	99	106	113	120	128	136	143	151	160	168	176	194	211
17	76	82	89	95	102	110	117	125	132	140	149	157	165	174	191	209
18	73	79	86	92	99	107	114	122	130	138	146	155	163	172	190	208
19	70	76	83	90	97	104	112	120	128	136	144	153	161	170	188	206
20	67	74	80	87	94	102	110	117	126	134	142	151	160	169	187	205
25	57	64	71	78	86	94	102	110	119	127	136	145	155	164	183	202
30	51	58	65	73	81	89	97	106	115	124	133	143	152	162	181	201
40	43	51	58	66	75	84	93	102	112	122	131	141	151	160	180	200

Example: £3,000 is borrowed to erect a building. The annual charge to service interest and capital repayment on the £3,000, repayable over 10 years at 12%, is 3 x £177 = £531. Where the write-off period of the building (10 years) is equal to the repayment period of the loan, then the average annual depreciation and interest will also equal £531.

The proportion of the total annual charge representing the average amount of capital repaid per annum can be readily determined by dividing the sum borrowed by the number of years of the loan: (in the above example this is £3,000 ÷ 10 = £300/year). The remainder is clearly the average amount of interest paid per annum: (in the above example, £531 — £300 = £231/year). The year to year variations between the two items (i.e. capital repaid and interest) are shown in the tables on pages 201 to 203, which demonstrate the way in which the capital repayment part increases and the interest part decreases over time.

Sinking Fund Table

The sum required to be set aside at the end of each year to make £1,000

No. of Years	Rate of Interest															
	3	4	5	6	7	8	9	10	11	12	13	14	15	16	18	20
5	188	185	181	177	174	170	167	164	161	157	154	151	148	145	140	134
6	155	151	147	143	140	136	133	130	126	123	120	117	114	111	106	101
7	131	127	123	119	116	112	109	105	102	99	96	93	90	88	82	77
8	112	109	105	101	97	94	91	87	84	81	78	76	73	70	65	61
9	98	94	91	87	83	80	77	74	71	68	65	62	60	57	52	48
10	87	83	80	76	72	69	66	63	60	57	54	52	49	47	43	39
11	78	74	70	67	63	60	57	54	51	48	46	43	41	39	35	31
12	70	67	63	59	56	53	50	47	44	41	39	37	34	32	29	25
13	64	60	56	53	50	47	44	41	38	36	33	31	29	27	24	21
14	59	55	51	48	44	41	38	36	33	31	29	27	25	23	20	17
15	54	50	46	43	40	37	34	31	29	27	25	23	21	19	16	14
16	50	46	42	39	36	33	30	28	26	23	21	20	18	16	14	11
17	46	42	39	35	32	30	27	25	22	20	19	17	15	14	11	9
18	43	39	36	32	29	27	24	22	20	18	16	15	13	12	10	8
19	40	36	33	30	27	24	22	20	18	16	14	13	11	10	8	6
20	37	34	30	27	24	22	20	17	16	14	12	11	10	9	7	5
25	27	24	21	18	16	14	12	10	9	7	6	5	5	4	3	2
30	21	18	15	13	11	9	7	6	5	4	3	3	2	2	1	1
40	13	11	8	6	5	4	3	2	2	1	1	1	1	—	—	—

Mortgage Repayment Data

Items per £1000 invested; where I = Interest, P = Principal repaid, L = Loan outstanding

Loan through	4%			5%			6%			8%			10%			12%		
	I	P	L	I	P	L	I	P	L	I	P	L	I	P	L	I	P	L
5 years																		
1	40	185	815	50	181	819	60	177	823	80	170	830	100	164	836	120	157	834
2	33	192	623	41	190	629	49	188	635	66	184	645	84	180	656	101	175	670
3	25	200	424	31	200	424	38	199	435	52	199	447	66	198	458	80	197	469
4	17	208	216	21	210	220	26	211	224	36	215	232	46	218	240	56	221	248
5	9	216	0	11	220	0	13	224	0	19	232	0	24	240	0	30	248	0
10 years																		
1	40	83	917	50	80	920	60	76	924	80	69	931	100	63	939	120	57	934
2	37	87	830	46	83	837	55	80	844	75	75	856	94	69	868	113	64	879
3	33	90	740	42	88	749	51	85	758	69	81	776	87	76	792	106	71	808
4	30	94	646	37	92	657	46	90	668	62	87	689	79	84	709	97	80	728
5	26	97	549	33	97	561	40	96	572	55	94	595	71	92	617	87	90	638
6	22	101	448	28	101	459	34	102	471	48	101	494	62	101	516	77	100	538
7	18	105	342	23	107	353	28	108	363	39	110	384	52	111	405	65	112	425
8	14	110	233	18	112	241	22	114	249	31	118	266	40	122	282	51	126	299
9	9	114	119	12	117	123	15	121	128	21	128	138	28	134	148	36	141	158
10	5	119	0	6	123	0	8	128	0	11	138	0	15	148	0	19	158	0

Mortgage Repayment Data (continued)

Loan through 20 years	4%			5%			6%			8%			10%			12%		
	I	P	L	I	P	L	I	P	L	I	P	L	I	P	L	I	P	L
1	40	34	966	50	30	970	60	27	973	80	22	978	100	17	983	120	14	986
5	34	39	818	43	37	833	53	34	847	72	30	872	92	26	893	112	22	912
10	26	48	597	33	47	620	41	46	642	58	44	683	76	41	722	95	38	756
15	15	58	328	20	60	347	26	61	367	38	64	407	51	66	445	66	68	483
20	3	71	0	4	76	0	5	82	0	8	94	0	11	107	0	14	120	0
25 years																		
1	40	24	976	50	21	979	60	18	982	80	14	986	100	10	990	120	7	993
5	36	28	870	45	25	884	55	23	897	75	19	920	95	15	938	116	12	952
10	30	34	712	38	33	736	47	31	760	66	27	802	86	24	838	107	21	868
15	22	42	519	29	41	548	37	41	576	54	40	629	72	39	677	91	37	720
20	13	51	285	18	53	307	23	55	330	35	59	374	48	62	418	63	65	460
25	2	62	0	3	68	0	4	74	0	7	87	0	10	100	0	14	114	0

Mortgage Repayment Data *(continued)*

Loan through 30 years	6%			8%			10%			12%			14%			16%		
	I	P	L	I	P	L	I	P	L	I	P	L	I	P	L	I	P	L
1	60	13	987	80	9	991	100	6	994	120	4	996	140	3	997	160	2	998
5	57	16	929	77	12	948	97	9	963	118	7	974	138	5	986	158	3	987
10	51	21	833	71	18	872	92	14	903	113	11	927	134	9	951	155	7	960
15	44	29	706	63	26	760	83	23	807	104	20	846	126	17	890	147	15	903
20	34	38	535	51	38	596	69	37	652	88	36	701	108	35	751	130	32	782
25	21	51	306	33	56	355	46	60	402	61	63	488	83	60	494	95	66	530
30	4	69	0	7	82	0	10	96	0	13	111	0	16	127	0	22	140	0
40 years																		
1	60	6	994	80	4	996	100	2	998	120	1	999	140	1	999	160	0	1000
5	58	8	964	79	5	977	99	3	986	119	2	992	139	2	995	160	1	997
10	56	11	915	76	8	944	97	5	964	118	4	977	138	3	989	159	2	991
15	52	15	850	73	11	895	94	9	928	115	6	951	136	5	973	157	3	978
20	47	20	762	67	17	823	88	14	871	110	11	906	130	11	942	153	7	951
25	40	26	645	59	24	718	80	22	778	102	20	826	123	18	874	145	15	894
30	31	35	489	48	36	563	66	36	628	86	35	685	109	32	742	129	31	775
35	20	47	280	31	53	335	45	58	388	60	61	437	85	56	487	95	66	525
40	4	63	0	6	78	0	9	93	0	13	108	0	18	123	0	22	138	0

Note—All figures rounded to nearest £.

Rates of Interest: Further Points

(i) *Rate of Interest on Bank Loans.* Typically 2.25% to 2.5% above Base Rate. Main range is 1.5% above to 3.5% above. Extremes are likely to be 1% above (minimum) and 5% above (maximum).

(ii) *Annual Percentage Rate (APR).* This is the effective rate of interest calculated on an annual basis and should be used when seeking to make a true comparison between interest charges on money borrowed from different sources. The APR allows for the fact that when interest is applied to accounts at half yearly, quarterly or monthly intervals an element of compounding will arise. For example, £100 borrowed for one year at a quoted annual nominal interest rate of 6% (e.g. 2% over base rate of 4%) with interest charged quarterly, will lead to an accumulated interest charge of £6.136 (i.e., giving an APR of just under 6.14%). The higher the annual nominal interest rate and the more frequently the interest charges are applied to the account, the more pronounced the compounding element becomes. For example, an annual nominal interest rate of 10% produces an APR of 10.25% with half yearly charging, 10.38% with quarterly charging and 10.47% with monthly charging and with a nominal rate as high as 20% the rates become 21%, 21.6% and 21.9% respectively.

In the case of some loans and hire purchase agreements, interest charges may be quoted as a flat rate on the original amount borrowed. The APR will be considerably greater than the flat rate if the loan is repaid by equal periodic instalments, comprising part capital and part interest, so that the borrowing is completely repaid by the end of the agreed term. For example, the APR for a loan at a flat rate of interest of 8% repaid by monthly instalments over 5 years will be 15%. The shorter the repayment period, and the more frequent the payments, the higher is the APR compared with the flat rate.

(iii) *The Real Rate of Interest.* When preparing simple profit and loss budgets to estimate the worthwhileness of an investment in a fixed asset (machinery, buildings, land), it is usual to price inputs and outputs at present-day values even when most costs and returns are expected to rise due to inflation over the life of the investment. Where this real terms approach is adopted a more realistic estimate of the effect on profitability can be gained by basing charges for capital on the real rate of interest rather than the APR. The real rate of interest is the APR adjusted for the annual rate at which prices relevant to the investment are expected to increase. A crude estimate of the real rate of interest can be obtained by simply subtracting the expected rate of price increase from the APR; for example, if the APR were 8% and the expected rate of inflation 3%, the real rate of interest would be $8 - 3 = 5\%$.

Financial Ratios

1. *Common Ratios*

The following ratios are often quoted as rough guidelines:

		% of Gross Output
Variable Costs		30-35%
Labour	15-17½%	
Machinery	15-17½%	} 35-40%
Sundry Fixed Costs	5%	
Rent & Interest		15%
Margin*		15%

* to cover drawings, tax, capital repayments, reinvestments

It has to be borne in mind, however, that these are indeed only rough guidelines and need to be considered with great care. Values vary, for example, with type of farming and size of farm. Furthermore, it is often unclear how certain items are being measured, especially whether unpaid manual labour of the farmer and family has been included or whether a rental value has been allowed for owner-occupied land.

2. Farm Survey Ratios

The following are rounded averages based on farm surveys in recent years on a large sample of all types of farm, assuming a Management and Investment Income (see page 231) of 10% of Total Output is made. It is to be noted that Total Output includes the market value of any production retained for use/consumption on the farm (e.g. cereals for feed or seed), Unpaid Labour (value of manual labour supplied by the farmer and spouse) is included. Rent includes the rental value of owner-occupied land and Interest charges are not included in the costs. Casual labour and all Contract work are included in fixed costs. Obviously, costs are a lower proportion and the margin a higher proportion in profitable years, and vice-versa in low profit years. Obviously, too, within years the more profitable farms have lower percentage costs, leaving higher percentage margins and vice-versa.

	% Total Output	% Total Gross Margin	% Total Fixed Costs
Variable Costs:			
(excl. casual labour and contract work)	32.5		
Fixed Costs:			
Labour: Paid (inc. casuals) }	20	30	33
Labour: Unpaid }			
Power & Machinery			
(inc. contract work)	20	30	33
Labour & Machinery	40	60	66
Rent/Rental Value	12.5	19	21
General Overheads	7.5	11	13
Total Fixed Costs	60	90	100
Margin	**7.5**	**10**	-

Total Gross Margin = 67.5% of Total Output

3. Lending Criteria

Another set of standards widely used by lending and leasing institutions looks at total Finance Charges (rent, interest, leasing charges, etc.), as a percentage of Gross Output and Gross Margin;

Finance as a % of Gross Output	Finance as a % of Gross Margin	Lending Criteria
0-10%	0-15%	Normally very safe
11-15%	16-22.5%	Common range, should be safe
16-20%	23-29%	Care required
20% plus	30% plus	Potentially dangerous

As lenders will be well aware, however, these ratios too must be regarded with caution and in conjunction with the farm's level of net worth (% equity) and its trend in recent years, recent trends in its profitability and the potential borrower's record of expenditure both on and off the farm, together with his or her character and potential. Also, of course, some enterprises / types of farming are more risky than others.

2. TAXATION

Note: no responsibility can be taken for any errors or omissions in the information presented in this section or for any action taken on the basis of the information provided. Professional advice should always be sought before taking any decision that may affect your tax position.

1. Income Tax

A. *Rates of Income Tax (2007-08)*

	Income Band	Dividends	Interest	Other Income
Starting rate	Up to £2,230	10	10	10
Basic rate	£2,231 to £34,600	10	20	22
Higher rate	Over £34,600	32.5	40	40

B. *Allowances and Reliefs (2007-08)*

(i) Personal Allowance: £5,225 (£7,550 if aged 65 to 74 and £7,690 if aged over 75 on 5th April 2008, subject to total income not exceeding the statutory income limit (£29,900 for 2007-08)).

(ii) Married Couple's Allowance: abolished from tax year ended 6th April 2001 except for couples where at least one spouse was born before 6th April 1935. From 2005-06 the allowance is available to couples in a civil partnership where at least one partner was born before 6th April 1935. The relief is given as a reduction in income tax restricted to the lower of 10% of the allowance (£2,440 for 2007-08) or the total tax liability.

(iii) Personal Pension Schemes. Tax relief is obtainable for contributions to a pension. The rules on maximum contributions have been simplified; there is an annual allowance of £225,000 (for 2007-08) and a lifetime allowance of £1,600,000. Maximum contributions under the simplified Stakeholder Pension rules are £3,600 per year.

2. Private Company Taxation

A. *Rates of Corporation Tax (FY07 – 1st April 2007-31st March 2008)*

Profits are chargeable to Corporation Tax at the following rates (the Starting rate of 0% was removed from 1st April 2006):

	Profits band	per cent tax	
		FY07	*FY08*
Small companies' rate	Up to £300,000	20	*21*
Upper marginal rate	£300,000 to £1.5m	32.5	*29.75*
Main companies' rate	Over £1.5m	30	*28*

B. *Company Taxation - Other Issues*

(i) *Capital Gains*: Capital gains of companies are charged at the appropriate rate of Corporation Tax.

(ii) *Quotas*: Milk quota purchased by a company after 1st April 2002 will attract Corporation Tax relief at the rate of depreciation selected in the accounting policies of the company or 4% per year if not depreciated in the accounts of the company.

(iii) *Distributions*: Dividends are not deductible in arriving at the amount of Corporation Tax profit. However, the recipient of distributions will be credited with a tax payment of 10% of distributions received, which will be deemed to discharge the liability of lower (10%) and basic rate (22%) taxpayers; however, higher rate taxpayers will have to pay additional tax of 25% of the net dividend; dividends are treated as the top slice of income.

(iv) *Losses*: Carry back restricted to one year. Losses can be carried forward and offset against profits of the same trade.

Editorial Note: *The increase in the rate of small companies Corporation Tax from 19% in FY06 to 21% in FY08 will make the benefits of incorporation less attractive. In addition, the reduction in the value of milk quotas make the benefits of incorporating to write-off the cost of the quota acquired by the company less attractive.*

3. Agricultural Businesses: Other Items

A. *Assessing Self-Employed Profits*

Since 1997-98 self-employed people have been assessed for tax in any tax year on the basis of the profits recorded in the annual accounts which end in that tax year, i.e. on a 'current year basis'.

B. *Livestock*

Dairy cows or breeding livestock may be treated on the herd basis or on a trading stock basis;

(i) *Herd basis:* valuation changes are not included in the trading account, nor are additions to the herd, but sales from the herd and replacements are. On the sale of all or a substantial proportion (normally taken as 20% or more) of the herd, no tax is paid on any profit over the original cost price, nor is there any relief for loss. ***Editorial Note:*** *The high values of cattle at present make it less likely that a new farming business will want to elect for the herd basis although each case must be judged on its merits.*

(ii) *Trading stock basis:* purchases, sales and valuation changes are all included in the trading account. Under this method stock should be valued at the lower of cost (or cost of production) and net realisable value. Where animals are home-produced and it is not possible to ascertain actual costs from farm records the 'deemed' cost may be used. This is 60% of market value for cattle and 75% for sheep and pigs.

C. *Stock Valuation: Crops*

Crops should generally be valued at the cost of production (or net realisable value, if lower). Costs which are directly attributable to buying, producing and growing the crops should be included. The deemed cost method allows 75% of market value to be used although this method should only be used where it is not possible to ascertain actual costs.

D. *Allowances for Capital Expenditure*

(i) *Machinery and Plant* (whether new or second hand). An annual writing down allowance of 25% is available on a reducing balance basis. However, small and medium-sized businesses are eligible to claim a first year allowance of 50%. The writing down allowances will normally be calculated on a "pool" basis. However, where it is expected that a machine will be sold within five years of acquisition and realise less than its written-down value for tax it will be possible for the taxpayer to elect to have allowances calculated separately for each machine. This system will enable balancing allowances to be claimed when a machine is sold for less than its written-down value. If at the end of five years the machine has not been sold its tax written-down value will be transferred to the main machinery pool. Motor cars costing more than £12,000 are included in a separate 'pool' in the year of purchase, on which a 25% writing down allowance is available. The allowance is restricted to a maximum of £3,000 for motor cars with a written-down value of more than £12,000. Special rules apply where a motor car is only partly used for business purposes. There is a 100% first year allowance for new cars with emissions of less than 120gm/km CO_2 registered after 16th April 2002.

(ii) *Machinery Leasing.* Tax allowances for rental payments on financial leases are spread to reflect the commercial depreciation of the asset. This may mean that full tax relief for rental payments may not be gained in the years in which the payments are made.

(iii) *Buildings*. Farm buildings, fencing, drainage and other improvements (including up to one-third of farmhouses) qualify for a writing-down allowance of 4% annually, given equally over 25 years. These annual allowances are to be phased out by the 2010-11 tax year.

Editorial Note: *The 2007 Budget saw the announcement of the phased withdrawal of Agricultural Buildings Allowances. The change includes the withdrawal of allowances on expenditure previously incurred. The changes make it even more important that any items of plant and equipment are identified in a building and the appropriate allowances claimed.*

E. Losses

Losses can normally be set off against other income in the year in which they are incurred and in the prior year. If other income is insufficient in the year when the loss occurs and in the prior year, any unrelieved losses can be carried forward and set off against future profits from farming. Special rules apply to prevent abuse of loss relief provisions by 'hobby' farmers who are not running their farms on a commercial basis with a view to producing a profit: normally losses are disallowed against other income after 5 consecutive years of loss.

Trading losses may be set against capital gains arising in the same year as the loss.

F. Profit Averaging

This relief is to enable farmers, other than companies, to average their taxable profits over two consecutive years. Where the difference between the profits of two consecutive years is 30% or more of the higher profits, the total profits for the two years are equally divided between the two years. Marginal relief is available where the difference is less than 30% but more than 25% of the higher profits. Profit for the purposes of tax averaging calculations is after the deduction of capital allowances. There is a two year limit in which to make the claim.

4. Capital Gains Tax

A. Application and Rates

Applies to capital gains made by an individual. Capital gains accruing to companies are chargeable to Corporation Tax. A capital gain is the difference between the acquisition value and the sale price subject to indexation allowance and/or taper relief. The first £9,200 of capital gains realised by an individual in a tax year are free of tax. Capital gains in excess of £9,200 are treated as the top slice of income and are therefore charged to tax at 10%, 22% or 40%.

Exempt assets include a principal private residence (e.g. farm house, if non-exclusive business occupation applies) if occupied as such, normal life assurance policies, animals and tangible movable properly (i.e. chattels) disposed of for £6,000 or less.

Capital Gains Tax is chargeable only on the disposal (including gifts) of assets. Capital Gains Tax is not payable on death.

Payment of Capital Gains Tax is due on 31st January following the tax year of disposal on the self-assessment return.

B. Reliefs

(i) *Losses:* Should a transaction produce a loss, this may be set against any long term chargeable gains arising in the same year or, if these are insufficient, those accruing in subsequent years. Losses brought forward will be used only to the extent necessary to reduce untaxed gains for the year to £9,200. Indexation allowances (for inflation) may not be utilised to create or increase a capital loss. Losses brought forward are set against any gains before applying tapering relief, so that claims need to be made very carefully.

Where a trading loss can be set against other income in the same or prior year for income tax purposes, any unused loss can be set against capital gains for those years.

(ii) *Improvements:* Spending that has increased the value of the asset can be offset against any gain. In the case of agricultural property, allowance would be made for any capital expenditure undertaken to improve the property, even though the expenditure may have obtained a buildings allowance referred to at 3(d) above.

(iii) *Indexation and Taper relief:* An indexation allowance for inflation applies to periods of ownership between 31st March 1982 and 1st April 1998 for individuals; for companies indexation carries on past 1st April 1998. The acquisition value of the asset (or its value at 31st March 1982, if it was owned prior to that date) is indexed-up for changes in the Retail Price Index. For assets owned on 31st March, 1982 and disposed of subsequently, providing an appropriate election is made (within two years), only the gain attributable to the period after that date is taxable, i.e. the chargeable gain is the gain from a valuation at 31st March, 1982 to the date of disposal.

Taper relief was introduced in 1998 to replace the indexation allowance and applies to periods of ownership after 5th April 1998. The taper relief reduces the amount of the gain that is liable to tax according to the length of the period of ownership. It is more generous for business assets than for non-business assets.

A business asset includes the following: 1. an asset used for the purposes of a trade carried on by the tax payer, or after 5 April 2004, any individual, trustee of personal representative; 2. an asset used for the purposes of a trade carried on by a 'qualifying company'; or 3. shares or securities in a 'qualifying company'.

A qualifying company is a trading company, or holding company of a trading group where one or more conditions are met, including: the company is unlisted (or an AIM company); or the tax payer is an employee of the company or a fellow group company (in this case, the company does not need to be a trading company provided the taxpayer holds no more than 10% of the share capital); or the taxpayer can exercise at least 5% of the voting rights.

The operation of taper relief for disposals after 6th April 2002 is illustrated below.

Number of complete years of ownership after 5th April 1998	Percentage of gain chargeable to tax	
	Business assets	Non-business assets
0	100%	100%
1	50%	100%
2	25%	100%
3	25%	95%
4	25%	90%
5	25%	85%
6	25%	80%
7	25%	75%
8	25%	70%
9	25%	65%
10 or more	25%	60%

(iv) *Rollover:* Payment of tax may be deferred on gains accruing from the sale of business assets (including land and buildings occupied and used for trade purposes, fixed plant and machinery, milk quotas, and from the sale of shares in a family business) if part or all of the proceeds are spent on acquiring new qualifying assets. The tax is deferred by deducting the gain from the acquisition price of the new asset. It can only be claimed if the new asset is acquired within 12 months before and 3 years after the disposal of the old assets. Disposal and acquisition dates for Capital Gains purposes are generally contract, not completion, dates.

(v) *Holdover:* Payments of tax may be deferred where disposal is by gift. This relief only applies to gifts of business assets, land which qualifies for agricultural property relief at either the 100% or 50% rate under Inheritance Tax (see next section) and gifts which lead to an immediate charge to Inheritance Tax (e.g. gifts into a discretionary trust). The amount of the chargeable gain which would normally have accrued to the donor will be held over; the value at which the donee is deemed to acquire the asset will be its market value reduced by the amount of the donor's chargeable gain held over. The held over gain is reduced by any time apportionment, indexation allowance, or any retirement relief available to the donor, but not taper relief. Where deferral is not available, payment of tax by interest bearing annual instalments over 10 years will be allowed for gifts of land, controlling share holdings and minority share holdings in unquoted companies.

5. Inheritance Tax

A. *Application and Rates*

This tax is charged on lifetime gifts and transfers on death. Rates for 2007-08 are as follows;

Slice of Chargeable Transfer	Rate per cent
£1- 300,000	0%
Over £300,000	40%

Outright gifts to individuals are exempt from tax at the time of the gift. If the donor lives for a further seven years then the transfer is fully exempt. Gifts into accumulation and maintenance trusts and interest in possession trusts no longer receive special treatment - all other gifts will be taxed at half the above rates at the time of the transfer.

Tax is charged on the value of an individual's estate at death plus the value of all gifts made within seven years of death. Allowance is made for any tax paid on lifetime gifts included in the value of the estate on death. Relief is given for outright gifts made more than three years before death according to the following scale:

Years between gift and death	Percentage of the full charge to tax
0-3	100
3-4	80
4-5	60
5-6	40
6-7	20

Exemptions include: transfers between husband and wife; the first £3,000 of gift made by a donor in the income tax year and separately up to £250 per year to any number of persons; gifts made out of income which form part of normal expenditure; marriage gifts within limits of £5,000 for a parent, £2,500 for a lineal ancestor and £1,000 for other donors.

B. *Reliefs*

(i) *Agricultural Property Relief (APR):* Relief may be available for agricultural land. Subject to a general rule that the agricultural land must have been occupied by the transferor (or by his controlled company) for two years, or owned by the transferor for 7 years and occupied for agricultural purposes by someone else before any relief is granted. The relief is at two different rates. If the basis of valuation is vacant possession (or there is the right to obtain it within 12 months), the taxable value of the land is reduced by 100%. If the basis of valuation is tenanted value, the taxable value of the land is reduced by 50% of that tenanted value. Ownership and occupation periods normally include prior periods of ownership or occupation by husbands and wives. From 1st September 1995, 100% relief applies to new lettings of agricultural land as Farm Business Tenancies.

Editorial Note: There has been some much publicised activity and tax cases concerning APR claims, particularly attempts by the Inland Revenue to reduce or deny the relief on claims for farmhouses. Care must be taken to protect the relief particularly where the attached land is either let out on a Farm Business Tenancy or under a contract farming arrangement.

(ii) *Business Property Relief (BPR):* Relief is also available in respect to 'business property' transferred during lifetime or on death. The relief extends to the business assets of a proprietor and the interest of a partner or controlling shareholder in the business capital of a company. The value of such property, providing certain tests are satisfied (e.g. it has been owned by the transferor for two years preceding transfer), is reduced by 100%. Where a partner or controlling shareholder owns assets (e.g. land) that the business uses, the value will be reduced by 50%. Shareholdings in unquoted companies receive a 100% reduction in market value.

Lifetime gifts of property eligible for Agricultural and Business Property Relief have to be retained (or replaced by similar property) until the death of the donor (or earlier death of the donee) if those reliefs are to be available when the tax (or additional tax) becomes payable subsequent to the donor's death

In the case of the transfer of property eligible for APR and BPR, the tax can be paid by annual instalments over ten years free of interest.

6. Stamp Taxes

A. Stamp Duty

Stamp Duty is charged at 0.5 per cent of consideration paid on the transfer of shares and securities.

B. Stamp Duty Land Tax

Stamp duty land tax is charged on the transfer of an interest in land; both sales and leases. With sales of property the tax is levied on a percentage of the sale value of the property (special rules apply to land in disadvantaged areas);

Residential property	Rate	Non-residential and mixed use	Rate
Value up to £125,000	nil	Value up to £150,000	nil
£125,000 to £250,000	1%	£150,000 to £250,000	1%
£250,000 to £500,000	3%	£250,000 to £500,000	3%
Over £500,000	4%	Over £500,000	4%

Stamp Duty Land Tax is payable on leases calculated according to the net present value of the rent payable over the term of the lease.

7. Value Added Tax

Agricultural businesses with a turnover of taxable goods and services in excess of £64,000 per annum (from 1st April 2006) are required to register for VAT. Businesses with a turnover below this limit may apply for voluntary registration. The standard rate of VAT is 17.5%. Most agricultural products are zero rated for VAT purposes. VAT has to be paid on certain inputs. Registered businesses are eligible to reclaim the tax paid where the goods or services purchased have been used in the production of zero-rated supplies.

A flat rate scheme is available to farmers as an alternative to registering for VAT. Farmers under the flat rate scheme do not have to submit tax returns or account for VAT and consequently cannot reclaim tax. They can, however, charge (and keep) a flat rate addition of 4% when they sell to VAT registered customers goods and services which qualify. This addition is not VAT but acts as compensation for losing input tax on purchases. The registered person paying the flat rate amount to the farmer can recover it as if it were VAT, subject to the normal rules for reclaiming. The local VAT office may refuse to issue a certificate to participate in the flat rate scheme if this would mean the farmer would recover substantially (£3,000) more than through the normal system.

On 25 April 2002 a new flat rate scheme was introduced for small businesses generally and is an alternative that farmers can use if they have taxable supplies of no more than £150,000 and a total business income of no more than £187,500. This scheme operates in a different way to the flat rate scheme for farmers in that a business charges the normal rate of VAT on sales. However, the VAT which the business has to remit to Customs and Excise is calculated by multiplying the value of gross sales by a rate specified for each particular trade sector. The rate for agriculture is 6% except for businesses supplying agricultural services, when the rate is 7.5%.

Editorial Note: *Farmers and landowners must always consider the VAT implications when considering any new or more farming activities on the land or within the buildings, particularly where supplies are made the public who cannot recover any VAT which may be charged on the service or goods provided from the farm.*

8. National Insurance Contributions (2007-08)

Class 1 (not contracted out).

Employee's weekly earnings	Employee	Employer
£100.00 or less	Nil	Nil
£100.01 to £670.00.	11%	12.8%
Over £670.00	1%	12.8%

Class 2.

Self-employed flat rate (exception
if earnings below £4,635 a year) . . . . £2.20 a week

Class 3.

Non-employed (voluntary) flat rate . . . . £7.80 a week

Class 4.

Self-employed. On profits or gains
between £5,225 and £34,840 . . . .   8%
over £34,840 . . . .   1%

Acknowledgment: The Author is grateful to *Howard Worth Chartered Accounts Agricultural Department* (Tel: 01606 75338) for their assistance in updating this section of the Pocketbook.

3. GRANTS

Grant aid and a number of other support measures for rural areas in England are predominantly provided under the umbrella of the English Rural Development Programme (ERDP) that was launched in the autumn of 2000. The ERDP comprises a package of schemes which reflect the switch in support away from agricultural production to more general support for the rural economy through measures designed to encourage business diversification and adding value to farm produce, and to protection of the environment. Following devolution, separate support arrangements apply in Wales and Scotland.

A new EU Rural Development Regulation has been agreed for the years 2007 to 2013. Each of the UK agricultural departments have been producing new Rural Development Programmes for this period. These programmes have to be approved by the EU Commission before any funding will be available. The submission of the Rural Development Programmes was held up due to delays in finalising the rates of 'voluntary modulation' (one source of the funding). DEFRA sent in the Rural Development Programme for England (RDPE) in mid-June. It is expected to take six months to gain EU approval, so it is likely to be December 2007 before any funding for schemes will start.

Although the RDPE has yet to be approved, it is understood that the Environmental Stewardship Scheme (ESS), including the Entry Level Stewardship, the Higher Level Stewardship and the Organic Entry Level Stewardship will continue with only minor changes. Similarly the English Woodland Grant Scheme will carry on. There is also a proposal for a national Energy Crops Scheme. Support for hill farming will continue in the form of Hill Farm Allowance (HFA) payments for 2008 and 2009, after which it will be replaced by an Uplands Entry Level Scheme, with options for hill areas being introduced into the existing ELS scheme. Support in the form of capital grants through diversification and economic development schemes is also proposed. The Regional Development Agencies will be responsible for these schemes and they will vary from region to region..

1. Land Based Schemes

A. *Environmental Stewardship Scheme (ESS)*

The Environmental Stewardship Scheme was launched in 2005 to replace the Environmental Sensitive Areas, Countryside Stewardship and Organic Farming schemes. The scheme is administered by Natural England and is the main agri-environmental scheme in England.
The scheme comprises three elements:-
- Entry Level Stewardship (ELS)
- Organic Entry Level Stewardship (OELS)
- Higher Level Stewardship (HLS)

ELS is intended to encourage a large number of farmers across a wide area to adopt simple environmental management practices such as hedgerow management, stone wall maintenance, low input grassland, buffer strips and arable options. The scheme is non-competitive and open to all as long as scheme requirements are met. Points are awarded for each management option adopted. There is a large range of management options including hedgerow management, one side 11 points/100m, both sides 22points/100m; 2m, 4m, 6m buffer strips attracting 10, 20 and 30 points /100m respectively; overwintered stubbles gain 120 points/ha and beetle banks 580 points/ha. Applicants have to achieve a minimum number of 30 points per hectare (8 points per ha for parcels of LFA land over 15 hectares) to be accepted into ELS. An annual payment of £30 per hectare will be made (£8 per hectare for parcels of land over 15ha within the LFA). ELS agreements last for five years.

OELS is open to all organic farmers with land which is registered as organic or in conversion and not currently receiving aid under the Organic Farming Scheme (see 1 E below). OELS has similar options to those under ELS and participants will receive annual payments of £30 per hectare for carrying out the organic options on the organic land plus an additional £30 per hectare for farming the land organically. There will also be an option to apply for organic conversion with a payment of £600 per hectare per year for top fruit orchards and £175 for improved land. To participate in this latter option land must not already have been converted to full organic production and applicants must have registered the land with an organic inspection body. OELS agreements last for five years.

HLS is targeted towards achieving significant environmental benefits in high priority areas with the objectives being wildlife conservation, protecting historic environments, maintaining and enhancing landscape quality, encouraging public access and resource protection. Applicants have to produce a Farm Environment Plan (FEP) and will usually have to participate in ELS. Only applications that give the best value in meeting the scheme aims will be accepted. Payment will depend on the management options adopted. HLS agreements will normally be for ten years with a break clause for either party after five years..

B. Woodland Schemes

The previous Woodland Grant Scheme (WGS) and the Farm Woodland Premium Scheme (FWPS) have been replaced by the English Woodland Grant Scheme (EWGS). In Wales the Better Woodlands for Wales scheme opened in April 2006. An outline of these schemes can be found on pages 66-68.

C. Environmentally Sensitive Areas (ESAs)

The first ESAs were designated in 1987. Currently there are 22 designated areas in England, covering some 10% of its agricultural land. Within these areas farmers were offered annual payments if they entered into 10 year agreements to manage their land, buildings, walls and other features in ways which will conserve the traditional environment. These agreements have now been superceded by the introduction of the Environmental Stewardship Scheme (ESS) (see 1A above). No more agreements are being offered, existing agreements will continue until the end of their term. Ageement holders will then be offered the option to enter land into the ESS.

D. Countryside Stewardship Scheme (CSS)

Once the flagship scheme offering both capital grants and annual payments for environmental measures. But now, similar to the ESA scheme, it is closed to new applicants following the introduction of the Enviromental Stewardship Scheme (ESS). Acceptance into the CSS was competitive and priority was given to proposals offering the best potential for environmental improvement and public benefit. Existing Agreements will continue until the end of their term at which point it may be possible to enter the land into the ESS. Land in the CSS is eligible for payment under the Single Payment Scheme as long as scheme rules are followed. Payments are reviewed every three years and can go up or down.

E. Organic Farming Scheme

This scheme is now closed to new applications in England. Current Agreements will continue until the end of their term. A similar scheme still operates in Wales. Support for organic farmers in England is available through the Organic Entry Level Stewardship (OELS), (see section 1 above)

F. Energy Crops Scheme

This scheme closed in June 2006. It operated in England and aimed to increase the area devoted to energy crops by providing support for establishing Short Rotation Coppice (SRC) (either willow or poplar) and Miscanthus (Elephant Grass).

A national Energy Crops Scheme covering the whole of England has been proposed under the new Rural Development Plan for England. At the time of writing, detailed scheme rules were not available, and it seems unlikely that grants will be available before December 2007. However, it has been indicated that the rates of grant under the new scheme will be as follows;

	£ per ha (acre)
Short Rotation Coppice	1,000 (405)
Miscanthus	800 (324)

Other scheme rules are likley to be similar to those seen under the previous Energy Crops Scheme. In order to be eligible for the scheme a minimum total area of three hectares must have been planted (although this can comprise of a number of smaller plots), and a contract, or letter of intent, from a crop end user was required. Normally the land being planted must have been within a reasonable distance to the end use site - 25 miles radius for large-scale projects and 10 miles for small-scale projects.

Land in the ECS can count towards the area to calculate your points target and associated payment under Entry Level Stewardship. But ELS options must not be located within parcels covered by the ECS agreement. It is possible to enter into boundary options on boundaries surrounding land within an ECS agreement. It may be possible to validate set-aside entitlements on land planted to energy crops under the Single Payment Scheme

Grant aid of up to 50 per cent (maximum £200,000) was available towards the cost of setting up groups producing SRC. Eligible expenditure includes legal costs, accommodation, office equipment, recruitment cost and harvesting machinery.

G. Hill Farm Allowance (HFA) Scheme

This scheme provides support for beef and sheep farming in the Less Favoured Areas. This scheme will continue for 2007, 2008 and 2009 after which it will be replaced by an 'Uplands Entry Level Stewardship'. It is expected that new options for hill farming will be introduced into the existing ELS scheme rather than a stand-alone scheme. For details of the current HFA scheme. See page 100-101.

2. Project Based Schemes

All the existing Project Based Schemes in England closed to new applications on 30th June 2006. Under the new RDPE for 2007 to 2013 the Regional Development Agencies (RDAs) will be responsible for delivering diversification and economic development schemes. Schemes may vary from region to region reflecting each RDA's spending priorities. It is expected that capital grants will be available for diversification projects and to improve the competitiveness of farming and forestry. Any new schemes are unlikely to be available before December 2007. At the time of writing scheme details were not available. Below is an outline of what was previously on offer.

A. Rural Enterprise Scheme

This scheme operated in England and aimed to improve rural economies and communities. It was open to farmers and other rural businesses and community groups. Grants were available for farm diversification projects, as well as services for the rural economy and population.

Rates of support were in three bands depending on the level of economic return generated, and ranged from 15% to 100%. Although there was no maximum or minimum project size, the maximum grant that any agricultural holding could receive under the ERDP was £500,000.

Grant aid to support farm improvement and diversification in Wales is provided by the Farm Improvement and Farm Enterprise Grant schemes and the Farming Connect banner.

B. Processing and Marketing Grant Scheme

This scheme operated throughout the UK, but is now closed. It provided capital grants on a competitive basis to individuals and groups of producers to encourage innovation and investment to achieve added value for agricultural products and to enhance market opportunities. Aid was available, at the rate of 30 per cent of eligible costs, on investments over £70,000 in England and £40,000 in Wales. The maximum grant for any one project was £1.2 million. Items eligible for grant aid included the cost of buildings (new and refurbishments) and new equipment. Consultants' and architects' fees may also have been eligible.

C. Vocational Training Scheme

This scheme operated in England. Payments were made for vocational training of farmers and other persons engaged in farming and forestry. Assistance was provided either to an individual or a group of individuals or businesses. Training must have been vocational and fall within specified areas. Up to 75% of eligible costs was funded. There was a minimum project size of 20 days training e.g. one person for 20 days or 20 people for one day.

In future, assistance for training in farming and forestry will be funded on a regional basis through the Regional Development Agencies (RDAs).

3. Other Grants

A number of other grants are available which fall outside the umbrella of the Rural Development Programme for England.

A. Fresh Fruit and Vegetable Aid Scheme

Producer organisations recognised under the European Commission Regulation 2200/96 may apply for a contribution towards an operation fund which the organisation has set up to finance a planned programme to improve performance in marketing, produce quality and environmental considerations. The contribution from the European Commission will be a maximum of 4.1 per cent of the producer organisation's marketed production or 50 per cent of eligible expenditure under the planned programme, whichever is the least. Further details are available from the Rural Payments Agency; (see www.rpa.gov.uk).

B. Agricultural Development Scheme

This scheme provided assistance to help farmers and growers in England improve their competitiveness through better marketing. It is currently closed to new entrants but may reopen at some point. The maximum grant was £0.5m and the maximum grant rate is 50% of eligible expenditure. The scheme was competitive and only the best applications in terms of value for money were awarded grants.

C. Farm Business Advice

The Farm Business Advice Service (FBAS) – 'Knowing your Options' which opened in September 2005, closed on 31st March 2007. Its aim was to provide farmers with advice on the implications of the Single Payment Scheme. The scheme was run regionally through the Regional Development Agencies (RDAs). The RDAs remain responsible for delivering farm business advice but at the time of writing no schemes had yet been launched.

D. Redundant Buildings Scheme

Grant aid towards the cost of converting redundant farm buildings may be available from Regional Development Agencies depending on the priorities for funding adopted in particular regions. Projects eligible for assistance include the conversion of redundant buildings for office, craft, manufacturing and retail purposes, tourism and leisure use. Conversion to residential accommodation will not be supported. Aid is usually up to 25% of eligible costs. The minimum grant is £2,500 and the maximum £60,000.

Environment Schemes Payments, 2005 (provisional)

		£ million
England:	Organic Farming Scheme	4.6
	Environmentally Sensitive Areas	69.8
	Countryside Stewardship	117.4
	Hill Farm Allowance	27.3
Wales:	Organic Farming Scheme	2.3
	Environmentally Sensitive Areas	8.5
	Tir Mynydd	35.8
	Tir Gofal	19.1
Scotland:	Organic Aid Scheme	2.5
	Environmentally Sensitive Areas	8.2
	Rural Stewardship	5.0
	Less Favoured Area Support Scheme	61.0
N. Ireland	Organic Farming Scheme	0.3
	New Environmentally Sensitive Areas	4.9
	Countryside Management Scheme	5.8
	Less Favoured Area Compensatory Allowances	21.8

Source: DEFRA, SEERAD, DARD, WAGDEPC. Agriculture in the UK 2006.

VIII. MISCELLANEOUS DATA

1. CONSERVATION COSTS

Note: Costs can vary quite widely, depending on geographical location and the type and size of the job.

(N.B. Abbreviations. DEFRA: Department of Environment, Food and Rural Affairs; CA: Countryside Agency; FC: Forestry Commission; EN: English Nature; BTCV: British Trust for Conservation Volunteers).

Hedge Cutting. From £260 per day at an average of 3 miles per day.

Hedge Laying. Contract labour, £7-£10 per metre (excluding stakes, bindings, burning debris), or £9.00 per hour. Contractor, 15 metres/day; BTCV, 5 metres/day per person. Nov./March. Every 8 to 20 years. Grant aid: CA, DEFRA, EN. Lantra quotes £1.50 a metre plus 60p a metre for stakers and pleachers, 40 metres a day.

Hedge Planting. Transplants av. £40/100; netlon guards av. 60p; canes av. 10p; fencing (labour and materials): stock proof £3.00/metre, rabbit proof (dug in) up to £5/metre. Overall, £2.00/metre unguarded and unfenced, £9.00/metre guarded and fenced. Contract labour: planting up to £2.20/metre, fencing up to £2.50/metre. Contractor 100-150 metres/day; BTCV 20 metres/day. Pref Oct./March. Above includes repair. Grant aid: CA, DEFRA, EN.

Hedge Coppicing. By hand: 2 men and a chain saw, £5/metre plus burning debris. Contractor: tractor mounted saw, driver and 2 men, 13 metres/ hour, £32/hour. Grant aid: CA, DEFRA.

Dry Stone Walling. Cost of stone approximately £80/tonne. Cost of building wall £67-£80 per square metre. Grant aid: CA, DEFRA.

Amenity Tree Planting; (half acre block or less). Transplants av. 75p; shelter plus stake and tie av. £1; stake av. 50p; whip av. 70p. (50p-£1); rabbit spiral guard 30p; netlon guard av. 50p (but 15p in a 50 m roll); cane av. 10p. Trees per man day: farmer 200, contractor 400; (large-scale, 33 man days/ha). Nov.-April. Grant aid: CA, DEFRA.

Shelter Belts. Per 100 metre length: 100 large species (oak, lime, etc.) £45; 66 medium species (cherry, birch, etc.) £38; 100 shrubs, £30; 166 tree stakes, shelters and ties, £250; (site preparation, weed control, labour and fencing extra). DEFRA standard costs £637.50/ha; windbreaks £33.85/ha. Grant aid: CA, DEFRA.

Woodland Establishment. Conifers £200/1000. To supply and plant oak or beech transplants (2-3ft tall) in tubes £3.00-£3.50 each, dependent on shelter size. Rabbit fencing £5.00/metre (dug in). Contract labour: conifers at 2m (inc. trees) £1,400/ha; broadleaves at 3m (inc. trees) £900/ha; forest transplants (not inc. trees) £270/1000. 12.5 days/ha (contractor). Nov-April. (Above not inc. maintenance). Grant aid: FC, CA, DEFRA.

Forestry: General. Contract labour: chain sawing £18/hr., brush cutting £10.50/hr, extracting timber/pulp £4-£10/tonne, chemical spot weeding 5.4p-7.4p/tree, rhodedendron control £600-£800/acre.

Pond Construction. Butyl lining (0.75mm) £4.84/m^2; other linings up to £3/m^2. Contract labour: 150 Komatsu £26/hr.; bulldozer D6 LGP £42/hr, 13t 360° excavator £36/hr (excluding haulage), Flailmowers from £16/hr. Autumn (dry ground conditions). Grant aid: DEFRA, CA (discretionary), EN (possibly).

Pond Maintenance. Hymac £37/hr.; Backhoe £21-23/hr. 5m²/day (BTCV); 100 m²/day (contractor). Timing: probably winter; time depends on ground condition and species whose life cycles may be disturbed. Every 5 to 50 years. Grant aid: CA, EN.

Ditch Maintenance. Backhoe excavator £20/hr; 13 tonne 360° excavator £30/hr.; labour £10/hr. Preferably in winter. Every 3 to 7 years on rotation. Grant aid: DEFRA (improvement plan), EN (conservation interest).

Pollarding and Tree Surgery. Pollard: £41-£62/stool; surgery: £155/ tree. Pollarding: 2 or 3 trees/day. Surgery: 2 days/tree. Winter. Pollard every 20-40 years. Grant aid: CA (discretionary).

Establishment of Wildlife Grassland Meadow. £149-236/ha for ground preparation, depending on weed burden; costs may be higher if follows set-aside, for heavy land or exceptional weed burden. Seed costs very variable, but as a guide: Perennial and annual wild flowers and grasses, £29.50/kg (25kg/ha); basic long season wildflower mix, £30 per 100g (250g/ha); neutral grassland stewardship mix, approx. £79/ha (at 25kg/ha).

Reducing Pesticide Drift. Use of appropriate spray nozzles: tilt jets £22.5-£25.5 for 6; lo-drift nozzles £15.5 for 6.

Permanent Grass Margins at Field Edges. To provide wildlife benefits and help control pernicious weeds, reducing herbicides at the field edge. A sterile strip provides virtually no wildlife benefit and the initial establishment costs may be offset by savings in maintenance costs in future years. Costs per 100 metres as follows. Establishment: 2m grass margins, 4.60-£6.00; 6m grass margins, £14-£18; beetle banks, £4-£5.70 (6m wide). Maintenance: 2m margins, 50p to 63p; 6m margins, £1.68-£1.88.

Fertilizer Losses at Field Boundaries. For a 12m spread pattern, at 150 kg/ ha, loss is approx. 30p per 100m per application, or £3 for a 6 ha field (450 x 150m). Loss avoided by driving further away from the field boundary/using a tilting hopper mechanism/using an appropriate border disc or deflector, costing £90.

Grant Aid. A summary of 'Grants for Landscape Conservation' is available from the CA, FC, DEFRA and EN. Countryside Agency grants are usually available through local authorities.

Acknowledgement. Above information supplied by Farming and Wildlife Advisory Group (FWAG). Sources: County FWAG personnel, BTCV, local authorities.

2. FERTILISER PRICES

A. *Compounds*

	Analysis			Price Per Tonne
N	**P₂O₅**	**K₂O**		**£**
0	24	24		199
0	18	36		195
0	20	30		193
0	30	15		205
0	30	20		214
5	24	24		209
8	24	24		215
10	24	24	(B)	219
10	10	30	(B)	168
12	15	20	(B)	170
13	13	20		165
14	14	21		185
15	19	19	(B)	182
16	16	16	(B)	185
20	5	15	(B)	155
20	10	10	(B)	156
21	8	11	(B)	165
24	4	4	(B)	147
25	5	5	(B)	153
24	0	17		158

B. *Straights*

Type	Price per tonne £
Ammonium Nitrate: UK (34.5% N.)	169
Ammonium Nitrate: Imported (34.5% N.) SP4/5	157
Sulphate of Ammonia (21% N.)	*145*
Urea (46% N.): granular/ prills	195
Liquid Nitrogen (28% N)	140
Triple Superphosphate (47% P₂O₅)	250
Muriate of Potash (Granular) (60% K₂O)	165

Average price (p) per kg:	N	:	49	(UK AN)
	P₂O₅	:	53	(triple supers).
	K2 O	:	28	(muriate).

The prices above are for fertilizer delivered in 600kg bags; delivery in bulk averages £6.50/tonne less; collection of bags by farmers £5 to £8/tonne less. They are spot prices in early August 2007; they vary according to area and bargaining power. (B) stands for blended; prices for granular (where available) average around £8/tonne more. They assume delivery in 25 tonne loads; add approximately £2/tonne for 10 tonne loads, £4 for 6-9 tonne loads, £6 for 4-5 tonne loads. Tight supplies and keen global demand indicate these prices may vary considerably from time of printing. Some products are also currently unavailable.

3. MANURIAL VALUE OF SLURRY AND FARMYARD MANURE

1. Composition (% by weight)

Undiluted Slurry (faeces plus urine, or droppings):

	N	P_2O_5	K_2O
Cow	0.5	0.2	0.5
Pig	0.6	0.2	0.2
Poultry	1.7	1.4	0.7

Farmyard Manure:

	N	P_2O_5	K_2O
Cattle	0.5	0.4	0.6
Pig	0.6	0.6	0.4
Poultry	1.8	1.8	1.2

2. Available Nutrients (kg)

Undiluted Slurry (per 10m³*):

	N	P_2O_5	K_2O
Cow	35	11	58
Pig	42	11	23
Poultry	118	82	82

(* = 10 tonnes; 10,000 litres)

Farmyard Manure (per 10 tonnes):

	N	P_2O_5	K_2O
Cattle	17	20	46
Pig	20	31	31
Poultry	110	92	92

3. Amount per head

(faeces plus urine, or droppings)

	litres per day	N	P_2O_5	K_2O
1 dairy cow	40	51	16	84
1 pig (dry meal fed)	4.5	6.8	1.8	3.7
100 laying hens	13	55	39	39

(kg per year (1))

(1) housed all year and no losses.

4. AGROCHEMICAL COSTS (2007)

Only the names of the active ingredients are given below, with their principal use. These materials should only be applied in accordance with the manufacturers' recommendations. Application rates can vary and there are differences between the prices of various proprietary brands. The list is not intended to be exhaustive and there is no implied criticism of materials omitted. Note, the variation in costs per hectare is primarily because of varying application rates rather than price variation between suppliers.

Crop	Function		Material	Approx. Cost £/ha per application
Cereals	Herbicides	General	MCPA	3.00-7.00
			Mecoprop-P	4.50-10.50
			Ioxynil+Bromoxynil	1.00-2.00
			Dicamba +Mecoprop-P + MCPA	16.00-20.00
			Metsulfuron-methyl	12.50-25.00
		Undersown Crops	MCPA+MCPB	46.50
		Blackgrass	Isoproturon	8.00-13.50
			Isoproturon + Diflufenican	4.00-21.00
			Clodinafop-propargyl + trifluralin + cloquintocet-mexyl	13.50
			Mesosulphuron + Idosulphuron	28.50
			Florasalum + Fluroxypyr	12.00-18.00
		Cleavers	Fluroxypyr	15.00-20.00
			Amidosulfuron	18.00
		Wild Oats	Diclofop-methyl + Fenoxaprop-P-ethyl	20.00-27.00
			Pinoxaden	13.00-34.00
		Wild Oats & Blackgrass	Clodinafop-propargyl	32.00
			Fenoxaprop-P-ethy	13.00-19.50
	Growth Regulator		Chlormequat	2.00
			Chlormequat + Choline Chloride	3.00
			Chlormequat + Choline Chloride + Imazaquin	10.50
			2-chlorethylphosphonic acid	5.50-11.00
			2-chloroethyl phosphonic acid + Mepiquat Chloride	7.00-14.00
			Trinexapac-ethyl	14.25-17.75
	Fungicides		Azoxystrobin	27.50
			Fenpropimorph	11.50-15.75
			Epoxiconazole	22.50
			Tebuconazole	15.00
			Prothioconazole	14.00-28.50
			Chlorothalonil	3.50
		Seed Dressing	Fuberidazole + Triadimenol + Imidacloprid	10.00-13.00
			Fuberidazole + Triadimenol	6.50-8.50

Crop	Function	Material	Approx. Cost £/ha per application
		Prythoconazole + Clothianidin	9.50-12.16
		Silthiofam	19.50-25.00
		Imidacloprid + tebuconazole + triazoxide	8.25-10.75
	Aphicide	Cypermethrin	0.75
		Deltamethrin	3.00-3.75
		Pirimicarb	8.00
		Chlorpyriphos	5.00-10.75
	Slug Killer	Metaldehyde	11.50
		Methiocarb	20.00
Oilseed Rape	Herbicides	Propyzamide	43.00-45.00
		Trifluralin	6.50
		Metazachlor	30.00-51.00
	Insecticide	Deltamethrin	3.75
		Pirimicarb	8.00-12.00
		Alphacypermethrin	2.50-5.25
	Fungicide	Iprodione + thiophate-methyl	24.50-36.50
		Tebuconazole	7.50-15.00
		Flusilazde + Carbendazim	13.75-18.00
		Metconazole	20.00
	Dessicant	Glyphosate	6.00
Potatoes	Herbicides:	Metribuzin	13.75-28.00
		Linuron	11.50-22.50
		Paraquat + Diquat	20.75
	Blight Control	Cymoxanil + Mancozeb	8.00
		Cymoxanil + Famoxadone	13.25-18.50
		Fluazinam	10.25
		Mancozeb+Metalaxyl	22.00
	Haulm Dessicant	Diquat	32.00
Sugar Beet	Herbicides: Pre-emergence	Chloridazon:	
		overall	24.00-56.00
		band spray	8.00-19.00
	Post-emergence	Phenmedipham:	6.50-11.00
		Triflusulfron-methyl	18.50
	Insecticide	Oxamyl	34.00-51.00
		Pirimicarb	8.00
Beans	Herbicide	Bentazone	56.00
		Pendimethalin	13.50-16.50
	Fungicide	Chlorothalonil	10.50

Crop	Function	Material	Approx. Cost £/ha per application
		Tebuconazole	15.00
		Azoxystobin	27.50
Peas	Herbicide	Pendimethalin + Imazamox	36.00
Beans and Peas	Insecticide	Pirimicarb	8.00
		Deltamethrin	3.00-4.50
Maize	Herbicide	Prosulfuron + Bromoxynil	24.00
		Nicosulfuron	24.00-36.00
Brassicas	Herbicides	Propachlor	57.00-82.00
		Trifluralin	6.25
Broadleaved Grass weeds and volunteer Crops			
	Cereals	Fluazifop-P-butyl	19.25-29.00
		Propaquizafop	12.50-27.00
		Cycloxydim	15.00-25.00
Grassland	Herbicides	MCPA	6.25-10.50
		MCPA + MCPB	34.00-46.75
General	Weed and Grass Killer		
	General	Paraquat	11.00-29.00
	Prior to Direct Drilling	Paraquat	22.00-40.00
	Couch Grass Control	Glyphosate	6.00-15.00
	WoodyWeed Control	Triclopyr	136-204
		Aminopyralid + Fluroxypyr	73.00

Note. The above prices are based largely on retail prices paid by farmers (2007) and reflect the discounts available where there are competing products from several manufacturers. The range in prices per hectare reflects the price variation and also the varying application rates.

Acknowledgement: Particular thanks to Bartolemews 01243 784 171

5. FEEDINGSTUFF PRICES

£ per tonne

			£ per tonne
Cattle	Dairy:	High Energy	120 - 145
		Medium Energy	115 - 135
		Low Energy	110 - 130
		Concentrate	215 - 235
	Beef:	Pellets	105 - 130
		Concentrate	195 - 210
	Calf:	Milk Substitute (bags)	1,200 - 1,600
		High Fat (bags)	885 - 1,250
		Calf Weaner Pellets	175 - 200
		Calf Rearer Nuts	130 - 155
Sheep	Lamb Pellets		105 - 125
	Medium energy sheep		90 - 115
	Sheep/lamb cake		90 - 110
	Ewe cake		85 - 120
Horses	Horse and Pony Pencils		205 - 215
Goats	Goat Nuts		230 - 240
Pigs	Piglet Weaner		230 - 250
	Sow Nuts		130 - 160
	Early Grower Pellets		175 - 215
	Grower/Finisher Pellets		155 - 175
	Sow Concentrate		250 - 270
	Grower Concentrate		260 - 275
Poultry	Chick and Rearer Feeds		140 - 170
	Layers Feeds		130 - 160
	Broiler Feeds		180 - 200
	Turkey Feeds		210
Straight Feeds	Fishmeal (English; 66/70%)		560 - 690
	Soya Bean Meal (Hipro; 44%)		145 - 170
	Rapeseed Meal (36%)		95 - 115
	Palm Kernel Meal/Cake (17%CP)		70 - 115
	Sunflower Seed Pellets (30/33%)		95 - 130
	Citrus Pulp Nuts/Pellets		90 - 135
	Wheatfeed		80 - 110
	Maize Gluten		95 - 135
	Molasses (Cane)		100 - 115
	Sugar Beet Pulp (Molassed Nuts/Pellets)		100 - 110
	Brewers' Grains		25 - 30
	Supergrains		30 - 40
	Fodder Beet		20 - 30

Compound feed prices are approximate ranges in August 2007; the range incorporates differences in the ingredients. Straight feed prices are ranges between February 2006 and August 2007.

They are (mainly) delivered prices for hauls more than 10 miles in 20-25 tonne loads. Discounts of £3 to £5/tonne for cash and £3 to £6 for deliveries within 10 miles of the mill at the company's convenience are usually available; they are not allowed for above. The additional farm delivered cost for bags ranges from £17.50 to £27.50 a tonne.

ME requirements for Friesian cows (590kg LW)

Liveweight Change (kg/day)	Maintenance	Milk yield (kg/day)			
		20	25	30	35
−0.5		147	172	196	221
0	62	161	186	210	235
+0.5		178	203	227	252

Source: Broster, W.H. and Alderman, G., Livestock Production Science, 4 (1977).

6. FEEDINGSTUFFS: NUTRITIVE VALUES

Typical Energy and Protein Contents of Some Common Feeds	Dry Matter Content	Metabolizable Energy MJ/kg	Crude Protein g/kg
Type of Feed	g/kg	DM	DM
Forages:			
Barley Straw	860	7.0	10
Grass Silage (typical clamp)	250	10.8	150
Hay (typical meadow)	850	8.8	100
Maize Silage	300	11.0	90
Pasture (rotational grazed)	180	11.5	160
Whole-crop Wheat (fermented)	400	10.5	95
Cereals:			
Barley	860	13.2	120
Oats	860	12.5	120
Wheat	860	13.6	130
Maize	880	13.8	90
Roots:			
Fodder Beet	180	12.0	60
Potatoes	200	13.3	100
Wet By-Products:			
Brewers'	260	11.5	250
Pressed Sugar Beet Pulp	260	12.5	100
Straights:			
Cane Molasses	750	12.7	40
Distillers Barley Grains	900	12.2	260
Distillers Maize Grains	900	14.0	310
Distillers Wheat Grains	900	13.5	340
Dried Citrus Pulp	900	12.6	70
Dried Molassed Sugar Beet Pulp	900	12.5	100
Extracted Rapeseed Meal	900	12.0	400
Extracted Soyabean Meal	900	13.4	530
Extracted Sunflower Meal	900	10.0	390
Field Beans	880	13.3	290
Lupin Seed Meal	900	14.2	350
Maize Gluten Feed	880	12.8	210
Palm Kernel Meal	900	11.4	200
Wheatfeed	880	11.3	190

For relative values of different feeds, see previous page.

7. SUMMARY OF OUTPUTS, GROSS MARGINS, AND STANDARD MAN DAYS

In the past, various Standard Outputs (S.O.s) and Standard Gross Margins (S.G.M.s) have been published, often by Government for the purposes of grant schemes, planning etc. This data is no longer produced, so this secton represent a summary of the author's estimates of Outputs and Gross Margins for 2008 of the enterprises included in this book. They are based on average performance under average conditions. Wide variations occur between farms. The Standard Man Day (S.M.D.) estimates are drawn from the labour use figures in Section IV, and are based on a standard 8-hour day. Some of these SMD figures are based on limited data only - though all that is available; these are subject to substantial variations with scale and production methods.

Crops (per hectare)	Output	Gr. Margin	S.M.D.s	
Winter Feed Wheat	825	522		
Winter Milling Wheat	846	517		
Spring Wheat.	627	381		
Winter Feed Barley	647	392	1.15 /	
Winter Malting Barley	621	391	1.75	(1)
Spring Malting Barley	593	400		
Winter Oats	644	446		
Spring Oats	545	369		
Winter Oilseed Rape	634	365	1.10	
Spring Oilseed Rape	390	222	1.00	
Linseed	350	212	1.00	
Winter Field Beans	475	309	0.90	
Spring Field Beans	461	308	0.95	
Dried Peas	485	285	1.60	
Lupins	395	190	1.50	
Vining Peas	1100	787	3.00	
Maincrop Potatoes	3738	1252	9.25	(2)
Early Potatoes	3000	1155	5.50	(2)
Sugar Beet	1304	617	3.00	
Herbage Seed (Ryegrass)	800	358	1.40	
Hops	5227	3970	9.50	(2)
Kale (grazed)	-	-	1.40	
Silage: one cut	-	-	1.60	(3)
two cuts	-	-	2.80	(3)
Grazing only	-	-	0.40	(3)
Hay for sale	500	350	1.80	(3)
Let Keep	175	150	0.40	(3)
Bare fallow / set-aside	-	-	0.20	
Rough Grazing	-	-	0.20	

Livestock (per head) (4, 5)				
Dairy Cows	1530	959	4.00	
Bulls	-	-	3.50	
Beef Cows (single suckler including calf):				
lowland	269	71	1.35	
upland/hill	263	73	1.68	

Cereal Beef (0-12 months) (6)	461	5	1.90
18-month Beef (6)	464	148	1.60
Grass Silage Beef (6)	456	111	1.90
Finishing Suckler bred stores: Grass	91	32	1.10
Winter	257	75	1.10
Calves; to 6 months (6)	151	28	1.20
Ewes: lowland	46	16.2	0.50
upland	40	13.8	0.45
hill	33	15.2	0.40
Rams	-	-	0.50
Winter Finishing Store Lambs	11.8	4.7	0.30
Sows (including weaners to 30kg)	711	241	2.25
Boars	-	-	2.00
Other Bacon Pigs	41.6	9.4	0.25
Laying Birds: battery cages	9.06	0.72	0.017
free range	15.65	6.10	0.06
Pullets reared (6)	2.25	0.52	0.005
Broilers (6)	1.04	0.07	0.002
Turkeys (6)	27.09	15.09	
Capons (6)	12.50	8.19	
Ducks (6)	11.20	7.25	
Geese (6)	32.50	26.0	

1. 1.25 if straw ploughed in; 2 if straw harvested. Highly mechanised larger farms will require no more than 0.75 S.M.D./ha of direct labour for cereals and other combinable crops (assuming straw ploughed in).

2. Excludes casual labour for harvesting.

3. Excludes any reseeding carried out – this is likley to be around 0.6 S.M.D./ha in the year reseeding is carried out.

4. In calculating the S.O.s and S.G.M.s for livestock, herd depreciation or livestock (e.g. calf) purchases or the value of transfers in have been deducted.

5. Note that for grazing livestock, the S.M.D. per head exclude field work, e.g. grass production and silage making, i.e. the labour for these has to be added to give total labour for these enterprises.

6. For these livestock, S.O., S.G.M. and S.M.D. per annum should be based on numbers produced (sold) during the year. For all other livestock, average numbers on the farm at any one time during the year should be used (i.e. average of numbers at end of each month).

7. 'Other Cattle' can refer to both beef animals and dairy followers (ref. detail on page 145).

For number of Standard Man-Days per worker per year, see page 130.

8. FARM RECORDS

The following records should be kept for management purposes:

1. Basic Whole Farm Financial Position

1. Cash Analysis Book, fully detailed.

2. Petty Cash Book.

3. Annual Valuation, including physical quantities, with crops in store and livestock at (near) market value, less any variable costs yet to be borne. Fertilizers, seeds, sprays, casual labour or contract work applied to growing crops should be recorded, but 'cultivations' and manurial residues can be ignored for management purposes.

4. Debtors and creditors at the end of the financial year.

2. Other Financial and Physical Records

1. Output (quantities and value) of each Crop and Livestock Enterprise for the 'Harvest Year' (or Production Cycle). It may be possible to get information of Sales from a fully detailed cash analysis book (although, for crops, the financial year figures will then have to be allocated between crops from the current harvest and those from the harvest in the previous financial year, in order to check on the accuracy of the opening valuation of crops in store; this is particularly a problem with Michaelmas ending accounts). The following records of Internal Transfers and Consumption will also be required:

   a. Numbers and Market Value of livestock transferred from one livestock category to another, e.g. dairy calves to Dairy Followers or Beef Enterprise, or dairy heifers to Dairy Enterprise.

   b. Quantity and Market Value of Cereals fed on farm and used for seed.

   c. Quantity and Market Value of Milk and other produce consumed by the farmer or his employees, used on the farm (e.g. milk fed to calves), or sold direct.

2. Monthly record of Livestock Numbers; preferably reconciled with the previous month according to births, purchases, deaths, sales and transfers.

3. Costs and Quantities of Concentrate Feed to each category of livestock, including Home-Grown Cereals fed on the farm.

4. Allocation of costs of seed, fertilizer, sprays, casual labour and contract work specific to an enterprise. This is in order to calculate gross margins, where required. It is less essential than the other records listed.

5. Breeding record for cows, including bulling dates, date(s) served, type of bull used, pregnancy testing, estimated calving date, actual calving date, and date when dried off.

6. For each crop, total output and yield per hectare, in both quantity and value. Include each field where the crop has been grown and its approximate yield, where this can be satisfactorily obtained.

7. For each field, keep one page to cover a period of say, ten years. Record on this, each year, crop grown, variety sown, fertilizer used, sprays used, date sown, date(s) harvested, approximate yield (if obtainable), and any other special notes that you feel may have significance for the future.

8. A rotation record. On a single page, if possible, list each field down the side and say, ten years along the top. Colour each field-year space according to the crop grown, e.g. barley yellow, potatoes red, etc.

9. DEFINITION OF FARM MANAGEMENT TERMS

Mainly abstracted from 'Terms and Definitions used in Farm and Horticulture Management', M.A.F.F., 1970.

1. Valuations and Capital

Valuations. Valuation is essentially a process of estimation. Thus alternative bases are sometimes possible, according to the purpose intended. The basis should be consistent throughout the period of any series of figures.

(i) Saleable crops in store. At estimated market value less costs still to be incurred, e.g. for storage and marketing. Both may be estimated either at the expected date of sale or at the date of valuation.

(ii) Growing crops. Preferably at variable costs to the date of valuation, although estimated total cost can alternatively be used.

(iii) Saleable crops ready for harvesting but still in the ground. Preferably valued as (i), less estimated harvesting costs, although they can alternatively be treated as (ii).

(iv) Fodder stocks (home-grown). Preferably at variable costs when calculating gross margins. Alternatively at estimated market value (based on hay-equivalent value according to quality). Fodder crops still in the ground, e.g. kale, treated as (ii).

(v) Stocks of purchased materials (including fodder). At cost net of discounts (where known) and subsidies.

(vi) Machinery and equipment. Original cost net of investment grants, less accumulated depreciation to date of valuation.

(vii)Livestock. At current market value, less cost of marketing. Fluctuations in market value expected to be temporary should be ignored.

Tenant's Capital. The estimated total value of capital on the farm, other than land and fixed equipment. There is no easy way of determining this sum precisely and estimates are made in several ways depending on the information available and the purpose for which the estimate is required. One method is to take the average of the opening and closing valuations (at either market value or cost) of livestock, crops, machinery and stores (feed, seed, fertilizers). See also pages 189-190.

Landlord's Capital. Value of the land and fixed equipment (including buildings).

2. Output Terms

Revenue (or Income). Receipts adjusted for debtors at the beginning and end of the accounting period. Items such as subsidies, grants, contract receipts and wayleaves are included.

Returns. Revenue adjusted for valuation changes (add closing, deduct opening, valuation).

Gross Output. Returns plus the value of produce consumed in the farmhouse or supplied to workers for which no payment is made, less purchases of livestock, livestock products and other produce bought for resale.

Enterprise Output. The total value of an enterprise, whether sold or retained on the farm. It therefore equals Gross Output of the enterprise plus the market value of any of the products kept on the farm (transfers out). Products transferred from another enterprise to be used in the production of the enterprise whose output is being calculated are deducted at market value (transfers in). Instead of the accounting year the 'harvest year' can be used for crops; valuations are then not relevant.

(Enterprise) Output from Forage. Primarily the sum of the enterprise outputs of grazing livestock, but includes keep let and occasional sales, e.g. of surplus hay,

230

together with an adjustment for changes in the valuation of stocks of home-grown fodder. However, fortuitous changes in stocks caused by yield variations due to the weather, the severity or length of the winter, or minor changes in livestock numbers or forage area can be either ignored (if small in relation to total annual usage) or included in miscellaneous output.

Adjusted Forage (Enterprise) Output is Output from Forage less rented keep and purchases of bulk fodder.

Net Output. Gross Output less the cost of purchased feed, livestock keep, seed, bulbs and plants.

Standard Output. The average enterprise output per hectare of a crop or per head of livestock calculated from either national or local average price and average yield data.

3. Input Terms

Expenditure. Payments adjusted for creditors at the beginning and end of the accounting period. Capital expenditure is not included.

Costs. Expenditure adjusted for valuation changes (add opening, deduct closing, valuation), with the following adjustments. Add: depreciation on capital expenditure including machinery, any loss made on machinery sales (add to depreciation) and the value of payments in kind to workers if not already included in their earnings. Deduct: purchases of livestock, livestock products and other produce bought for resale, any profit made on machinery (deduct from depreciation), allowance for private use of farm vehicles (deduct from machinery costs), the value of purchased stores used in the farmhouse (e.g. electricity) or sold off the farm (deduct from the relevant item).

Inputs. Costs with the following adjustments, made in order to put all farms on a similar basis for comparative purposes. Add: the value of unpaid family labour, including the manual labour of the farmer and his wife, and, in the case of owner-occupiers, an estimated rental value (based on average rents of similar farms in the area), less any cottage rents received. Deduct: any mortgage payments and other expenses of owner-occupation, interest payments and the cost of paid management. A proportion of the rental value of the farmhouse may also be deducted.

Fixed Costs. See pages 1-2, 169.

Variable Costs. See page 1.

4. Margin Terms

Management and Investment Income. Gross Output less Inputs. It represents the reward to management and the return on tenant's capital invested in the farm, whether borrowed or not. It is mainly used for comparative purposes, all farms having been put on a similar financial basis by the adjustments made to costs in calculating Inputs.

Net Farm Income. Management and Investment Income, less paid management, plus the value of the manual labour of the farmer and his wife. It represents the return to all tenant's type capital and the reward to the farmer for his manual labour and management.

Profit (or Loss). Gross Output less Costs. This represents the surplus or deficit before imputing any notional charges such as rental value or unpaid labour. In the accounts of owner-occupiers it includes any profit accruing from the ownership of land.

Gross Margin. See page 1.

Net Margin. A term sometimes used to denote Gross Margin less direct labour and machinery costs charged to an individual enterprise. This is not, however, nationally accepted terminology.

5. Area Terms

Total Hectares. All hectares comprising the farm.

Hectares. Total hectares less the area of woods, waste land, roads, buildings, etc.

Adjusted Hectares. Hectares reduced by the conversion of rough grazings into the equivalent hectares of average quality grassland. This is the figure often used for lowland farms when calculating 'per hectare' results.

Forage Hectares. Total hectares of forage crops grown, less any hectares exclusively used by pigs or poultry and the area equivalent of any home-grown fodder fed to barley beef. Usually, too, the area of rough grazings is converted to its grassland equivalent (see Adjusted Hectares). Forage crops are all crops, grass and rough grazings grown specifically for grazing livestock, other than catch crops and crops harvested as grain and pulses.

Adjusted Forage Hectares. Forage hectares adjusted as follows. Add area equivalent of keep rented, deduct area equivalent of keep let; deduct the area equivalent of occasional sales of fodder, e.g. surplus hay, and seed cuts (note: hay and seed grown regularly for sale should be regarded as cash crops, not forage crops); add or deduct the area equivalent of planned changes in the valuation of stocks of home-grown fodder (fortuitous changes in stocks resulting from weather conditions may be ignored); convert rough grazings into their grassland equivalent if not already done. The following adjustments also may be made: add the area equivalent of catch crops and of grazing from cash crops of hay or seed: add the area equivalent of purchased fodder.

In calculations such as Gross Margins per Forage Hectare, Adjusted Forage Hectares are usually used. If the area equivalent of purchased fodder has been added the cost of purchased fodder must not be charged as a variable cost: this is probably the best calculation for comparative purposes. Alternatively, when considering all the grazing enterprises taken together, purchased fodder can be deducted as a variable cost and no addition made for its area equivalent.

Source: DEFRA Statistics.

10. AGRISTATS

Some basic agricultural statistics relating to U.K. agriculture. (All figures are for the U.K. in 2006 unless otherwise stated.)

A. Structure

1. **Agriculture's Economic Contribution** (2006)

   Agriculture's contribution to total economy Gross   £ 5,580 million
   Value Added (provisional):   0.5%

2. **Agricultural Workforce** (2006)

   (a) *Agriculture's proportion of total workforce in employment:*   1.7%

   (b) *Numbers of Persons Engaged in Agriculture (June) (to nearest '00):*

A: Employed:	Male	Female	Total
Regular Full-time	54,000	10,000	64,000
Regular Part-time*	24,000	17,000	41,000
Seasonal, Casual and Gang	44,000	20,000	64,000
Salaried Managers			15,000
Total Employees			184,000
B: Farmers, Partners Directors and their Spouses			
Full-time			152,000
Part-time*...			198,000
Total Farmers, Partners Directors and their Spouses			350,000
Total Labour Force**			534,000

   *   Part-time is 39 hours or less per week in England and Wales, less than 38 in Scotland and less than 30 in Northern Ireland.

   **   Total labour force excludes schoolchildren but includes 'official' trainees.

3. **Livestock Numbers** (June '000 Head)

	2001	2006
Total Cattle and Calves	10,602	10,270
of which Dairy Cows	2,251	2,066
Beef Cows	1,708	1,733
Heifers in Calf	701	645
Total Sheep and Lambs	36,716	34,722
of which Female Breeding Flock	17,921	16,637
Total Pigs	5,845	4,933
of which Female Breeding Flock	598	468
Poultry Broilers	112,531	110,672
Laying Flock	29,895	28,632
Growing Pullets	9,367	9,625
Farmed Deer	31	36
Goats	71	98

4. Crop Areas (June)

	Area ('000 ha) 2001	Area ('000 ha) 2006	% Total Area 2006	% Crops & Grass 2006*
Wheat	1,635	1,833	9.8	15.8
Barley (% winter in brackets)	1,245 (37)	881 (44)	4.7	7.6
Oats	112	121	0.6	1.0
Mixed Corn, Triticale and Rye	21	25	0.1	0.2
Total Cereals (excluding maize)	3,013	2,860	15.3	24.7
Potatoes	165	140	0.7	1.2
Sugar Beet (England and Wales only)	177	130	0.7	1.1
Oilseed Rape (non Set-aside) (% winter in brackets)	404 (90)	500 (94)	2.7	4.3
Peas harvested dry (GB only)	102	47	0.3	0.4
Field Beans (GB only)	173	184	1.0	1.6
Linseed (non Set-aside)	31	33	0.2	0.3
Vegetables & Salad grown in the open	120	119	0.6	1.0
Orchards, Small Fruit and Grapes . . .	37	34	0.2	0.2
Other Horticulture	136	14	0.1	0.1
Maize (excl. Scotland in 2001)	129	137	0.7	1.2
Other Crops	86	141	0.8	2.4
Bare Fallow	43	150	0.8	1.3
Total Tillage	4,497	4,489	24.0	38.7
Temporary Grass (under 5 years old)	1,205	1,137	6.1	9.8
Total Arable	4,455	5,626	30.1	48.5
Permanent Grass (5 years, and over) .	5,584	5,967	31.9	51.5
(Total Grass (excluding Rough Grazing))	(6,789)	(7,104)	38.0	.
Total Tillage & Grass (excl. R.G.). . .	11,286	11,594	62.0	100.0
Rough Grazing**	5,661	5,732	30.6	.
Set-aside (incl. any in non-food crops)	800	513	2.7	.
Woodland	514	606	3.2	.
Other Land on agricultural holdings .	288	268	1.4	.
Total Agricultural Area***	18,549	18,713	100.0	.

*   Excluding Rough Grazing

**   Including 1,241,000 ha of common grazing.

*** Urban land and forest each approximately 2.0 million ha; other non-agricultural land approximately 1.5 million ha; total U.K. land area including inland waters: 24.1 million.

5. Size Structure

(a) *Number and Size Distribution of UK Holdings, 2005* (latest data):

Size group	Total land area			Tillage and grass area		
(ha)	No. ('000)	%	% area	No. ('000)	%	% area
0.1 to 19.9	183.3	58.9	5.3	133.0	53.0	
20.0 to 49.9	49.3	15.8	9.4	48.6	19.3	
50.0 to 99.9	36.8	11.8	15.2	36.4	14.5	
100 and over	41.7	13.4	70.1	33.2	13.2	
Total	311.1	100.0	100.0	251.2	100.0	100.0

Average area (ha/[acres]) per holding: 56.6 (140); tillage and grass 45.7 (113).

Size of Business (ESU)	'000 of Holdings	% of holdings	% of total ESU
Under 8	197.5	63.5	2.5
8 to 40	55.4	17.8	13.1
40 to 100	33.1	10.6	28.3
100 to 200	16.1	5.2	26.3
200 and over	9.0	2.9	29.8
Total	311.1	100.0	100.0

Average size of holdings: 26.3. Average size over 8 ESU (which is judged to be the minimum for full-time holdings, which are 37.7% of all holdings) = 67.4 ESU, 124.6 ha (308 acres). ESU = European Size Unit (the number provides a measure of the financial potential of the holding, based on standardised gross margins).

(b) *Number and Size distribution of holdings in England and Wales, 2000 (latest data)*

Size group	By total land area				By tillage and grass area			
(ha)	Holdings		Hectares		Holdings		Hectares	
	'000	%	'0,000	%	'000	%	'0,000	%
Under 10.......	62.8	36.0	212	2.0	53.2	33.6	195	2.3
10 to 30	35.2	20.2	646	6.2	33.9	21.4	628	7.3
30 to 50	19.6	11.2	771	7.4	19.9	12.6	779	9.1
50 to 100	27.0	15.5	1937	18.6	26.6	16.8	1900	22.2
100 to 200	19.0	10.9	2641	25.3	17.0	10.7	2340	27.3
200 to 300......	5.5	3.2	1342	12.9	4.4	2.8	1056	12.3
300 to 500	3.7	2.1	1386	13.3	2.5	1.6	916	10.7
500 to 700......	1.0	0.6	592	5.7	0.6	0.4	344	4.0
700 and over....	0.8	0.5	897	8.6	0.4	0.3	411	4.8
Total	174.6	100	10425	100	158.5	100	8570	100

6. Average Size of Enterprises

Hectares	2000	2005		2000	2005
			Dairy Cows	73	84
Cereals (excl. maize)...	50.7	51.7	Beef Cows..........	27	29
Oilseed Rape	25.4	35.0	Breeding Sheep	240	214
Potatoes	11.2	13.4	Breeding Pigs	82	82
Sugar Beet	20.0	22.7	Fattening Pigs	480	355
			Laying Fowls	1,295	1,095
			Broilers	40,834	36,141

7. *Tenure* (England and Wales, 2000 – latest data available)

Tenure	No. of Holdings	Area owned (%)	Area rented (%)
Wholly owned	119,254 (68.2)	4,969 (47.2)	-
Mainly owned	19,850 (11.4)	1,805 (17.1)	456 (4.3)
Wholly rented	22,643 (13.0)	-	1,826 (17.3)
Mainly rented	13,010 (7.4)	345 (3.3)	1,137 (10.8)
Total	174,757 (100)	7,119 (67.6)	3,419 (32.4)*

N.B. Mixed tenure holdings: mainly owned = over 50% owned;
mainly rented = over 50% rented.

Wholly or mainly owned, 79.6% of holdings; wholly or mainly rented, 20.4%

* N.B. As the above figures for rented land include family arrangements (e.g. farmers, or family farming companies, renting from other members of the family, or family shareholders) the percentage of 'truly' rented land is almost certainly a few percentage points less than the figures given above.

B. Finance

1. *Inputs and Outputs* (2006)

Inputs	£m	Outputs	£m	%
Animal Feed	2,423	Wheat	1,158	7.9
Seeds	329	Barley	412	2.8
Fertilisers	787	Oats and other cereals....	45	0.3
Pesticides	561	Oilseed rape...........	307	2.1
Hired Labour	2,161	Potatoes	625	4.3
Consumption of Fixed Capital*	2,755	Sugar beet	168	1.1
Maintenance: materials	680	Fresh vegetables	986	6.7
Maintenance: buildings	360	Fruit	377	2.6
Fuels	566	Plants and flowers.......	744	5.1
Electricity	246	Cattle	1,568	10.7
Agricultural services........	662	Sheep	702	4.8
Veterinary expenses	278	Pigs.................	687	4.7
Net rent	205	Poultry	1,315	9.0
Interest	571	Milk and milk products ..	2,501	17.1
Other goods and services.....	2,350	Eggs	357	2.4
Adjustments	6	Miscellaneous..........	2,686	18.3
Total Inputs	14,937	Total Gross Output......	14,638	100.0
Total Income From Farming	2,718	Single Payment & subsidies	3,017	
	17,655	Total Gross Output	17,655	
		Total Crops	3,076	21.0
		Total Horticulture........	2,107	14.4
		Total Livestock	5,245	35.8
		Total Livestock Products .	2,903	19.8
		Other	1,307	8.9

* including 679 buildings and 1,201 equipment.

Note. The above layout differs substantially from that published by DEFRA.

2. Income from Farming

(a) *Index of UK Total Income from Farming* in Real Terms (av. 1974-76 = 100)*

Year	Index	Year	Index	Year	Index	Year	Index
1975 ...	93	1983 ...	65	1991 ...	49	1999 ...	40
1976 ...	109	1984 ...	82	1992 ...	64	2000 ...	30
1977 ...	98	1985 ...	44	1993 ...	88	2001 ...	34
1978 ...	86	1986 ...	50	1994 ...	95	2002 ...	41
1979 ...	71	1987 ...	57	1995 ...	109	2003 ...	54
1980 ...	56	1988 ...	52	1996 ...	97	2004 ...	47
1981 ...	64	1989 ...	55	1997 ...	57	2005 ...	40
1982 ...	78	1990 ...	47	1998 ...	40	2006.....	43

* 'TIFF' = business profits plus income to farmers, partners and directors and others with an entrepreneurial interest in the business. It refers only to farming, i.e. diversification incomes and expenditures are excluded. There are no imputed charges (such as a rental value for owned land or value of the farmer's own labour).

(b) *Recent TIFF Values (£ million)*

	Actual	At 2006 Prices
1995 (the 1992-1997 peak)	5,205	6,913
2001	1,877	2,144
2002	2,348	2,639
2003	3,140	3,429
2004	2,824	2,996
2005	2,465	2,542
2006 (provisional)	2,718	2,718

(c) *Index of UK Farming Income* in Real Terms (av. 1940-69 = 100)*

Year	Index	Year	Index	Year	Index	Year	Index
1940-49	101	1977 ...	98	1987 ...	50	1997 ...	52
1950-59	100	1978 ...	89	1988 ...	34	1998 ...	37
1960-69	99	1979 ...	73	1989 ...	45	1999 ...	37
1970 ...	95	1980 ...	56	1990 ...	43	2000 ...	28
1971 ...	96	1981 ...	66	1991 ...	41	2000 ...	31
1972 ...	110	1982 ...	77	1992 ...	56	2002 ...	38
1973 ...	138	1983 ...	57	1993 ...	82	2003 ...	50
1974 ...	103	1984 ...	86	1994 ...	88	2004 ...	44
1975 ...	98	1985 ...	37	1995 ...	101	2005 ...	37
1976 ...	113	1986 ...	46	1996 ...	90	2006 ...	40

* As this figure is no longer produced by DEFRA the figures from 1997 onwards are only approximate. Up to that year a figure for 'Labour: family, partners and director' was deducted from Total Income from Farming (TIFF) to give Farming Income.

3. Indices of UK Net Farm Income in Real Terms by Main Types of Farming
(£s, at 200/06 prices)

Farm Type	2001/02	2002/03	2003/04	2004/05	2005/06	2006/07
Dairy	31,300	15,500	22,300	24,300	24,500	19,100
Grazing Livestock (LFA)	6,400	14,200	15,100	13,400	9,300	9,000
Grazing L'stock (Lowland)	1,400	7,300	7,500	5,400	4,100	7,500
Cereals	5,500	12,000	35,500	14,000	12,700	27,000
General Cropping ...	15,800	12,700	53,800	27,100	22,500	47,700
Specialist Pigs	22,200	25,600	34,000	25,800	29,000	23,700
Specialist Poultry ...	24,500	90,900	52,800	92,100	97,500	74,700
Mixed	5,900	11,300	23,900	15,200	15,600	20,100
ALL TYPES						
(inc. Horticulture)	14,400	14,900	25,300	18,400	17,100	20,600

1. In calculating net farm income various adjustments are made to the accounts, e.g. an imputed rent for owned land is deducted but interest payments are not deducted, nor is the value of unpaid labour of the farmer and spouse. Accounting years end of average in February.

2. The 2001/02 figures above exclude farms subjected to foot-and-mouth disease cull.

4. Balance Sheet of UK Agriculture (2005)

			£m	£m
Assets:	Fixed:	Land and buildings	119,427	
		Plant, machinery and vehicles	7,125	
		Breeding livestock	3,978	
	Total Fixed Assets:			*130,530*
	Current	Trading livestock	2,320	
		Crops and stores	2,042	
		Debtors and cash deposits	5,598	
	Total Current Assets:			*9,959*
	Total Assets:			**140,490**
Liabilities:	Long &	Bank loans	2,403	
	Medium-term:	AMC and SASC	1,363	
		Other	1,333	
	Total Long and Medium Term Liabilities			*5,099*
	Short-term	Bank overdrafts	3,485	
		Trade credit	1,388	
		Hire purchase and leasing	723	
		Other	128	
	Total Short-term Liabilities:			*5,724*
	Total Liabilities:			**10,823**
Net Worth:	....			**129,667**

% Equity (Net worth as a % of Total Assets):		*92.3%*
Total Income from Farming (TIFF) 2006 as a % of a) Net Worth:		*2.08%*
b) Total Assets:		*1.92%*

(Note: no charge has been made for farmers' own labour or management*)*

Bank Lending to Agriculture, Hunting and Forestry (2006 year avearge): .. *£9,375m*

C. Miscellaneous

1. UK Crop Yields and Prices, 2002-2006 (2006 Provisional)

Average Yields (harvest years) (tonnes per hectare)	2002	2003	2004	2005	2006	Average 2002-06
Wheat	8.0	7.8	7.8	8.0	8.0	7.9
Barley (all)	5.6	5.9	5.8	5.9	5.9	5.8
Winter Barley	6.3	6.3	6.4	6.5	6.7	6.4
Spring Barley	4.9	5.7	5.3	5.4	5.3	5.3
Oats	6.0	6.2	5.8	5.8	6.0	6.0
Oilseed Rape (excl. set-aside)	3.5	3.4	3.0	3.3	3.3	3.3
Linseed (excl. set-aside)	1.3	1.7	1.7	1.7	1.4	1.6
Field Beans (for stockfeed)	3.9	3.9	3.7	3.8	3.4	3.7
Dried Peas (for stockfeed)	3.4	3.9	3.5	3.8	3.3	3.6
Potatoes (all)	44.0	40.7	42.5	42.3	40.4	42.0
Early Potatoes	16.4	20.0	17.4	15.1	16.5	17.1
Maincrop Potatoes	46.7	42.9	45.2	45.1	42.5	44.5
Sugar Beet (adj. to 16% sugar)	56.5	56.6	58.7	57.3	54.7	56.8

Average Prices (calendar years) (£ per tonne)		2002	2003	2004	2005	2006	Average 2002-2006
Wheat	milling	71	83	86	73	83	79
	feed	63	75	76	66	79	72
Barley	malting	72	82	80	77	92	81
	feed	58	71	70	65	74	68
Oats	milling	57	63	64	70	79	67
	feed	54	61	63	68	81	65
Oilseed Rape (excl. set-aside)		140	160	163	131	164	152
Linseed (excl. set-aside)		165	170	175	180	163	171
Field Beans (for stockfeed)		73	92	82	84	85	83
Dried Peas (for stockfeed)		76	94	85	87	80	84
Potatoes (all, inc seed)		81	103	117	98	124	105
	Earlies	110	132	178	105	194	144
	Maincrop	75	99	111	95	121	100
Sugar Beet (per adjusted tonne)		30	31	31	31	24	29

2. Self-sufficiency (2006 provisional, [2002 in brackets])

(a) *Total Food* all food types .... 58.1% *(62.4%)*

indigenous type food .... 71.5% *(75.5%)*

(b) *Individual Products (production as a % of total new supply for use in the UK):*

	2001	2006		2001	2006
Wheat	104	107	Beef and Veal	73	81
Barley	109	109	Mutton and Lamb	79	89
Oats	116	100	Pork	76	62
Total Cereals	99	101	Bacon and Ham	43	44
Oilseed Rape	75	105	Poultrymeat	90	87
Potatoes	84	83	Butter	64	53
Sugar	63	70	Cheese	65	60
Fresh Vegetables	67	61	Cream	138	122
Fresh Fruit	10	11	Hen Eggs	89	89

3. Food Consumption and Expenditure, UK 2005-06

(a) *Food and Drink Consumed Within the Household*

Average quantity consumed / expenditure per person per week:

	2004-05 kg per week	2005-06 kg per week	2005-06 £ per week
Milk and Cream (litres)	1.984	2.027	1.64
Cheese	0.110	0.116	0.63
Meat	1.049	1.047	4.95
Fish	0.158	0.167	1.04
Eggs (number)	1.56	2.00	0.19
Fats	0.182	0.183	0.38
Sugars and Preserves..............	0.134	0.129	0.17
Potatoes	0.822	0.842	1.01
Other Vegetables	1.106	1.156	1.94
Fruit..........................	1.168	1.292	1.88
Bread	0.695	0.701	0.97
All Other Cereals (inc. Pasta & Pizza) .	0.882	0.695	2.34
Beverages (litres)	0.056	0.057	0.41
Soft Drinks (litres)	1.832	1.718	0.77
Alcoholic Drinks (litres)	0.763	0.739	2.65
Confectionery	0.131	0.123	0.78
Other Food.....................	-	0.710	1.24
Total	-	-	23.05

(b) *Food and Drink Consumed Outside the Household*

	£ per week
Food and Drink excl. Alcohol	7.79
Alcoholic Drinks	3.62
Total	11.41

(c) *Total Food and Drink*

	£ per week
Food and Drink excl. Alcohol	28.70
Alcoholic Drinks	6.27
Total	34.97

Sources: Agriculture in the UK: 2005 (DEFRA etc.). All items except for the following:

A5 (part), A7: Other DEFRA etc. Statistics.

B4, Bank Lending: Bank of England, Financial Statistics Division.

C3 and C4: Family Food Survey, DEFRA.

11. RATE OF INFLATION; PRICE AND COST INDICES

1. Retail Price Index (all items)

Year	% increase on year earlier	Index (1970 = 100)	Index (1980 = 100)	Year	% increase on year earlier	Index (1970 = 100)	Index (1990 = 100)
1990.....	9.5	682	189	1999.....	1.5	893	247
1991.....	5.9	722	200	2000.....	3.0	920	254
1992.....	3.7	749	207	2001.....	1.8	937	259
1993.....	1.6	761	210	2002.....	1.7	952	263
1994.....	2.4	779	215	2003.....	2.9	980	271
1995.....	3.5	806	223	2004.....	3.0	1010	279
1996.....	2.4	825	228	2005.....	2.8	1040	287
1997.....	3.1	851	235	2006.......	3.0	1071	296
1998.....	3.4	880	243	2007 (f'cast)	2.5	1098	303

*   Index in 1965: 80; index in 1962: 70. 1970-1994 figures available in earlier editions.

2. UK Annual Price and Cost Indicies, 2001-2005 (2000 = 100)

A. Producer Prices	2002	2003	2004	2005	2006
Feed Wheat	96.6	105.3	117.6	98.2	112.1
Feed Barley	88.1	104.3	108.3	99.1	107.9
All Cereals	95.0	105.2	114.2	99.1	111.0
Oilseed Rape	121.2	140.3	136.1	112.9	134.5
Potatoes (maincrop)	90.6	106.0	141.6	109.7	141.7
Sugar Beet	114.8	112.1	115.4	116.3	110.0
Desert Apples	111.3	124.6	120.9	116.5	122.5
All Fresh Fruit	113.9	124.2	112.4	120.1	120.8
All Fresh Vegetables	112.7	125.5	113.7	120.2	130.7
All Crop Products	104.0	110.7	115.0	108.4	117.9
Milk	101.0	106.4	109.0	109.0	106.0
Cattle	103.8	106.7	113.4	114.6	123.9
Sheep	118.5	132.5	131.5	122.9	125.5
Wool	96.4	108.4	107.3	99.7	33.6
Pigs........................	98.7	109.0	109.3	109.8	110.9
Poultry	97.2	99.4	101.2	100.6	106.5
Eggs	109.5	130.7	135.1	121.1	126.0
All Animal Products	102.7	109.4	112.0	110.4	111.6
All Products	103.3	109.9	113.2	109.6	114.4
B. Input Prices					
Seeds	105.5	116.0	110.3	108.1	108.6
Fertilisers	110.3	119.0	130.5	143.3	151.4
Plant Protection Products	95.8	95.7	100.6	102.9	103.4
Energy and Lubricants	92.4	100.5	108.8	137.4	149.5
Animal Feeding Stuffs	103.5	104.9	111.6	102.9	107.4
Maintenance and Repair of Plant ..	109.4	116.0	122.5	130.3	137.8
Machinery and Other Equipment .	95.7	95.1	96.1	103.8	108.2
Buildings	107.8	112.1	118.1	123.7	130.9
General Expenses	105.5	105.2	114.0	114.6	119.3

12. METRIC CONVERSION FACTORS

Metric to Imperial   *Imperial to Metric*

Area

1 hectare (10,000m^2) . . . . . 2.471 acres	1 acre . . . . 0.405 ha
	1 square mile . . . . 259 ha
1 square km . . . . 0.386 sq. mile	1 square mile . . . . 2.590 sq. km
1 square m . . . . 1.196 sq. yard	1 square yard . . . . 0.836 sq. m
1 square m . . . . 10.764 sq. feet	1 square foot . . . . 0.093 sq. m

(m = metre, km = kilometre)

Length

1 mm . . . . 0.039 inch	1 inch . . . . 25.4 mm
1 cm . . . . 0.394 inch	1 inch . . . . 2.54 cm
1 m . . . . 3.281 feet	1 foot . . . . 0.305 m
1 m . . . . 1.094 yard	1 yard . . . . 0.914 m
1 km . . . . 0.6214 mile	1 mile . . . . 1.609 km

(mm = millimetre, cm = centimetre)

Volume

1 millilitre . . . . 0.0352 fluid oz	1 fluid oz . . . . 28.413 ml
1 litre . . . . 35.2 fluid oz	1 fluid oz . . . . 0.028 litre
1 litre . . . . 1.76 pints	1 pint . . . . 0.568 litre
1 litre . . . . 0.22 gallon	1 gallon . . . . 4.546 litres

[Milk: 1 litre = 1.03 kg (.971 kg/litre); 1 kg = 1.709 pints, 0.214 gal.; 1 tonne = 213.63 gal; 1 pint = 0.585 kg; 1 gallon = 4.681 kg]

1 cubic m . . . . 35.31 cu feet	1 cubic foot . . . . 0.028 cu m
1 cubic m . . . . 1.307 cu yard	1 cubic yard . . . . 0.765 cu m
1 cubic m . . . . 220 gallons	1 gallon . . . . 0.005 cu m

Weight

1 gram . . . . 0.0353 oz	1 oz . . . . 28.35 gm
1 kg 35.274oz	
1 kg . . . . 2.205 lb	1 lb . . . . 0.454 kg
50 kg . . . . 0.984 cwt	
1 tonne (1,000 kg) . . . . 19.68 cwt	1 cwt . . . . 50.80 kg
1 tonne . . . . 0.984 ton	1 ton . . . . 1.016 tonne

Yields and Rates of Use

1 tonne/ha . . . . .0.398 ton/acre	1 ton/acre . . . . 2.511 tonnes/ha
1 tonne/ha . . . . 7.95 cwt/acre	1 cwt/acre . . . . 0.125 tonne/ha
1 gram/ha . . . . 0.014 oz/acre	1 oz/acre . . . . 70.053 g/ha
1 kg/ha . . . . 0.892 lb/acre	1 lb/acre . . . . 1.121 g/ha
1 kg/ha . . . . 0.008 cwt/acre	1 cwt/acre . . . . 125.5 g/ha
1 kg/ha (fert.) . . . . 0.797 unit/acre	1 unit/acre . . . . 1.255 kg/ha
1 litre/ha . . . . 0.712 pint/acre	1 pint/acre . . . . 1.404 litre/ha
1 litre/ha . . . . 0.089 gal/acre	1 gal/acre . . . . 11.24 litres/ha

Power, Pressure, Temperature

1 Kw . . . . 1.341 hp	1 hp . . . . 0.746 kW
1 kilojoule . . . . 0.948 Btu	1 Btu . . . . 1.055 kilojoule
1 therm . . . . 10,000 Btu	1 Btu . . . . 0.0001 therm
1 lb f ft . . . . 1.356 Nm	1 Nm . . . . 0.738 lb f ft
1 bar . . . . 14.705 lb/sq.in.	1 lb/sq.in. . . . . 0.068 bar
°C to °F . . . . x1.8, +32	°F to °C . . . . -32, ÷1.8

13. USEFUL ADDRESSES AND TELEPHONE NUMBERS

1. General

ADAS
Headquarters: Woodthorne, Wergs Road, Wolverhampton WV6 8TQ   01902 754190

Advisory Committee on Organic Standards (ACOS)
DEFRA, Area 5F, Ergon House, Horseferry Road, London SW1P 2AL   020 7238 5605

Agricultural Central Trading Ltd. (Act)
90 The Broadway, Chesham, Bucks. HP5 lEG   01494 784931

Agricultural Engineers' Association
Samuelson House, Paxton Road, Orton Centre, Peterborough,
Cambs. PE2 5LT   01733 371381

Agricultural Law Association
6 St. Peters Close, Chislehurst, Kent BR7 6PD   020 8467 0722

Agricultural Industries Confederation (AIC)
Confederation House, East of England Showground, Peterborough,
PE2 6XE   01733 385230

Agricultural Wages Board
Ergon House, Area 3A, Horseferry Road, London SWlP 2AL   020 7238 6523

Association of Independent Crop Consultants
Agriculture Place, Heath Farm, Heath Road East, Petersfield,
Hampshire, GU31 4HT   01730 710095

BBC Radio 4 Farming To-day
The Mail Box, Birmingham B1 1RF   0121 432 8888

British Agricultural and Garden Machinery Association (BAGMA)
1st Floor, Entrance B, Salamander Quay West, Park Lane,
Harefield, Middlesex UB9 6NZ   0870 205 2834

British Association of Seed Producers
Manor House, Woodhall Spa, Lincolnshire, LN10 6PX.   01526 352368

British Cereal Exports
HGCA, Caledonia House, 223 Pentonville Road, London N1 9HY   020 7520 3927

British Crop Protection Council (BCPC)
7 Omni Business Park, Omega Park, Alton, Hampshire GU34 2QD   01420 593200

British Deer Society
Burgate Manor, Fordingbridge, Hampshire SP6 1EF   01425 655434

British Egg Industry Council (BEIC)
2nd Floor, 89 Charterhouse Street, London EC1M 6HR   020 7608 3760

British Grassland Society
PO Box 237, University of Reading, 1 Earley Gate, Berks. RG6 6AR   0118 931 8189

British Institute of Agricultural Consultants (BIAC)
The Estate Office, Torry Hill, Milstead, Sittingbourne,
Kent ME9 0SP   01795 830100

British Pig Association
Trumpington Mews, 40b High Street, Trumpington, Cambs. CB2 2LS   01223 845100

British Potato Council
4300 Nash Court, John Smith Drive, Oxford Business Park
South, Oxford OX4 2RT   01865 714455

British Poultry Council
Europoint House, 5 Lavington Street, London SE1 0NZ   020 7202 4760

British Sheep Dairying Association
The Sheep Centre, Malvern, Worcs. WR13 6PH   01684 892661

British Society of Plant Breeders
Woolpack Chambers, Market Street, Ely, Cambs. CB7 4ND   01353 653200

British Sugar
PP Box 26, Oundle Road, Peterborough, Cambs. PE2 9QU   01733 563171

British Veterinary Association
7 Mansfield Street, London WlG 9NQ   020 7636 6541

British Wool Marketing Board
Wool House, Roydsdale Way, Euroway Trading Estate,
Bradford, West Yorkshire BD4 6SE   01274 688666

CAB International
Nosworthy Way, Wallingford, Oxon OX10 8DE   01491 832111

Campaign to Protect Rural England (CPRE)
128 Southwark Street, London SE1 0SW   020 7981 2800

Central Association of Agricultural Valuers (CAAV)
Market Chambers, 35 Market Place, Coleford, Gloucestershire
GL16 8AA   01594 832979

Centre for Agricultural Strategy
University of Reading, P.O. Box 237, Earley Gate, Reading,
Berks. RG6 6AT   0118 931 8152

Country Land and Business Association (CLA)
16 Belgrave Square, London SWlX 8PQ   020 7235 0511

Crop Protection Association UK
4 Lincoln Court, Lincoln Road, Peterborough, Combs PE1 2RP   01733 349225

Dairy Industry Association Ltd.
93 Baker Street, London W1V 6RL   020 7486 7244

Department of Agriculture and Rural Development (DARDNI)
Dundonald House, Upper Newtownards Road, Belfast BT4 3SB   028 9052 0100

Department of Environment, Food and Rural Affairs (DEFRA)
Nobel House, 17 Smith Square, London SW1P 3JR   020 7270 3000

English Heritage
23 Savile Row, London WlS 2ET   020 7973 3000

English Hops and Herbs Ltd
Hop Pocket Lane, Paddock Wood, Tonbridge, Kent TN12 6DQ   01892 833 415
www.botanix.co.uk,   intray@botanix.co.uk

Environment Agency
Rio House, Waterside Drive, Aztec West, Almonsbury, Bristol
BS32 4UD   0870 850 6506

European Commission (London Office)
Jean Monnet House, 8 Storey's Gate, London SW1P 3AT   020 7973 1992

FACE (Farming and Countryside Education)
National Agricultural Centre, Stoneleigh Park, Warks. CV8 2LZ 024 7685 8261

Family Farmers' Association
Osborne Newton, Aveton Gifford, Kingsbridge, Devon TQ7 4PE   01548 852794

Farmers Club
3 Whitehall Court, London SWlA 2EL   020 7930 3751

Farmers Union of Wales
Llys Amaeth, Plas Gogerddon, Aberystwyth, Ceredigion SY23 3BT 01970 820820

Farming and Wildlife Advisory Group (FWAG)
National Agricultural Centre, Stoneleigh Park, Warks. CV8 2RX   024 7669 6699

Food and Drink Federation
Federation House, 6 Catherine Street, London WC2B 5JJ   020 7836 2460

Food from Britain
4th Floor, Manning House, 22 Carlisle Place, London SW1P 1JA   020 7233 5111

Food Standards Agency
Aviation House, 125 Kingsway, London WC2B 6NH   020 7276 8000

Forestry Commission
231 Corstorphine Road, Edinburgh EH12 7AT   0131 334 0303

Grain and Feed Trade Association (GAFTA)
GAFTA House, 6 Chapel Place, Rivington Street, London EC2A 3SH   020 7814 9666

Guild of Agricultural Journalists
Isfield Cottage, Church Road, Crowborough, East Sussex TN6 1BN   01892 611618

Health and Safety Executive (Agriculture Sector)
National Agricultural Centre, Stoneleigh Park, Warks. CV8 2LG   024 7669 8350

Home Grown Cereals Authority
Caledonia House, 223 Pentonville Road, London N1 9NG   020 7520 3926
Price Information Service   020 7520 3972

Horticultural Development Council
Bradbourne House, Tithe Barn, East Malling, Kent ME19 6DZ   01732 848383

Institution of Agricultural Engineers
West End Road, Silsoe, Bedford MK45 4DU   01525 861096

Institute of Agricultural Management
Farm Management Unit, University of Reading, PO Box 236,
Reading RG6 6AT   0118 931 6578

Institute of Agricultural Secretaries and Administrators
National Agricultural Centre, Stoneleigh Park, Warks. CV8 2LZ   024 7669 6592

Institute of Chartered Foresters
7a St. Colme Street, Edinburgh EH3 6AA   0131 225 2705

International Grains Council
1 Canada Square, Canary Wharf, London E14 5AE   020 7513 1122

Land Drainage Contractors Association
National Agricultural Centre, Stoneleigh Park, Warks. CV8 2LG   01327 263264

Land Heritage
Summerhill Farm, Hittisleigh, Devon EX6 6LP   01647 24511

Lands Improvement Holdings plc
1 Buckingham Place, London SW1E 6HR   020 7222 5331

Lantra
Lantra House, National Agricultural Centre, Stoneleigh Park,
Warks. CV8 2LG   024 7669 6996

LEAF (Linking Environment and Farming)
National Agricultural Centre, Stoneleigh Park, Warks. CV8 2LZ   024 7641 3911

London Commodity Exchange (Euronext Liffe)
Cannon Bridge House, 1 Cousin Lane, London EC4R 3XX   020 7623 0444

Meat and Livestock Commission (MLC)
PO Box 44, Winterhill House, Snowdon Drive, Milton Keynes
MK6 1AX   01908 677577

Milk Development Council (MDC)
Stroud Road, Cirencester, Glos GL7 6JN   01285 646500

National Agricultural Centre (NAC)
Stoneleigh Park, Warks. CV8 2LZ   024 7669 6969

National Association of Agricultural Contractors (NAAC)
Samuelson House, Paxton Road, Orton Centre, Peterborough PE2 5LT   01733 362920

National Association of British & Irish Millers (NABIM)
21 Arlington Street, London SW1A 1RN   020 7493 2521

National Beef Association
Mart Centre, Tyne Green, Hexham, NE46 3SG   01434 601005

National Cattle Association (Dairy)
Brick House, Risbury, Leominster, Herefordshire HR6 0NQ   01568 760632

National Dairy Council
164 Shaftesbury Avenue, London WC2H 8HL   020 7395 4030

National Farmers' Retail and Markets Association (FARMA)
The Greenhouse, PO Box 575, Southampton, Hants. SO15 7BZ   0845 458 8420

National Farmers' Union (NFU)
Agriculture House, Stoneleigh Park, Warks. CV8 2LZ   024 7685 8500
London Office, Kings Buildings, 16 Smith Square, London SW1P 3JJ   020 7808 6600

National Non-Food Crops Centre
Innovation Centre, York Science Park, Innovation Way, Heslington,
York YO10 5DG   01904 435182

NFU Scotland
Rural Centre, West Mains, Ingliston, Midlothian EH28 8LT   0131 472 4000

National Federation of Young Farmers Clubs
YFC Centre, National Agricultural Centre, Stoneleigh Park,
Warks. CV8 2LG   024 7685 7200

National Office of Animal Health (NOAH)
3 Crossfield Chambers, Gladbeck Way, Enfield, Middlesex EN2 7HF   020 8367 3131

National Sheep Association
The Sheep Centre, Malvern, Worcs. WR13 6PH   01684 892661

National Trust
36 Queen Anne's Gate, London SW1H 9AS   020 7222 9251

Natural England
1 High Street Parade, East Parade, Sheffield S1 2GA   01733 455192

Processed Vegetable Growers' Association Limited (PGVA)
133 Eastgate, Louth, Lincolnshire LN11 9QG   01507 602427

Royal Agricultural Benevolent Institution (RABI)
Shaw House, 27 West Way, Oxford OX2 0QH   01865 724931

Royal Agricultural Society of England (RASE)
National Agricultural Centre, Stoneleigh Park, Warks. CV8 2LZ   024 7669 6969

Royal Association of British Dairy Farmers
Unit 31, Stoneleigh Deer Park, Stareton, Kenilworth, Warks CV8 2LY   0845 458 2711

Royal Forestry Society of England, Wales and N.I.
102 High Street, Tring, Herts. HP23 4AF   01442 822028

Royal Highland and Agricultural Society of Scotland
Ingliston, Edinburgh EH28 8NF   0131 335 6200

Royal Horticultural Society
80 Vincent Square, London SW1P 2PE   020 7834 4333

Royal Institution of Chartered Surveyors (RICS)
12 Great George Street, Parliament Square, London SW1P 3AD   020 7222 7000

Royal Society for the Protection of Birds
The Lodge, Sandy, Bedfordshire SG19 2DL   01767 680551

Royal Welsh Agricultural Society
Llanelwedd, Builth Wells, Powys LD2 3SY   01982 553683

Rural, Agricultural and Allied Workers Trade Group (TGWU)
Transport House, 128 Theobalds Road, Holborn, London WC1X 8TN   020 7611 2500

Rural Payments Agency
Kings House, 33 Kings Road, Reading RG1 3BU   0118 958 3626

Scottish Executive Environment and Rural Affairs Department (SEERAD)
Pentland House, 47 Robb's Loan, Edinburgh EH14 1TY   0131 556 8400

Tenant Farmers' Association
7 Brewery Court, Theale, Reading, Berks. RG7 5AJ   0118 930 6130

The Stationery Office
The Publications Centre, PO Box 276, London SW8 5DT   0870 600 5522

Ulster Farmers Union
475 Antrim Road, Belfast BT15 3DA   028 9037 0222

United Farmers Trading Agency (UFTA) Ltd.
Hancock House, Smallgate, Beccles, Suffolk NR34 9AE.   01502 717877

Welsh Assembly Government, Agriculture and Rural Affairs Department
Crown Offices, Cathays Park, Cardiff, CF10 3NQ   029 2082 5111

Women's Food and Farming Union
National Agricultural Centre, Stoneleigh Park, Warks. CV8 2LZ   024 7669 3171

2. University Agricultural Economics
(Farm Business Survey work)

ENGLAND AND WALES

Northern: School of Agriculture, Food and Rural Development, University of Newcastle, Newcastle-upon-Tyne NE1 7RU   0191 222 6902

North Eastern: Rural Business Research Unit, Askham Bryan College, Askham Bryan, York YO23 3FR   01904 772233

East Midlands: Rural Business Research Unit, University of Nottingham, Sutton Bonington Campus, Loughborough, Leics. LE12 5RD   0115 951 6070

Eastern: Rural Business Unit, Centre for Rural Economics Research, 16-21 Silver Street, Cambridge CB3 9EP   01223 337166

South Eastern: Farm Survey Section, Imperial College London, Wye Campus, Ashford, Kent TN25 5AH   020 7594 2925

Southern: Department of Agriculture and Food Economics The University of Reading, 4 Earley Gate, Whiteknights, PO Box 237, Reading RG6 6AR   01189 875123

South Western: Centre for Rural Research, The University of Exeter, Lafrowda House, St. German's Road, Exeter EX4 6TL   01392 263836

Wales: Institute of Rural Studies, University of Wales, Aberystwyth, Llanbadarn Campus, Aberystwyth, Ceredigion SY23 3AL   01970 622253

SCOTLAND (SAC Farm Business Services)

Scottish Agricultural College
Regional Offices:
North: SAC Aberdeen, Ferguson Building, Craibstone Estate, Bucksburn, Aberdeen AB21 9YA   01224 711000
East: SAC Edinburgh, Bush Estate, Penecuik, Midlothian, EH26 0PH   0131 535 3440
West: SAC Auchincruive, Ayr KA6 5HW   01292 520331

NORTHERN IRELAND (Advisory Services also)

Economics & Statistics Division, DARDNI, Dundonald House, Upper Newtownards Road, Belfast BT4 3SB   028 9052 0100

3. Commercial Banks: Agricultural Departments

Agricultural Mortgage Corporation (AMC)
Charlton Place, Charlton Road, Andover, Hants. SP10 1RE   01264 334747

Bank of Scotland
Agricultural Business, City House, City Road, Chester CH88 3AN   0845 3072852

Barclays Bank
24th Floor, 1 Churchill Place, London, E14 5HP   020 7166 5515

Clydesdale Bank
AgriBusiness Banking Centre, 10 Fleet Place, London EC4M 7RB   020 7395 5662

Farming and Agricultural Finance Limited (FAF)
PO Box 234, Upminster, Essex RM14 2WS   0800 225567

HSBC Bank
Agriculture Head Office, 51 De Montford Street, Leicester LE1 7BB   0116 281 8328

Lloyds TSB Group
Business Banking Agricultural, PO Box 112, Canons House,
Canons Way, Bristol BS99 7LB   0117 943 3114

National Westminster Bank
Agricultural Services, Gogaburn Business House C, PO Box 1000
Edinburgh EH12 1HQ   0131 626 0151

The Royal Bank of Scotland
Agricultural Services, Gogaburn Business House C, PO Box 1000
Edinburgh EH12 1HQ   0131 626 0151

4. Research Organisations

Biotechnology and Biological Sciences Research Council (BBSRC)
Polaris House, North Star Avenue, Swindon, Wilts. SN2 IUH   01793 413200

Babraham Institute
Babraham, Cambridge CB2 4AT   01223 496000

Broom's Barn Research Station
Higham, Bury St. Edmunds, Suffolk IP28 6NP   01284 812200

CEDAR (Centre for Dairy Research)
Arborfield Hall Farm, Reading Road, Arborfield, Reading,
RG2 9HX   0118 976 0964

East Malling Research
East Malling, Kent ME19 6BJ   01732 843833

Elm Farm Research Centre
Hamstead Marshall, Newbury, Berkshire RG15 0HR   01488 658298

Hannah Research Institute
Ayr, Scotland KA6 5HL   01292 674000

Institute for Animal Health
Compton, Newbury, Berks. RG20 7NN   01635 578411

Institute of Food Research
Norwich Research Park, Colney, Norwich NR4 7UA   01603 255000

Institute of Grassland and Environmental Research (IGER)
Aberystwyth Research Centre, Plas Gogerddan, Aberystwyth,
Ceredigion SY23 3EB   01970 823000
North Wyke Research Station, Okehampton, Devon EX20 2SB   01837 883500

Kingshay Farming Trust
Bridge Farm, West Bradley, Glastonbury, Somerset BA6 8LU   01458 851555

Macauley Land Use Research Institute
Craigiebuckler, Aberdeen AB15 8QH   01224 318611

Morley Research Centre
Morley St. Botolph, Wymondham, Norfolk NR18 9DB   01953 713200

NIAB
Huntingdon Road, Cambridge CB3 0LE   01223 342200

Processors and Growers Research Organisation (PGRO)
The Research Station, Great North Road, Thornhaugh,
Peterborough PE8 6HJ   01780 782585

Roslin Institute
Roslin, Midlothian EH25 9PS   0131 527 4200

Rothamsted Research
Harpenden, Hertfordshire AL5 2JQ   01582 763133

Rowett Research Institute
Greenburn Road, Bucksburn, Aberdeen AB21 9SB 01224 712751

Scottish Crop Research Institute (SCRI)
Mylnefield, Invergowrie, Dundee DD2 5DA 01382 562731

The Arable Group (TAG)
Manor Farm, Lower End, Doglingworth, Cirencester, Glos. GL7 7AH 01285 652184

5. National Agricultural Colleges

Cranfield University, Silsoe Campus
Silsoe, Bedford MK45 4DT 01525 863000

Harper Adams University College
Edgmond, Newport, Shropshire TF10 8NB 01952 820280

Institute of Rural Sciences
Llanbadarn Campus, Aberystwyth, Ceredigion SY23 3AL 01970 624471

Royal Agricultural College
Stroud Road, Cirencester, Glos. GL7 6JS 01285 652531

Scottish Agricultural College (student recruitment)
Auchincruive Campus, Ayr KA6 5HW 0800 269453

Shuttleworth College
Old Warden Park, Biggleswade, Beds. SG18 9EA 01767 626222

Writtle College
Lordship Road, Writtle, Chelmsford, Essex CM1 3RR 01245 424200

INDEX